Othello

6

Satomi Ikezawa

TRANSLATED AND ADAPTED BY
William Flanagan

LETTERED BY
Michaelis/Carpelis Design

DEL
REY

NE BOOKS • NEW YORK

2005 Del Rey® Books Trade Paperback Edition

Copyright © 2005 by Satomi Ikezawa.

Published in the United States by Del Rey Books, an imprint of The Random House Publishing Group, a division of Random House, Inc., New York.

Del Rey is a registered trademark and the Del Rey colophon is a trademark of Random House, Inc.

Originally published in Japan by Kodansha Ltd., Tokyo in 2004 by Satomi Ikezawa. This publication—rights arranged through Kodansha Ltd.

Library of Congress Control Number: 2004096774

ISBN 0-345-48438-X

Printed in the United States of America

www.delreymanga.com

9 8 7 6 5 4 3 2 1

Translator and adapter—William Flanagan
Lettering—Michaelis/Carpelis Design

Contents

Honorifics
iv

A Note from the Author
vi

Othello Volumn 6
1

About the author
164

Translation Notes
165

Honorifics

Throughout the Del Rey Manga books, you will find Japanese honorifics left intact in the translations. For those not familiar with how the Japanese use honorifics and, more importantly, how they differ from American honorifics, we present this brief overview.

Politeness has always been a critical facet of Japanese culture. Ever since the feudal era, when Japan was a highly stratified society, use of honorifics—which can be defined as polite speech that indicates relationship or status—has played an essential role in the Japanese language. When addressing someone in Japanese, an honorific usually takes the form of a suffix attached to one's name (example: "Asuna-san"), or as a title at the end of one's name or in place of the name itself (example: "Negi-sensei," or simply "Sensei!").

Honorifics can be expressions of respect or endearment. In the context of manga and anime, honorifics give insight into the nature of the relationship between characters. Many translations into English leave out these important honorifics, and therefore distort the "feel" of the original Japanese. Because Japanese honorifics contain nuances that English honorifics lack, it is our policy at Del Rey not to translate them. Here, instead, is a guide to some of the honorifics you may encounter in Del Rey Manga.

-san: This is the most common honorific and is equivalent to Mr., Miss, Ms., or Mrs. It is the all-purpose honorific and can be used in any situation where politeness is required.

-sama: This is one level higher than "-san" It is used to confer great respect.

-dono: This comes from the word "tono," which means "lord." It is an even higher level than "-sama" and confers utmost respect.

-kun: This suffix is used at the end of boys' names to express familiarity or endearment. It is also sometimes used by men among friends, or when addressing someone younger or of a lower station.

-chan: This is used to express endearment, mostly toward girls. It is also used for little boys, pets, and even among lovers. It gives a sense of childish cuteness.

Bozu: This is an informal way to refer to a boy, similar to the English term "kid" or "squirt."

Sempai/Senpai: This title suggests that the addressee is one's senior in a group or organization. It is most often used in a school setting, where underclassmen refer to their upperclassmen as "sempai." It can also be used in the workplace, such as when a newer employee addresses an employee who has seniority in the company.

Kohai: This is the opposite of "sempai" and is used toward underclassmen in school or newcomers in the workplace. It connotes that the addressee is of a lower station.

Sensei: Literally meaning "one who has come before," this title is used for teachers, doctors, or masters of any profession or art.

[blank]: Usually forgotten in these lists, but perhaps the most significant difference between Japanese and English. The lack of honorific means that the speaker has permission to address the person in a very intimate way. Usually, only family, spouses, or very close friends have this kind of permission. Known as *yobisute,* it can be gratifying when someone who has earned the intimacy starts to call one by one's name without an honorific. But when that intimacy hasn't been earned, it can also be very insulting.

A Note from the Author

♡ When I was drawing the live performances, I went to the real thing with an instrument and a digital camera and took pictures. Then I used those pictures as the basis for my drawings. But I was really embarrassed when I had to act out the scene where Nana belts out her song. When you draw manga, you really need the heart of an actor... But when I printed out the picture of me singing full out, and the entire time I was using it to draw, I couldn't help but blush.

Satomi Ikezawa

OTHELLO
オセロ。

OTHELLO
オセロ。
Satomi
Ikezawa

6

CONTENTS

Chapter 21
Man and Woman..........................3

Chapter 22
When She Knows the Secret............ 43

Chapter 23
Yaya's Breakdown?!.................... 83

Chapter 24
Nana's Rampage?!......................123

Chapter 21
Man and Woman

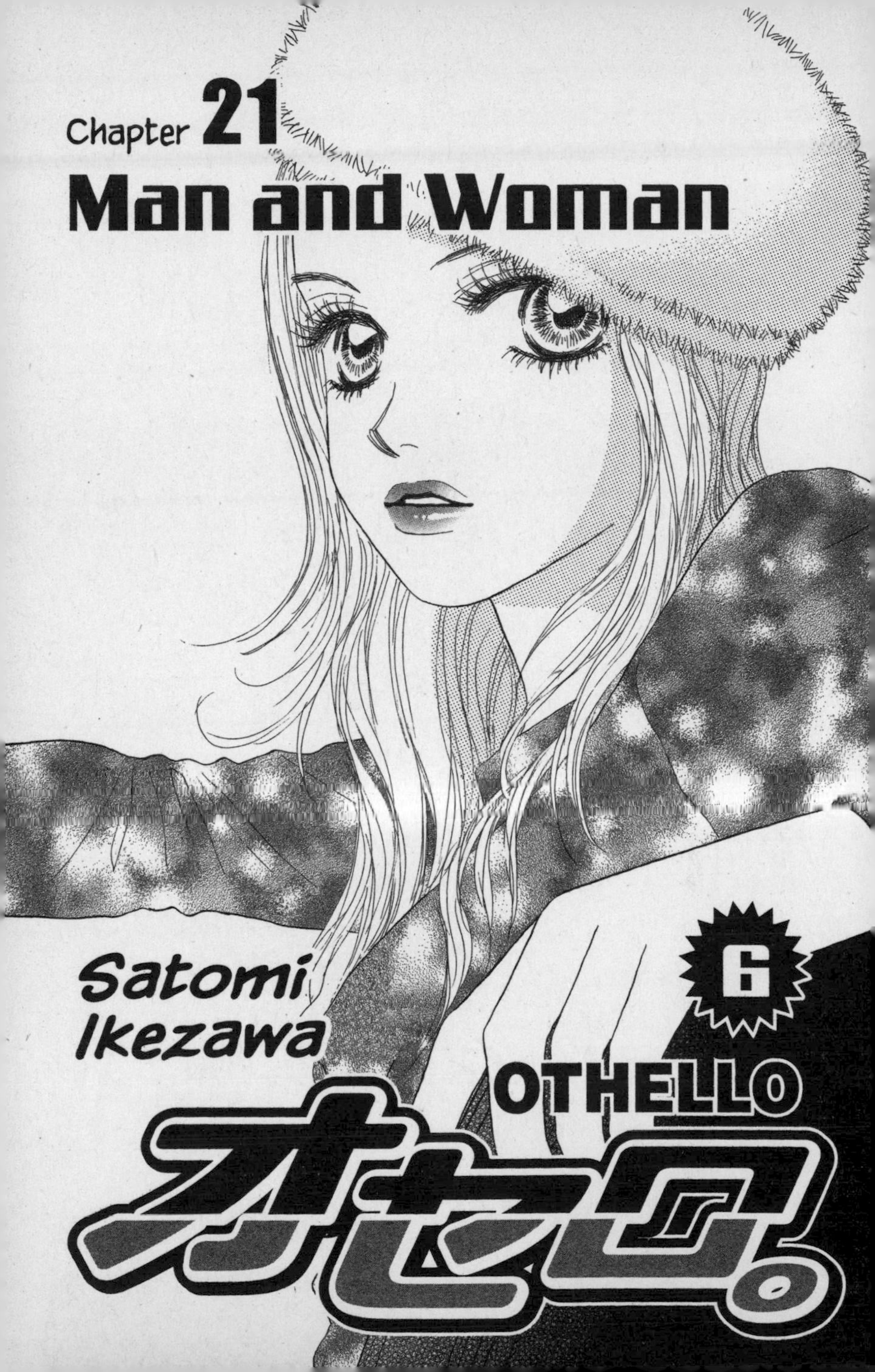
Satomi Ikezawa
6
OTHELLO
オセロ。

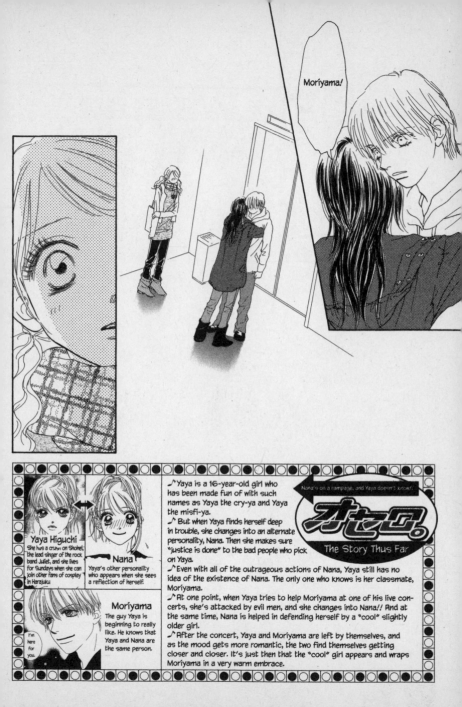

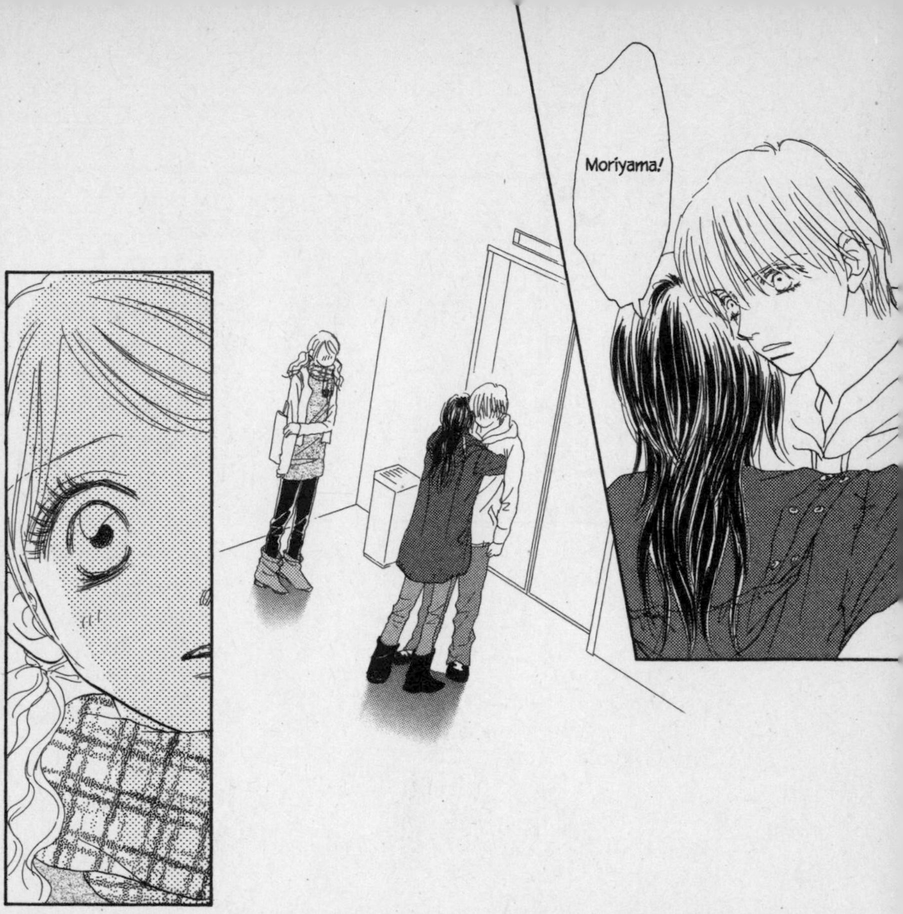
Moriyama!

Nana's on a rampage, and Yaya doesn't know!!

オセロ。

The Story Thus Far

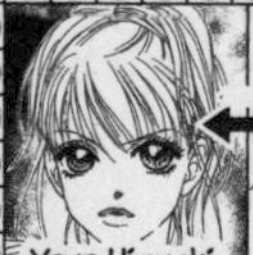

Yaya Higuchi

She has a crush on Shohei, the lead singer of the rock band Juliet, and she lives for Sundays when she can join other fans of cosplay in Harajuku

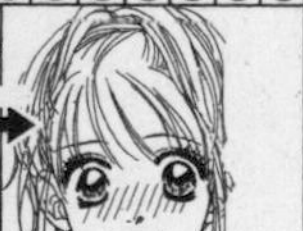

Nana

Yaya's other personality who appears when she sees a reflection of herself.

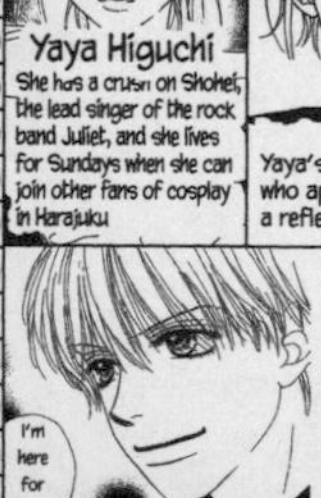
I'm here for you.

Moriyama

The guy Yaya is beginning to really like. He knows that Yaya and Nana are the same person.

♪ Yaya is a 16-year-old girl who has been made fun of with such names as Yaya the cry-ya and Yaya the misfi-ya.

♪ But when Yaya finds herself deep in trouble, she changes into an alternate personality, Nana. Then she makes sure "justice is done" to the bad people who pick on Yaya.

♪ Even with all of the outrageous actions of Nana, Yaya still has no idea of the existence of Nana. The only one who knows is her classmate, Moriyama.

♪ At one point, when Yaya tries to help Moriyama at one of his live concerts, she's attacked by evil men, and she changes into Nana!! And at the same time, Nana is helped in defending herself by a "cool" slightly older girl.

♪ After the concert, Yaya and Moriyama are left by themselves, and as the mood gets more romantic, the two find themselves getting closer and closer. It's just then that the "cool" girl appears and wraps Moriyama in a very warm embrace.

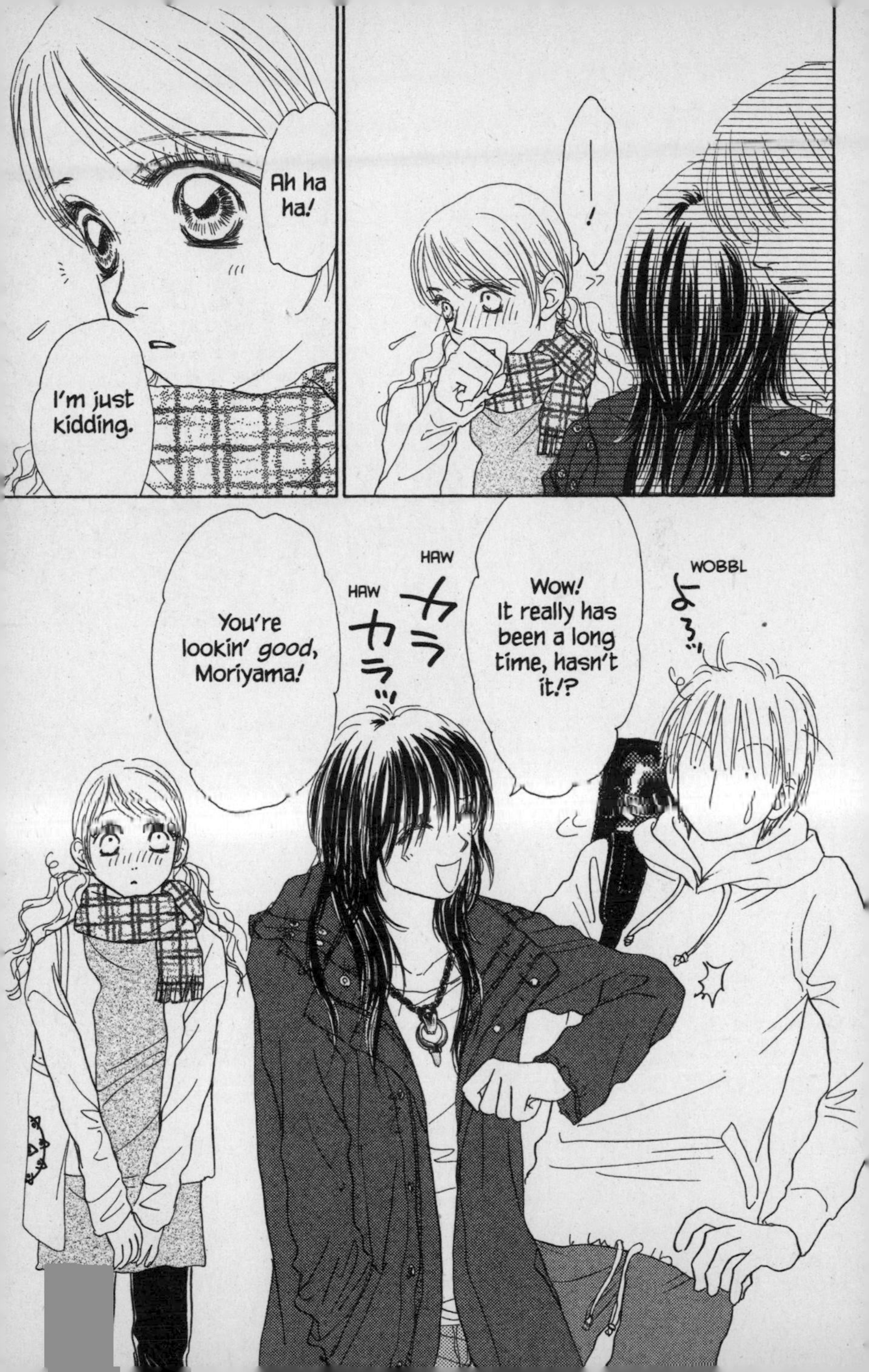
!
Ah ha ha!
I'm just kidding.
WOBBL
よろ…
Wow! It really has been a long time, hasn't it!?
HAW
カラ
HAW
カラッ
You're lookin' *good*, Moriyama!

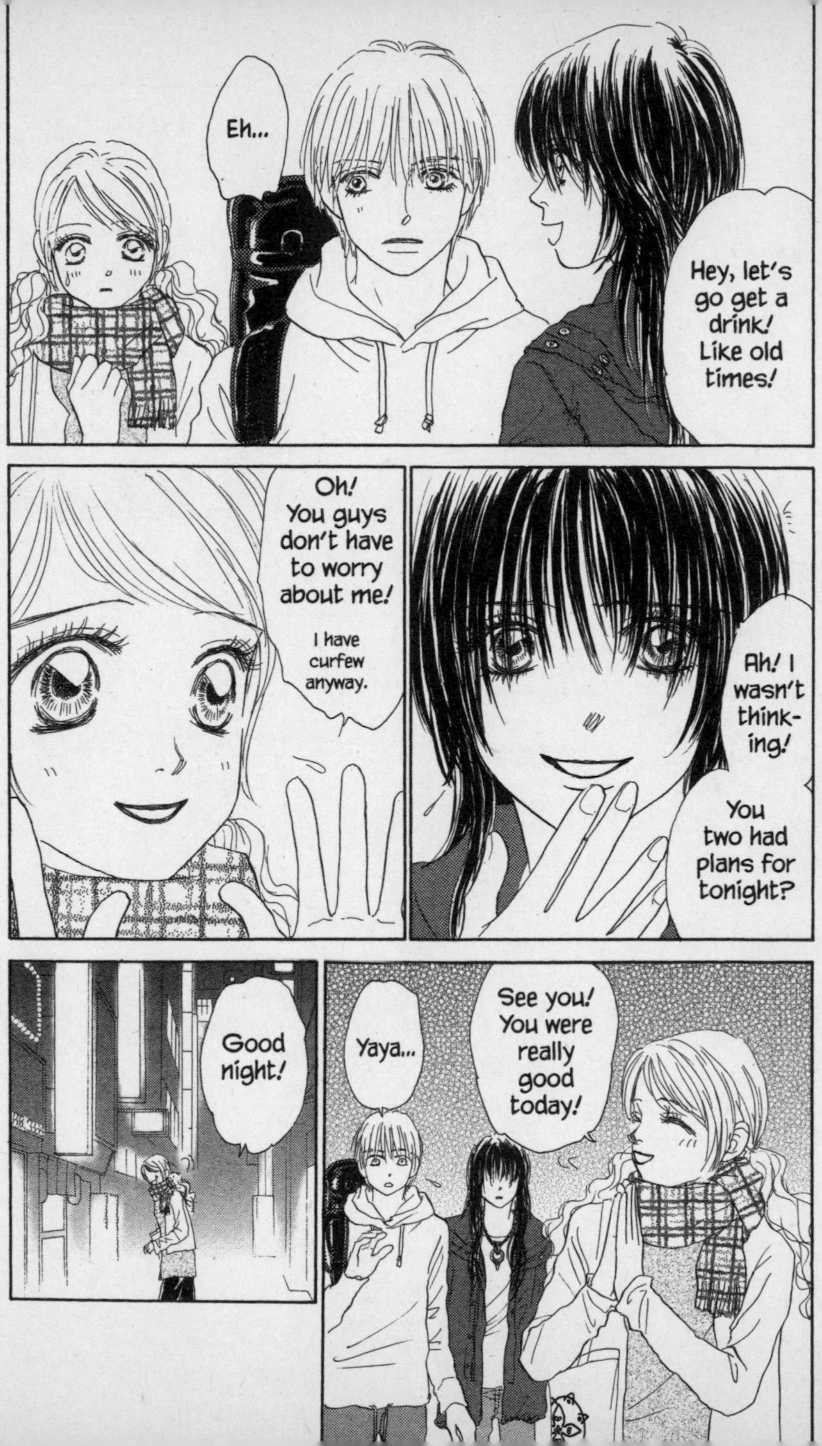
Hey, let's go get a drink! Like old times!
Eh...
Ah! I wasn't think-ing!
You two had plans for tonight?
Oh! You guys don't have to worry about me!
I have curfew anyway.
See you! You were really good today!
Yaya...
Good night!

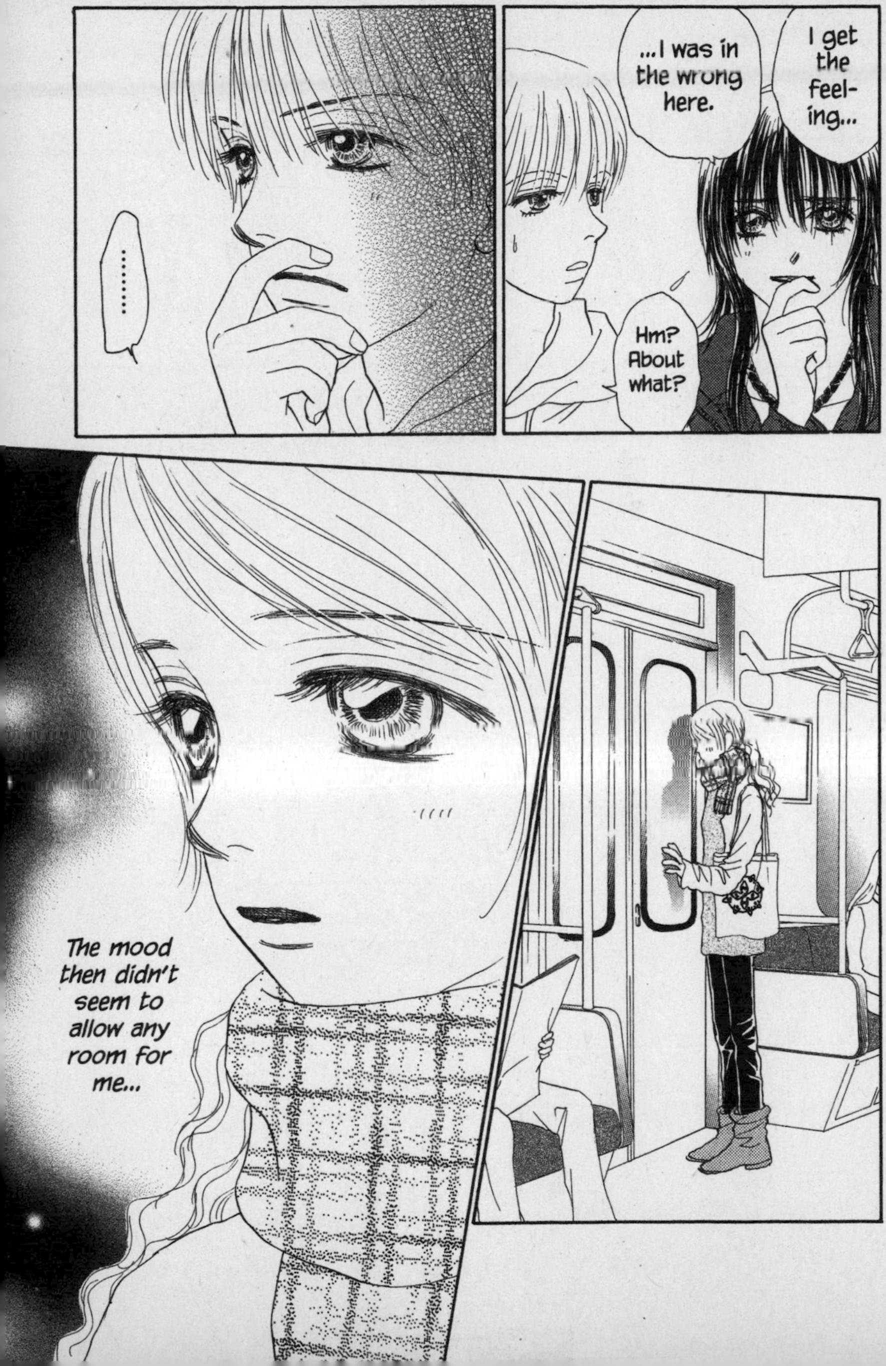

I get the feel-ing...
...I was in the wrong here.
Hm? About what?
......
The mood then didn't seem to allow any room for me...

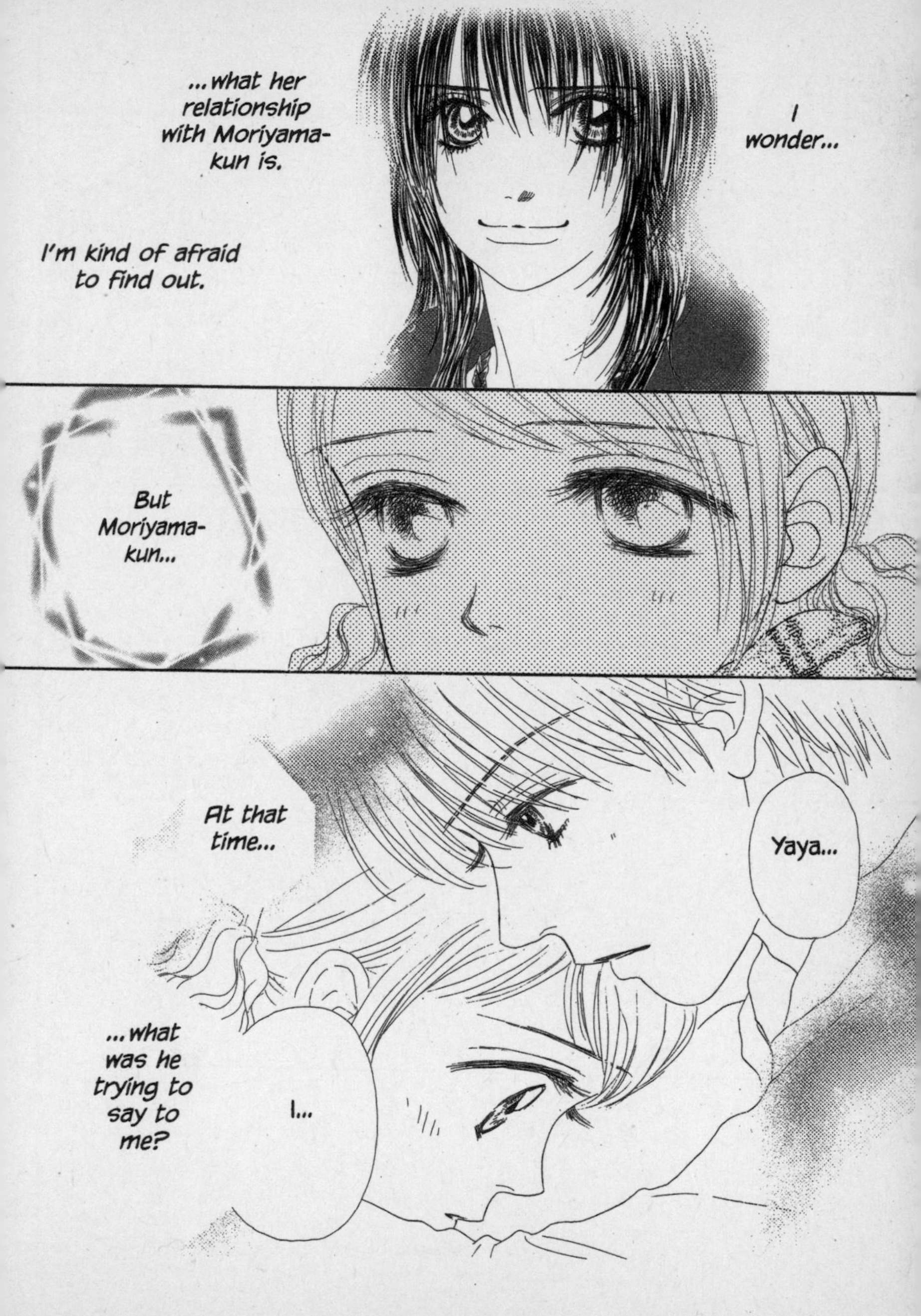
I wonder...
...what her relationship with Moriyama-kun is.
I'm kind of afraid to find out.
But Moriyama-kun...
Yaya...
At that time...
I...
...what was he trying to say to me?

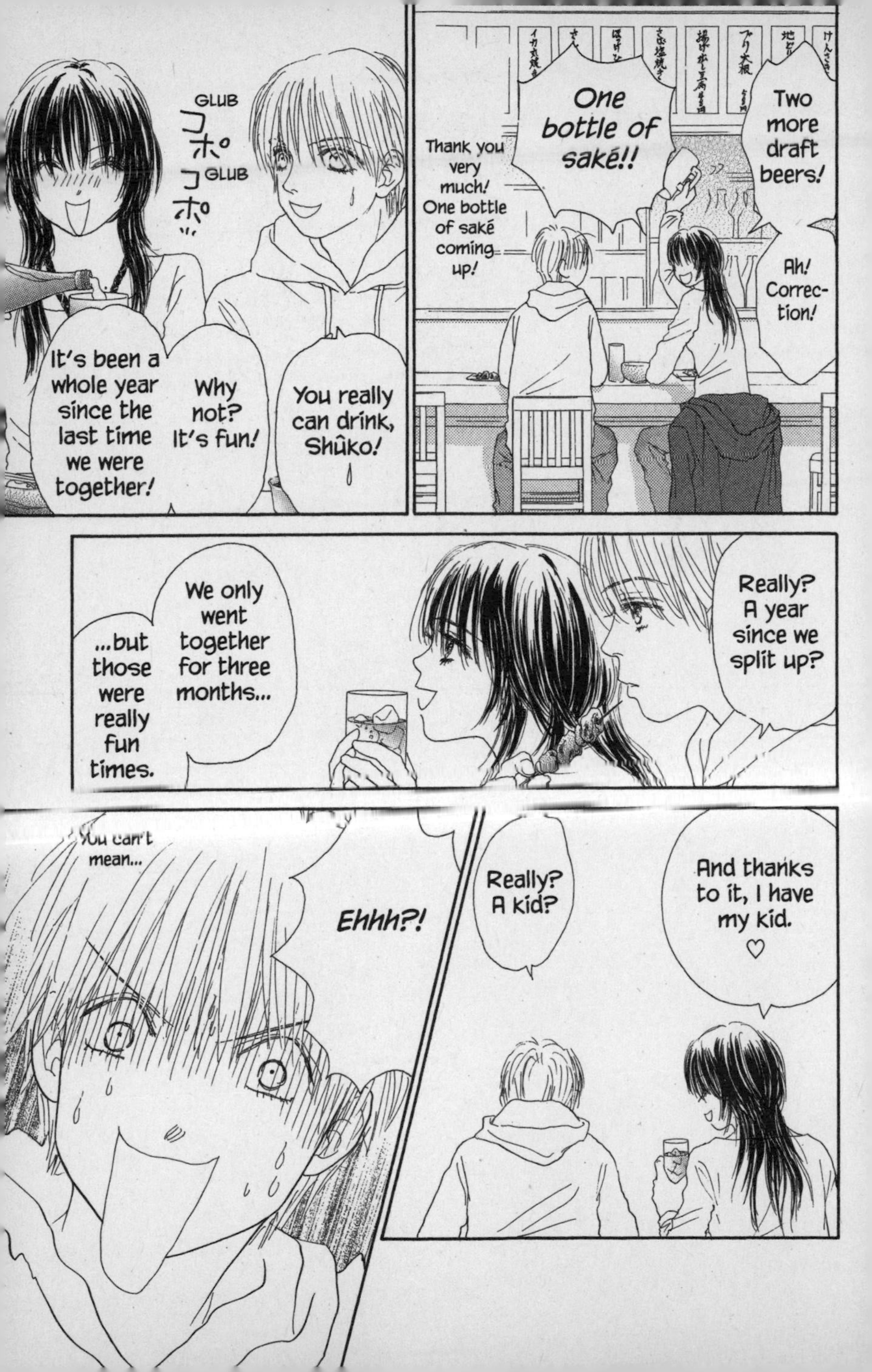
Two more draft beers!
Ah! Correction!
One bottle of saké!!
Thank you very much! One bottle of saké coming up!
GLUB コポ GLUB コポ
You really can drink, Shûko!
Why not? It's fun!
It's been a whole year since the last time we were together!
Really? A year since we split up?
We only went together for three months...
...but those were really fun times.
And thanks to it, I have my kid. ♡
Really? A kid?
Ehhh?!
You can't mean...

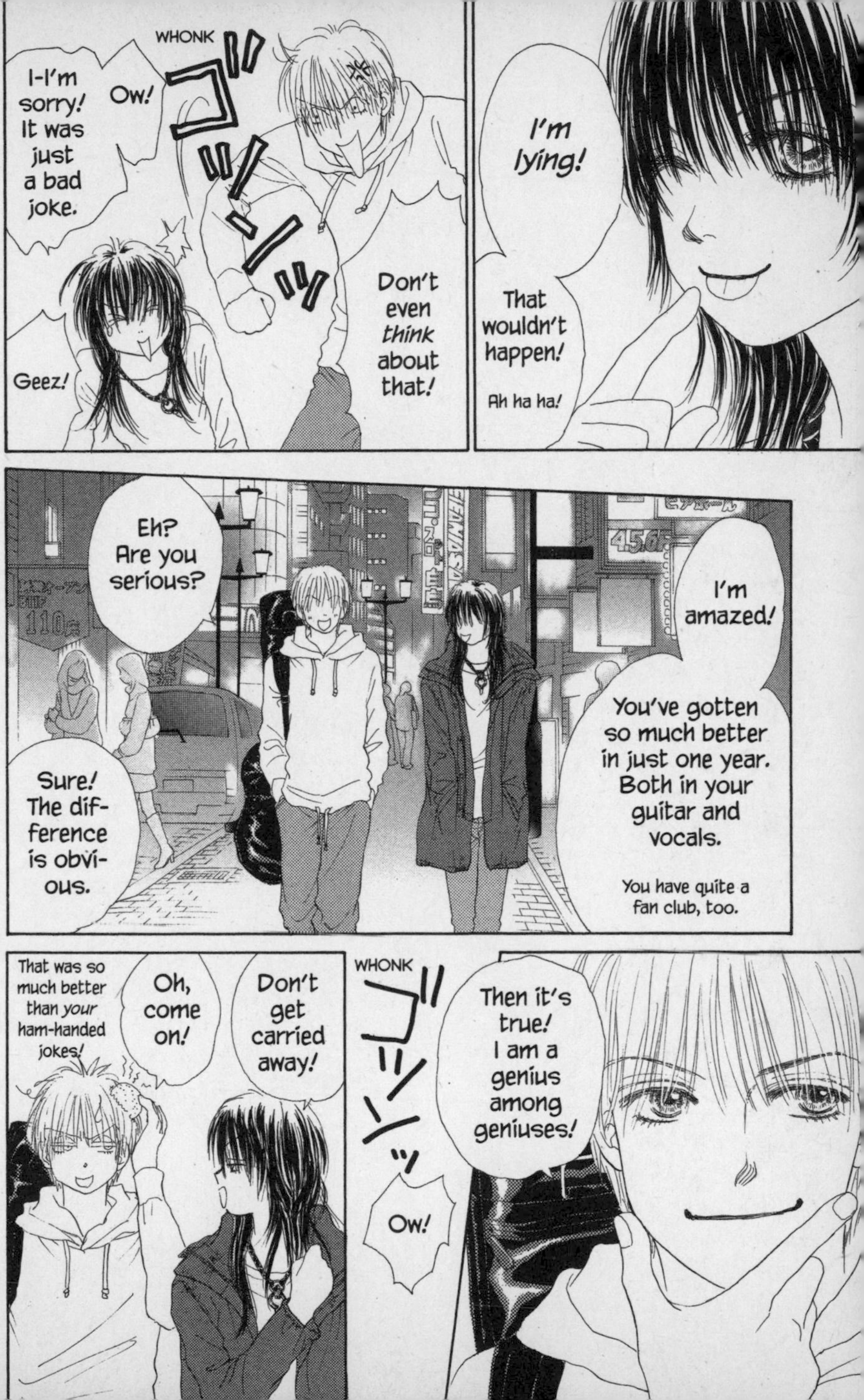
I'm lying!
That wouldn't happen!
Ah ha ha!
WHONK
Don't even *think* about that!
Ow!
I-I'm sorry! It was just a bad joke.
Geez!
I'm amazed!
You've gotten so much better in just one year. Both in your guitar and vocals.
You have quite a fan club, too.
Eh? Are you serious?
Sure! The difference is obvious.
Then it's true! I am a genius among geniuses!
WHONK
Ow!
Don't get carried away!
Oh, come on!
That was so much better than *your* ham-handed jokes!

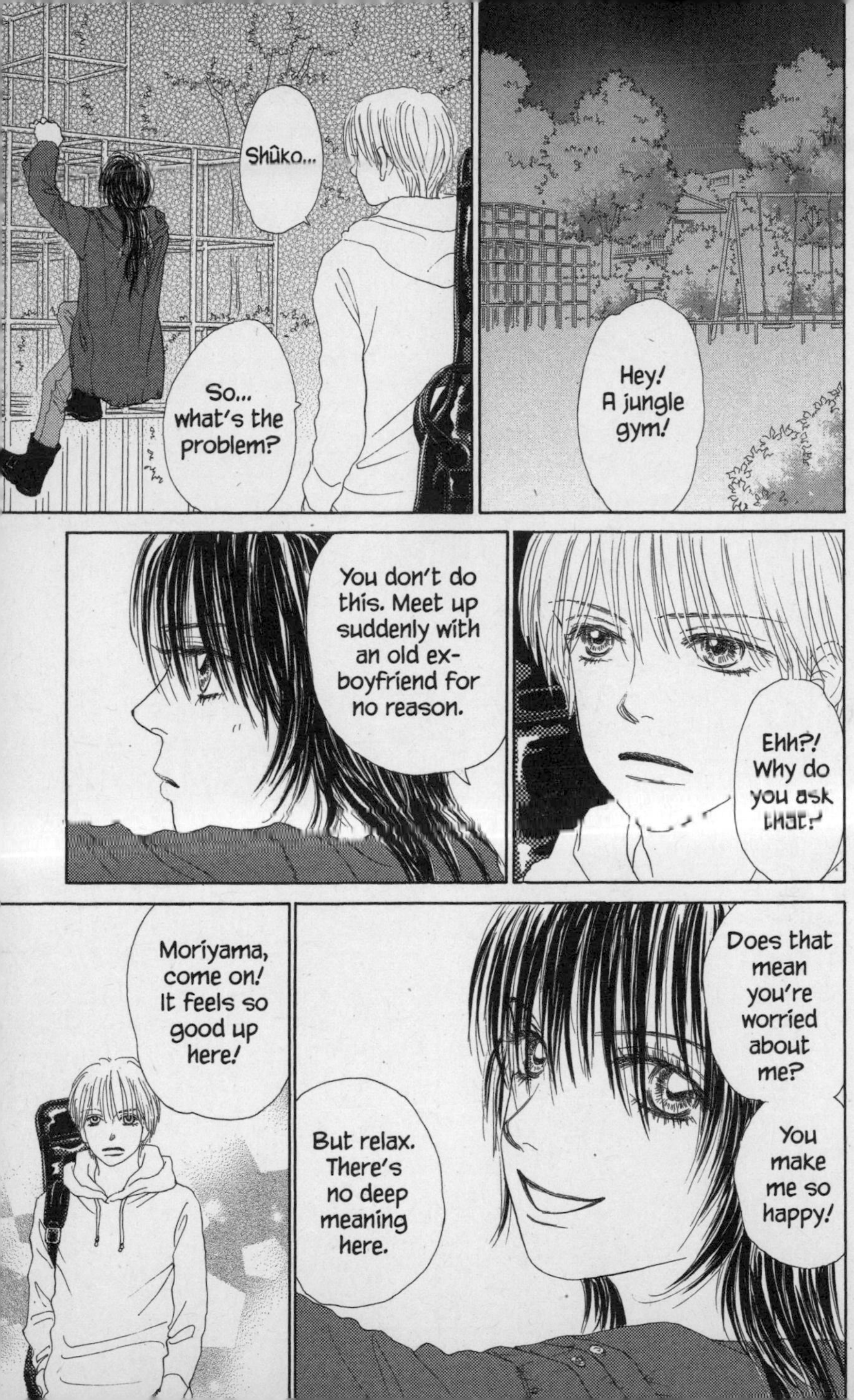
Hey! A jungle gym!
Shûko...
So... what's the problem?
Ehh?! Why do you ask that?
You don't do this. Meet up suddenly with an old ex-boyfriend for no reason.
Does that mean you're worried about me?
You make me so happy!
But relax. There's no deep meaning here.
Moriyama, come on! It feels so good up here!

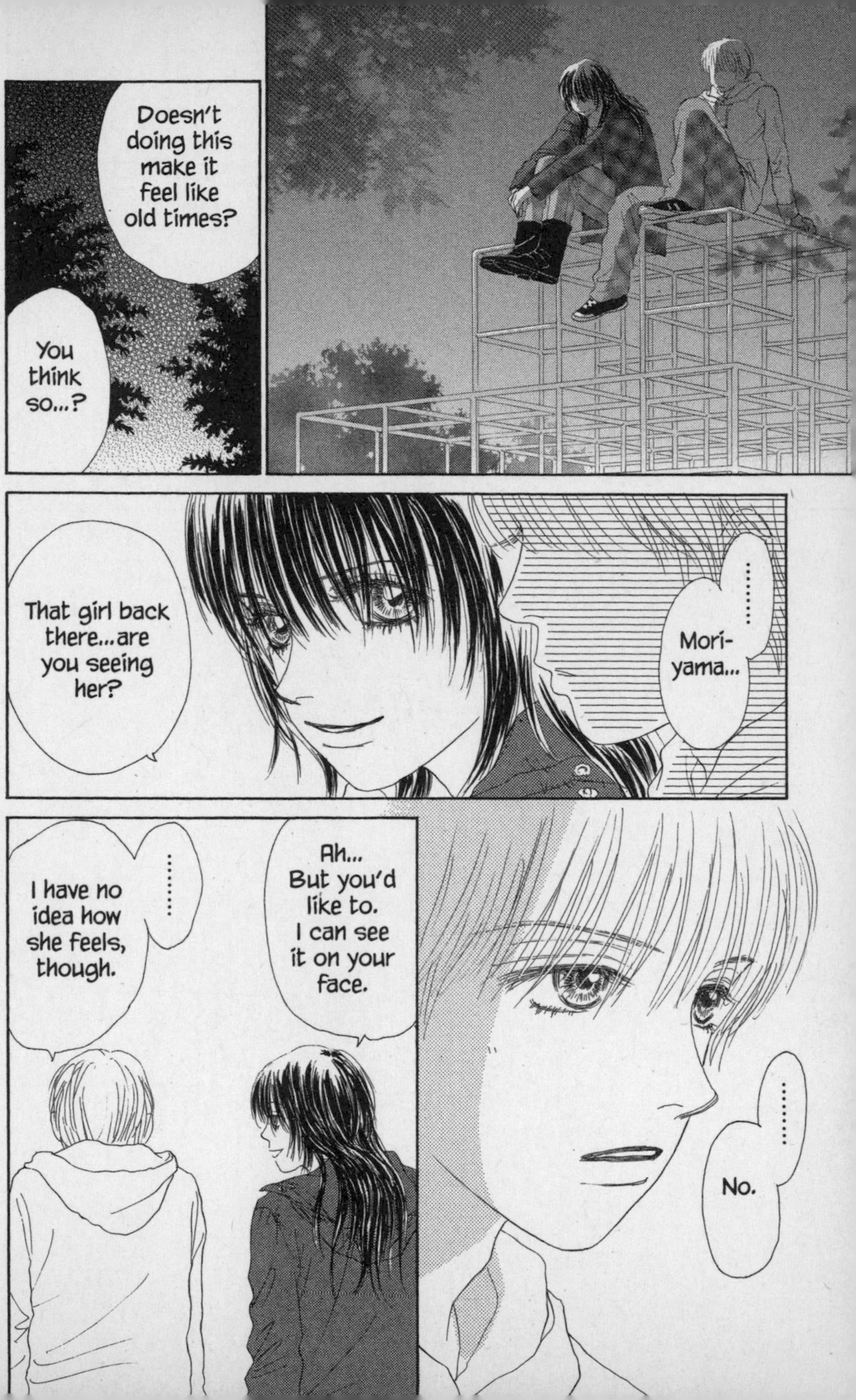
Doesn't doing this make it feel like old times?
You think so...?
...... Mori-yama...
That girl back there...are you seeing her?
......
No.
Ah... But you'd like to. I can see it on your face.
......
I have no idea how she feels, though.

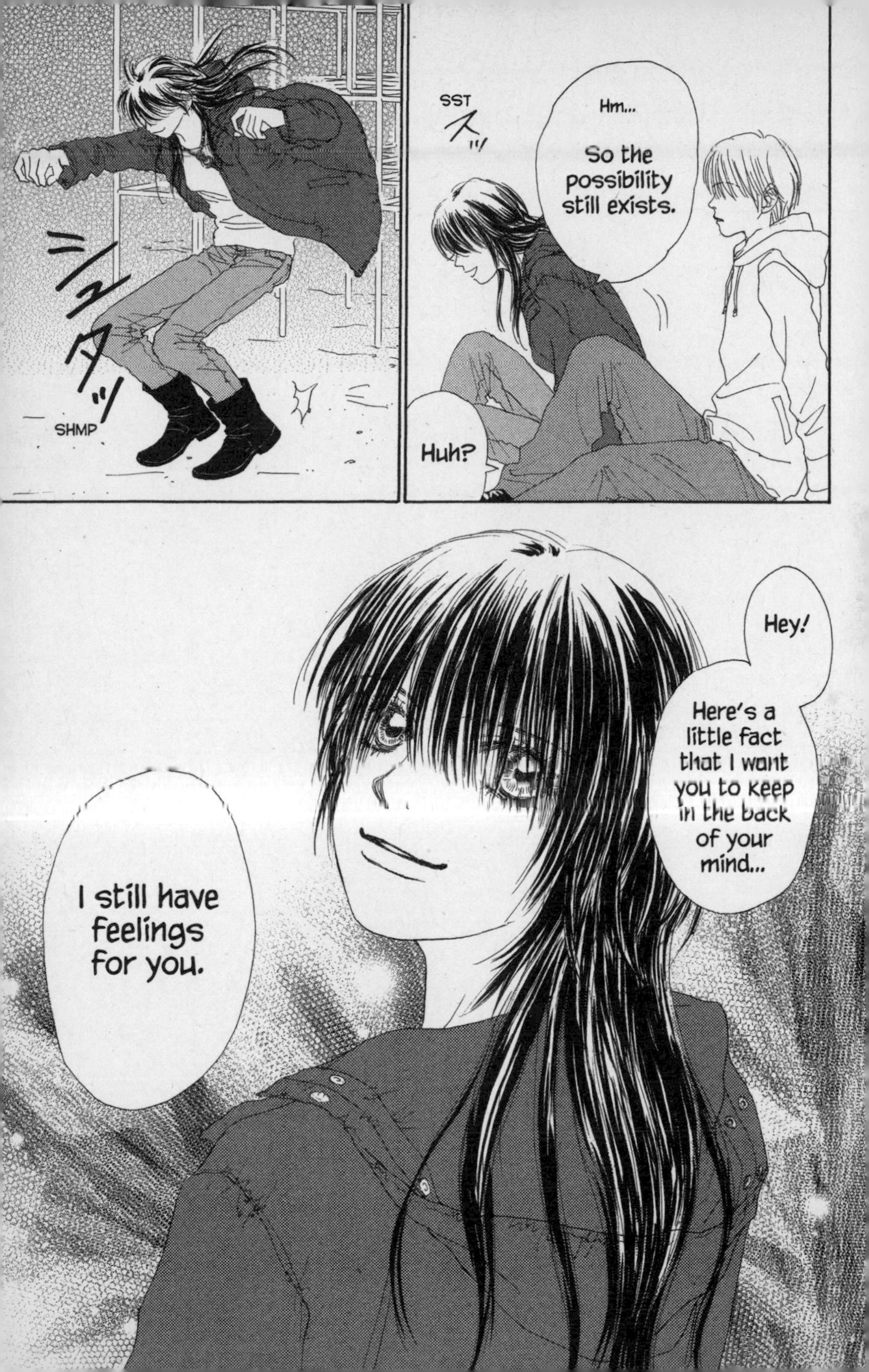
SST
スッ
Hm...
So the possibility still exists.
Huh?
シュタッ
SHMP
Hey!
Here's a little fact that I want you to keep in the back of your mind...
I still have feelings for you.

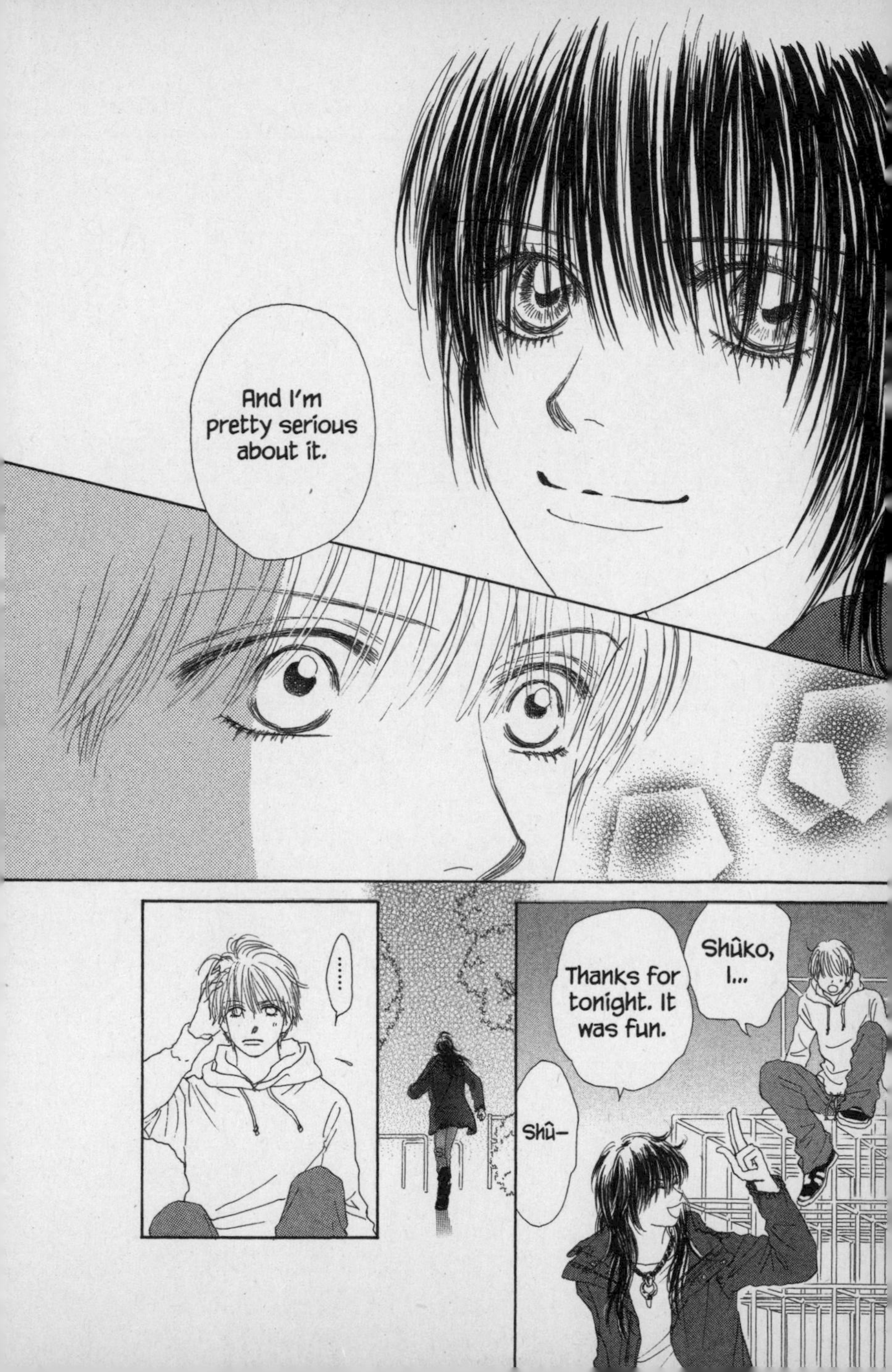
And I'm pretty serious about it.
Shûko, I...
Thanks for tonight. It was fun.
Shû-
......

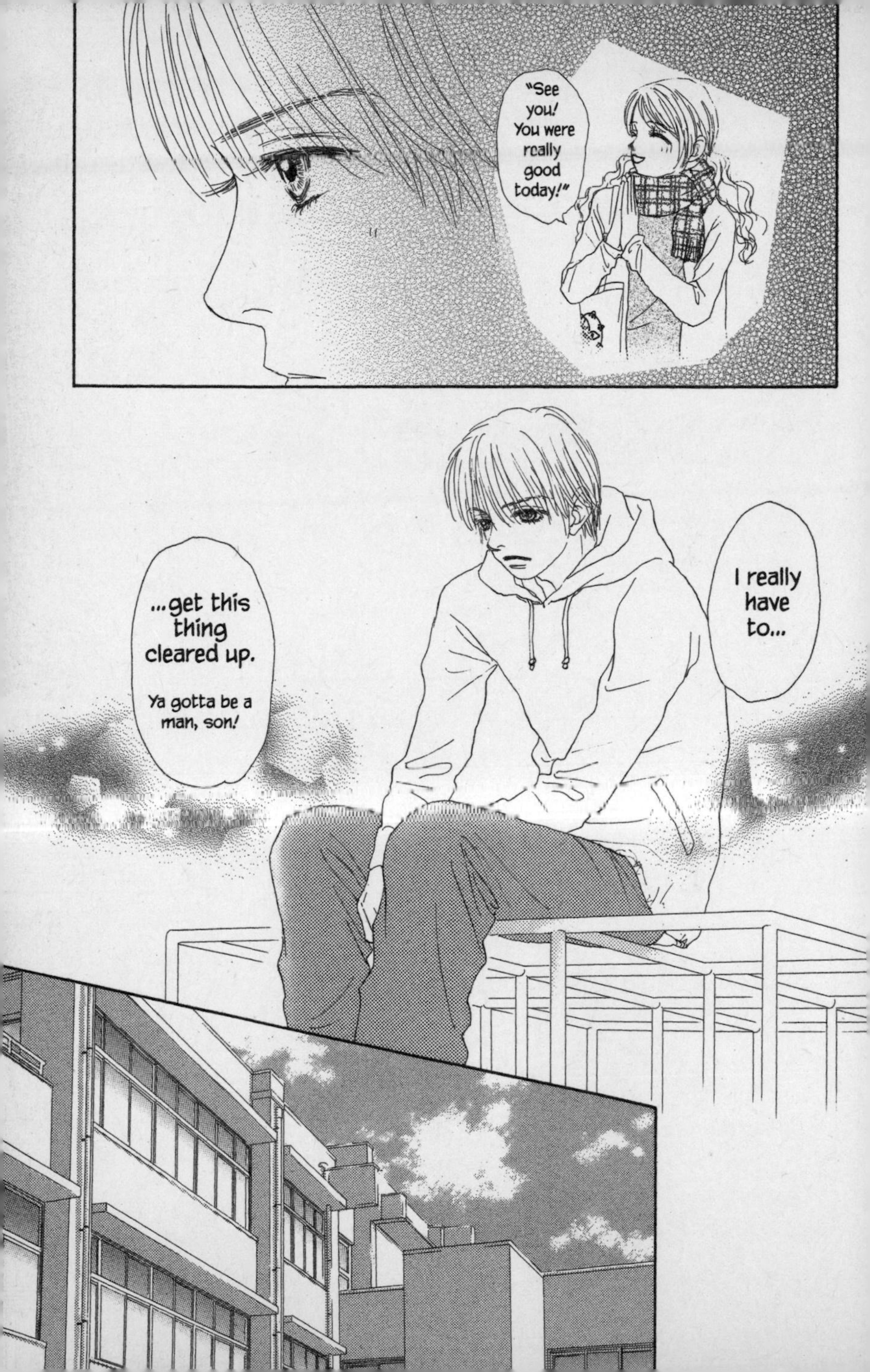
"See you! You were really good today!"
I really have to...
...get this thing cleared up.
Ya gotta be a man, son!

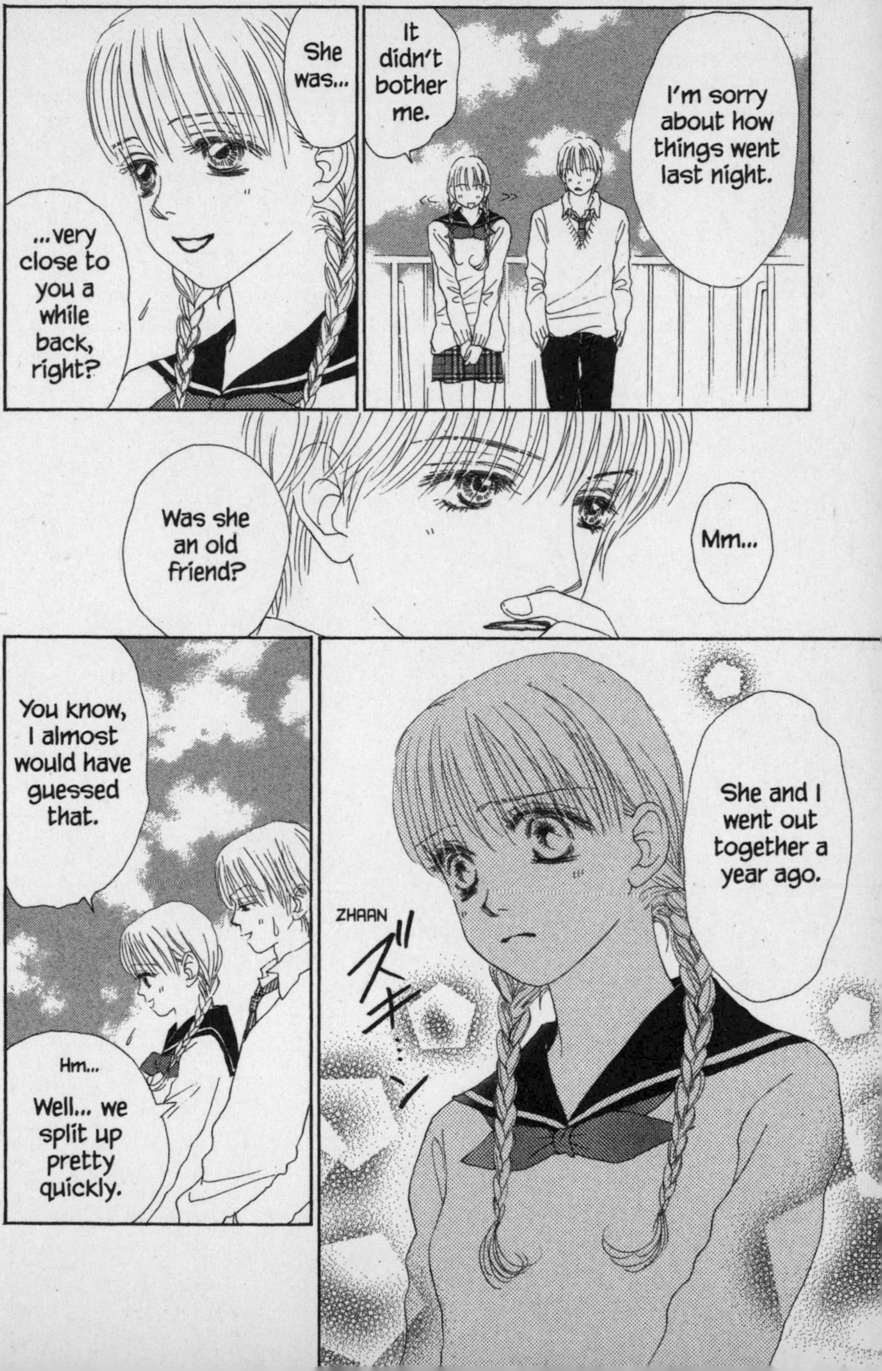
I'm sorry about how things went last night.
It didn't bother me.
She was...
...very close to you a while back, right?
Was she an old friend?
Mm...
She and I went out together a year ago.
ZHAAN
You know, I almost would have guessed that.
Hm...
Well... we split up pretty quickly.

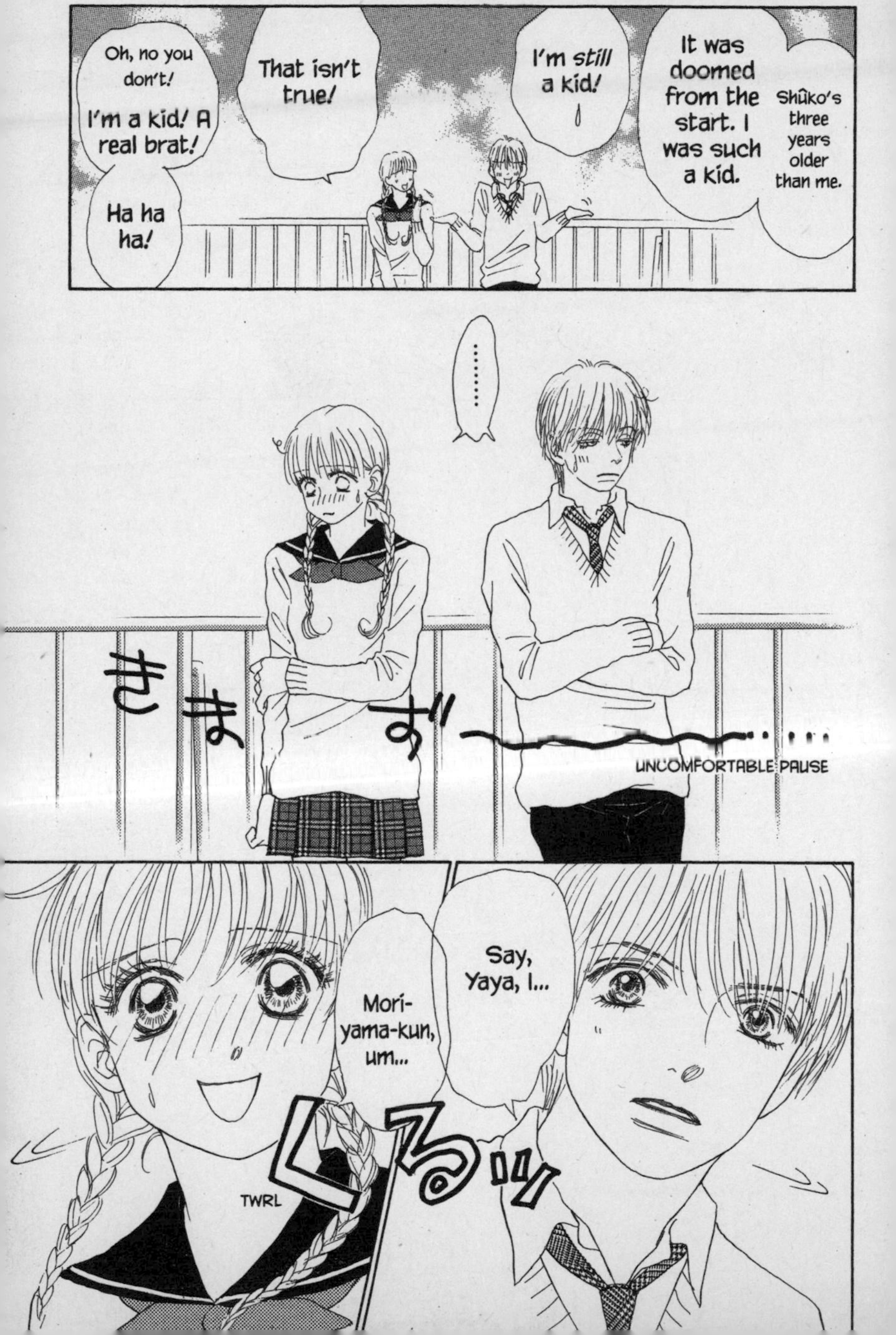
Shûko's three years older than me.
It was doomed from the start. I was such a kid.
I'm *still* a kid!
That isn't true!
Oh, no you don't!
I'm a kid! A real brat!
Ha ha ha!
......
きまずー……
UNCOMFORTABLE PAUSE
Say, Yaya, I...
Mori-yama-kun, um...
TWRL

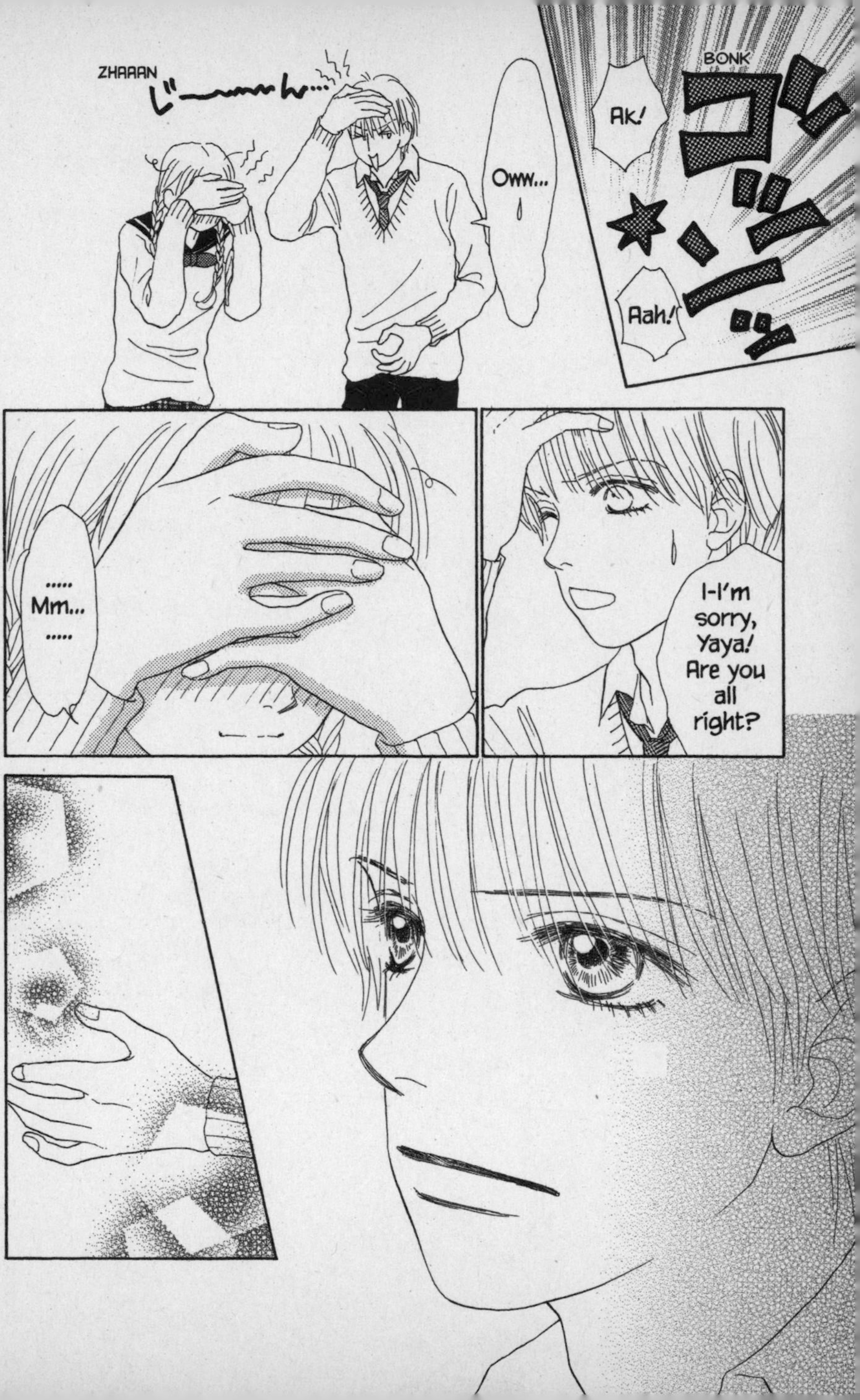
BONK
Ak!
Aah!
Oww...
ZHAAAN
I-I'm sorry, Yaya! Are you all right?
..... Mm... .....

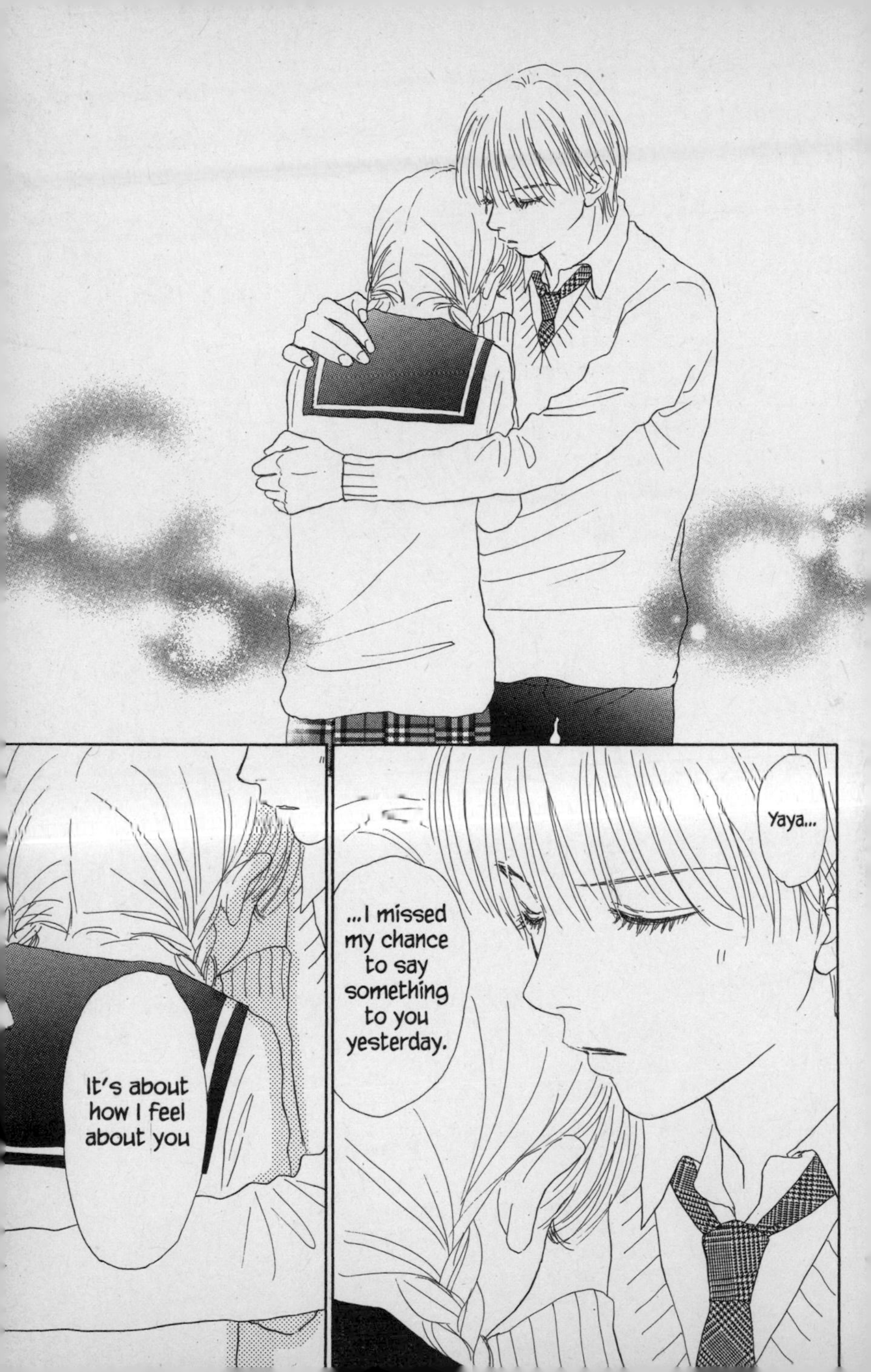
Yaya...
...I missed my chance to say something to you yesterday.
It's about how I feel about you

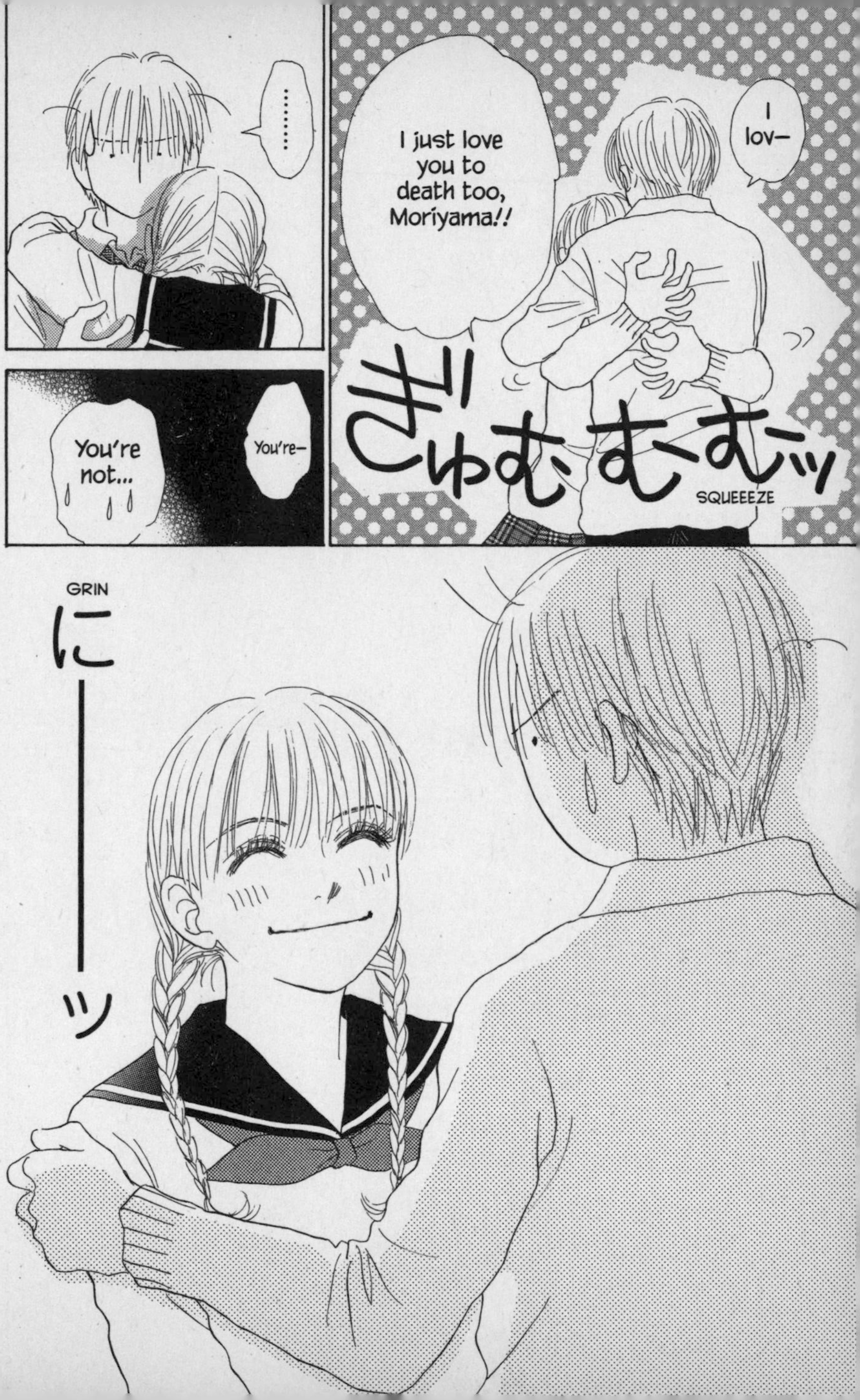
I lov—
I just love you to death too, Moriyama!!
ぎゅむむーむーッ
SQUEEEZE
……
You're—
You're not...
にーーッ
GRIN

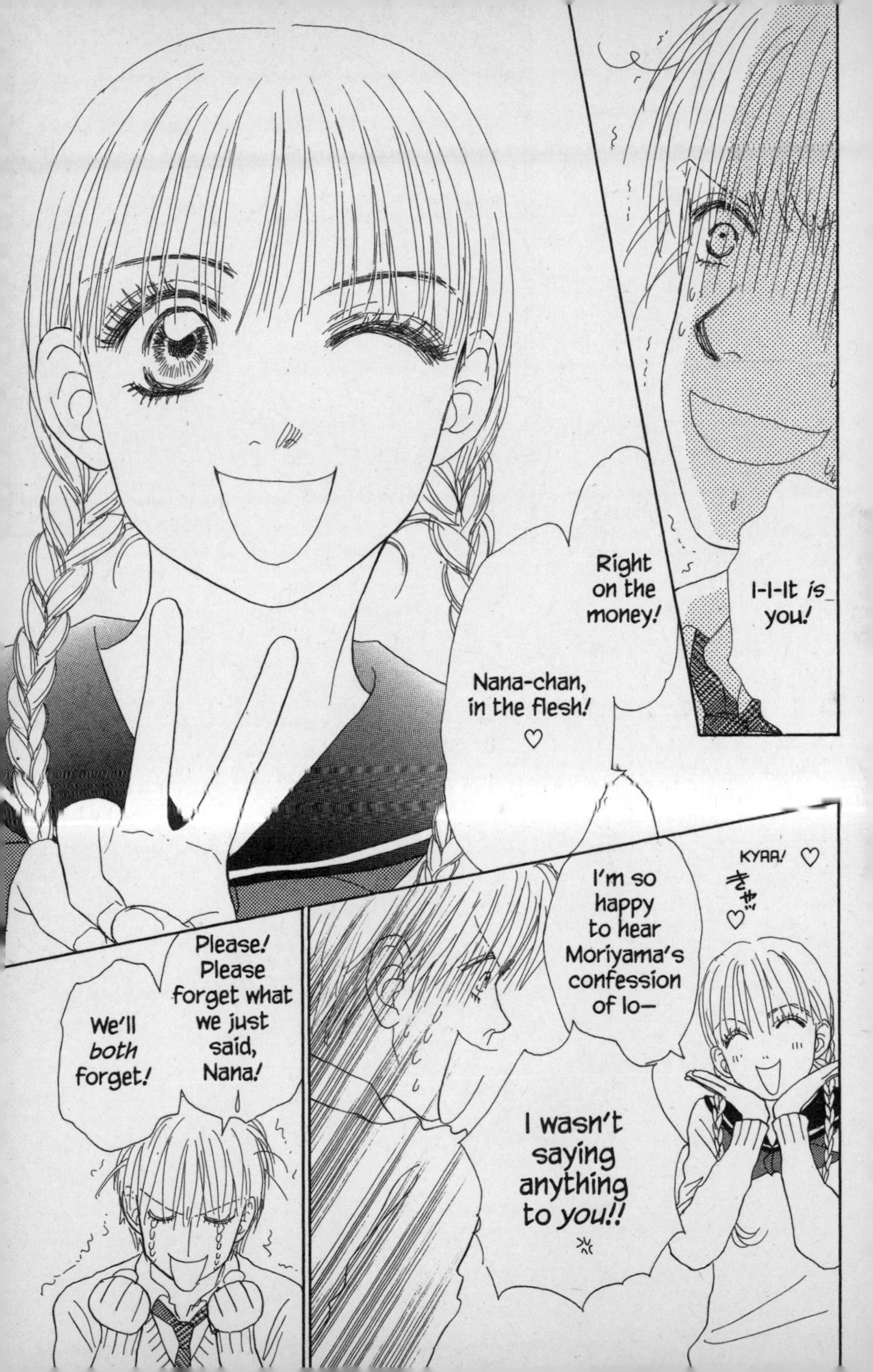

I-I-It *is_* you!
Right on the money!
Nana-chan, in the flesh! ♡
KYAA! ♡
I'm so happy to hear Moriyama's confession of lo—
I wasn't saying anything to *you*!!
Please! Please forget what we just said, Nana!
We'll *both* forget!

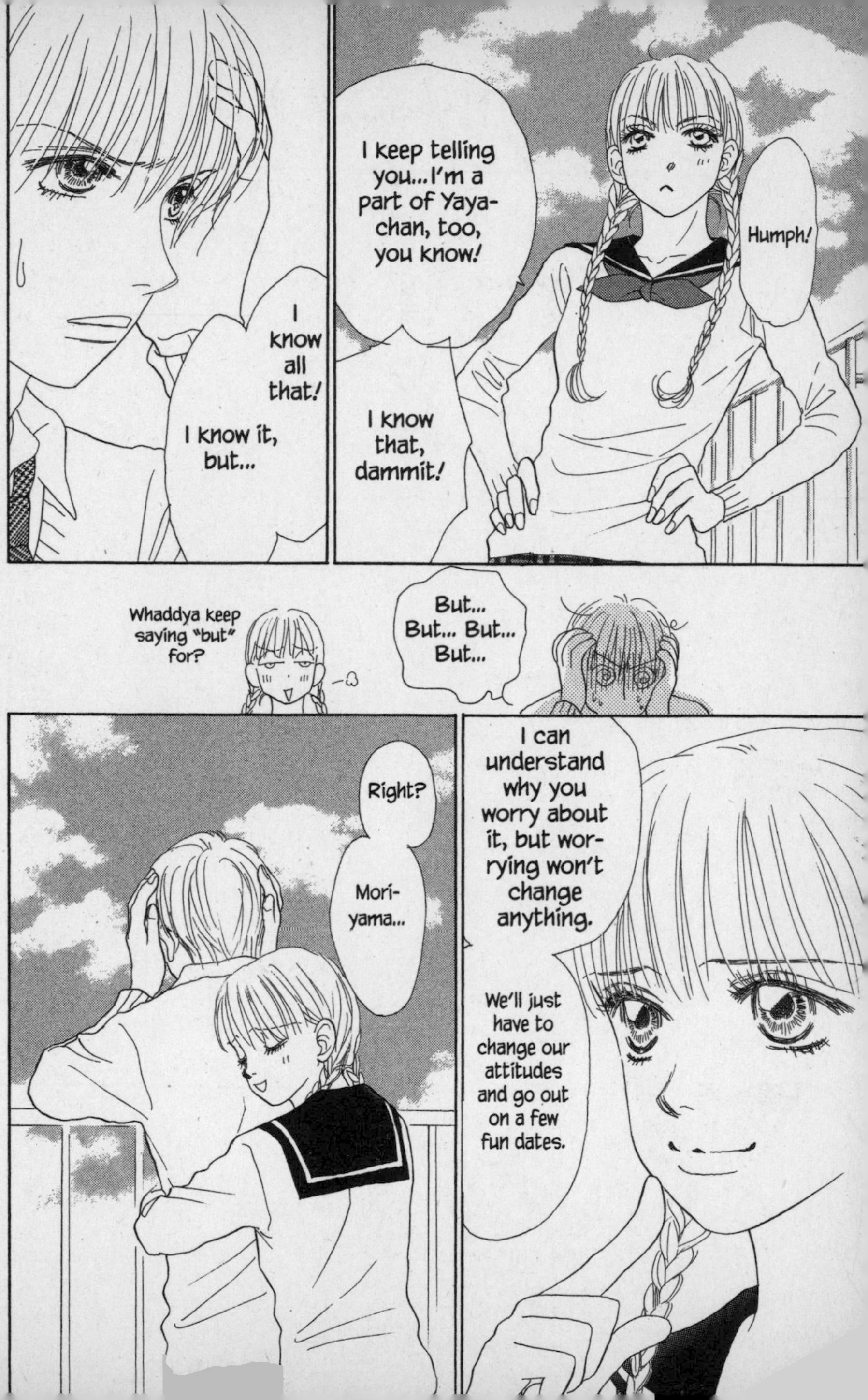
I keep telling you...I'm a part of Yaya-chan, too, you know!
Humph!
I know that, dammit!
I know all that!
I know it, but...
But... But... But... But...
Whaddya keep saying "but" for?
I can understand why you worry about it, but worrying won't change anything.
We'll just have to change our attitudes and go out on a few fun dates.
Right?
Mori-yama...

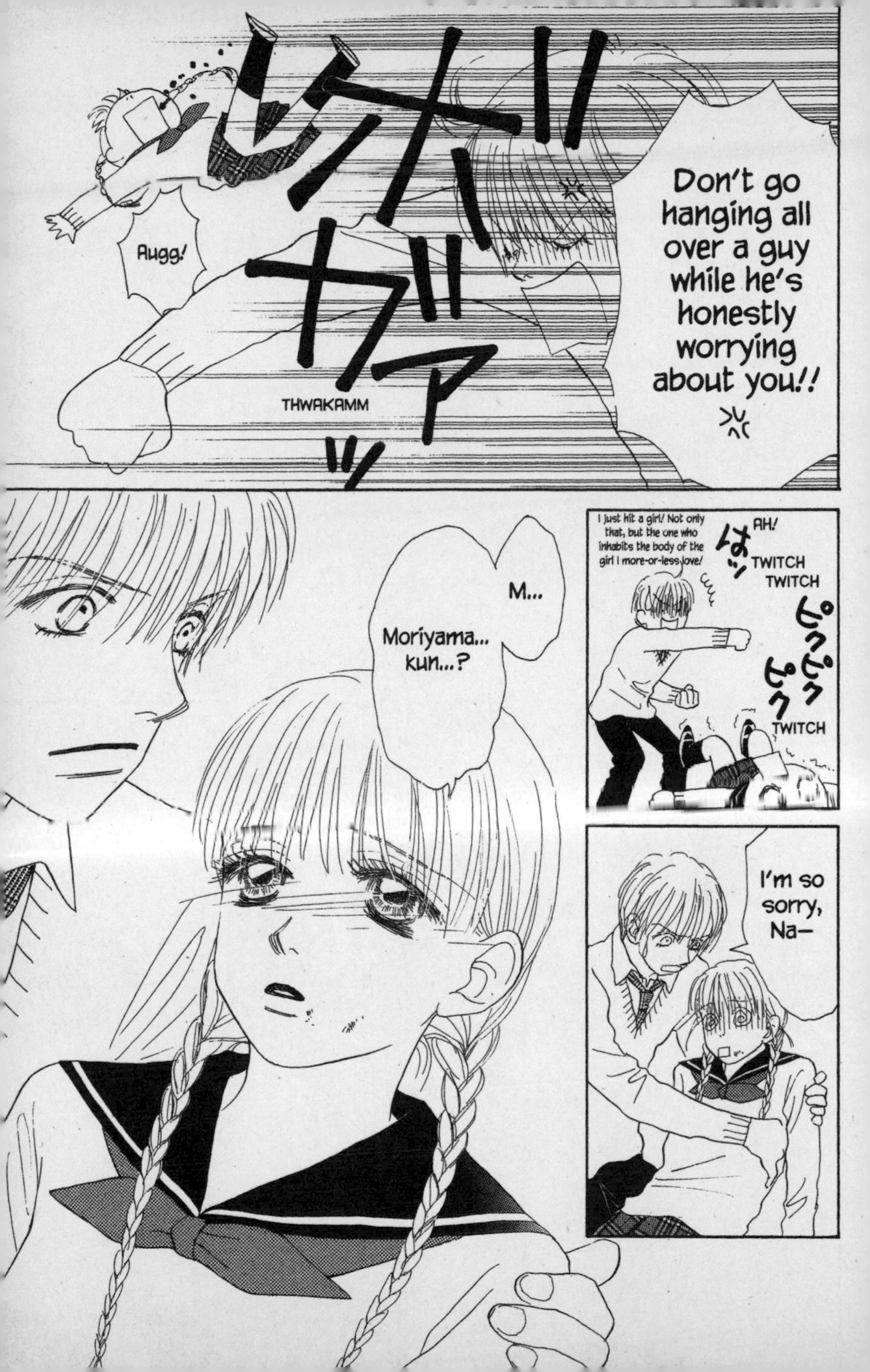

Don't go hanging all over a guy while he's honestly worrying about you!!
THWAKAMM
Augg!
AH!
はッ
I just hit a girl! Not only that, but the one who inhabits the body of the girl I more-or-less love!
TWITCH TWITCH
ピクピク
ピク
TWITCH
I'm so sorry, Na–
M...
Moriyama... kun...?

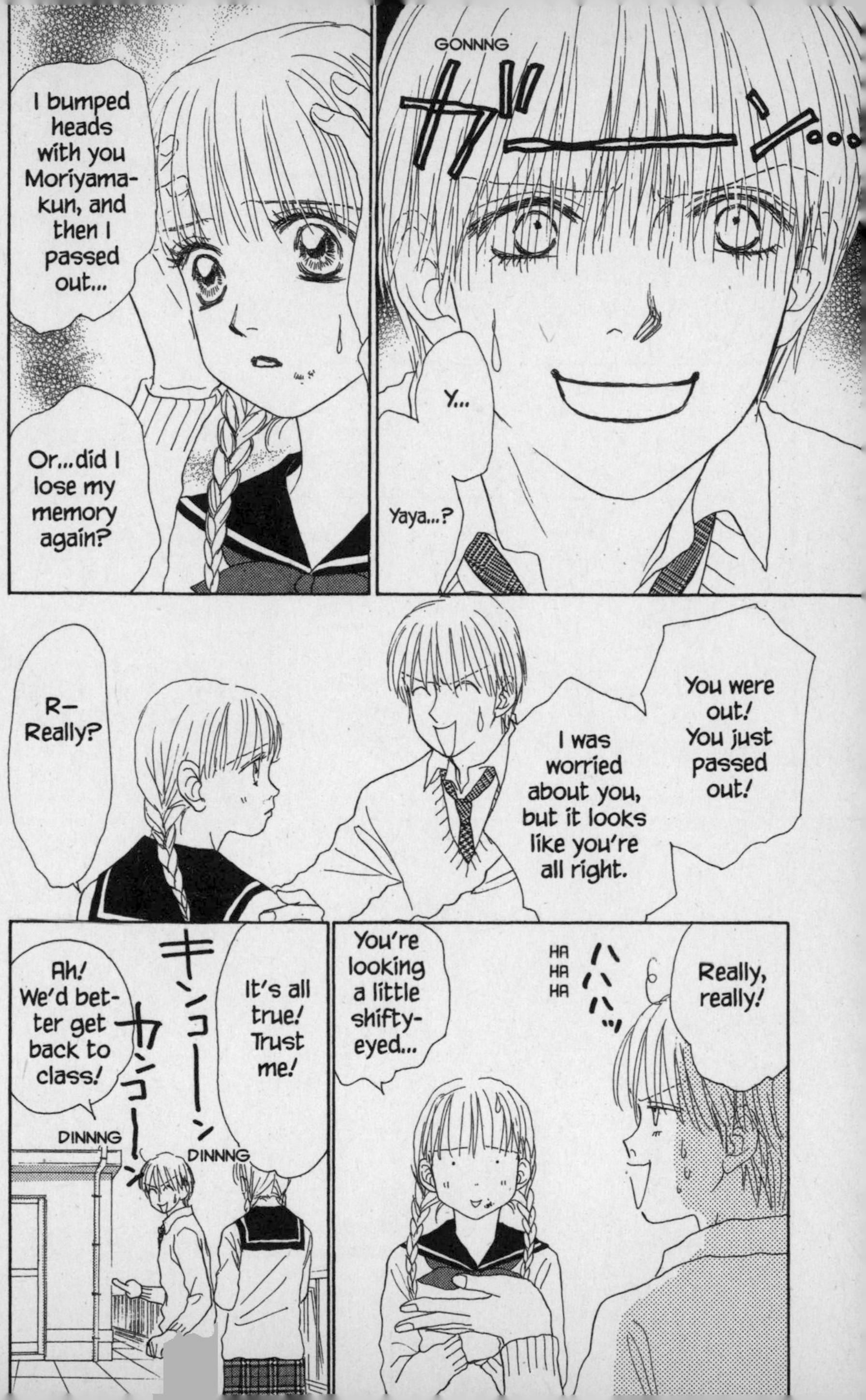
GONNNG
Y...
Yaya...?
I bumped heads with you Moriyama-kun, and then I passed out...
Or...did I lose my memory again?
You were out! You just passed out!
I was worried about you, but it looks like you're all right.
R—Really?
Really, really!
HA HA HA
You're looking a little shifty-eyed...
It's all true! Trust me!
DINNNG
DINNNG
Ah! We'd better get back to class!

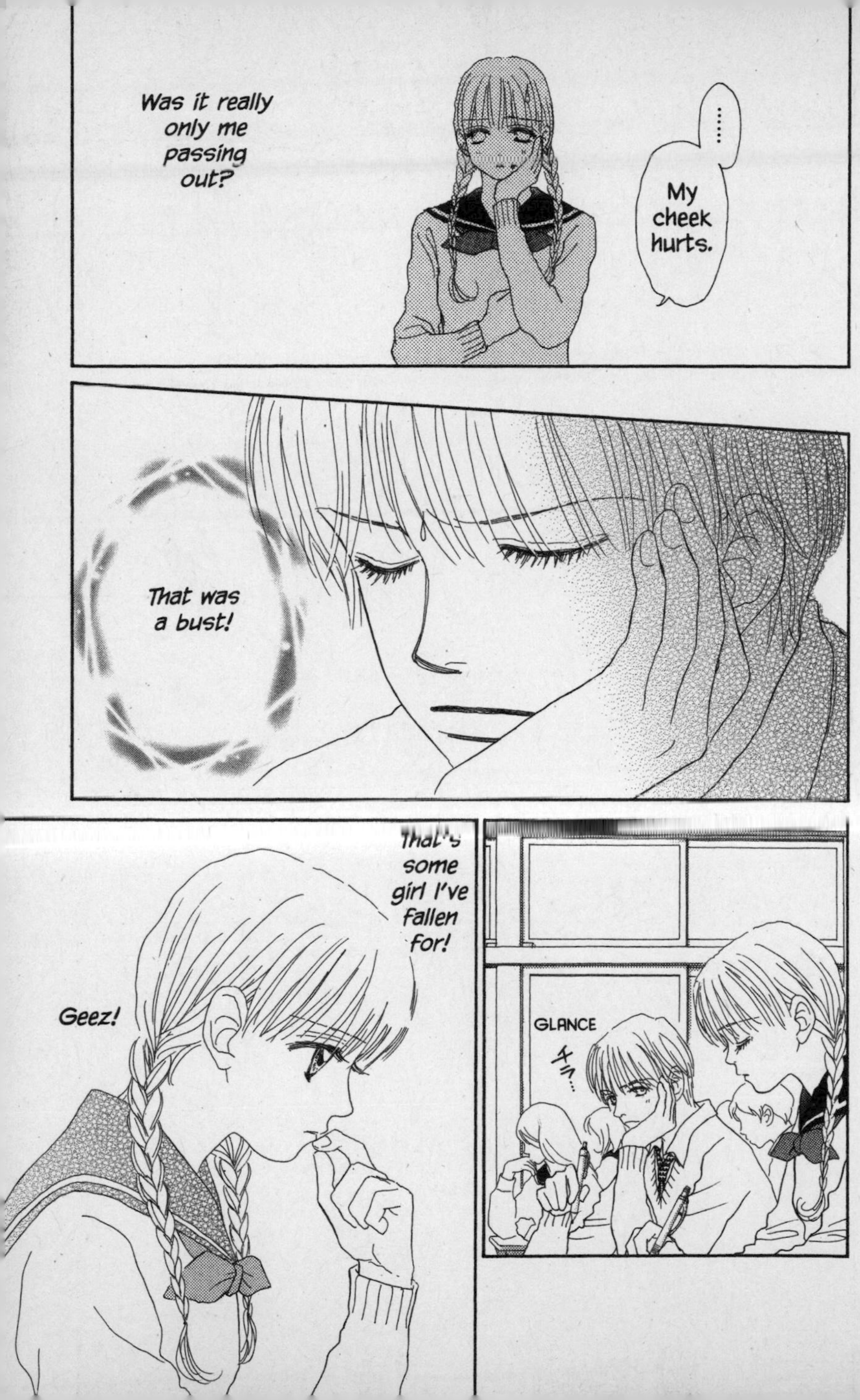
......
My cheek hurts.
Was it really only me passing out?
That was a bust!
GLANCE
チラ…
That's some girl I've fallen for!
Geez!

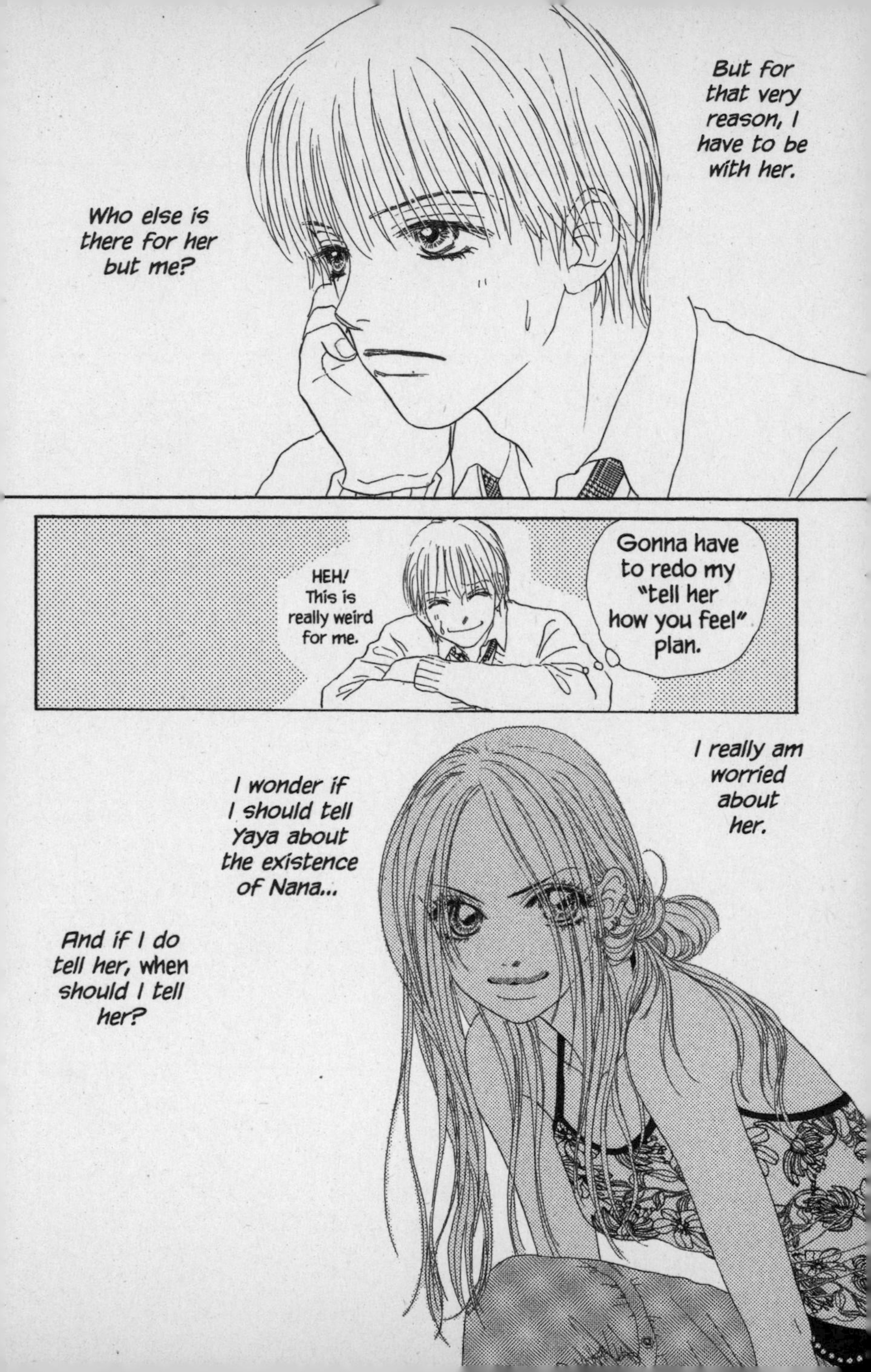

But for that very reason, I have to be with her.
Who else is there for her but me?
Gonna have to redo my "tell her how you feel" plan.
HEH! This is really weird for me.
I really am worried about her.
I wonder if I should tell Yaya about the existence of Nana...
And if I do tell her, when should I tell her?

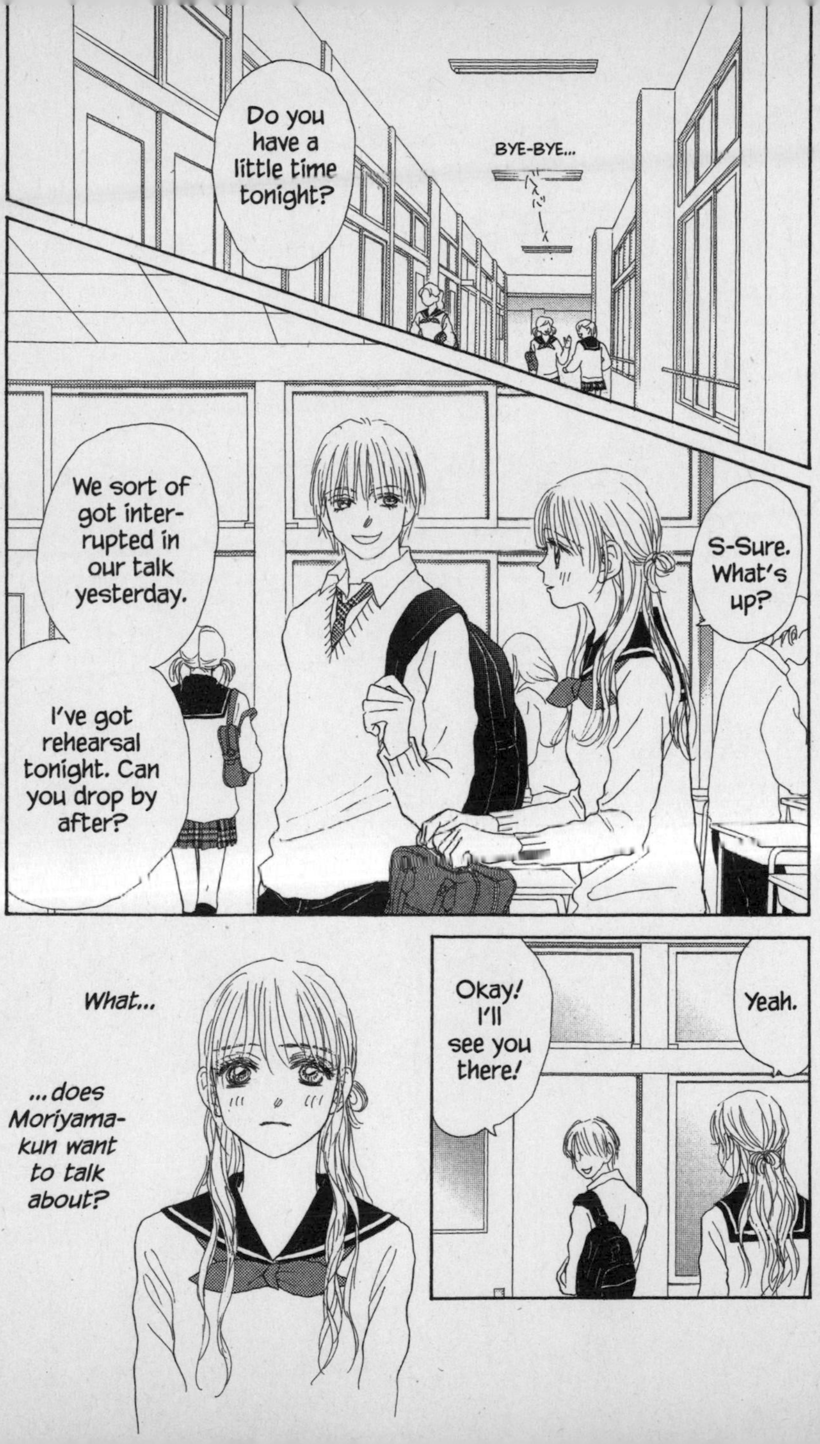
BYE-BYE...
Do you have a little time tonight?
S-Sure. What's up?
We sort of got interrupted in our talk yesterday.
I've got rehearsal tonight. Can you drop by after?
Yeah.
Okay! I'll see you there!
What...
...does Moriyama-kun want to talk about?

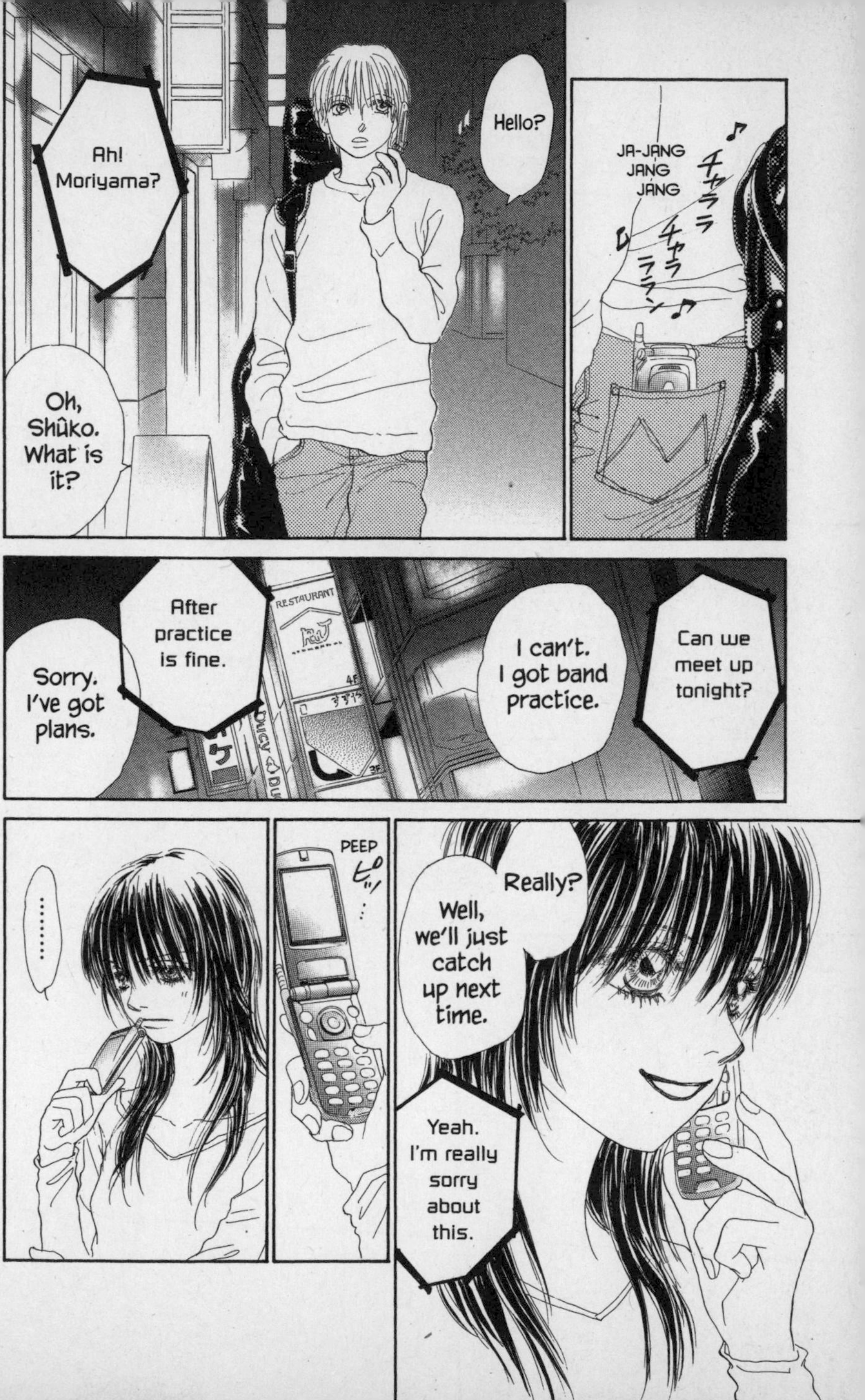
JA-JANG JANG JANG
チャララ チャララララン
Hello?
Ah! Moriyama?
Oh, Shûko. What is it?
Can we meet up tonight?
I can't. I got band practice.
After practice is fine.
Sorry. I've got plans.
Really?
Well, we'll just catch up next time.
Yeah. I'm really sorry about this.
PEEP
ピッ
...
......

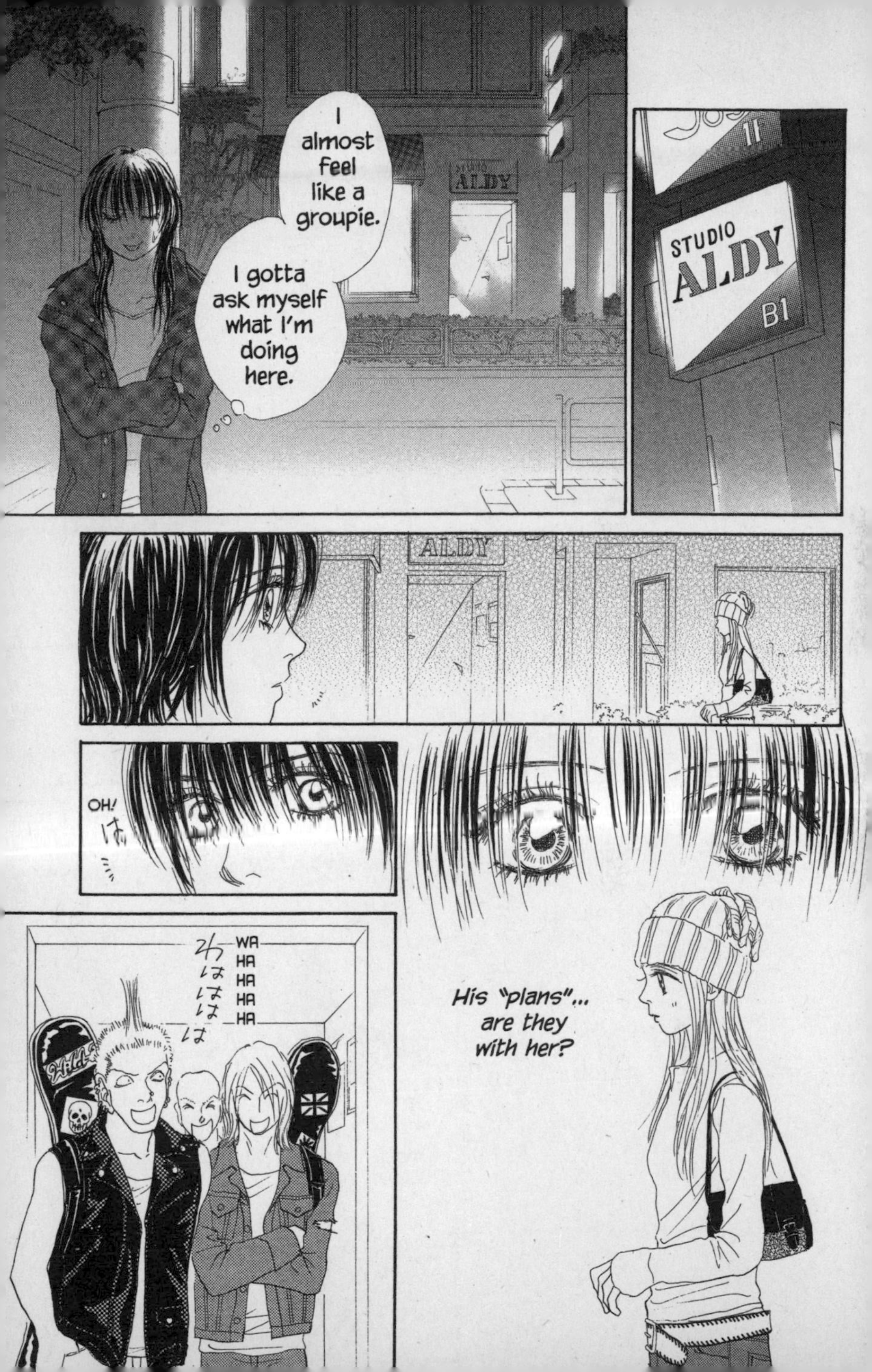

1F
STUDIO ALDY
B1
I almost feel like a groupie.
I gotta ask myself what I'm doing here.
ALDY
OH!
は
His "plans"... are they with her?
WA HA HA HA HA
わはははは

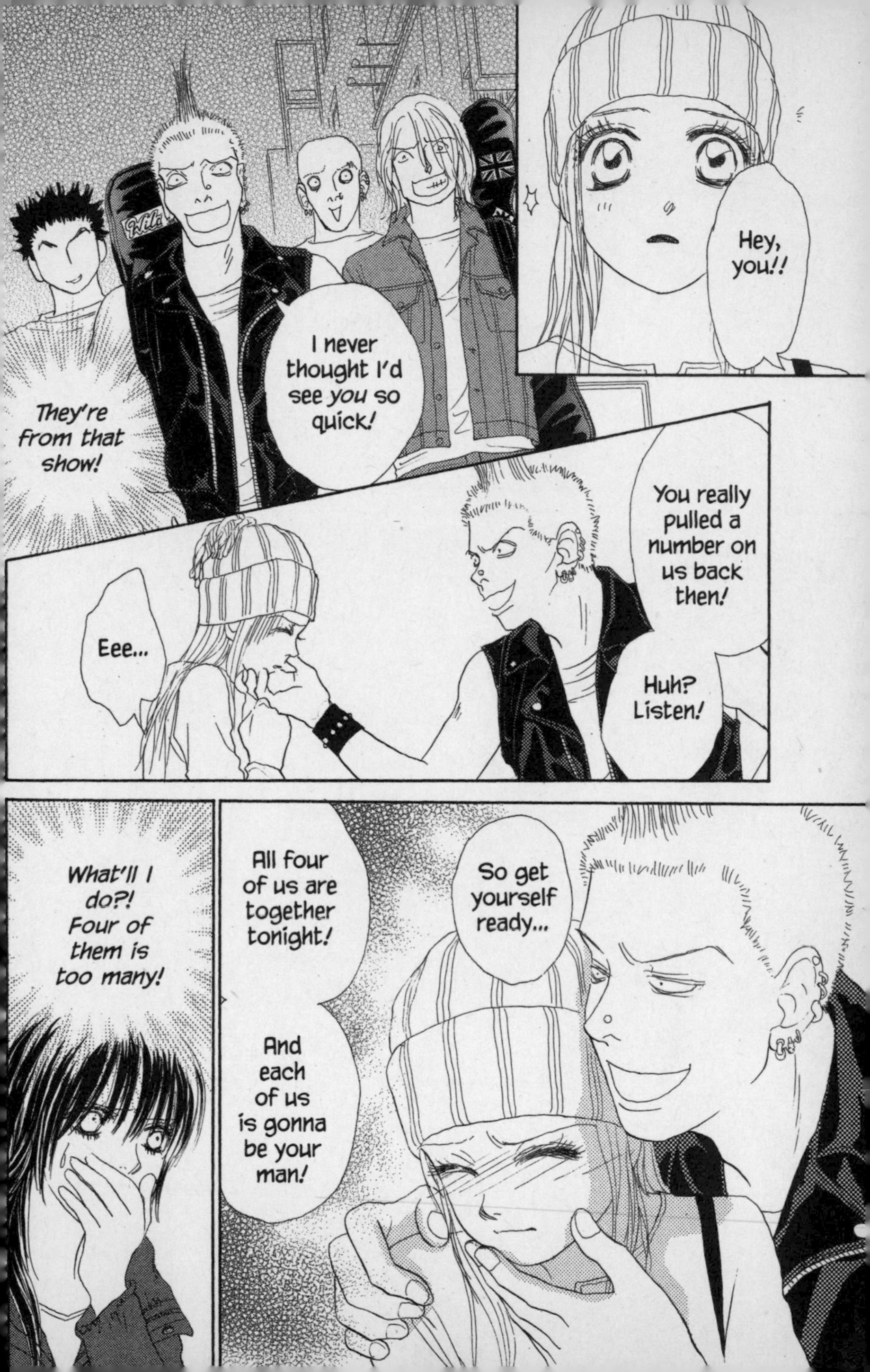
Hey, you!!
I never thought I'd see *you* so quick!
They're from that show!
You really pulled a number on us back then!
Huh? Listen!
Eee...
So get yourself ready...
All four of us are together tonight!
And each of us is gonna be your man!
What'll I do?! Four of them is too many!

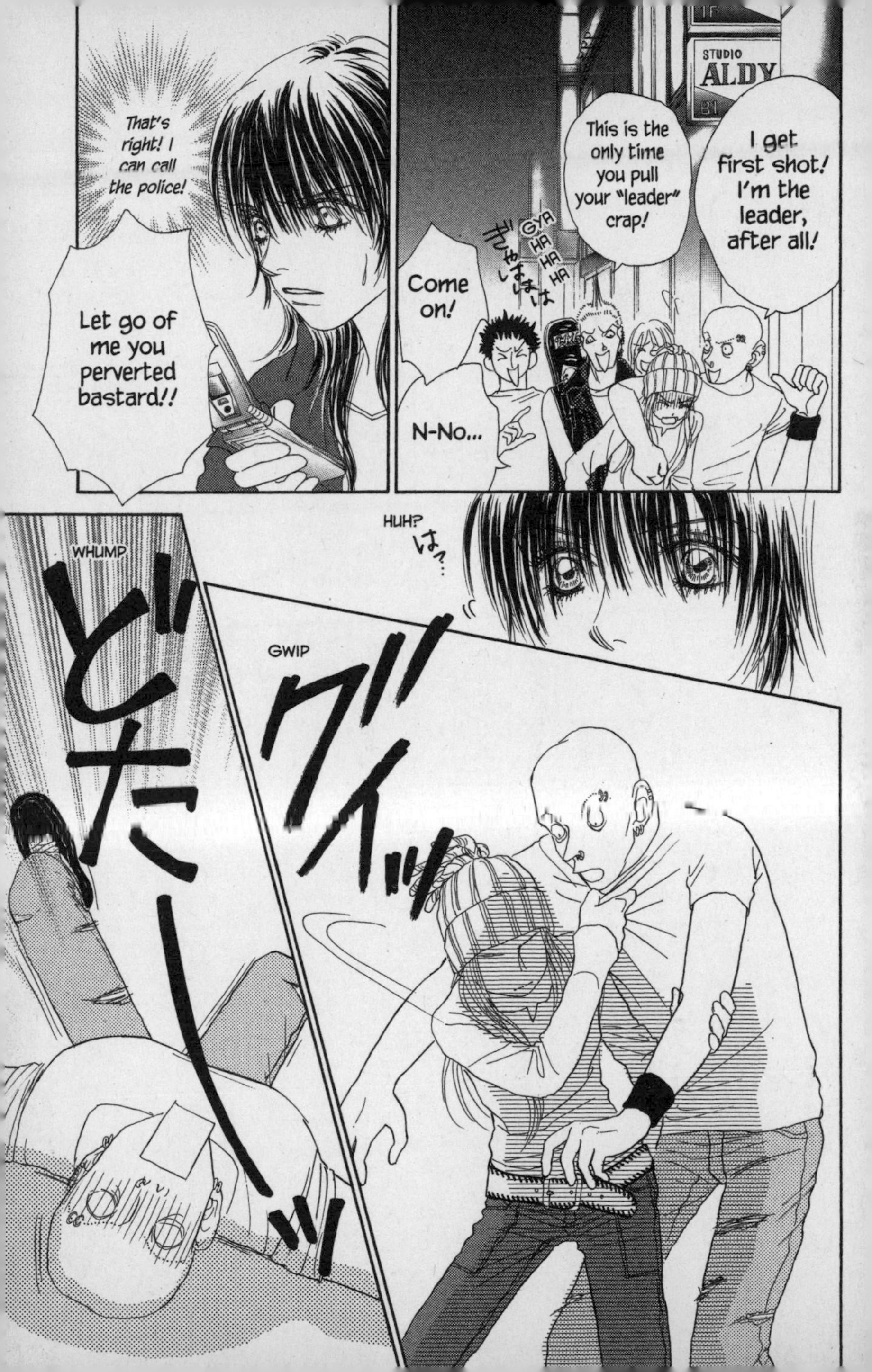
STUDIO
ALDY
I get first shot! I'm the leader, after all!
This is the only time you pull your "leader" crap!
GYA HA HA HA
Come on!
N-No...
That's right! I can call the police!
Let go of me you perverted bastard!!
HUH?
は?
GWIP
グイッ
WHUMP
どたーッ

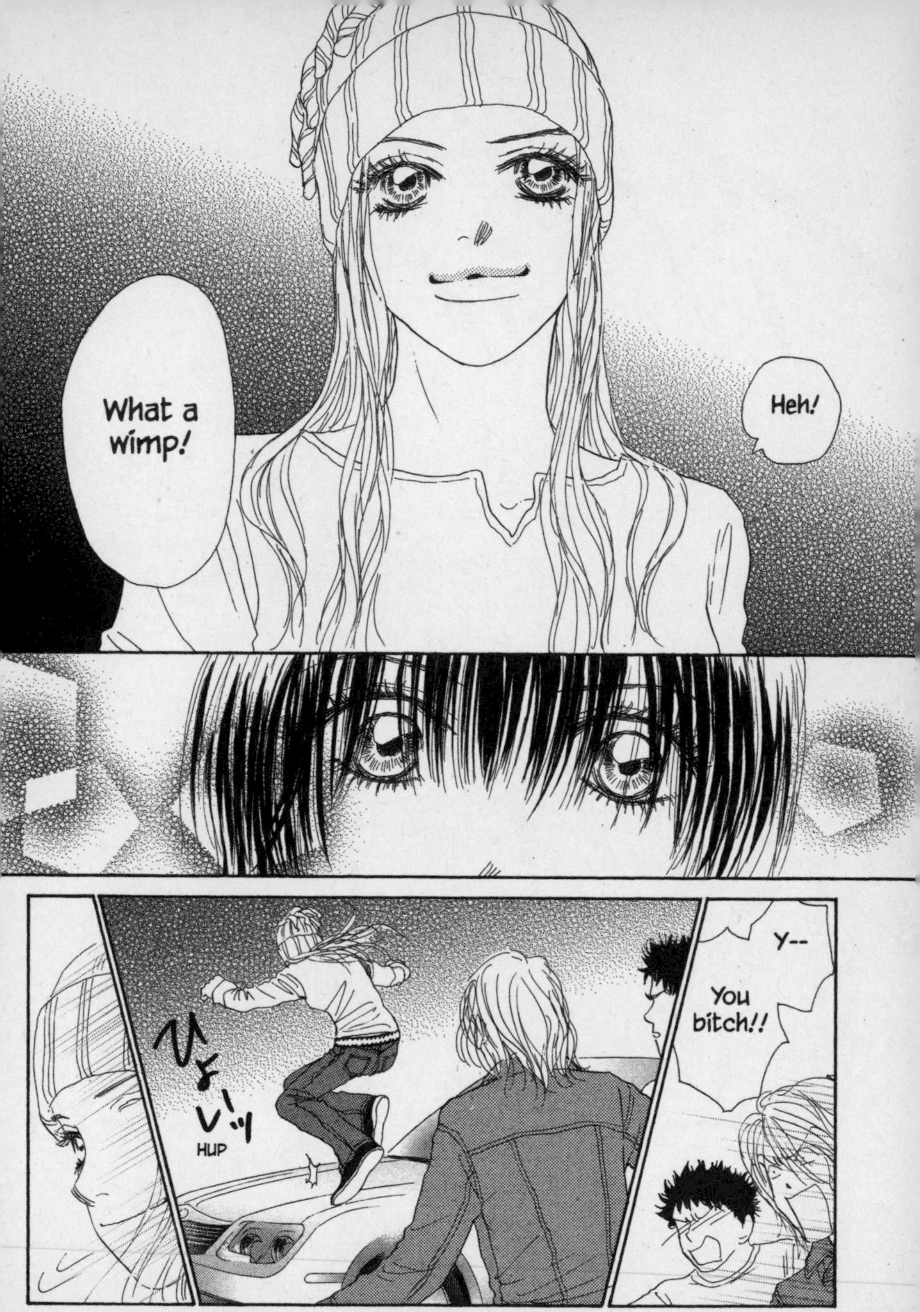
Heh!
What a wimp!
Y--
You bitch!!
HUP

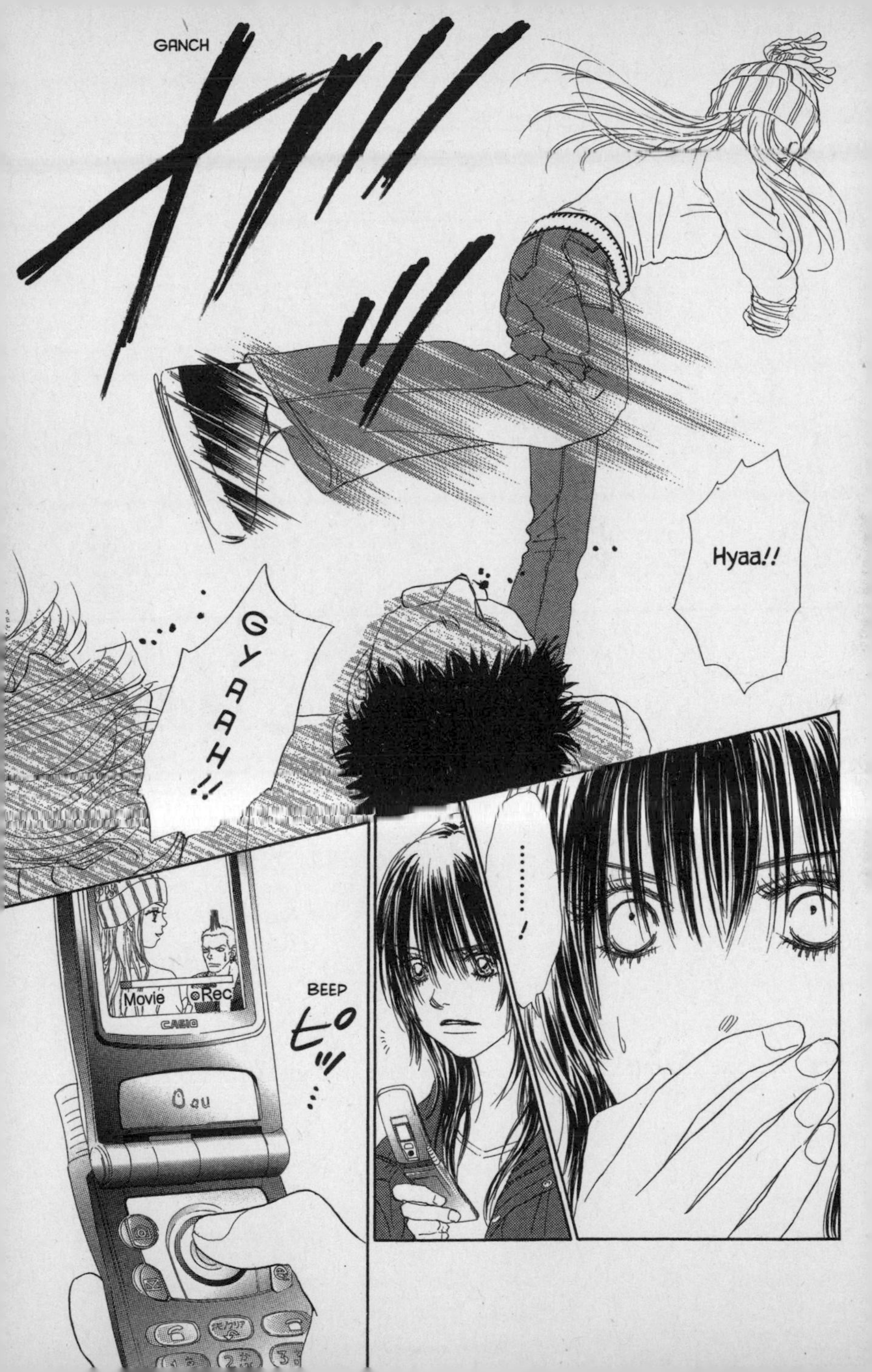
GANCH
Hyaa!!
GYAAAH!!
......!
Movie
Rec
CASIO
BEEP

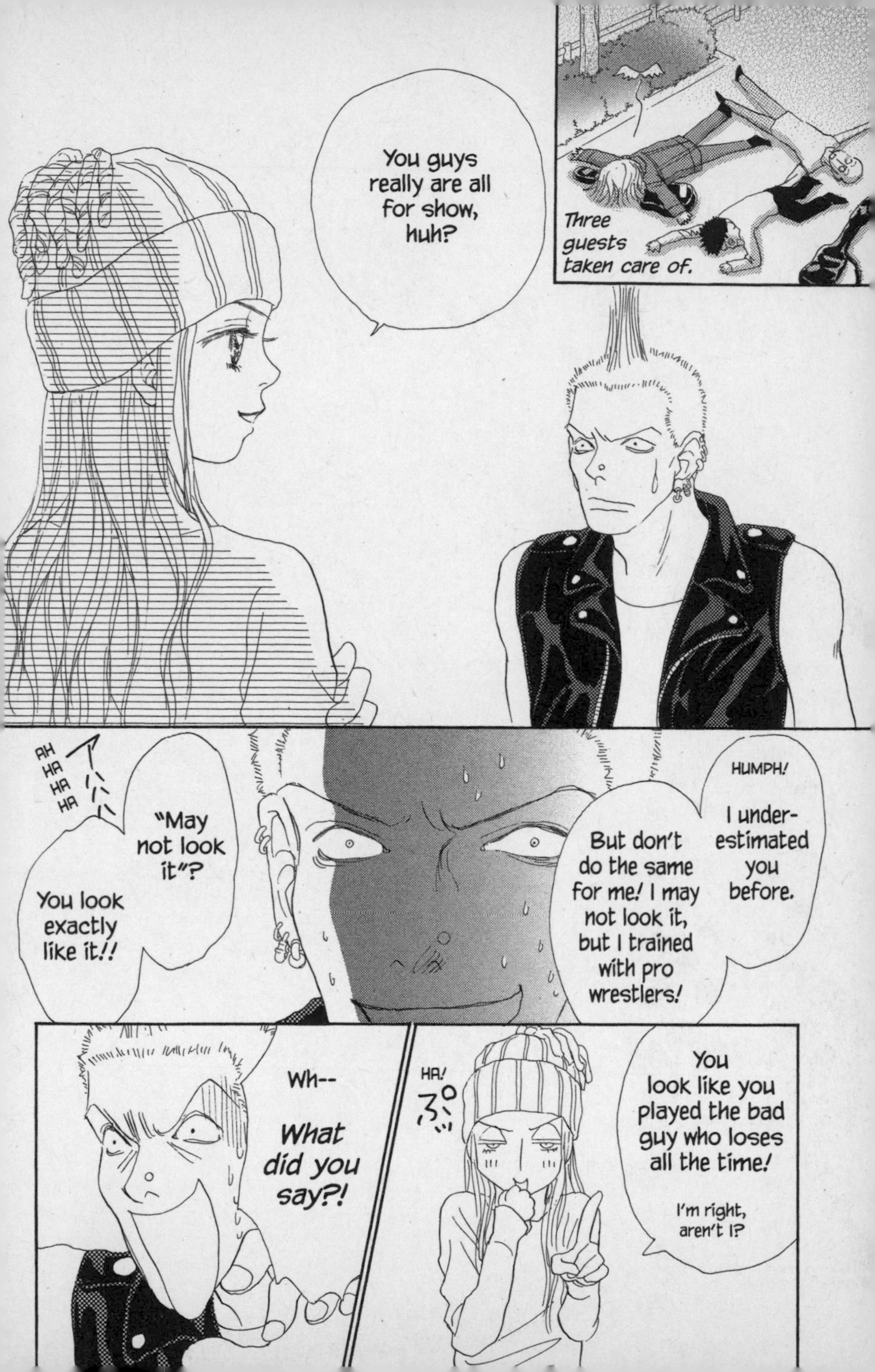
Three guests taken care of.
You guys really are all for show, huh?
HUMPH!
I underestimated you before.
But don't do the same for me! I may not look it, but I trained with pro wrestlers!
AH HA HA HA
"May not look it"?
You look exactly like it!!
HA!
You look like you played the bad guy who loses all the time!
I'm right, aren't I?
Wh--
What did you say?!

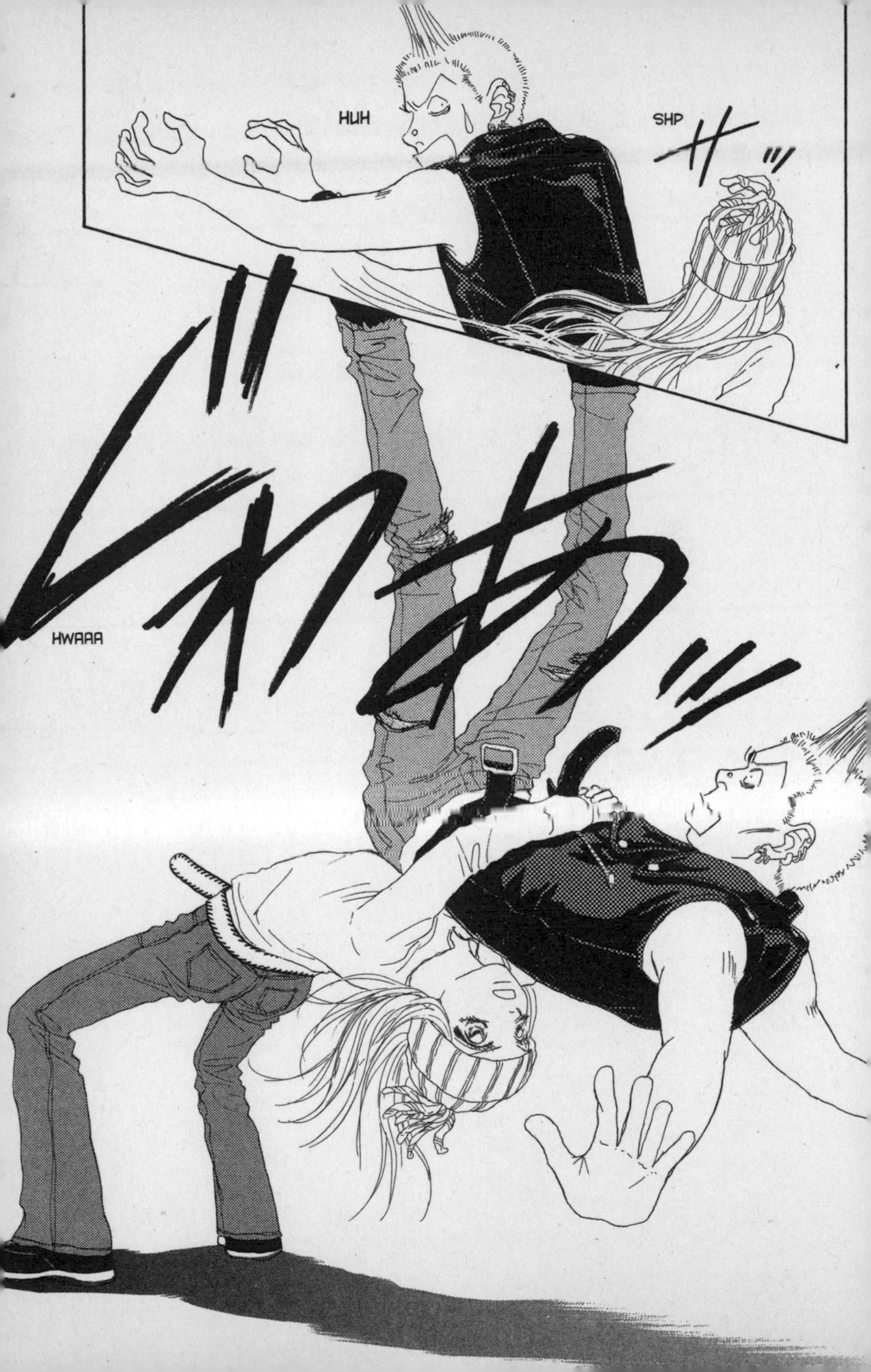
SHP
HUH
HWAAA

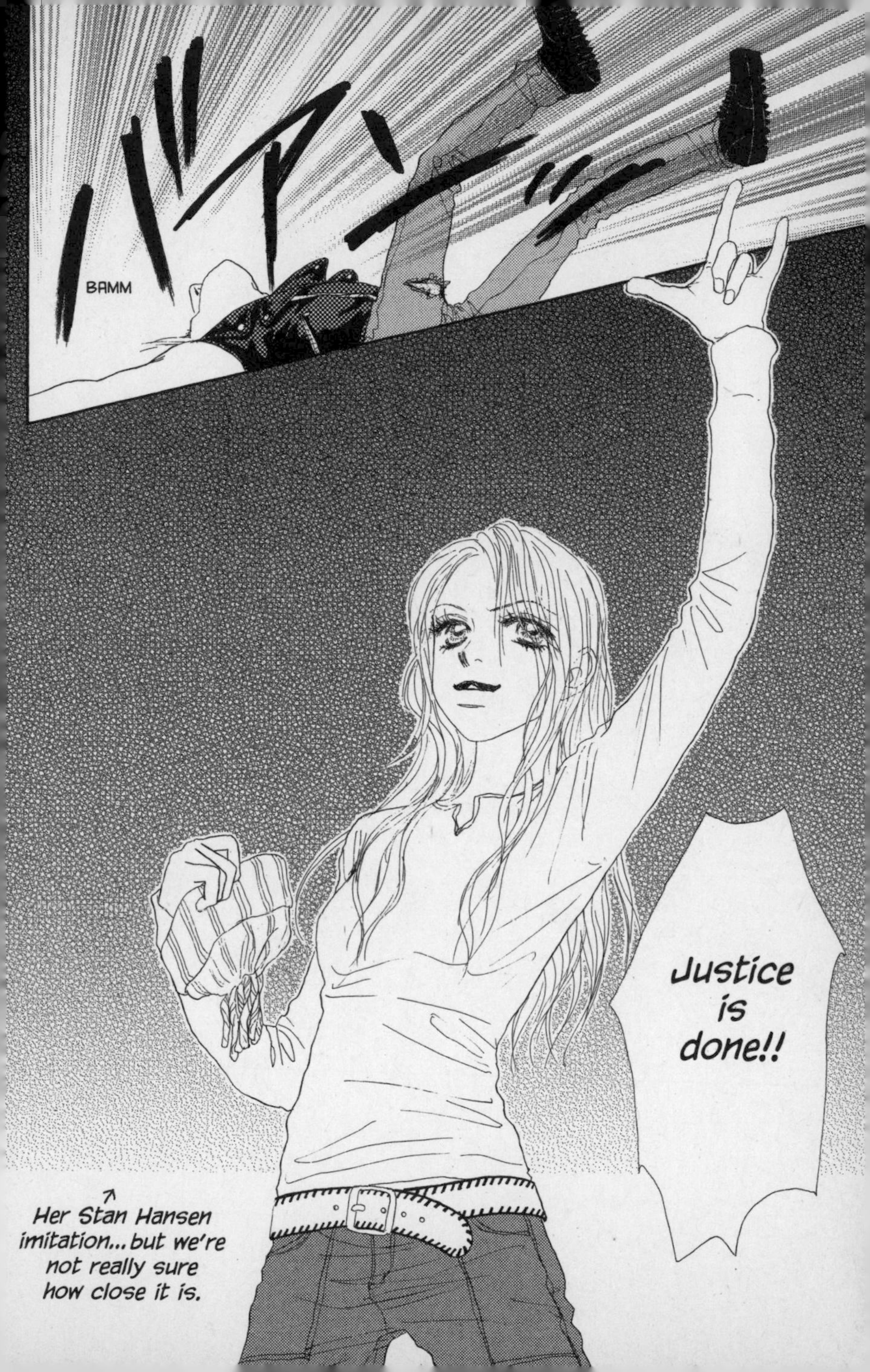
BAMM
Justice is done!!
Her Stan Hansen imitation...but we're not really sure how close it is.

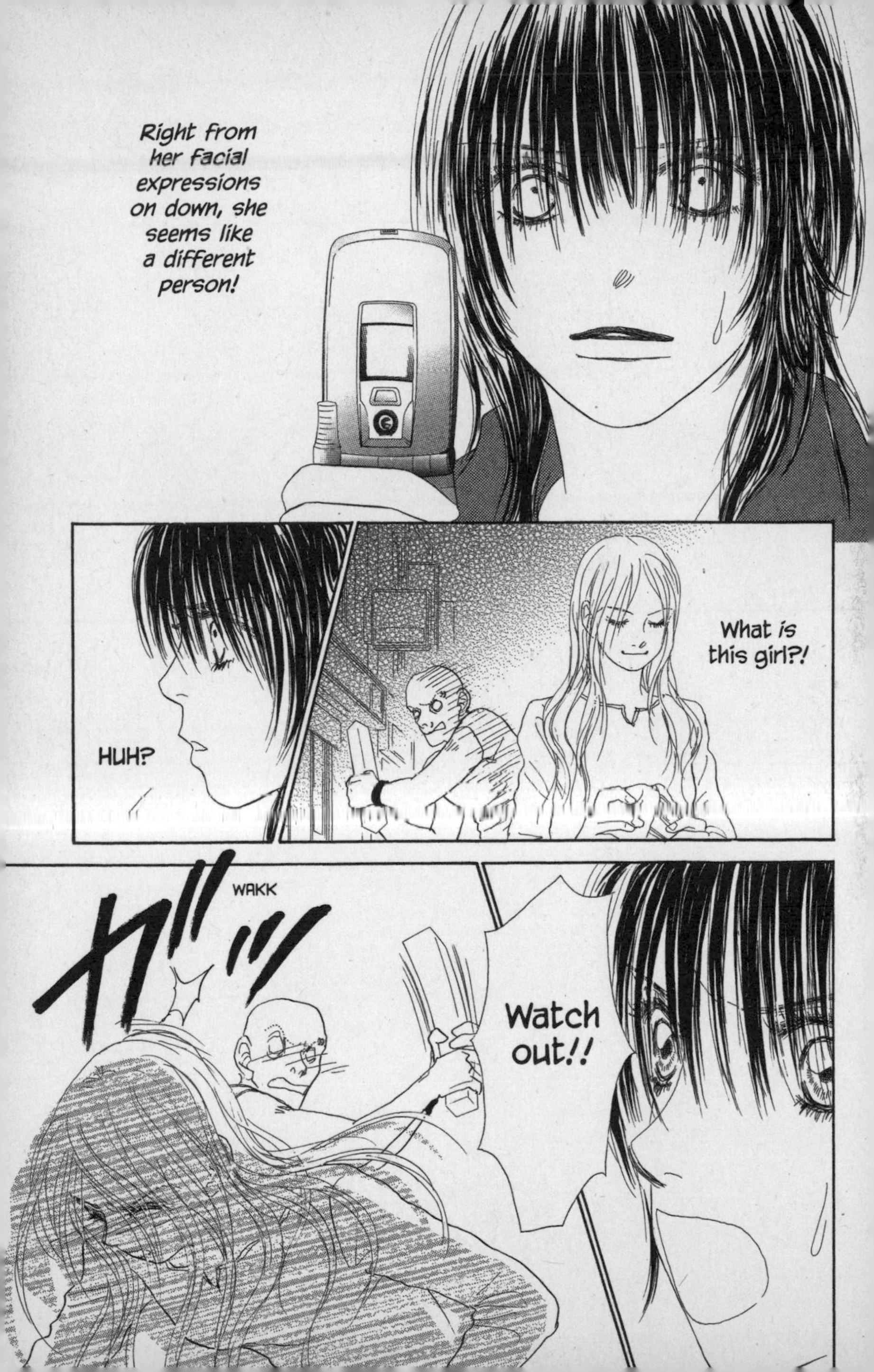
Right from her facial expressions on down, she seems like a different person!
What is this girl?!
HUH?
Watch out!!
WAKK

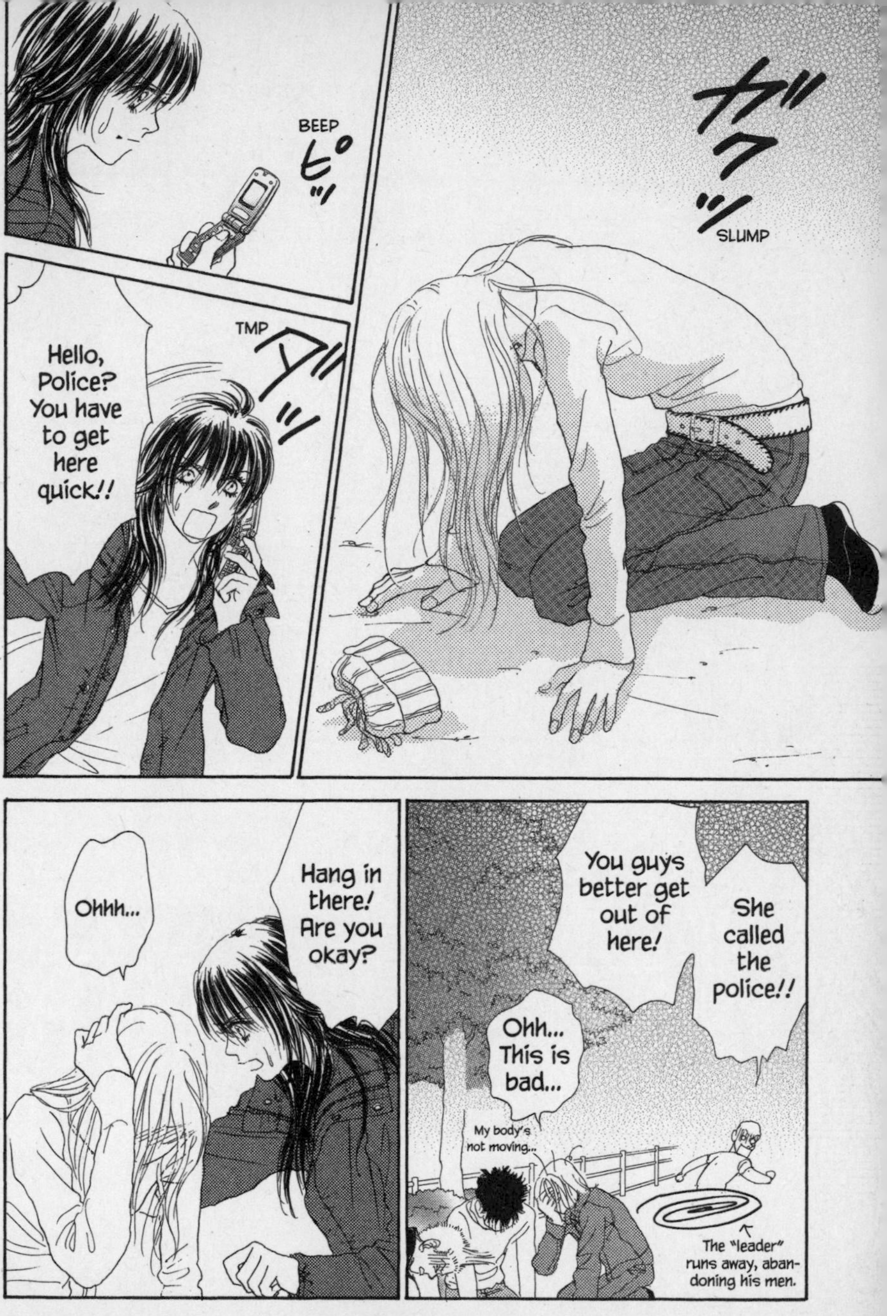
ガクッ
SLUMP
BEEP
ピッ
TMP
Hello, Police? You have to get here quick!!
She called the police!!
You guys better get out of here!
Ohh... This is bad...
My body's not moving...
The "leader" runs away, abandoning his men.
Hang in there! Are you okay?
Ohhh...

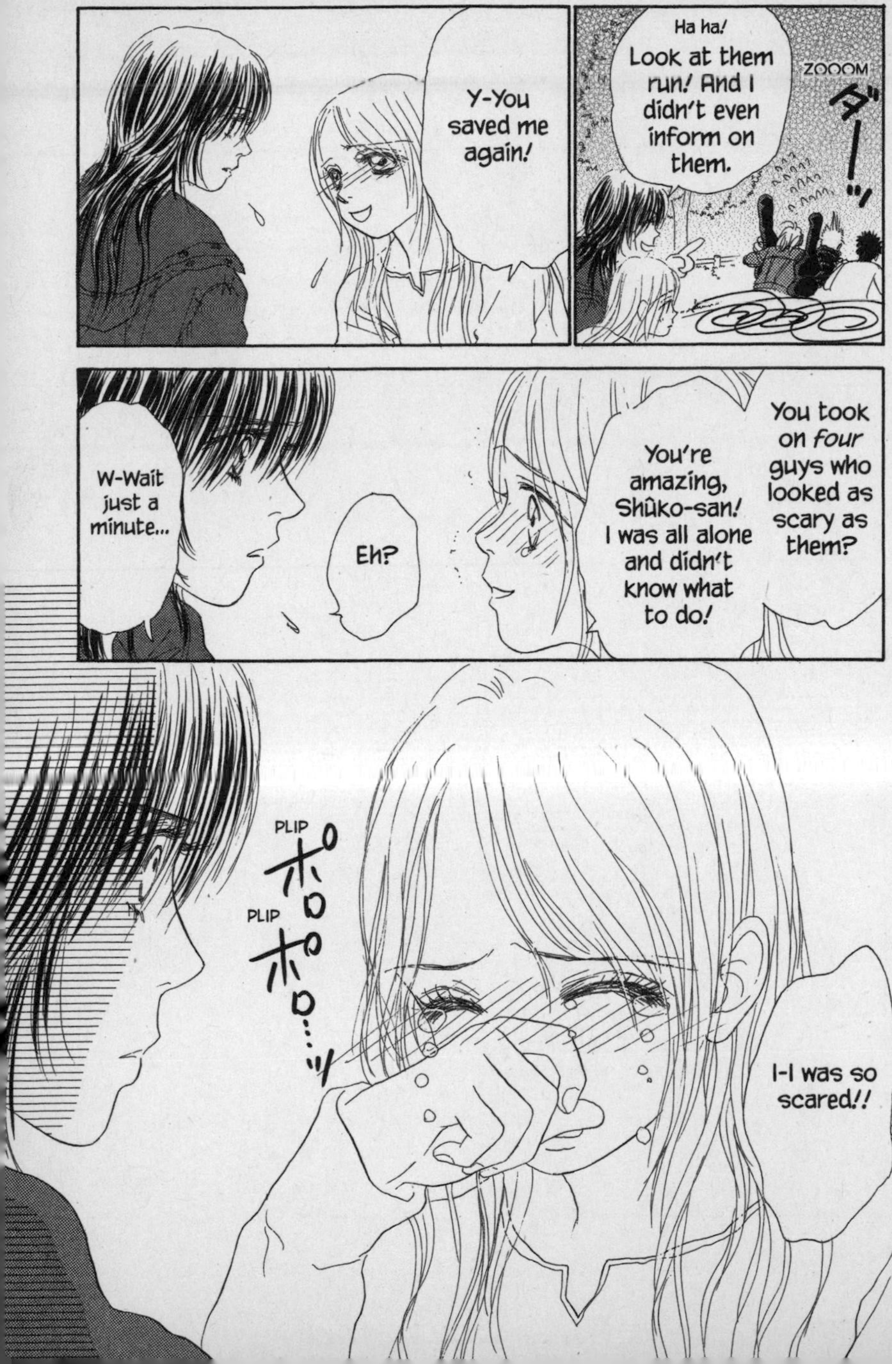
Ha ha! Look at them run! And I didn't even inform on them.
ZOOOM
Y-You saved me again!
You took on *four* guys who looked as scary as them?
You're amazing, Shûko-san! I was all alone and didn't know what to do!
Eh?
W-Wait just a minute...
I-I was so scared!!
PLIP
PLIP

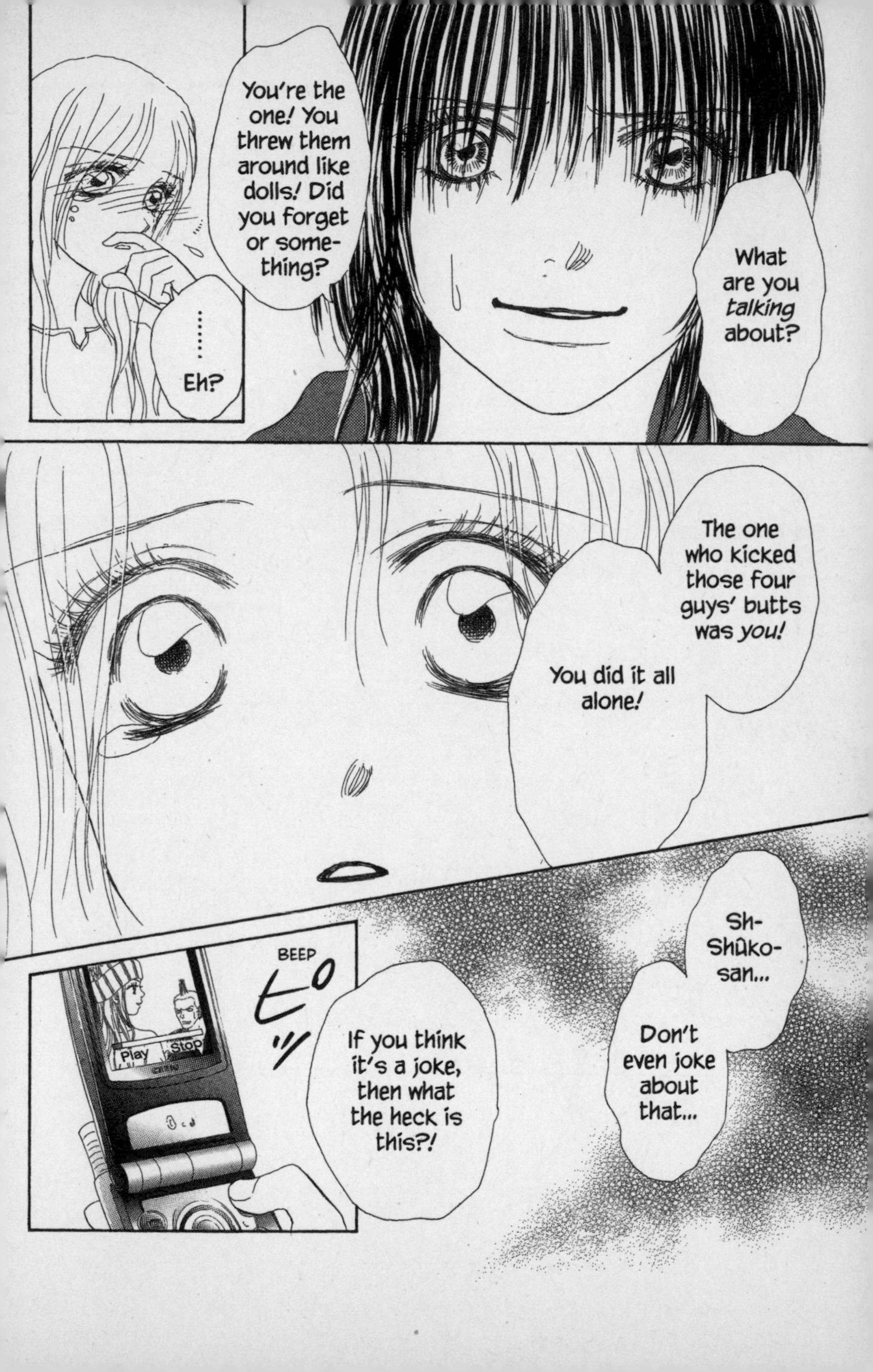
What are you talking about?
You're the one! You threw them around like dolls! Did you forget or something?
......
Eh?
The one who kicked those four guys' butts was you!
You did it all alone!
Sh-Shûko-san...
Don't even joke about that...
BEEP
If you think it's a joke, then what the heck is this?!
Play
Stop

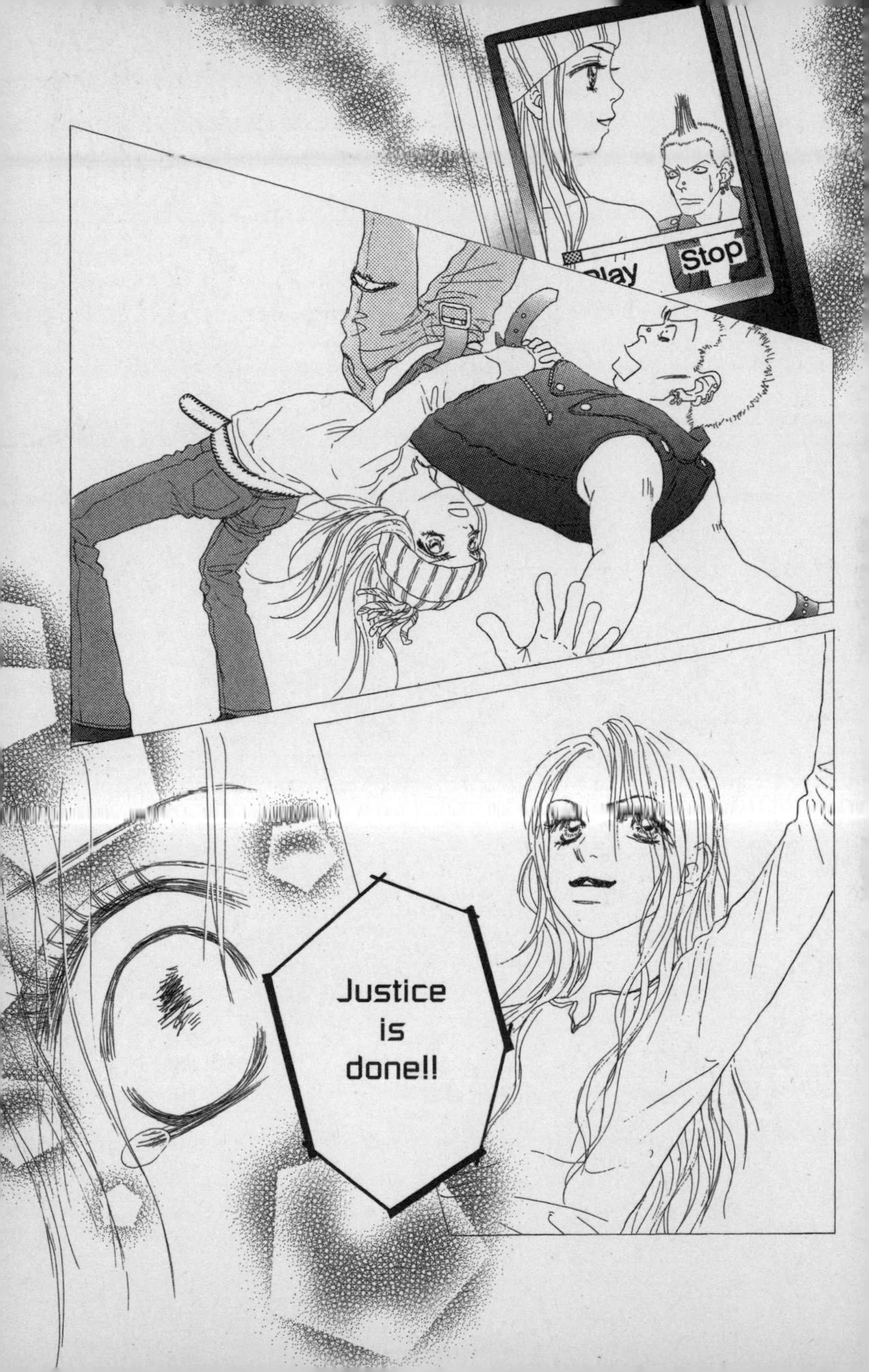
Play
Stop
Justice is done!!

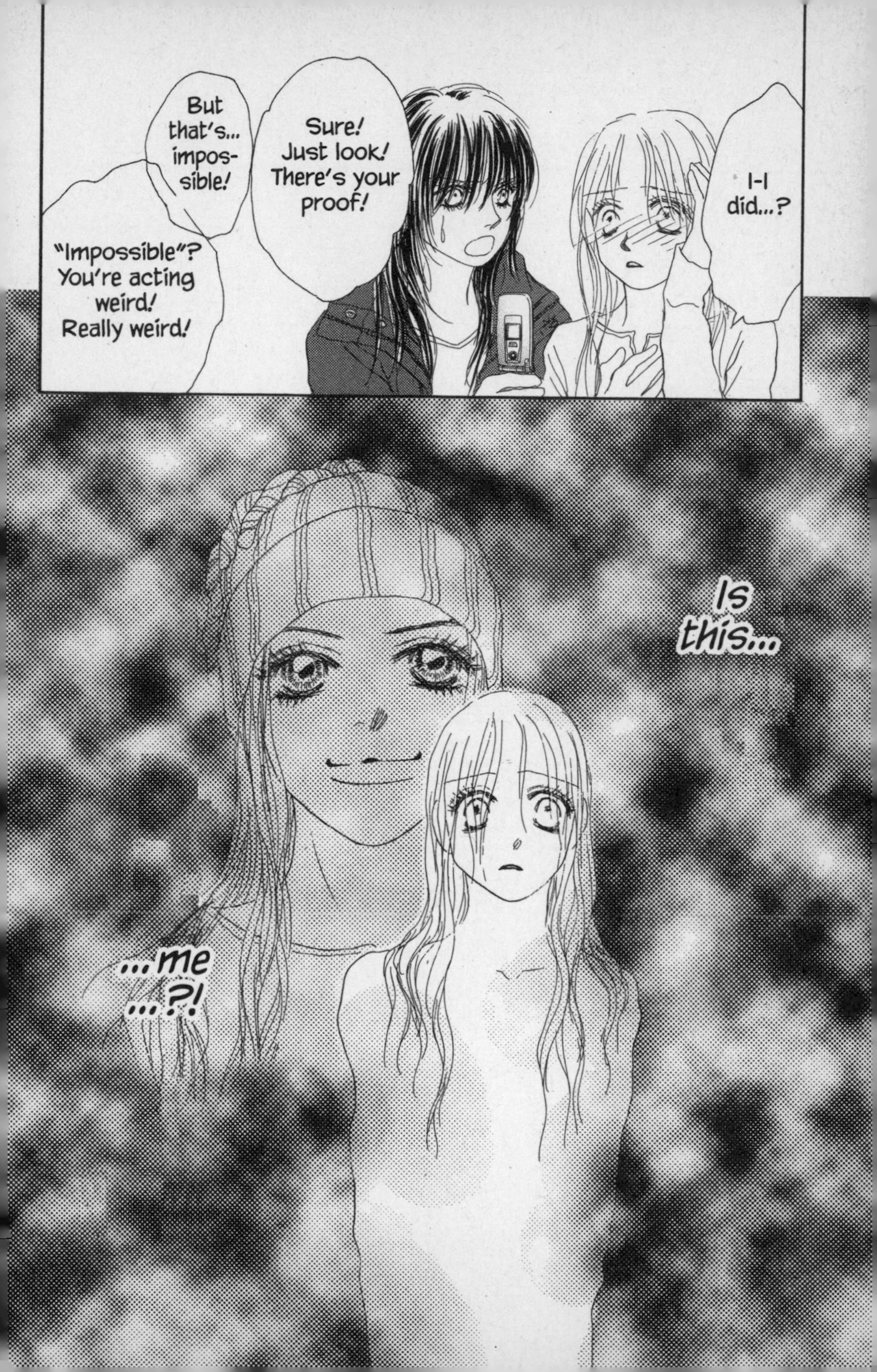
I-I did...?
Sure! Just look! There's your proof!
But that's... impos-sible!
"Impossible"? You're acting weird! Really weird!
Is this...
...me ...?!

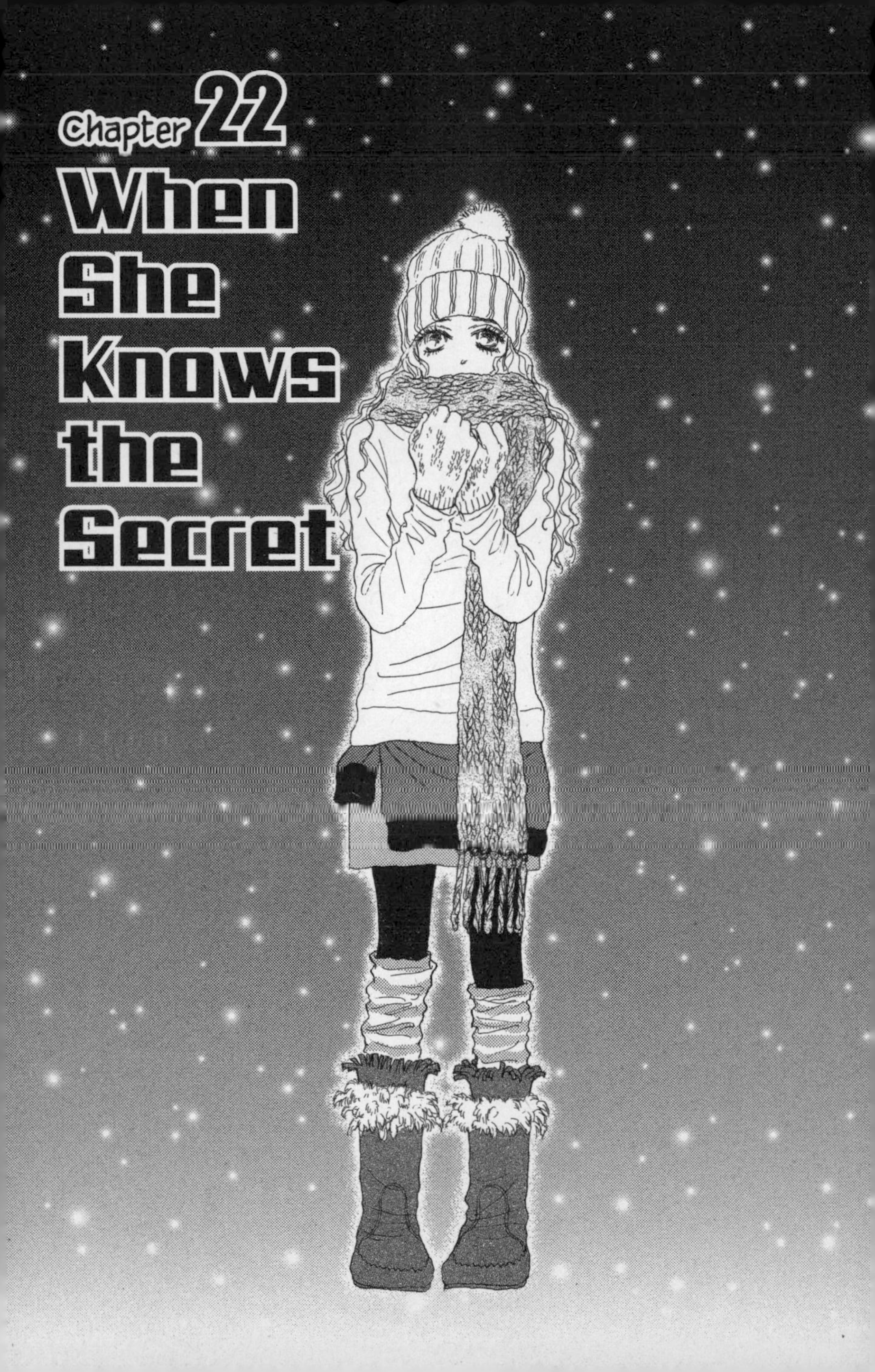
Chapter 22
When She Knows the Secret

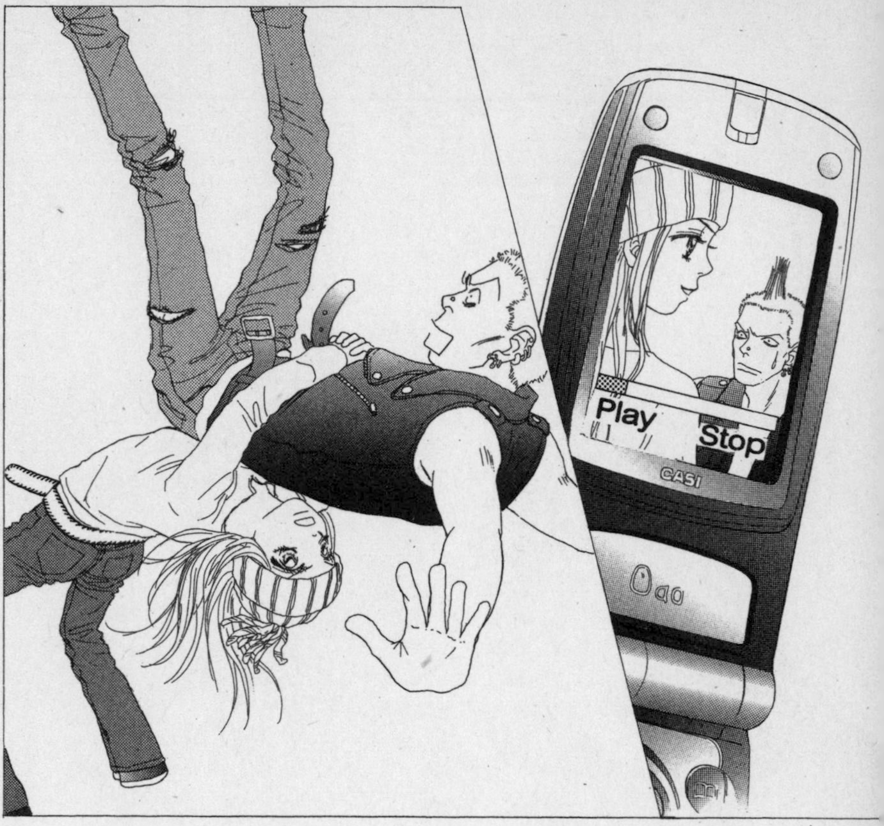
Play
Stop
CASI

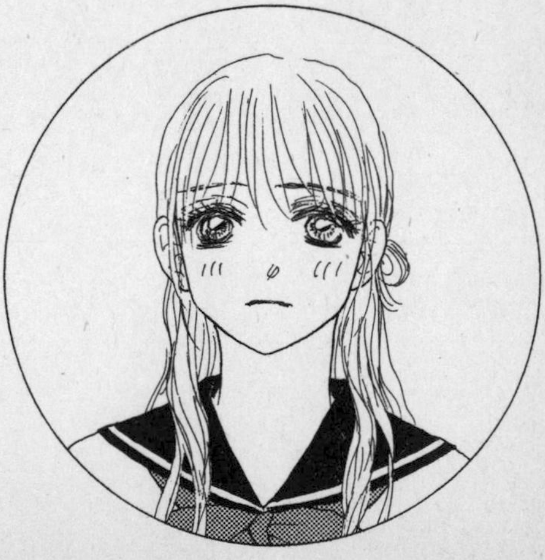

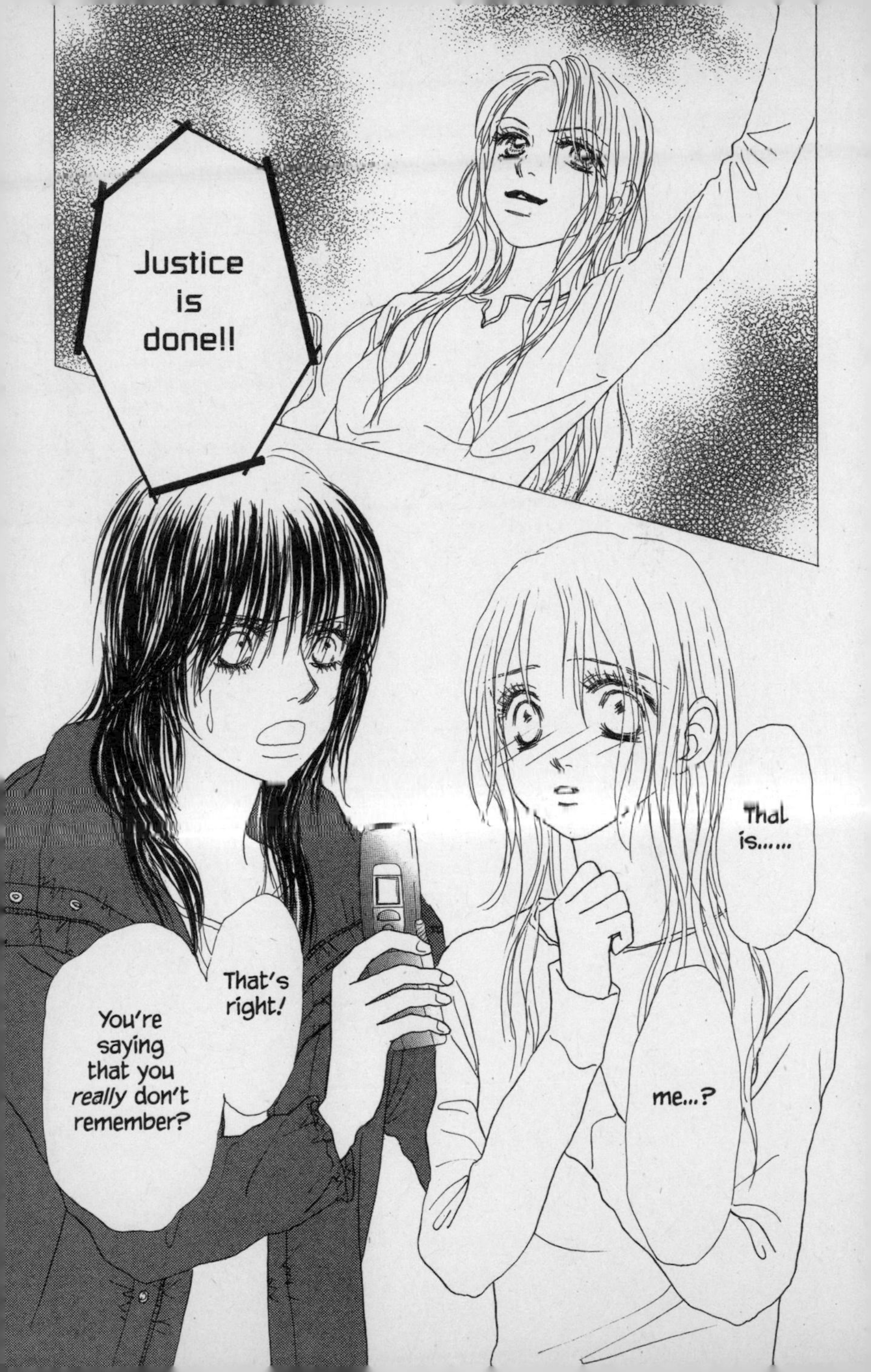
Justice is done!!
That is...... me...?
That's right! You're saying that you *really* don't remember?

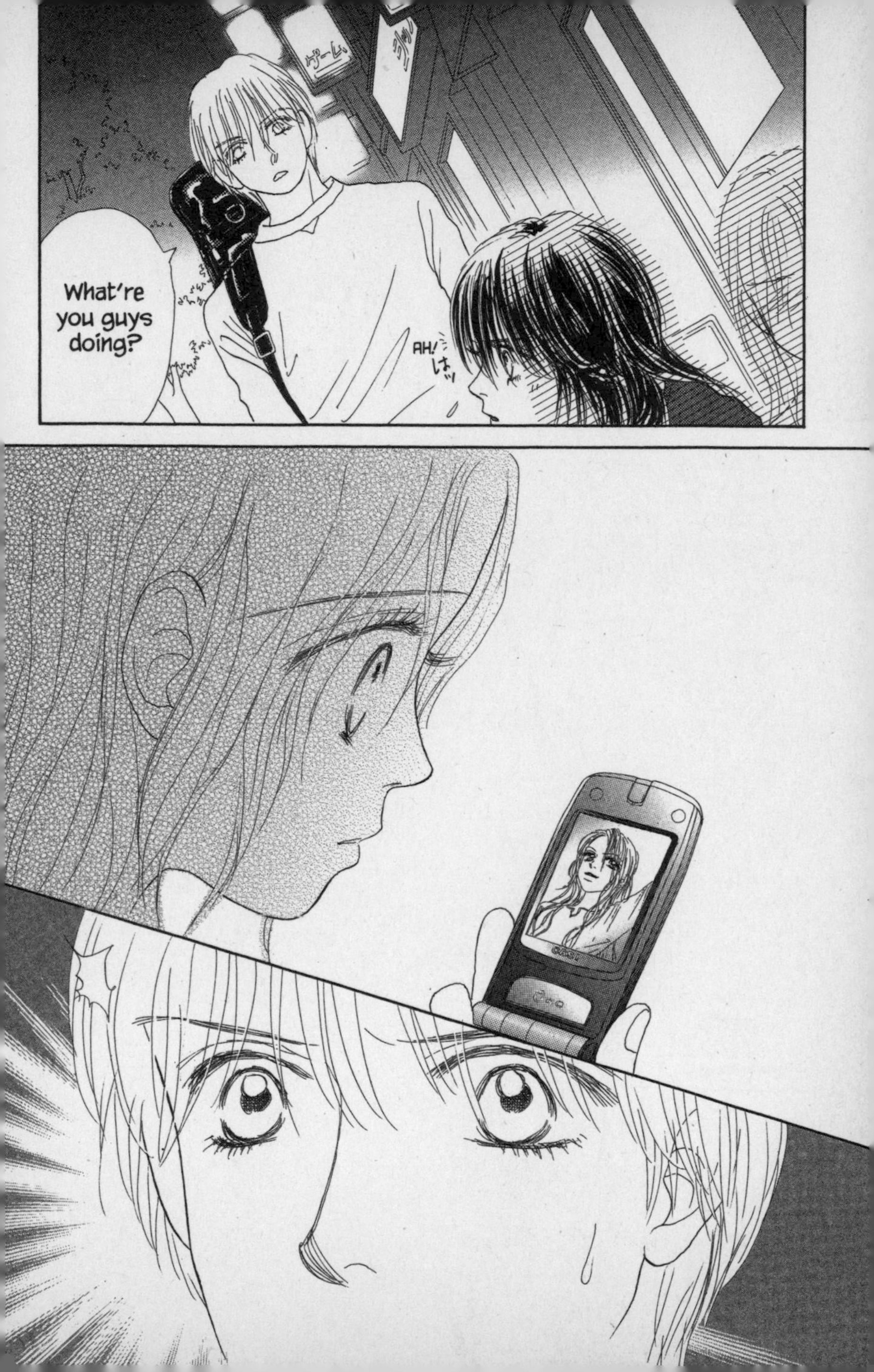
What're you guys doing?
AH! はッ

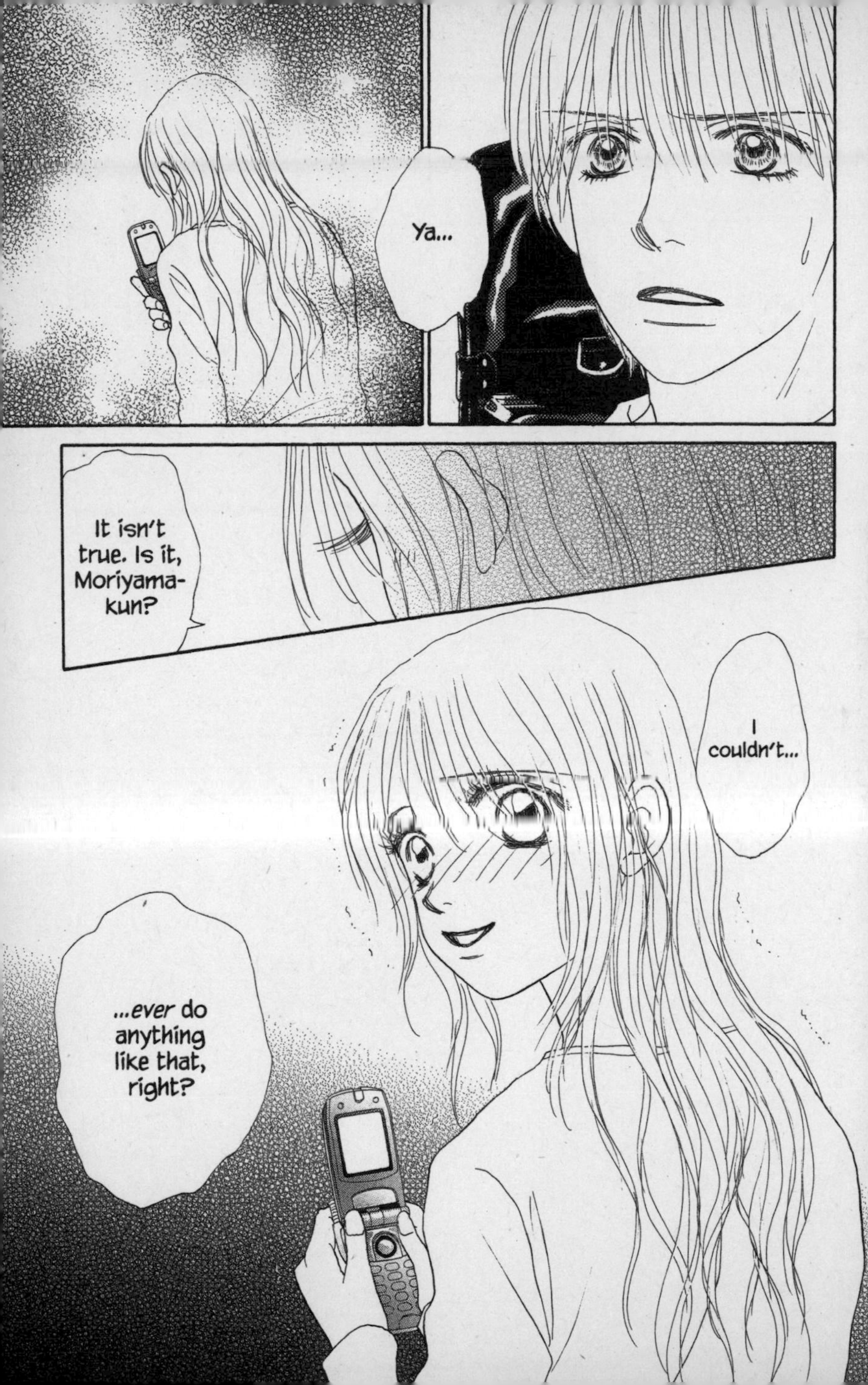
Ya...
It isn't true. Is it, Moriyama-kun?
I couldn't...
...*ever* do anything like that, right?

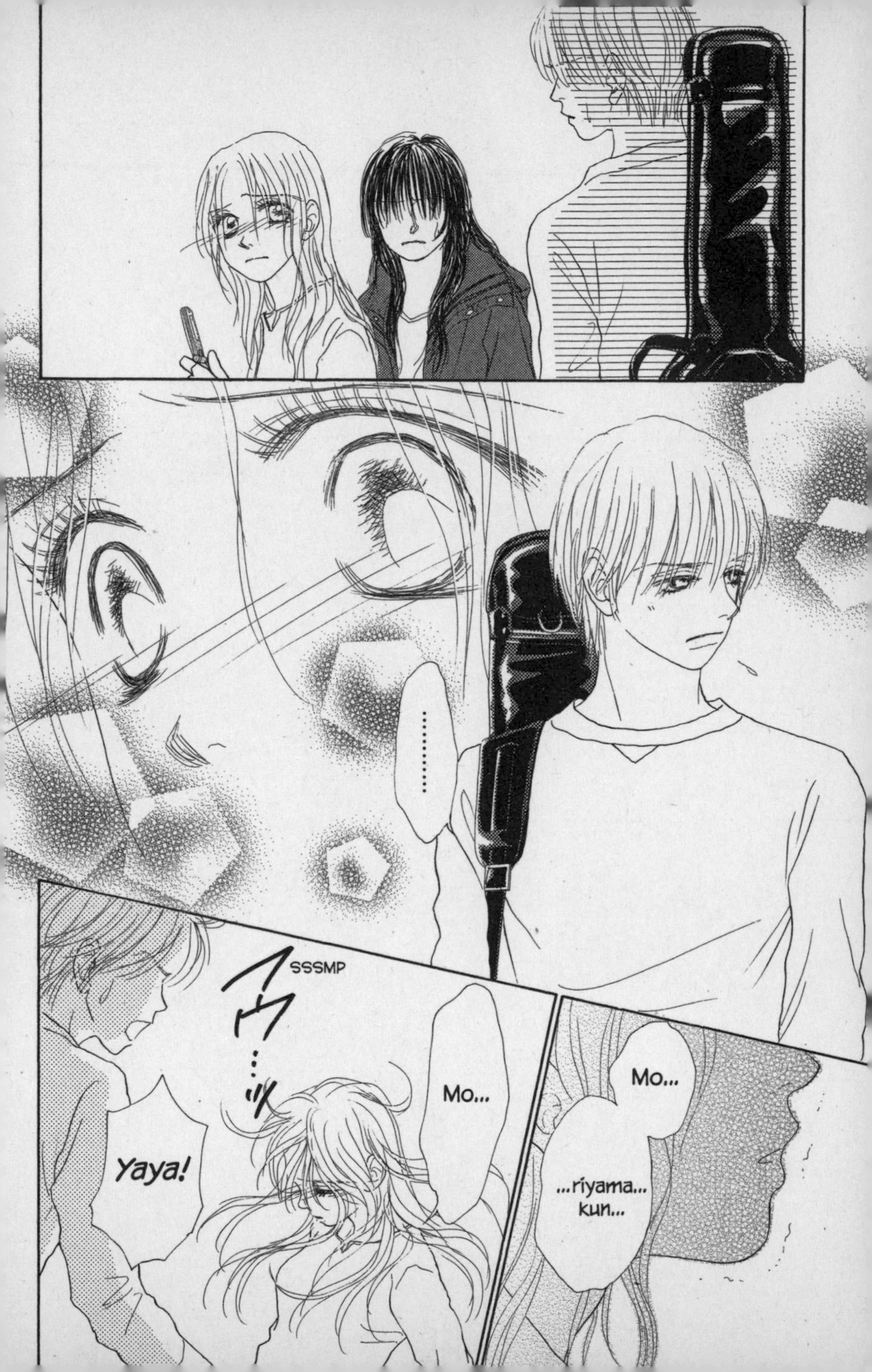
......
Mo...
...riyama... kun...
Mo...
SSSMP
Yaya!

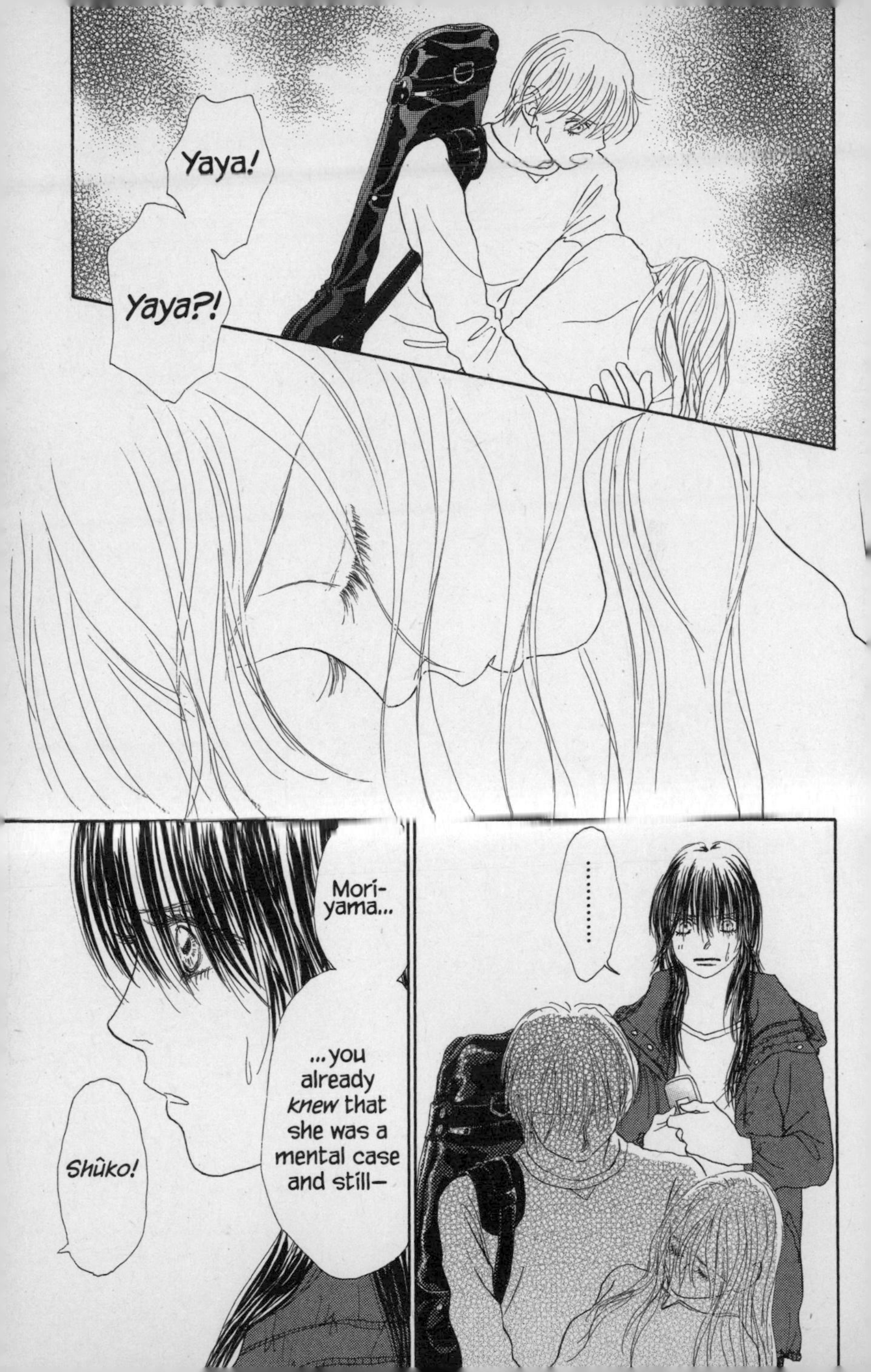
Yaya!
Yaya?!
......
Mori-yama...
...you already *knew* that she was a mental case and still—
Shûko!

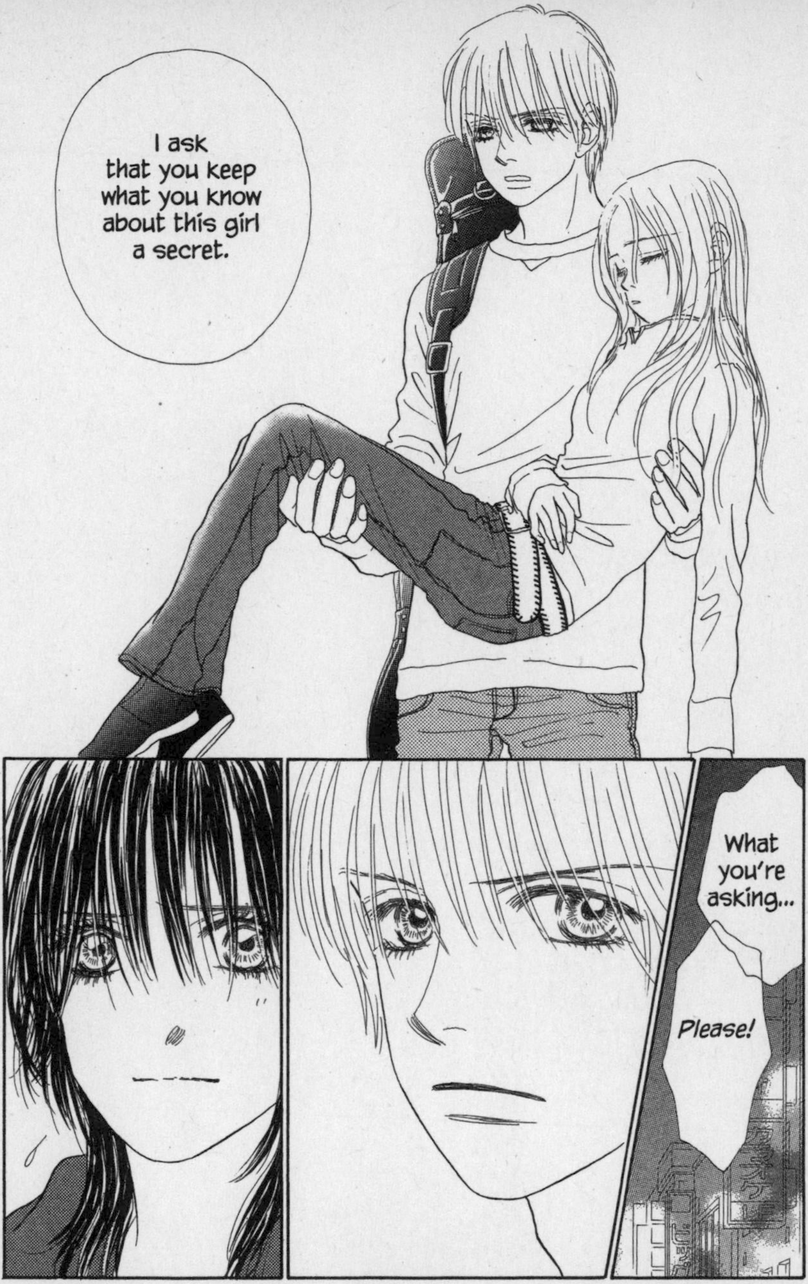
I ask that you keep what you know about this girl a secret.
What you're asking...
Please!

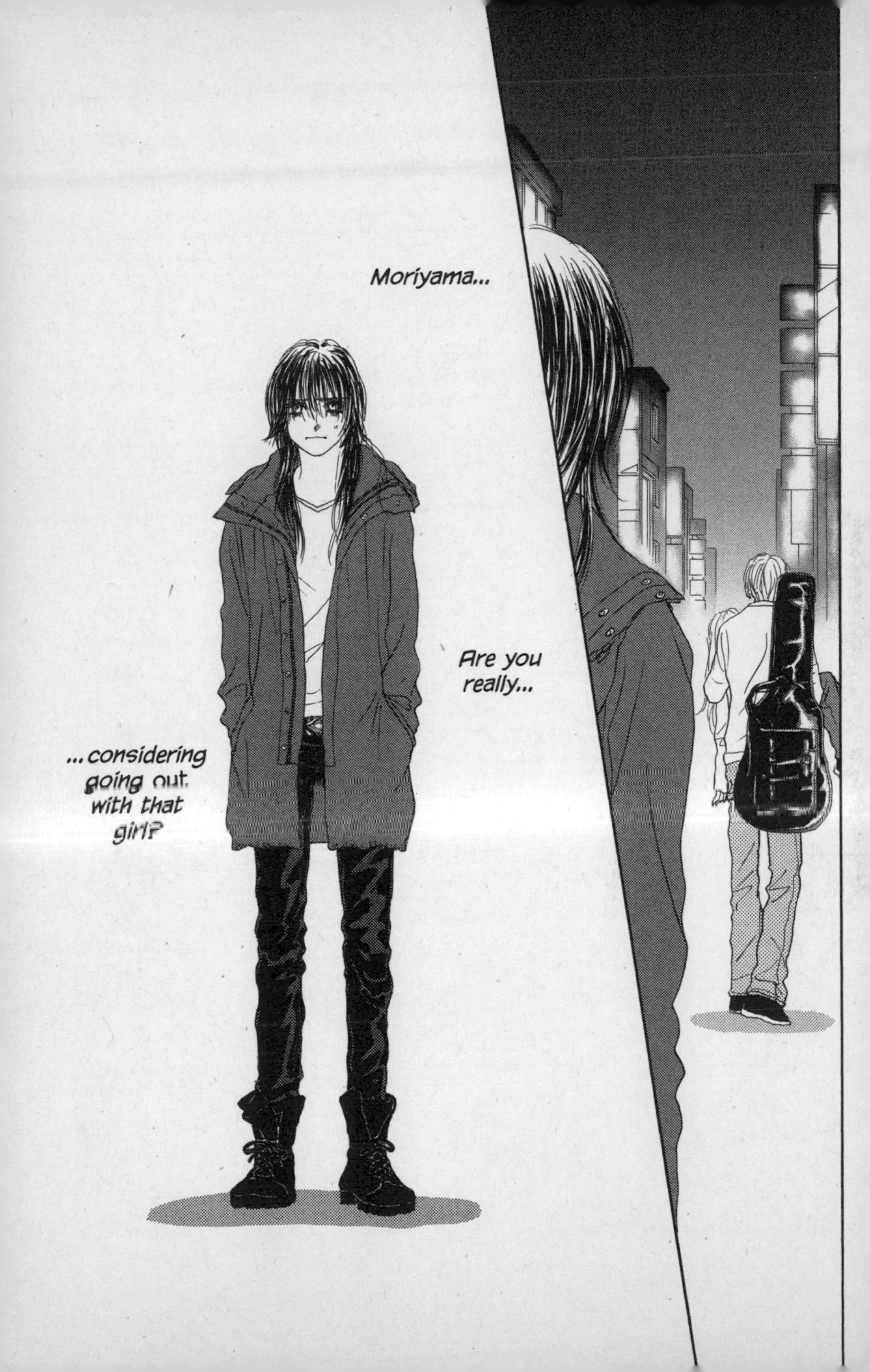
Moriyama...
Are you really...
...considering going out with that girl?

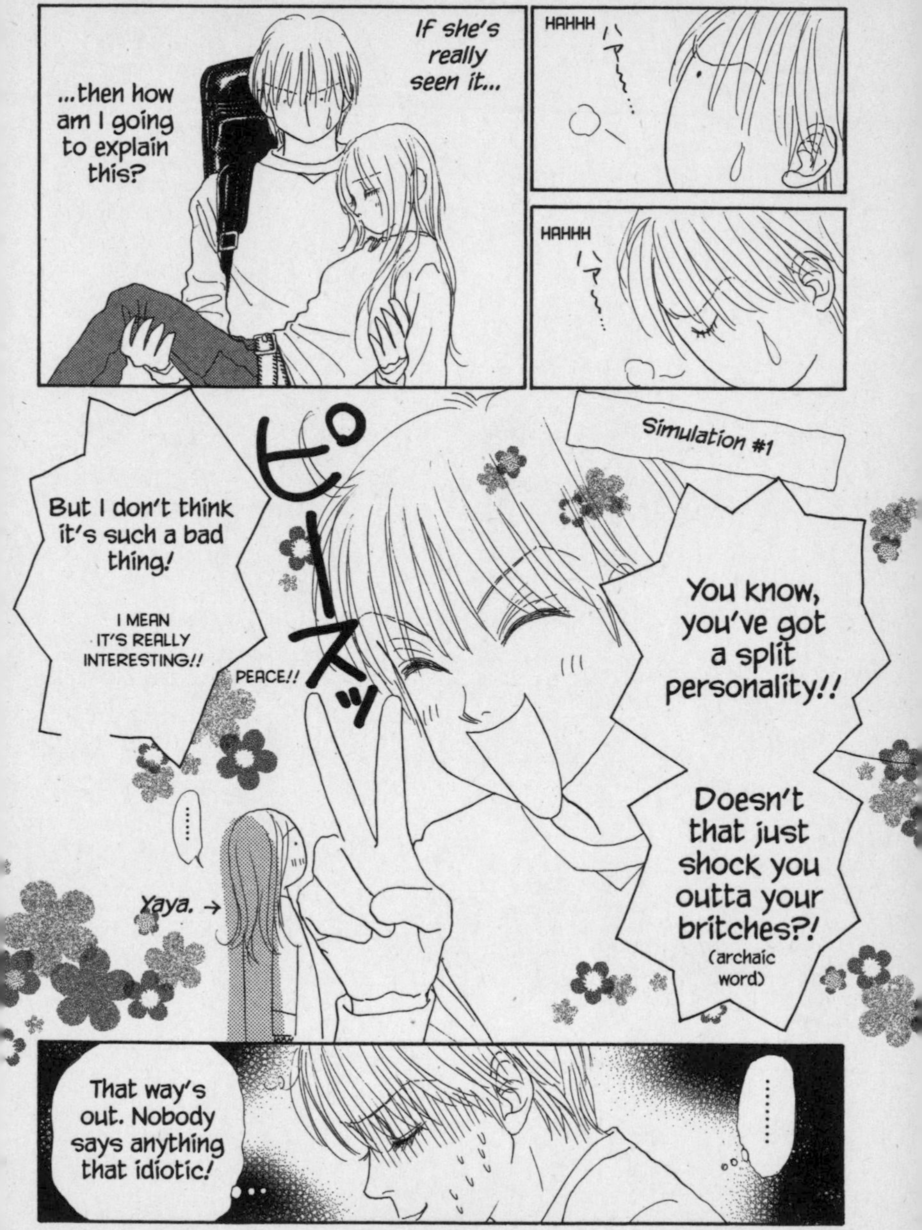

HAHHH
ハァ〜…
HAHHH
ハァ〜…
If she's really seen it...
...then how am I going to explain this?
Simulation #1
You know, you've got a split personality!!
Doesn't that just shock you outta your britches?!
(archaic word)
ピースッ
PEACE!!
But I don't think it's such a bad thing!
I MEAN IT'S REALLY INTERESTING!!
......
Yaya. →
......
That way's out. Nobody says anything that idiotic!

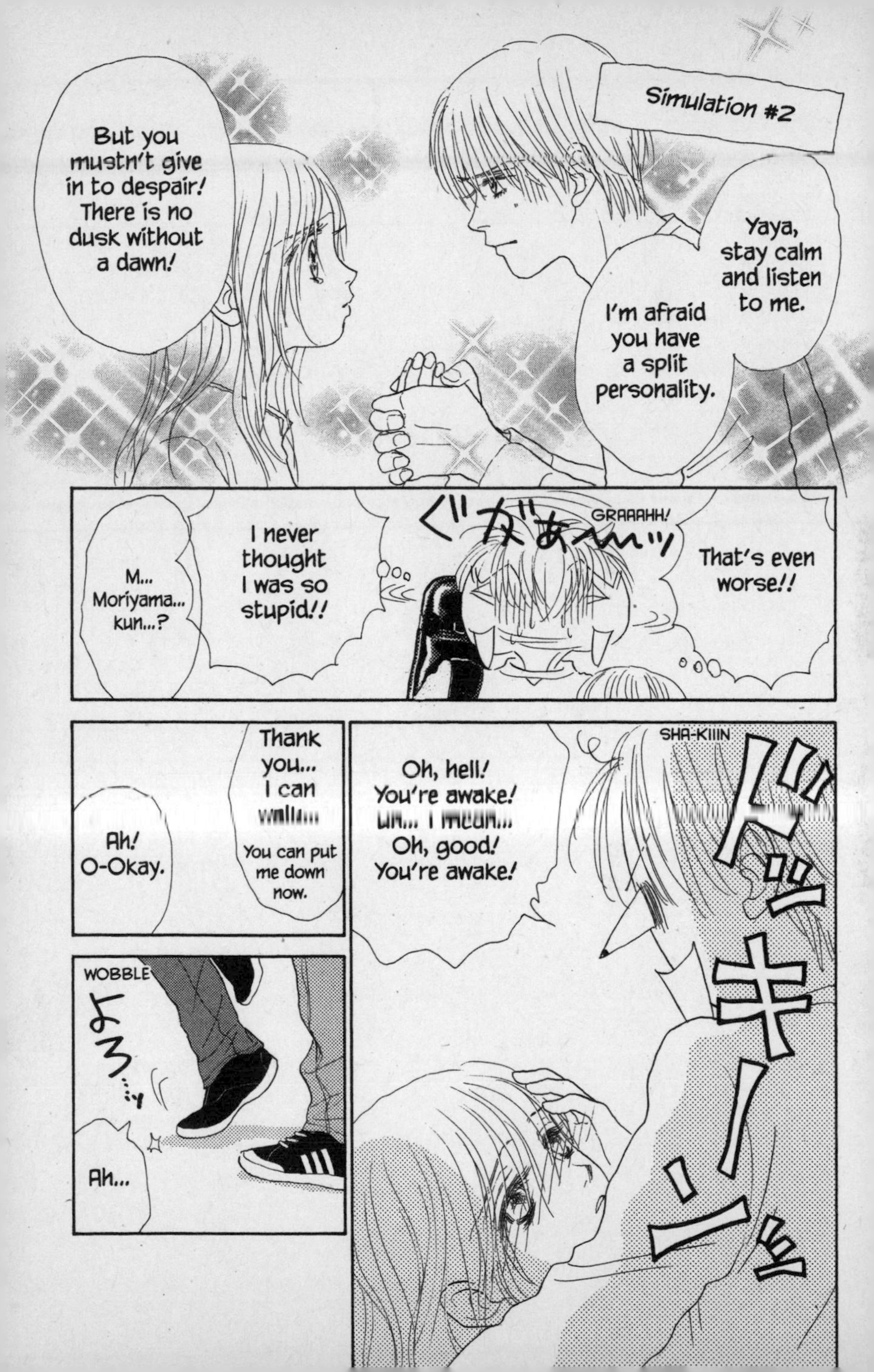
Simulation #2
Yaya, stay calm and listen to me.
I'm afraid you have a split personality.
But you mustn't give in to despair! There is no dusk without a dawn!
That's even worse!!
GRAAAHH!
I never thought I was so stupid!!
M... Moriyama... kun...?
SHA-KIIN
Oh, hell! You're awake! Uh... I mean... Oh, good! You're awake!
Thank you... I can walk...
You can put me down now.
Ah! O-Okay.
WOBBLE
Ah...

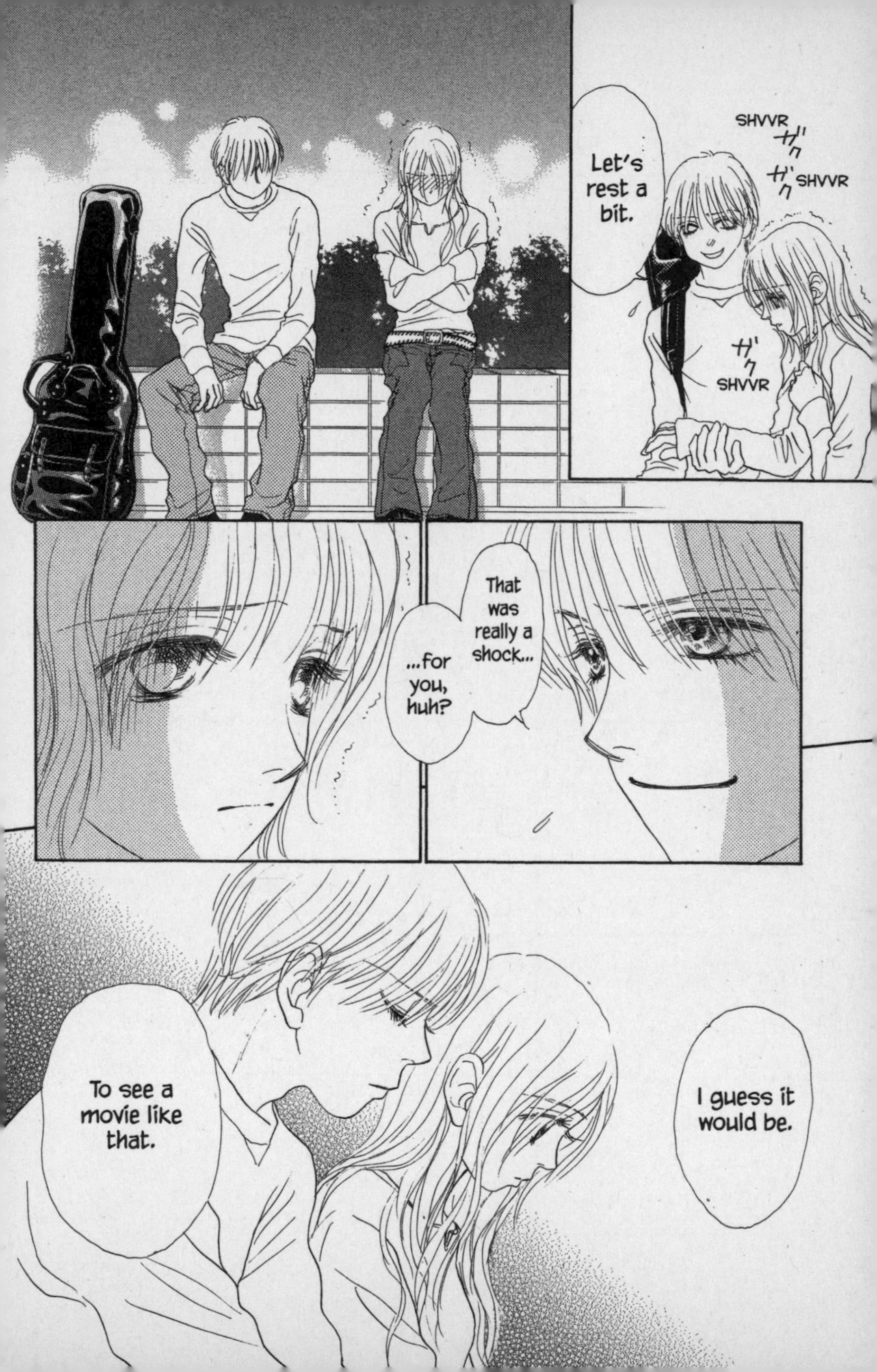
Let's rest a bit.
SHVVR
ガク
ガク SHVVR
ガク SHVVR
That was really a shock...
...for you, huh?
I guess it would be.
To see a movie like that.

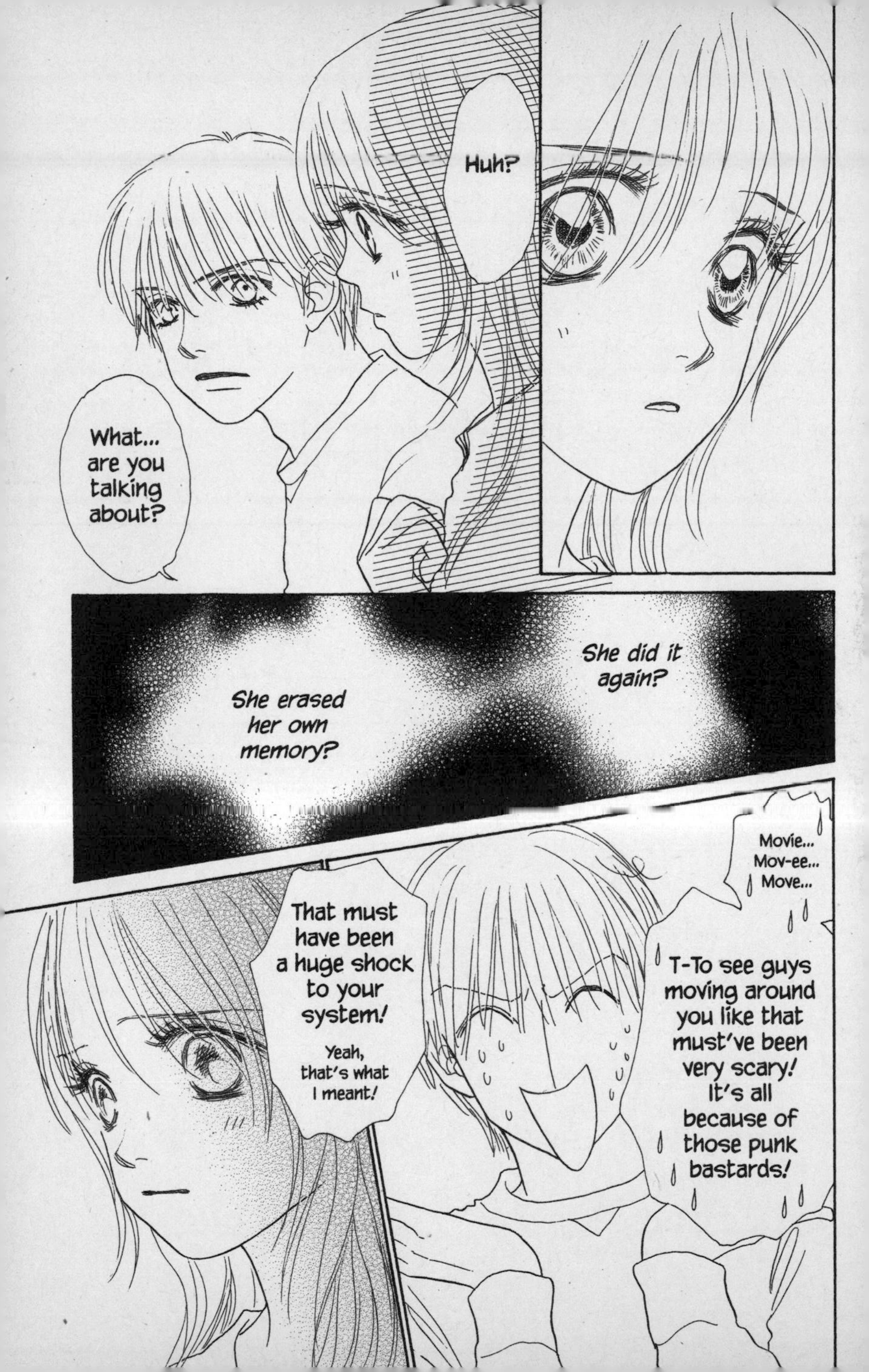
Huh?
What... are you talking about?
She did it again?
She erased her own memory?
Movie... Mov-ee... Move...
T-To see guys moving around you like that must've been very scary! It's all because of those punk bastards!
That must have been a huge shock to your system!
Yeah, that's what I meant!

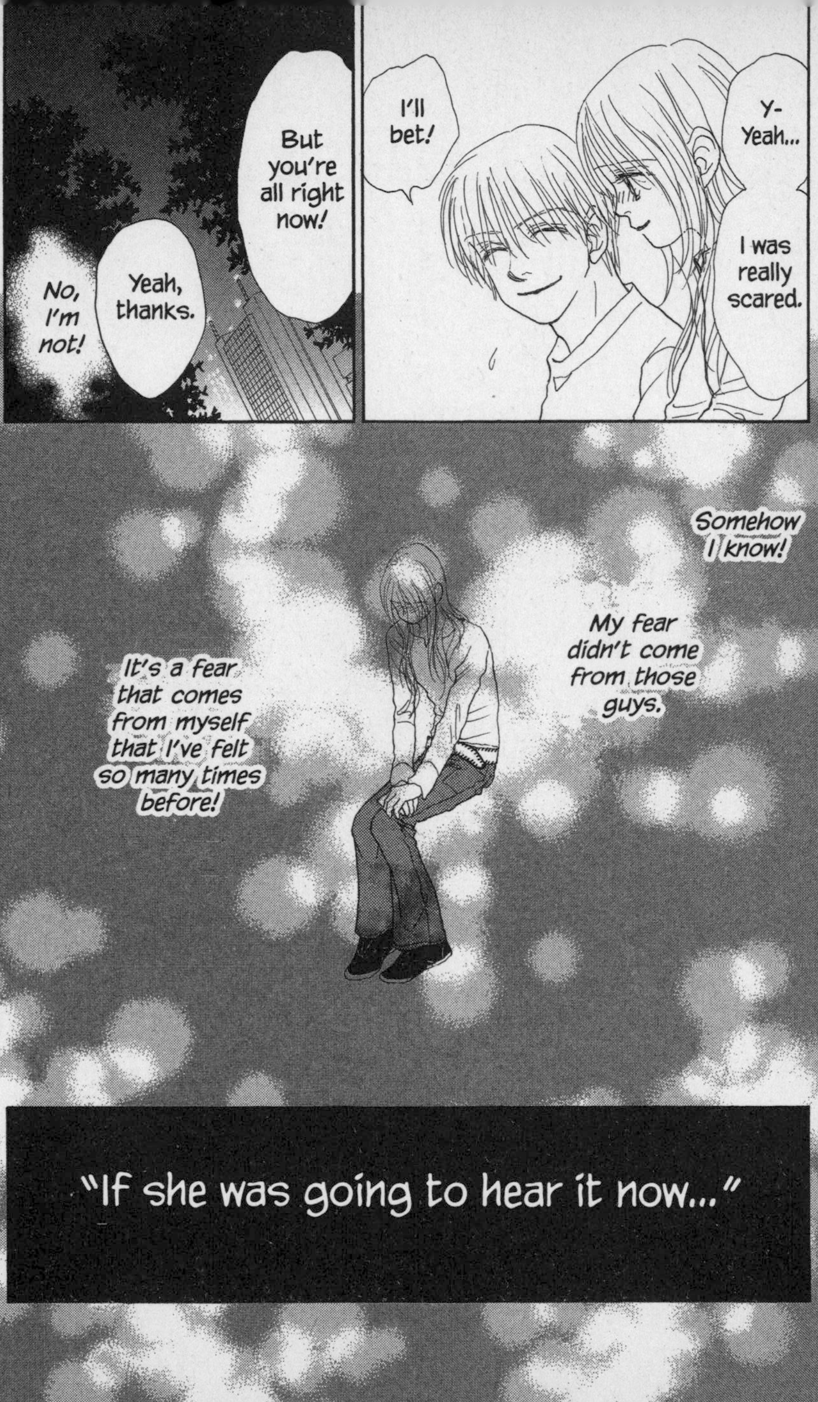
Y-
Yeah...
I was really scared.
I'll bet!
But you're all right now!
Yeah, thanks.
No, I'm not!
Somehow I know!
My fear didn't come from those guys.
It's a fear that comes from myself that I've felt so many times before!
"If she was going to hear it now..."

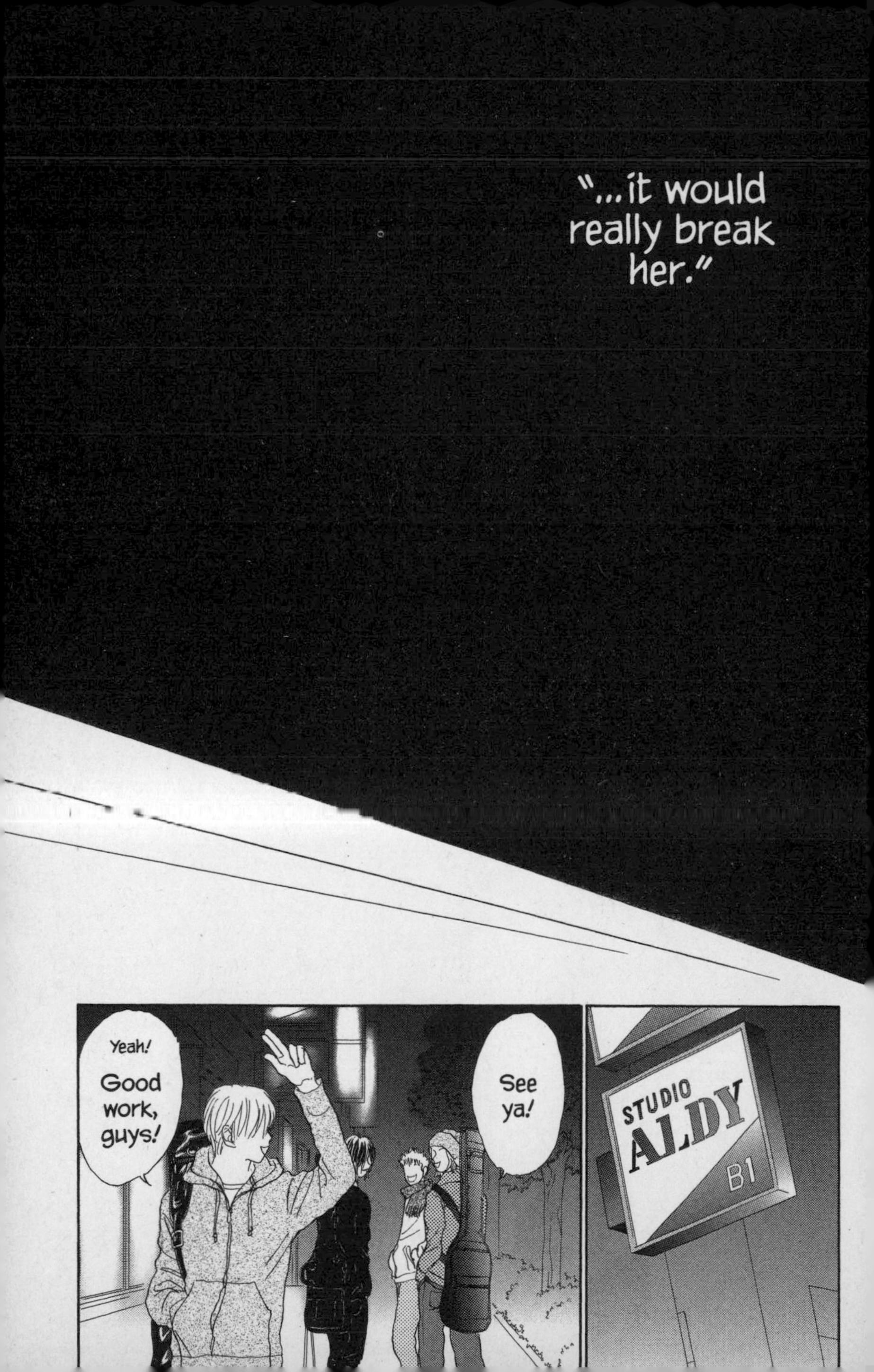
"...it would really break her."
STUDIO ALDY
B1
See ya!
Yeah! Good work, guys!

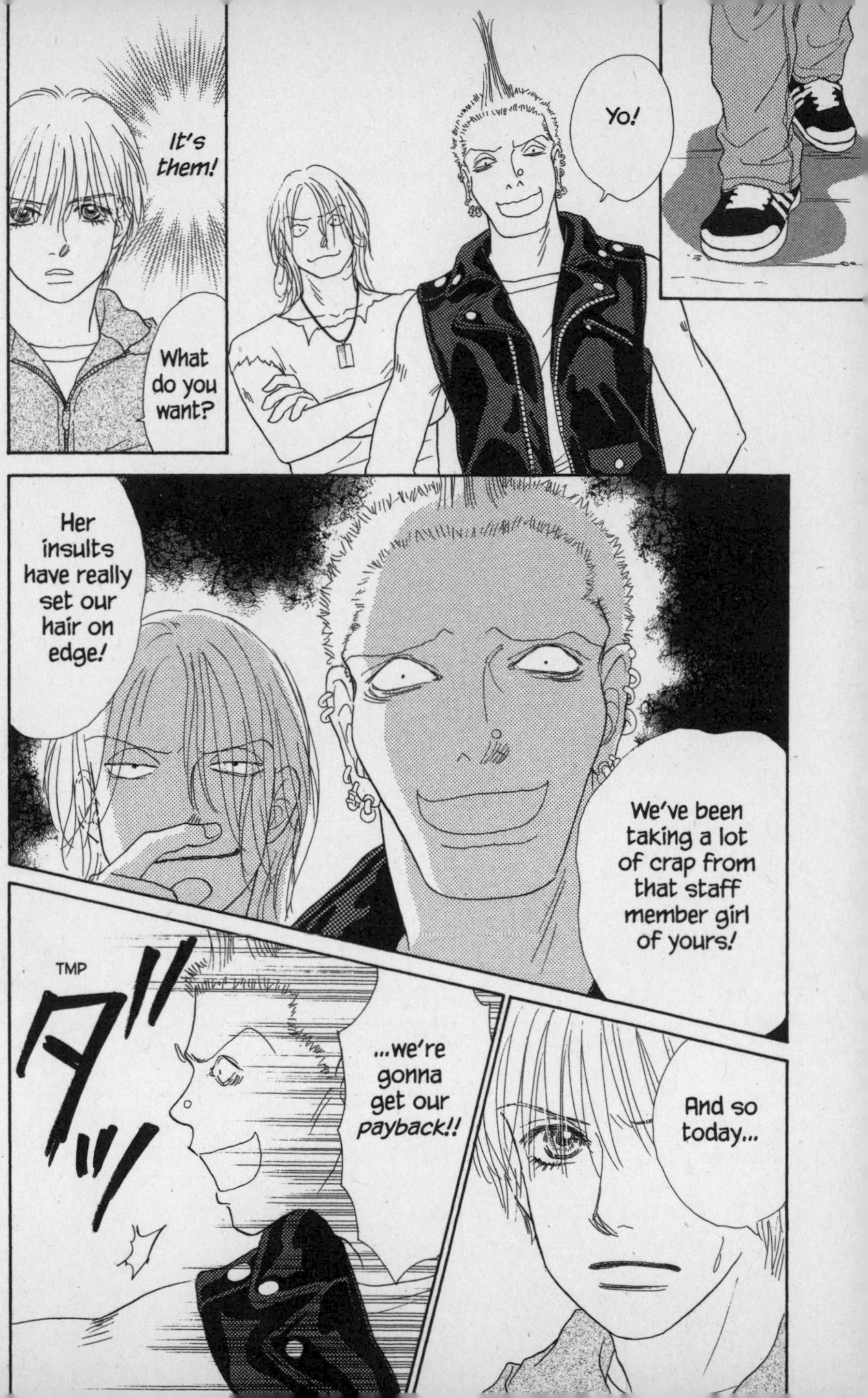
Yo!
It's them!
What do you want?
We've been taking a lot of crap from that staff member girl of yours!
Her insults have really set our hair on edge!
And so today...
...we're gonna get our payback!!
TMP
ダッ

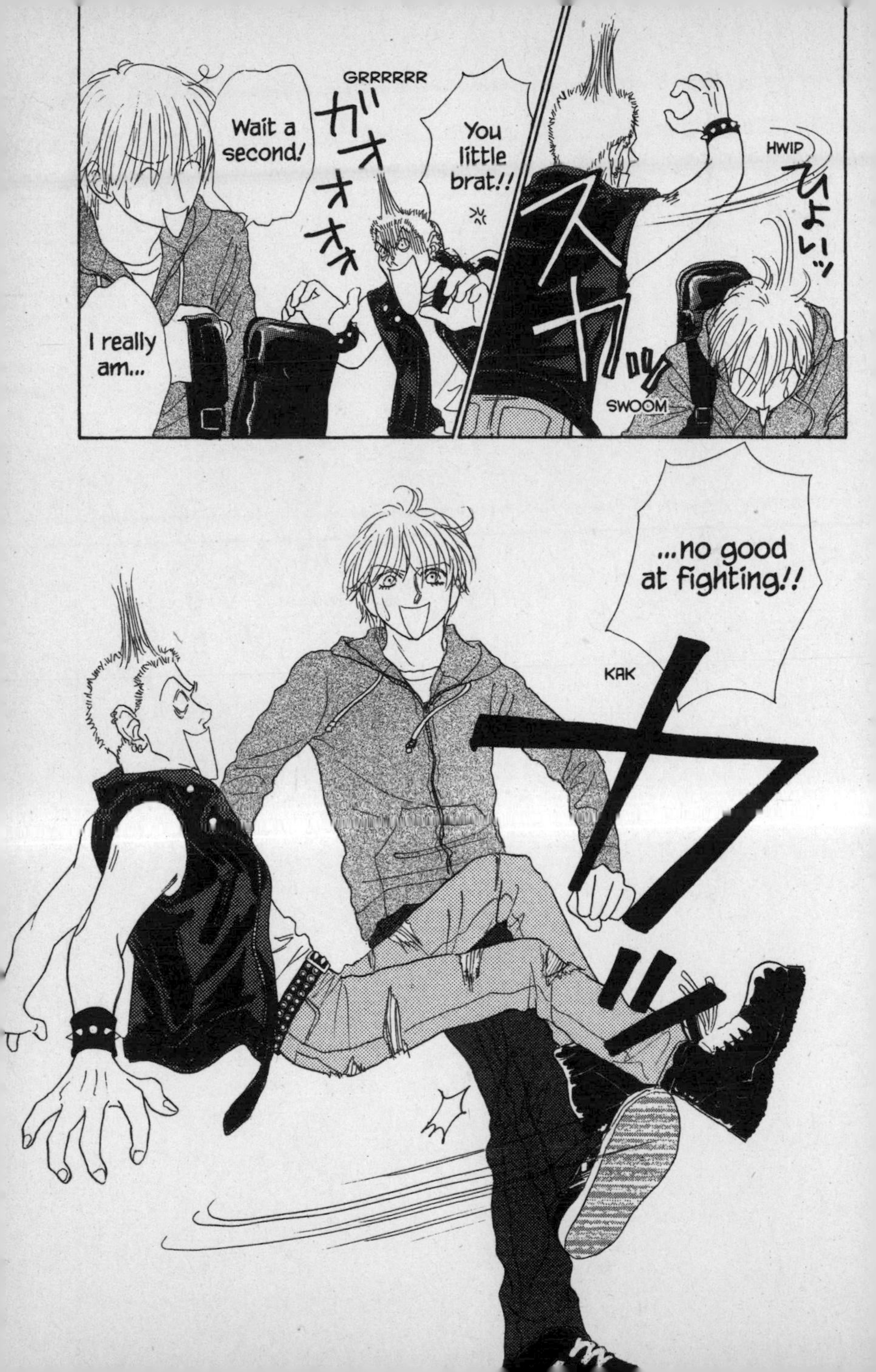
HWIP
ひょいッ
スカッ
SWOOM
You little brat!!
GRRRRRR
ガオオォ
Wait a second!
I really am...
...no good at fighting!!
KAK
カッ

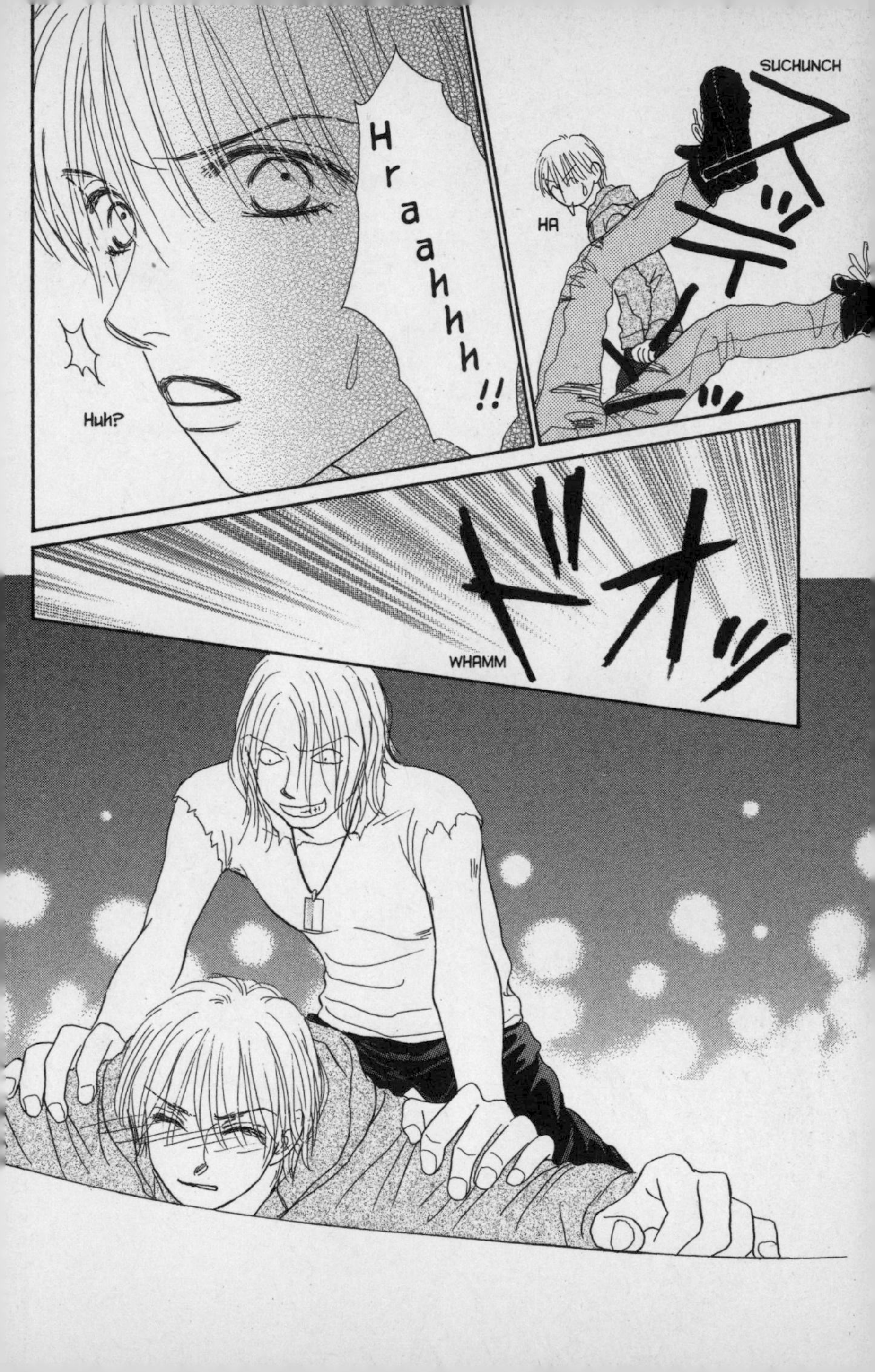
SUCHUNCH
HA
Hraahhh!!
Huh?
WHAMM

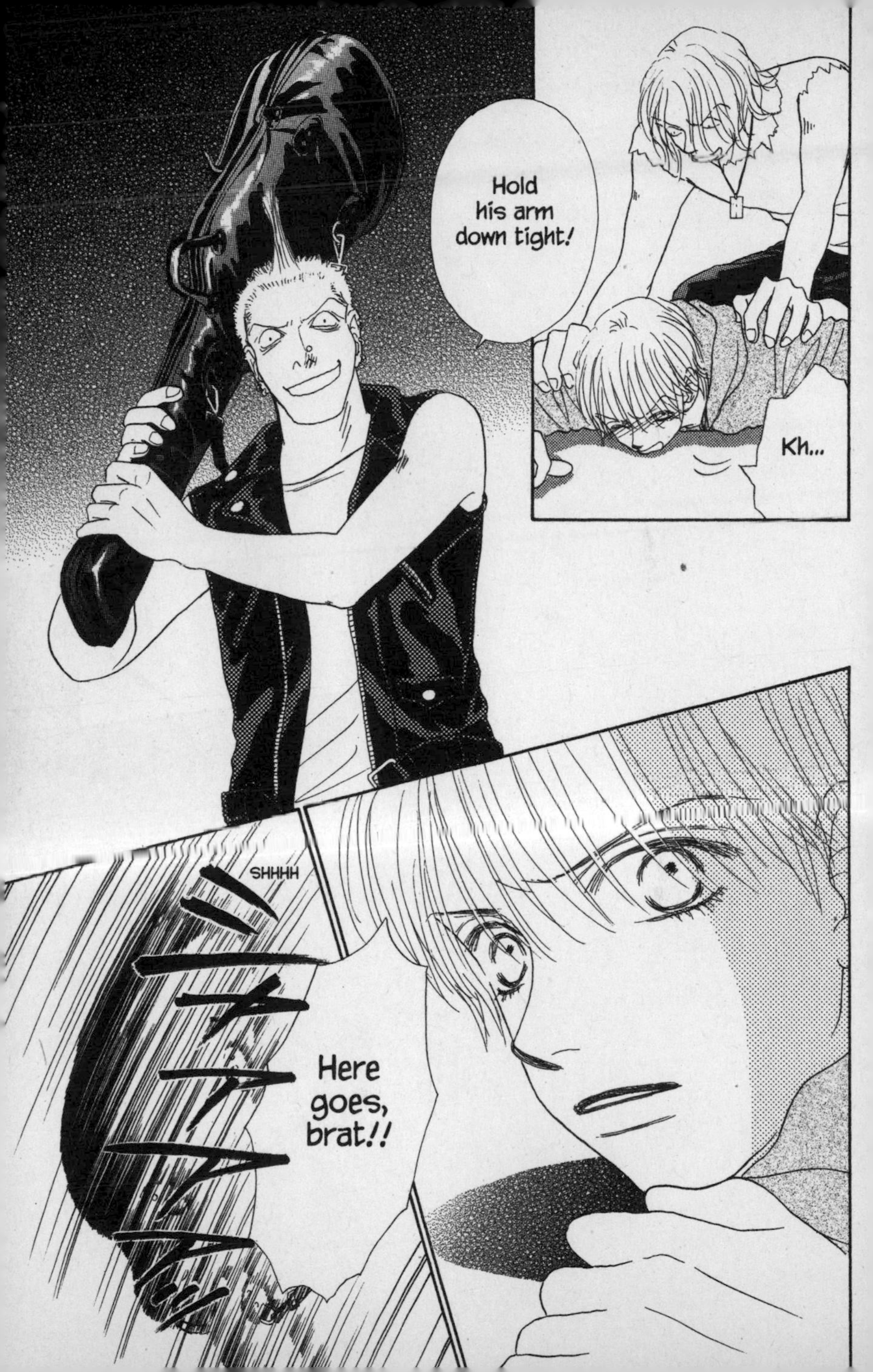
Hold his arm down tight!
Kh...
SHHHH
Here goes, brat!!

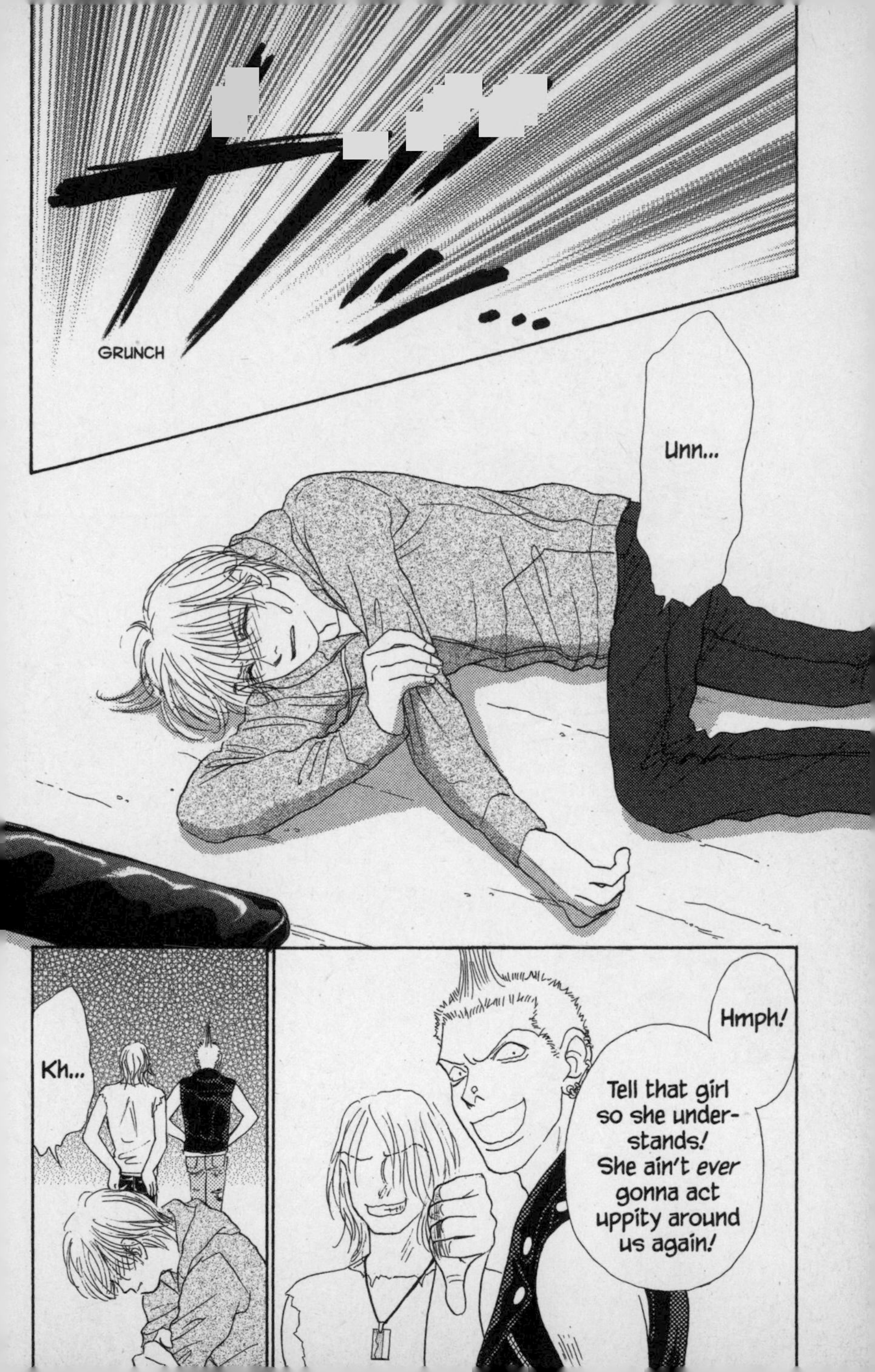
GRUNCH
Unn...
Hmph!
Tell that girl so she understands! She ain't *ever* gonna act uppity around us again!
Kh...

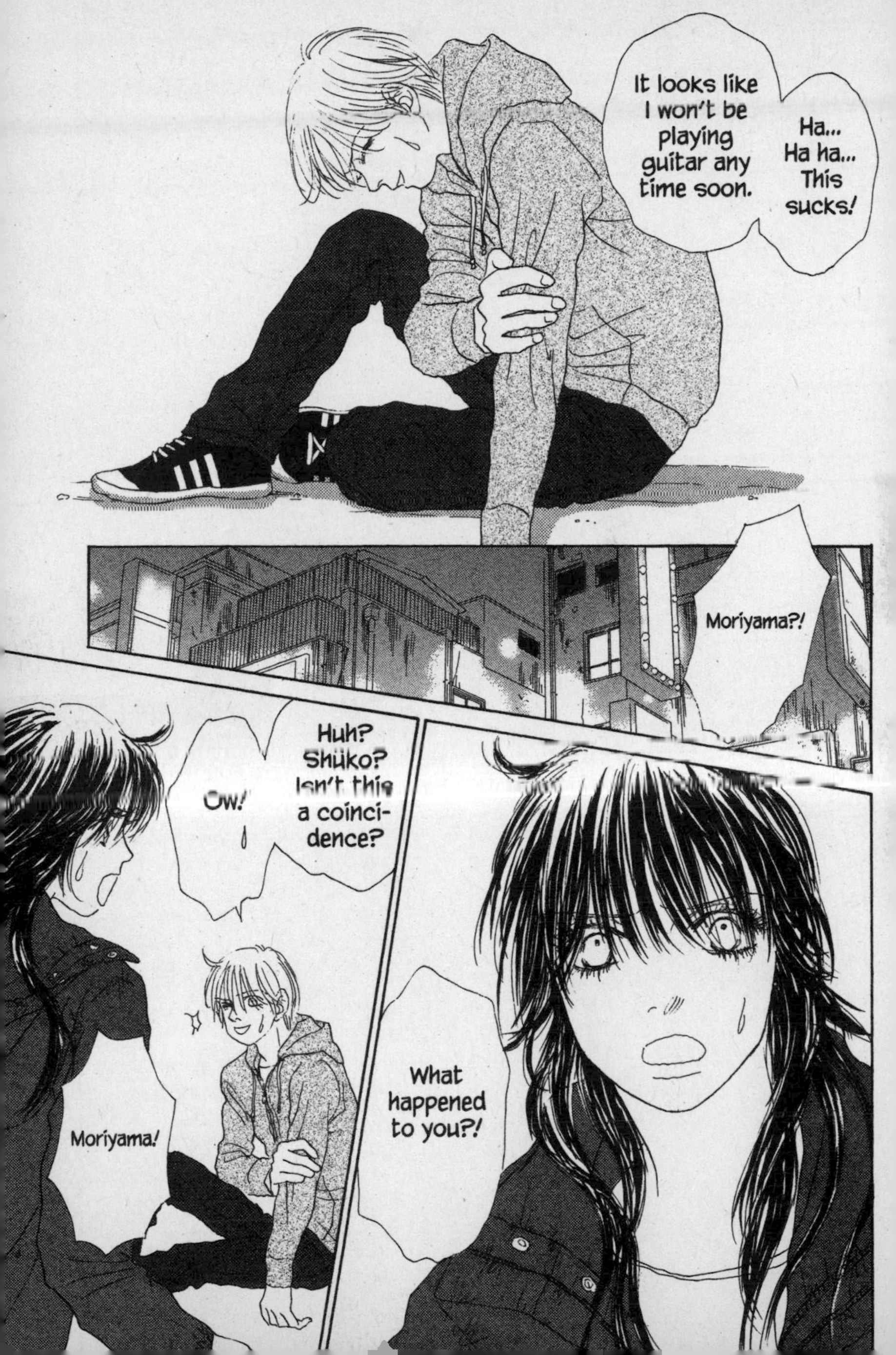
Ha... Ha ha... This sucks!
It looks like I won't be playing guitar any time soon.
Moriyama?!
What happened to you?!
Huh? Shūko? Isn't this a coincidence?
Ow!
Moriyama!

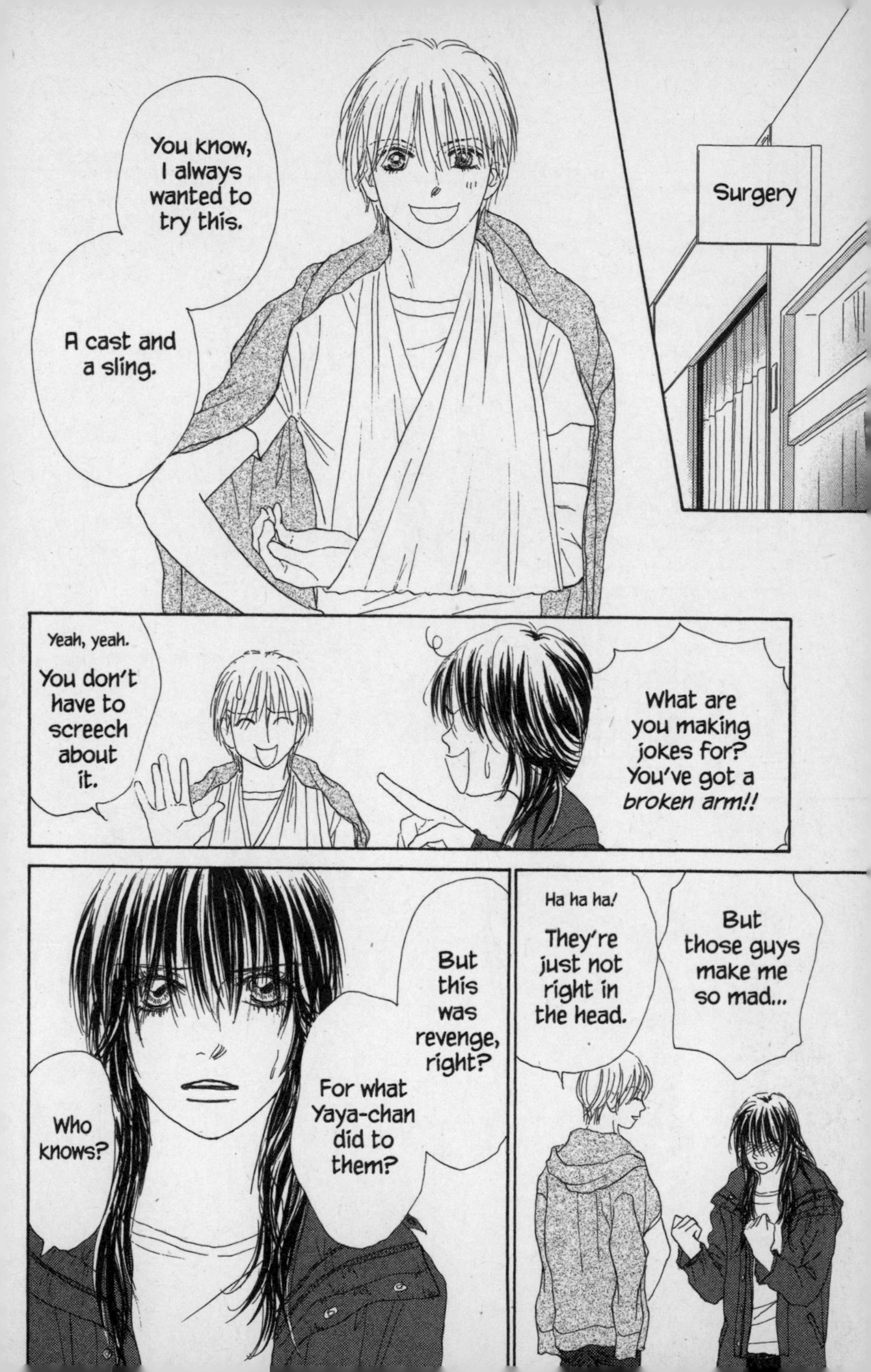
Surgery
You know, I always wanted to try this.
A cast and a sling.
What are you making jokes for? You've got a *broken arm!!*
Yeah, yeah.
You don't have to screech about it.
But those guys make me so mad...
Ha ha ha!
They're just not right in the head.
But this was revenge, right?
For what Yaya-chan did to them?
Who knows?

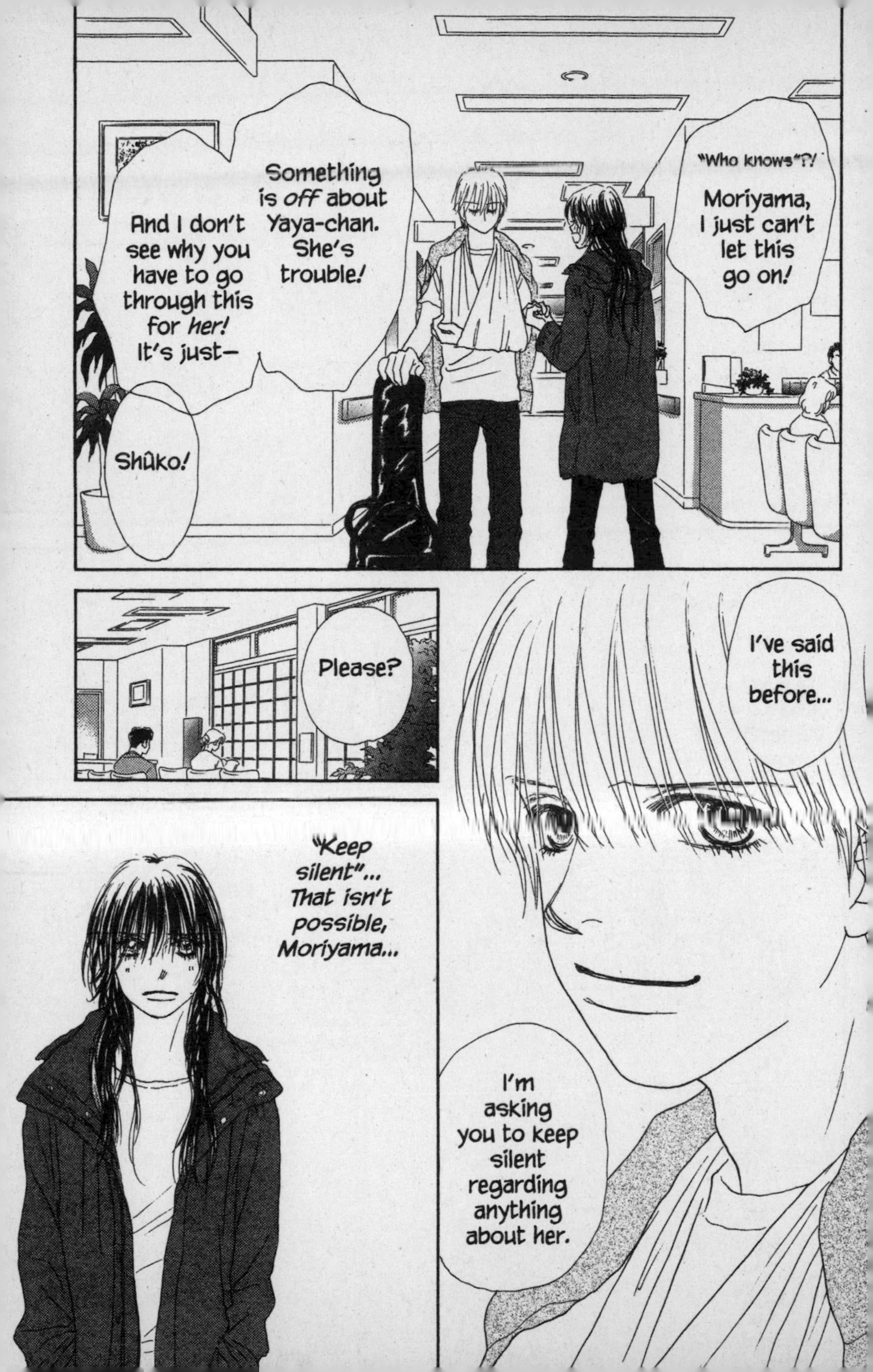
"Who knows"?! Moriyama, I just can't let this go on!
Something is *off* about Yaya-chan. She's trouble!
And I don't see why you have to go through this for *her*! It's just—
Shûko!
I've said this before...
I'm asking you to keep silent regarding anything about her.
Please?
"Keep silent"... That isn't possible, Moriyama...

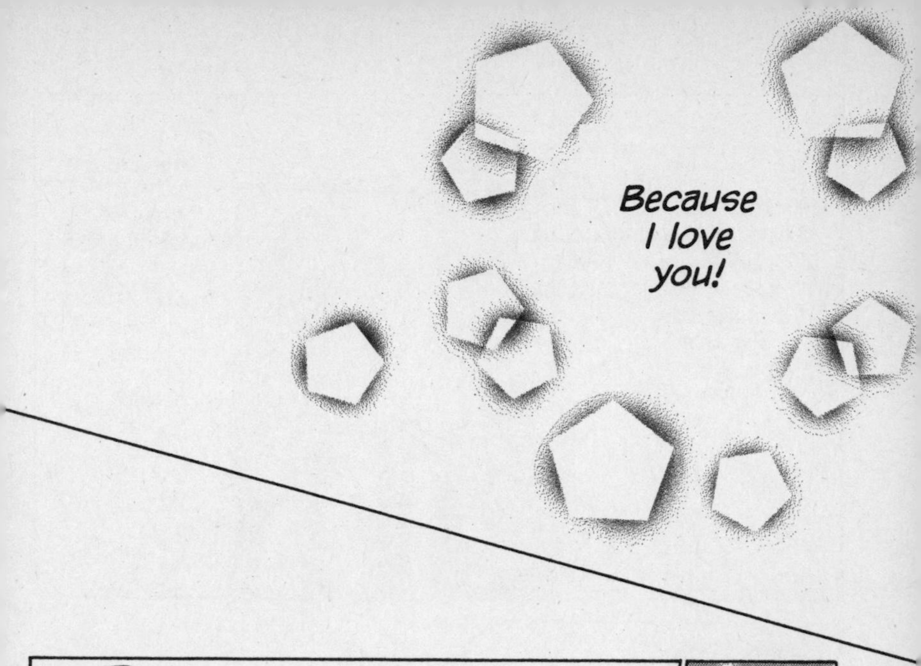
Because I love you!

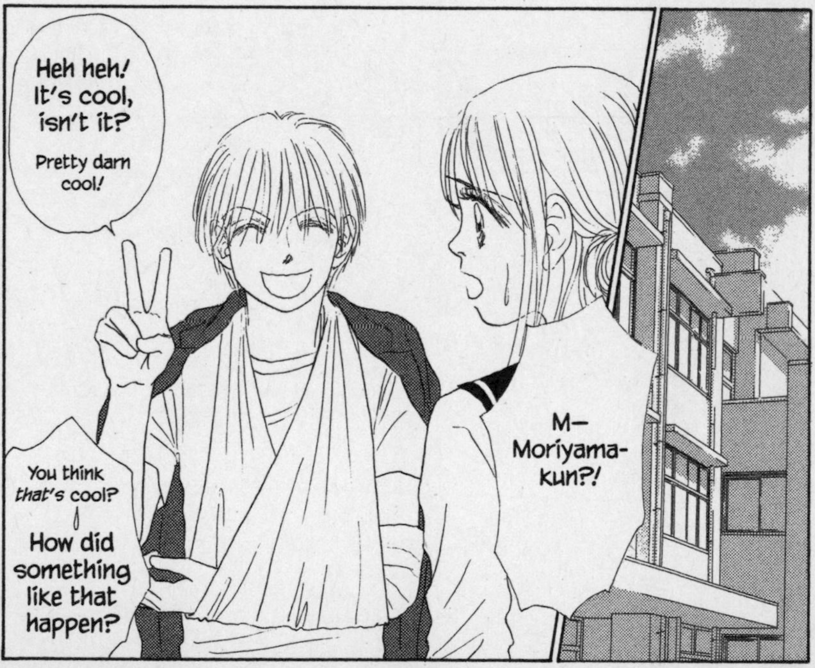
M—Moriyama-kun?!
Heh heh! It's cool, isn't it?
Pretty darn cool!
You think *that's* cool? How did something like that happen?

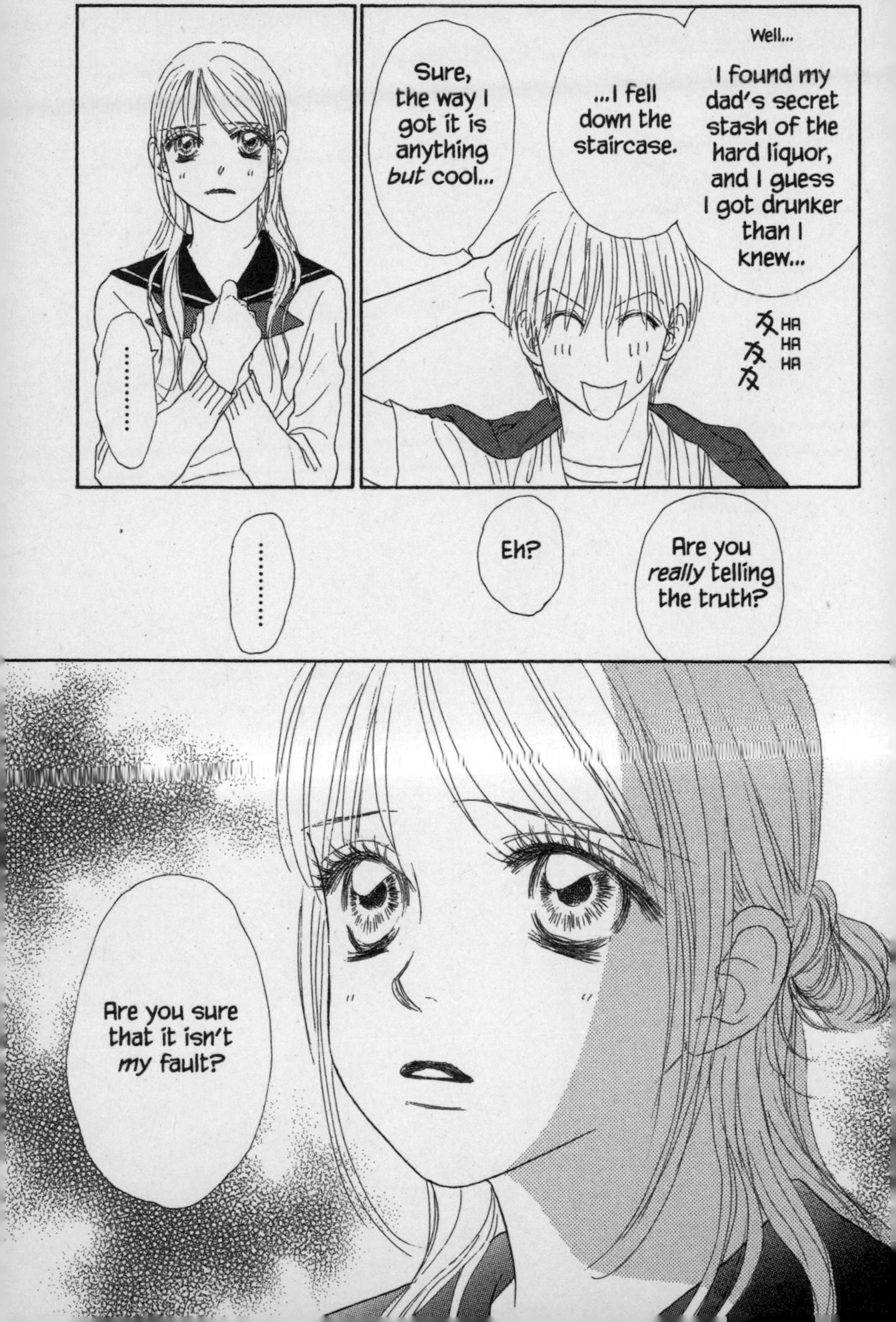
Well...
I found my dad's secret stash of the hard liquor, and I guess I got drunker than I knew...
...I fell down the staircase.
Sure, the way I got it is anything *but* cool...
HA HA HA
......
Are you *really* telling the truth?
Eh?
......
Are you sure that it isn't *my* fault?

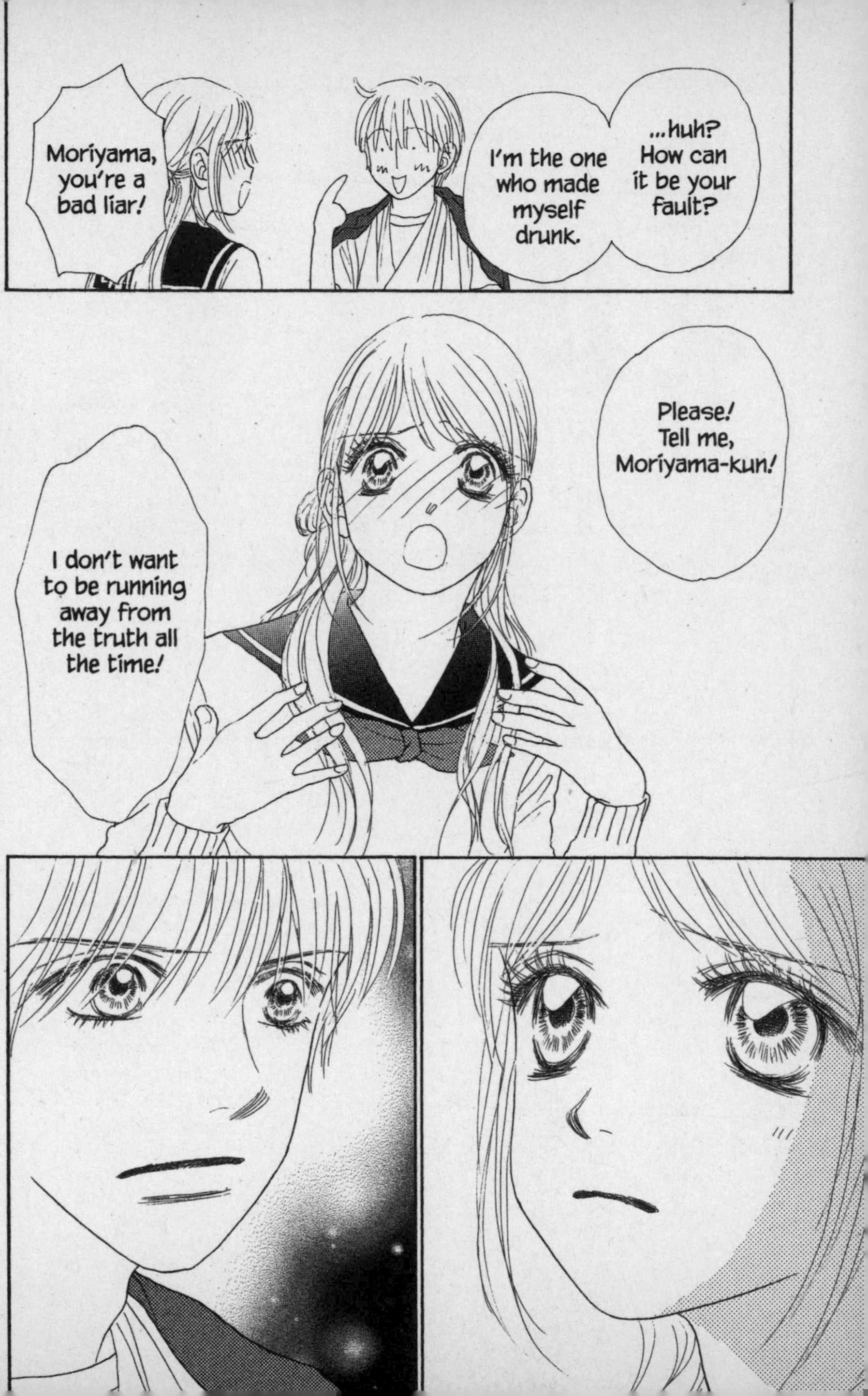
...huh? How can it be your fault?
I'm the one who made myself drunk.
Moriyama, you're a bad liar!
Please! Tell me, Moriyama-kun!
I don't want to be running away from the truth all the time!

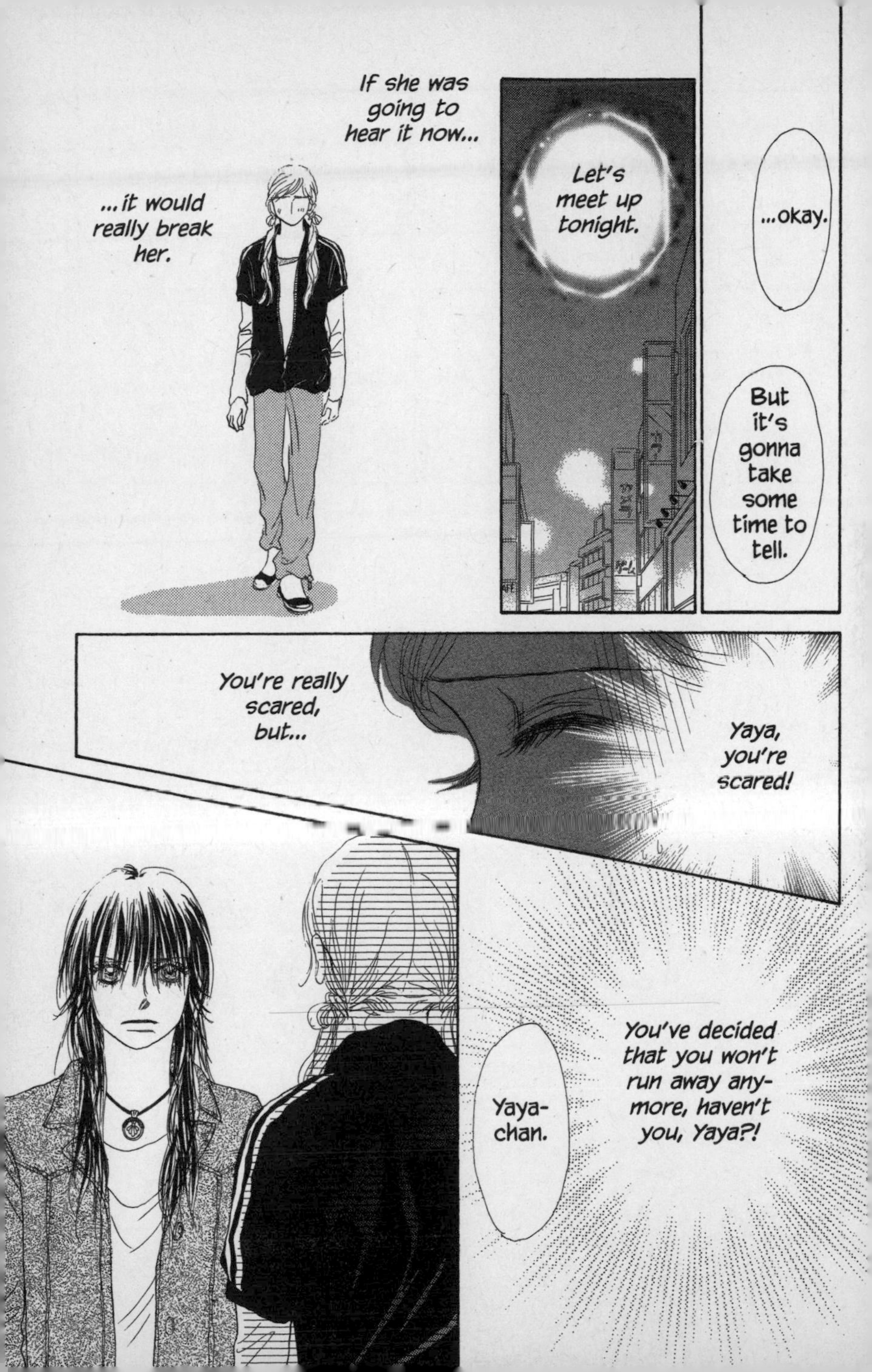
...okay.
But it's gonna take some time to tell.
Let's meet up tonight.
If she was going to hear it now...
...it would really break her.
Yaya, you're scared!
You're really scared, but...
You've decided that you won't run away any-more, haven't you, Yaya?!
Yaya-chan.

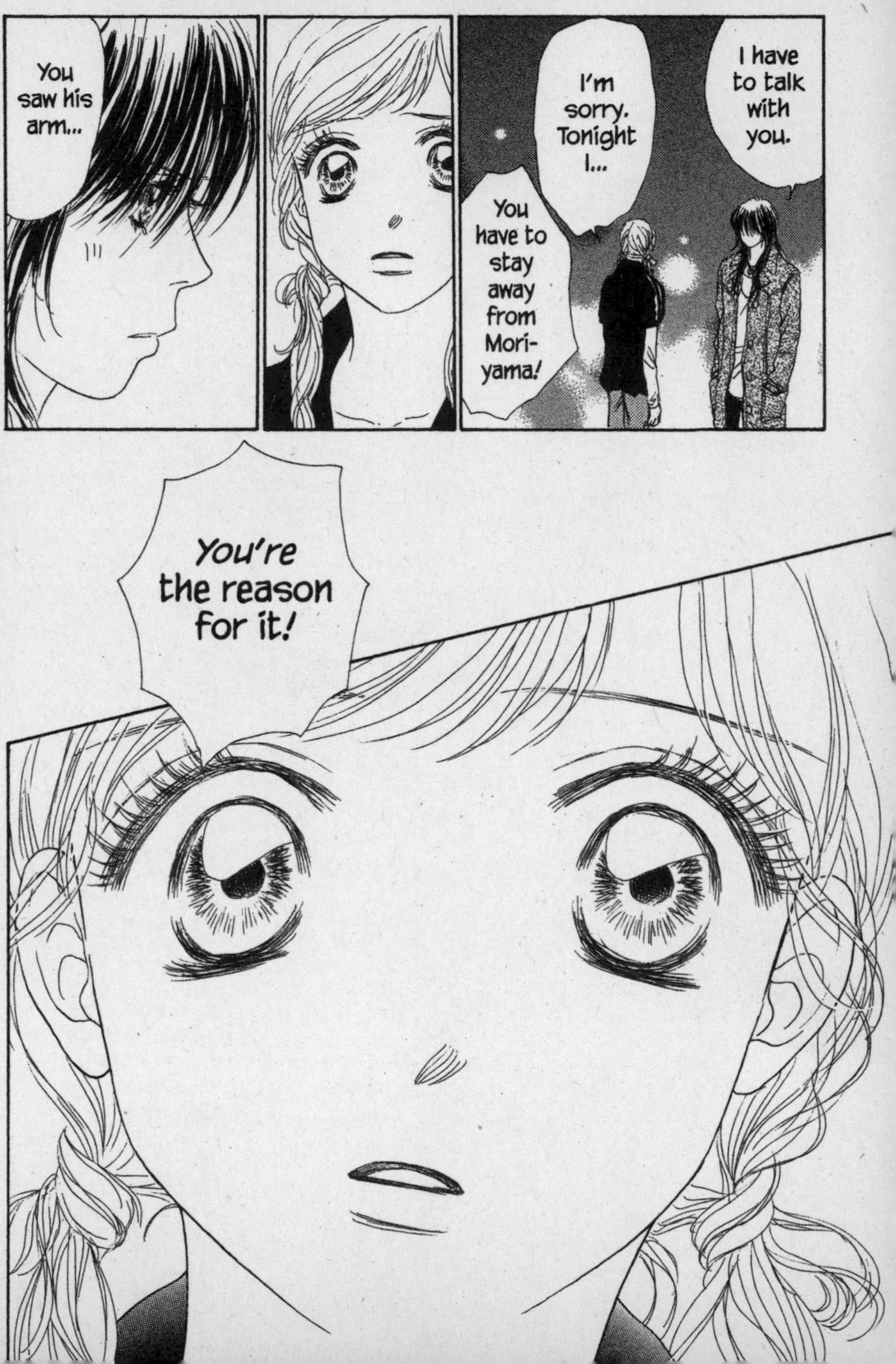
I have to talk with you.
I'm sorry. Tonight I...
You have to stay away from Mori-yama!
You saw his arm...
You're the reason for it!

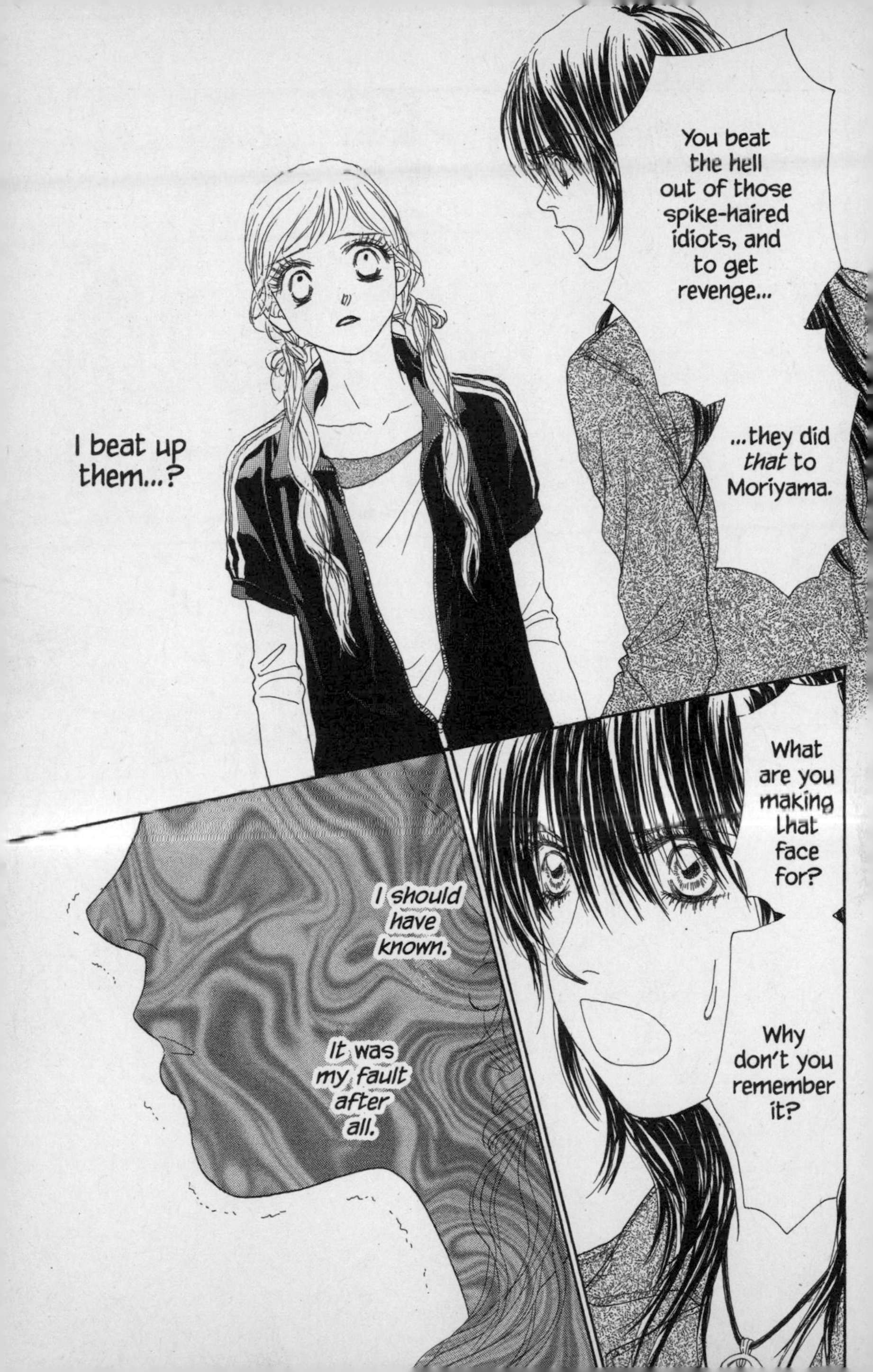
You beat the hell out of those spike-haired idiots, and to get revenge...
...they did *that* to Moriyama.
I beat up them...?
What are you making that face for?
Why don't you remember it?
I should have known.
It was my fault after all.

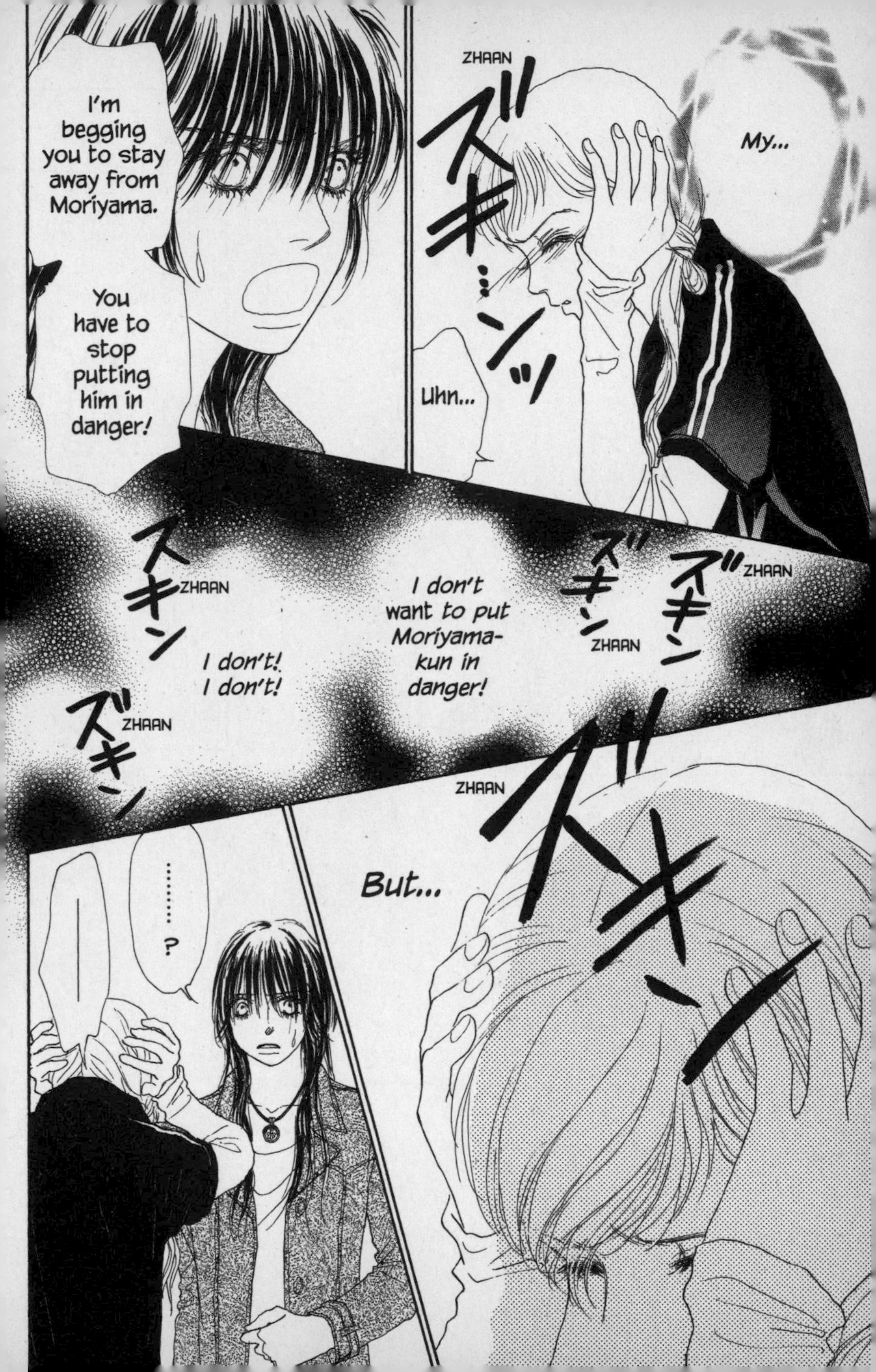
My...
ZHAAN
Uhn...
I'm begging you to stay away from Moriyama.
You have to stop putting him in danger!
ZHAAN
ZHAAN
I don't want to put Moriyama-kun in danger!
I don't! I don't!
ZHAAN
ZHAAN
ZHAAN
But...
......?

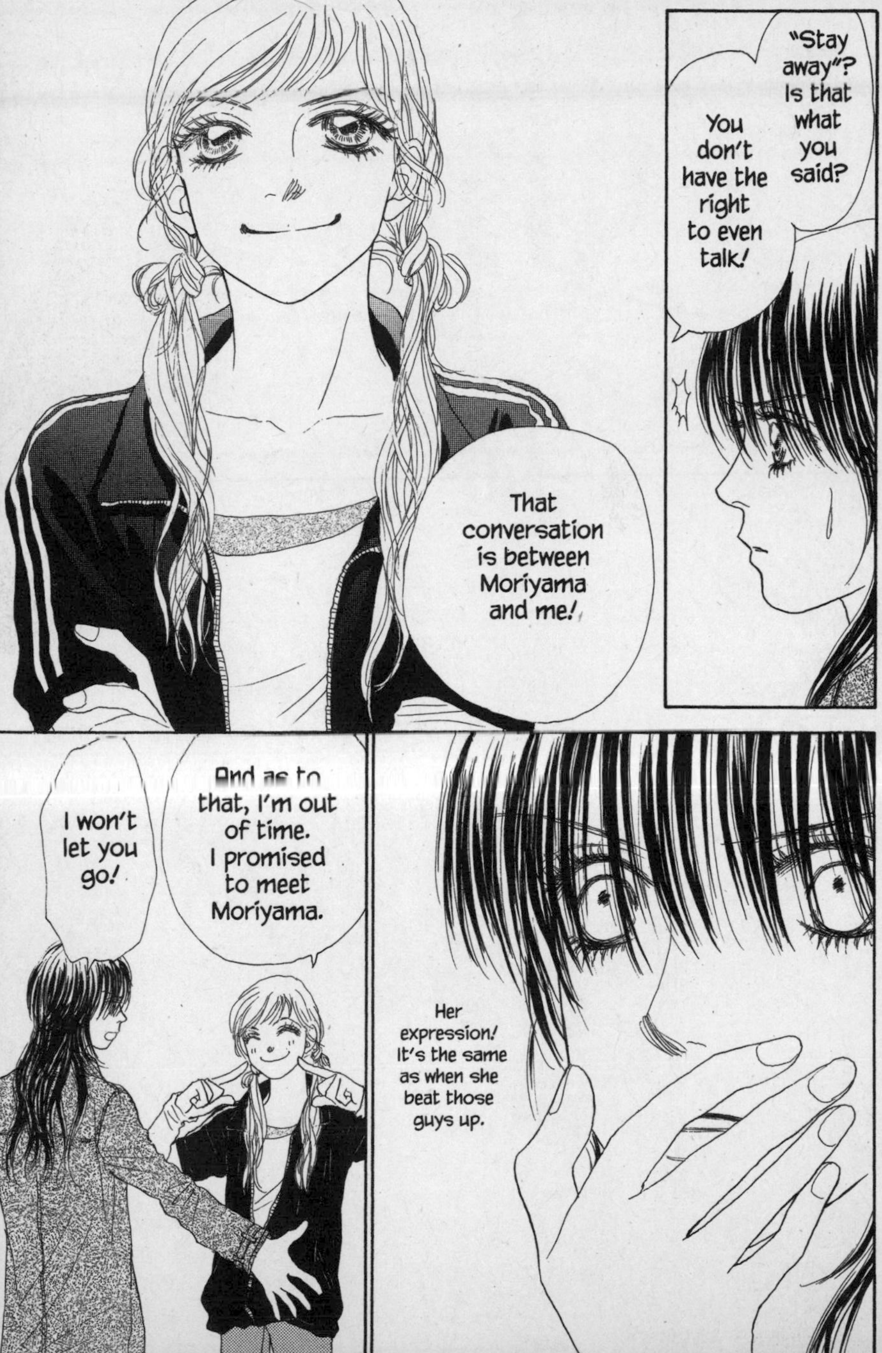
"Stay away"? Is that what you said?
You don't have the right to even talk!
That conversation is between Moriyama and me!
Her expression! It's the same as when she beat those guys up.
And as to that, I'm out of time. I promised to meet Moriyama.
I won't let you go!

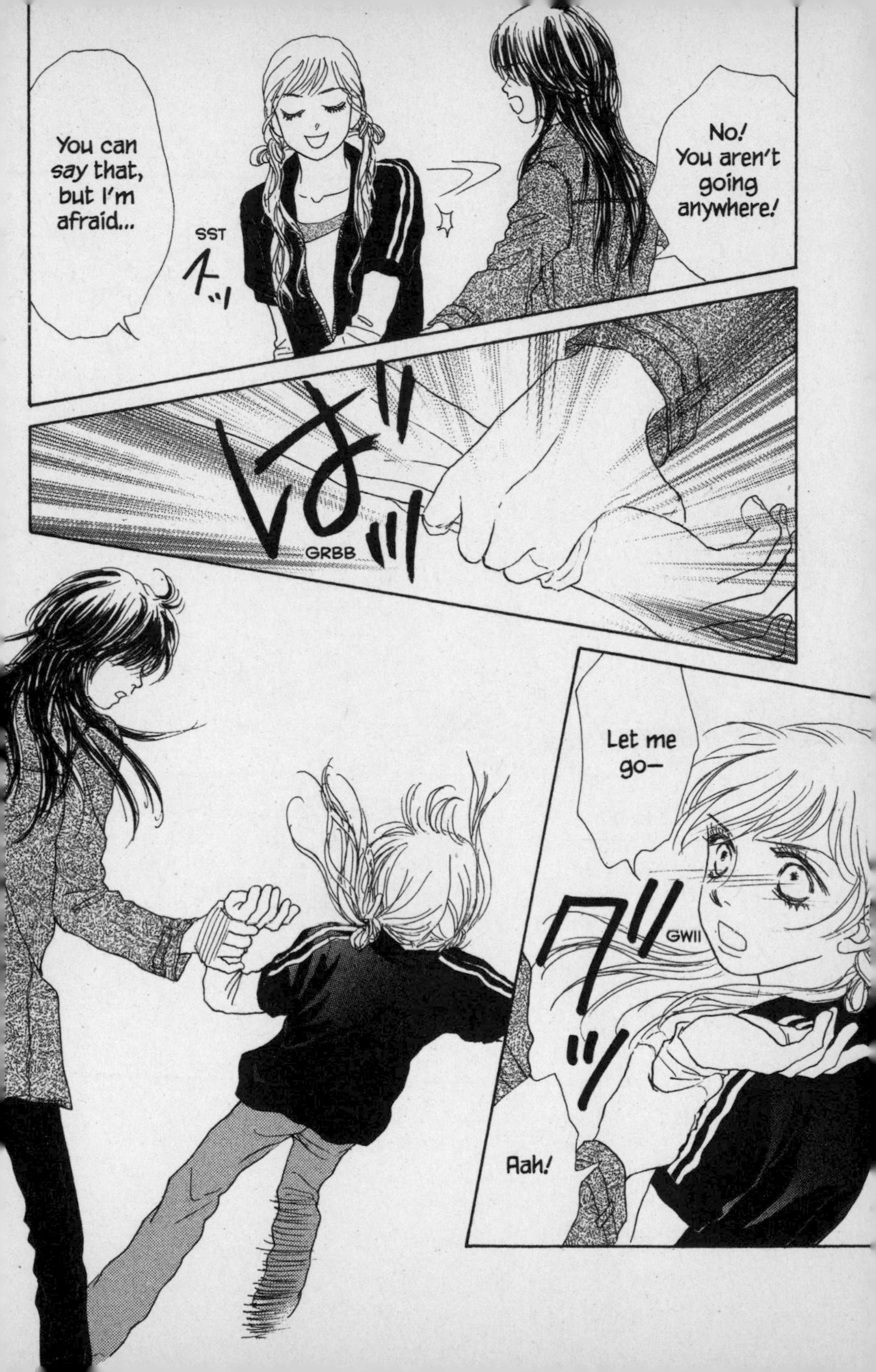
You can say that, but I'm afraid...
SST
No! You aren't going anywhere!
GRBB
Let me go–
GWII
Aah!

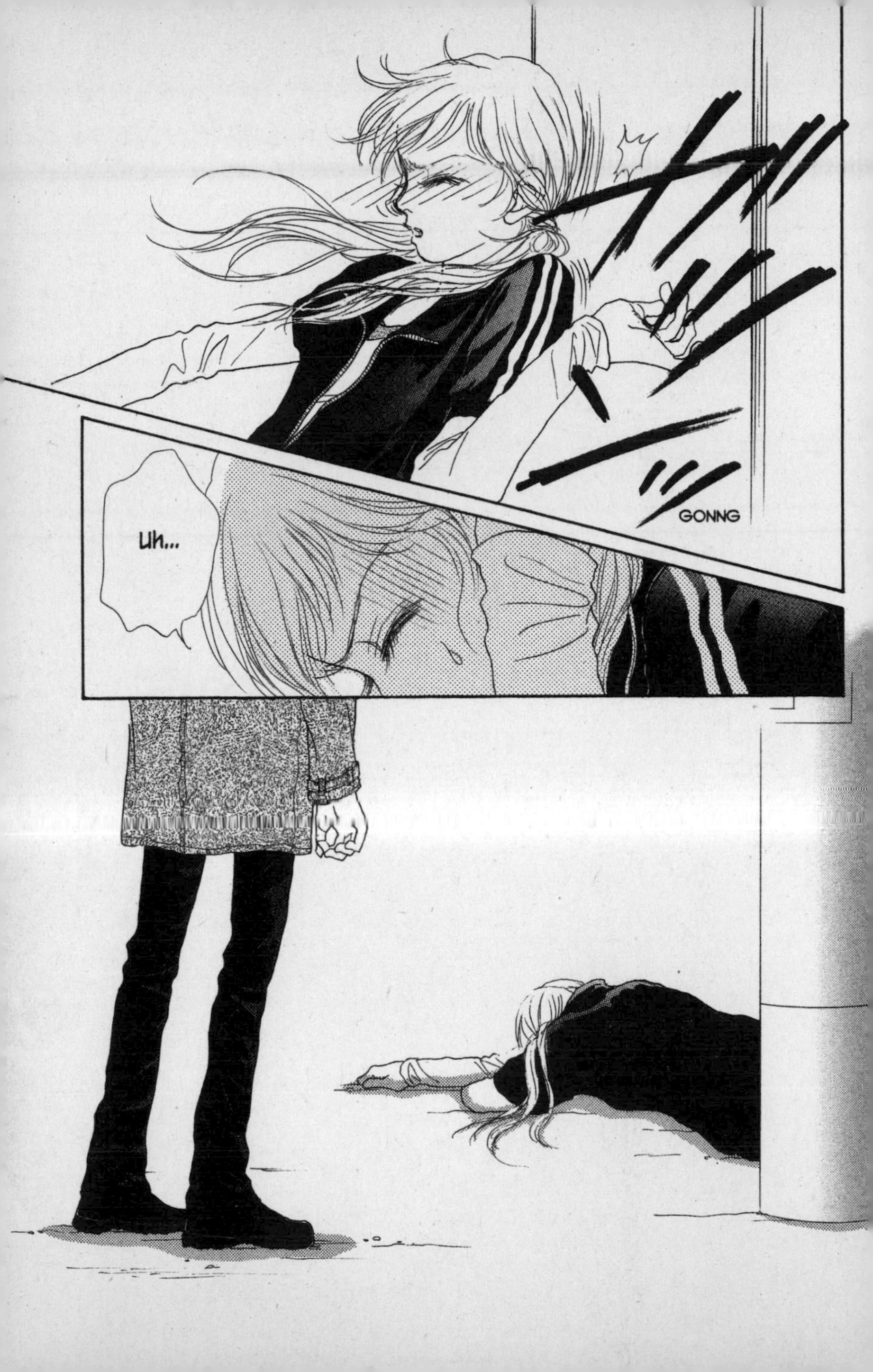
GONNG
Uh...

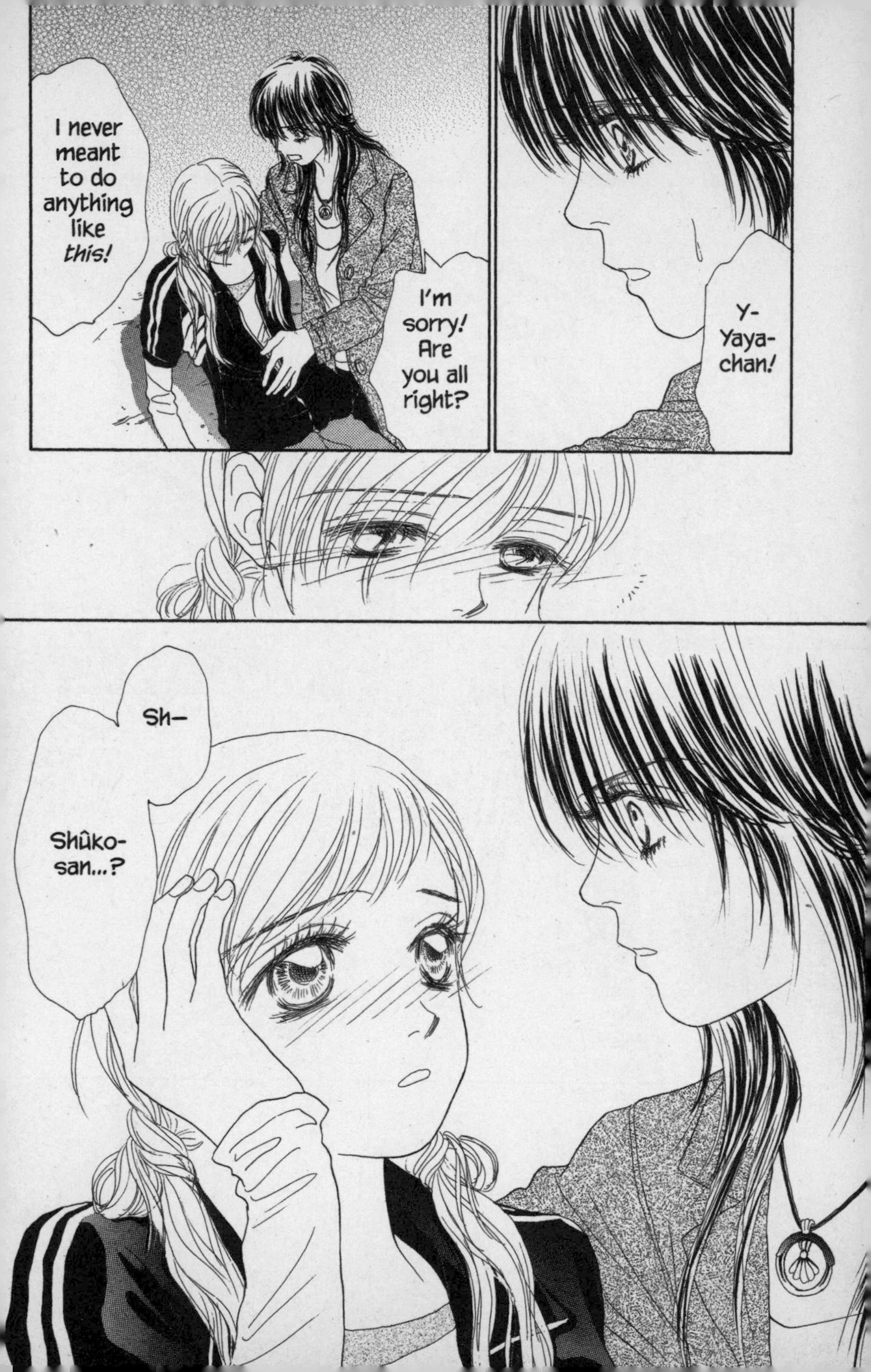
Y- Yaya-chan!
I'm sorry! Are you all right?
I never meant to do anything like *this!*
Sh- Shûko-san...?

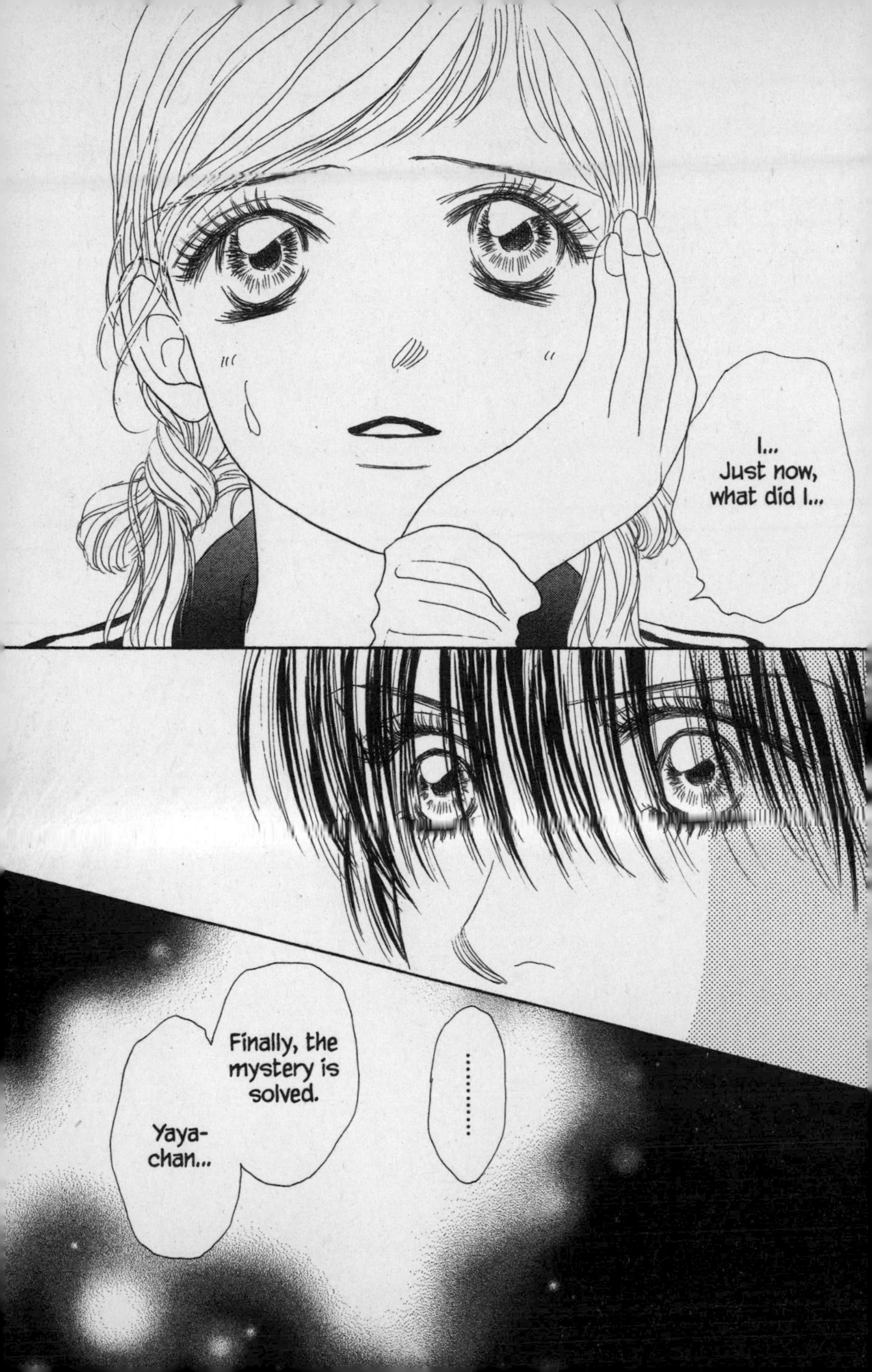
I...
Just now, what did I...
......
Finally, the mystery is solved.
Yaya-chan...

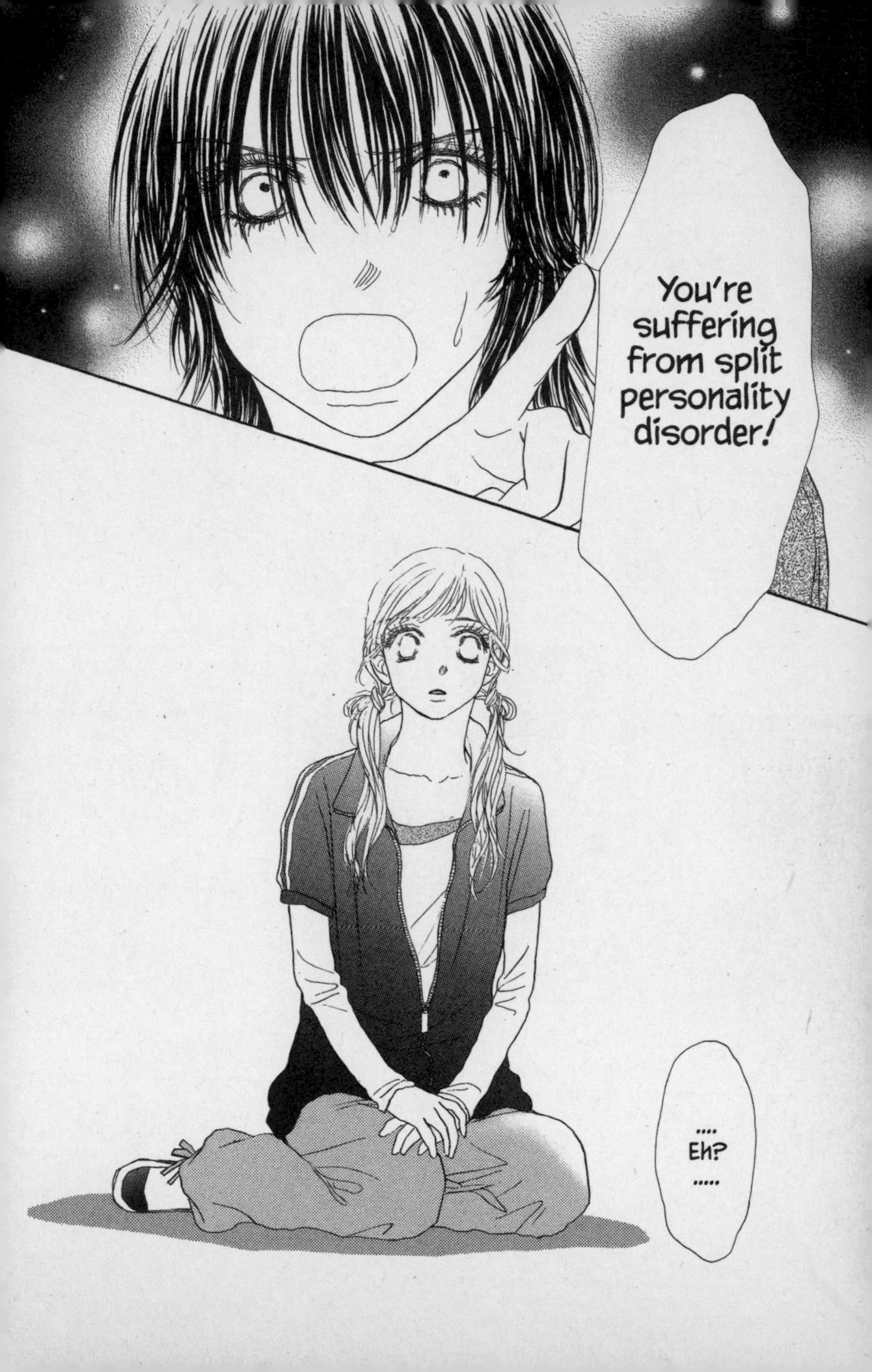
You're suffering from split personality disorder!
.... Eh? .....

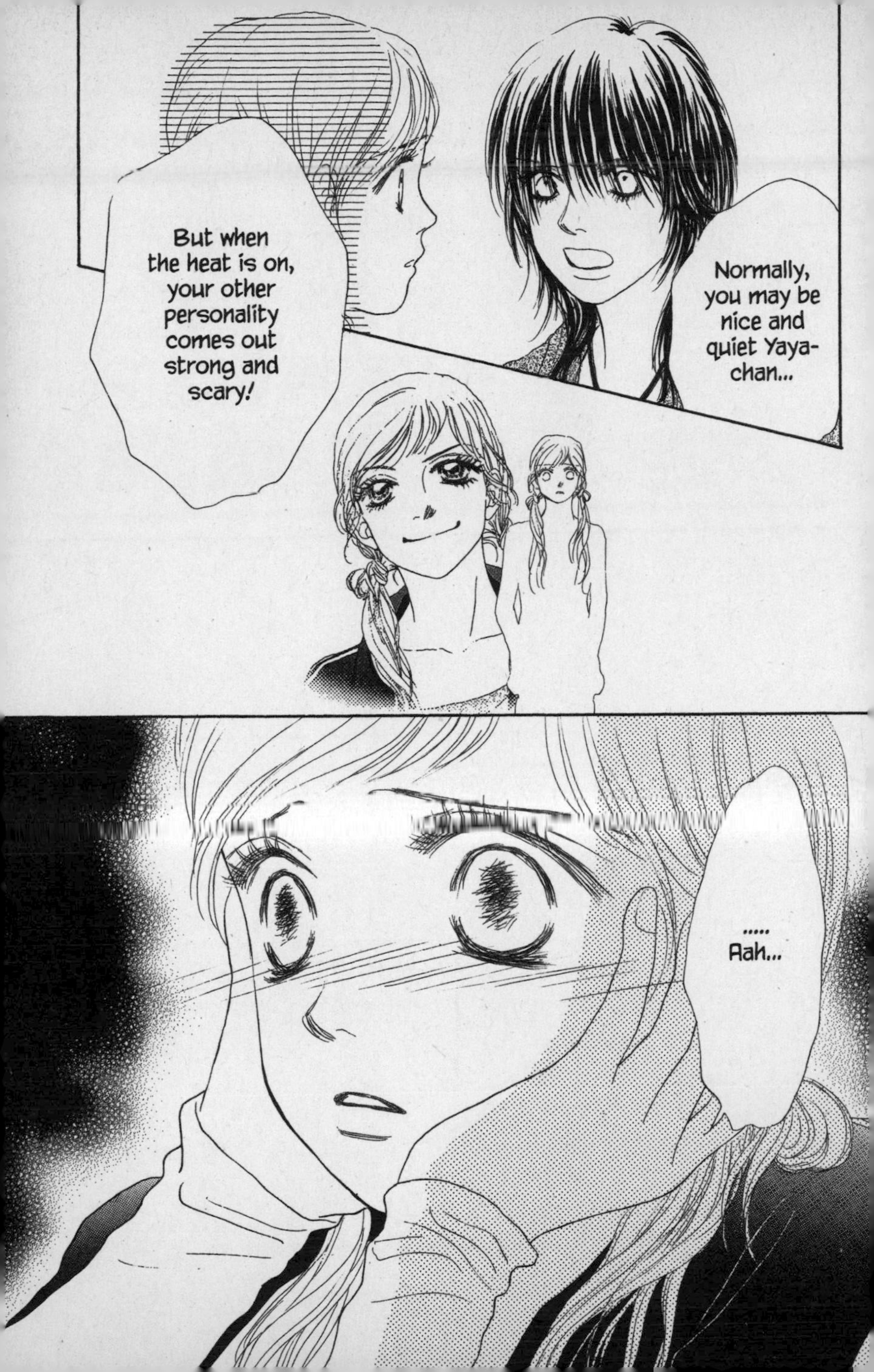
Normally, you may be nice and quiet Yaya-chan...
But when the heat is on, your other personality comes out strong and scary!
..... Aah...

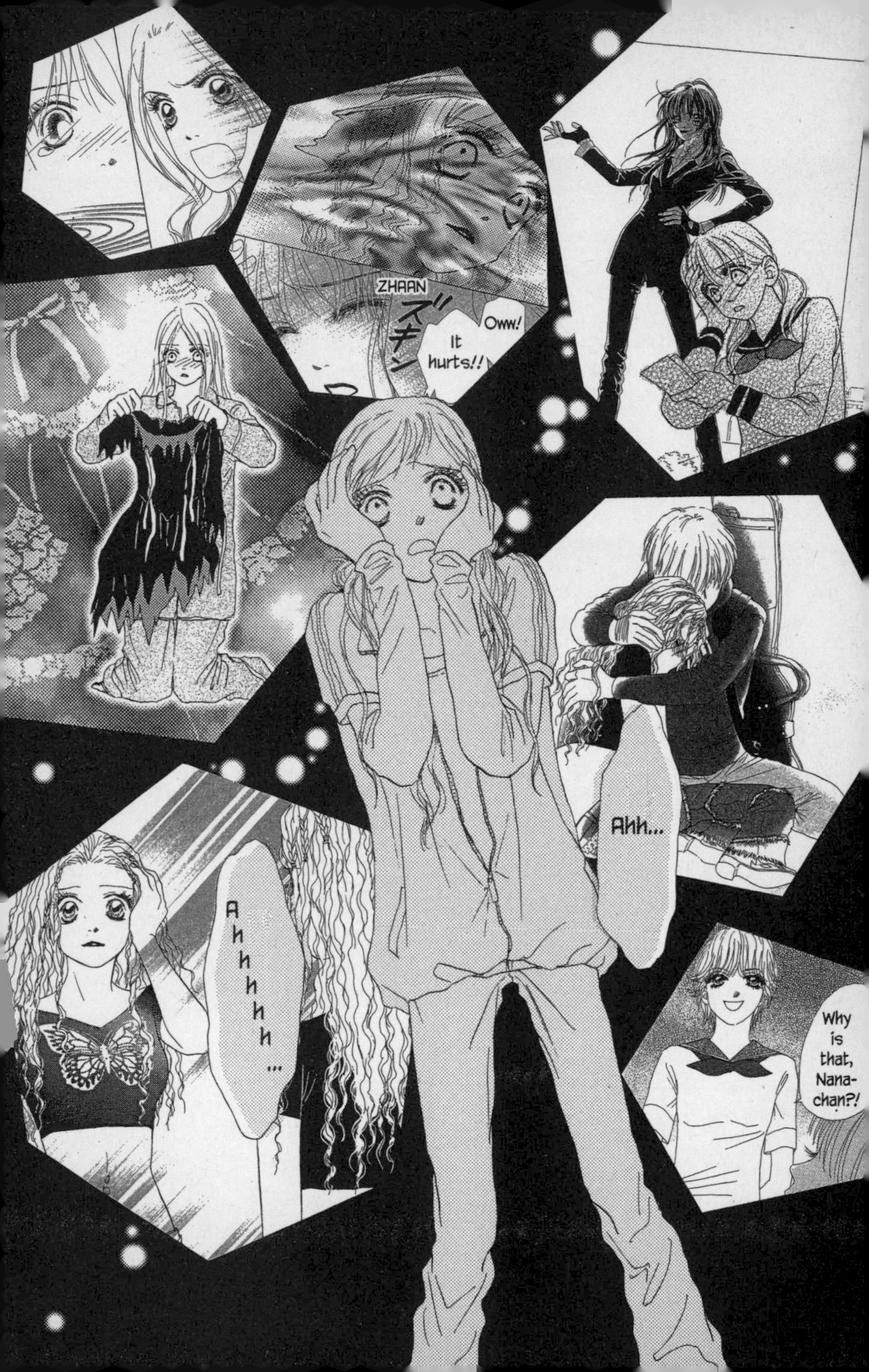
ZHAAN
ズキン
Oww! It hurts!!
Ahh...
Why is that, Nana-chan?!
Ahhhhhh...

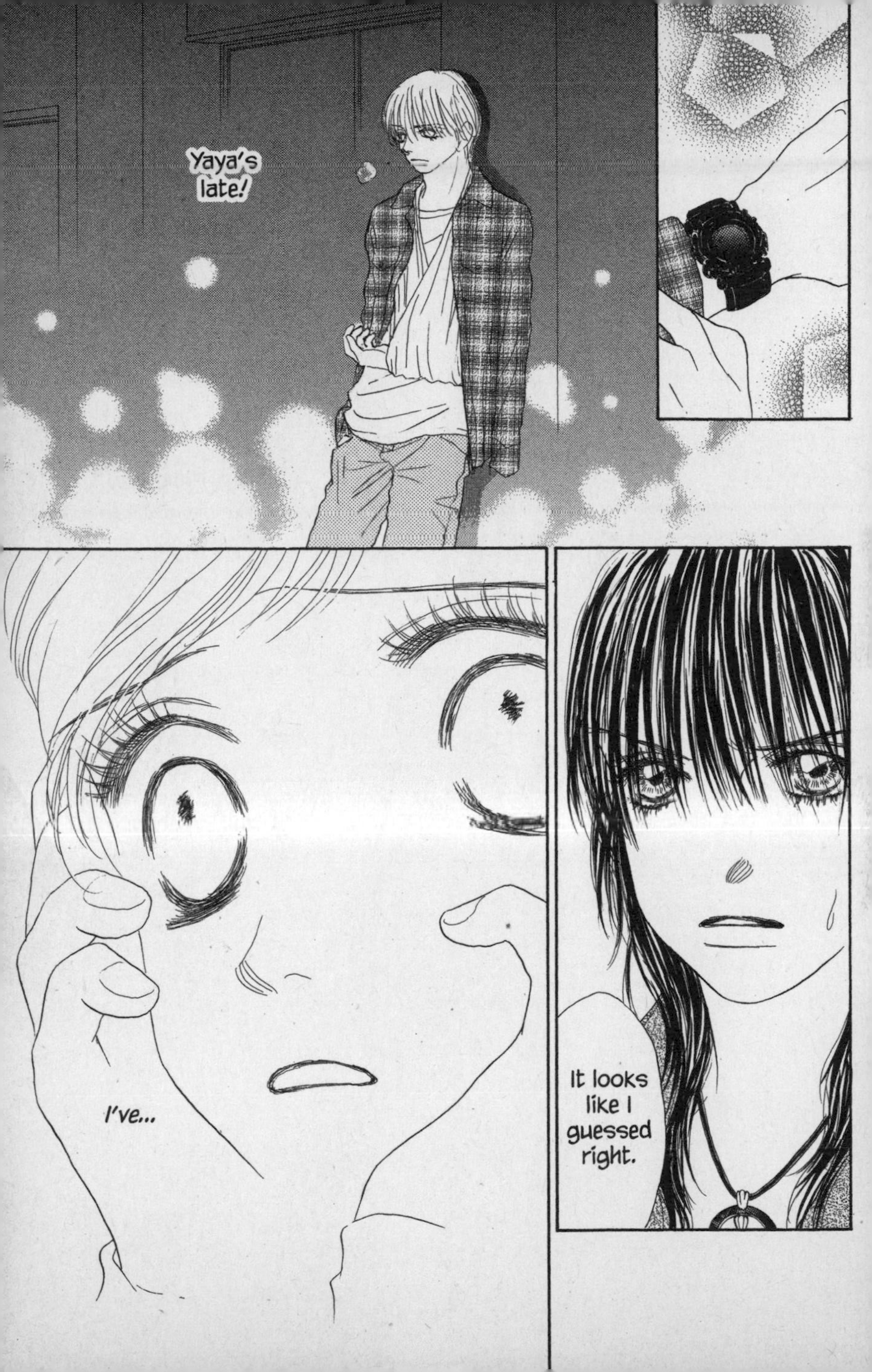
Yaya's late!
It looks like I guessed right.
I've...

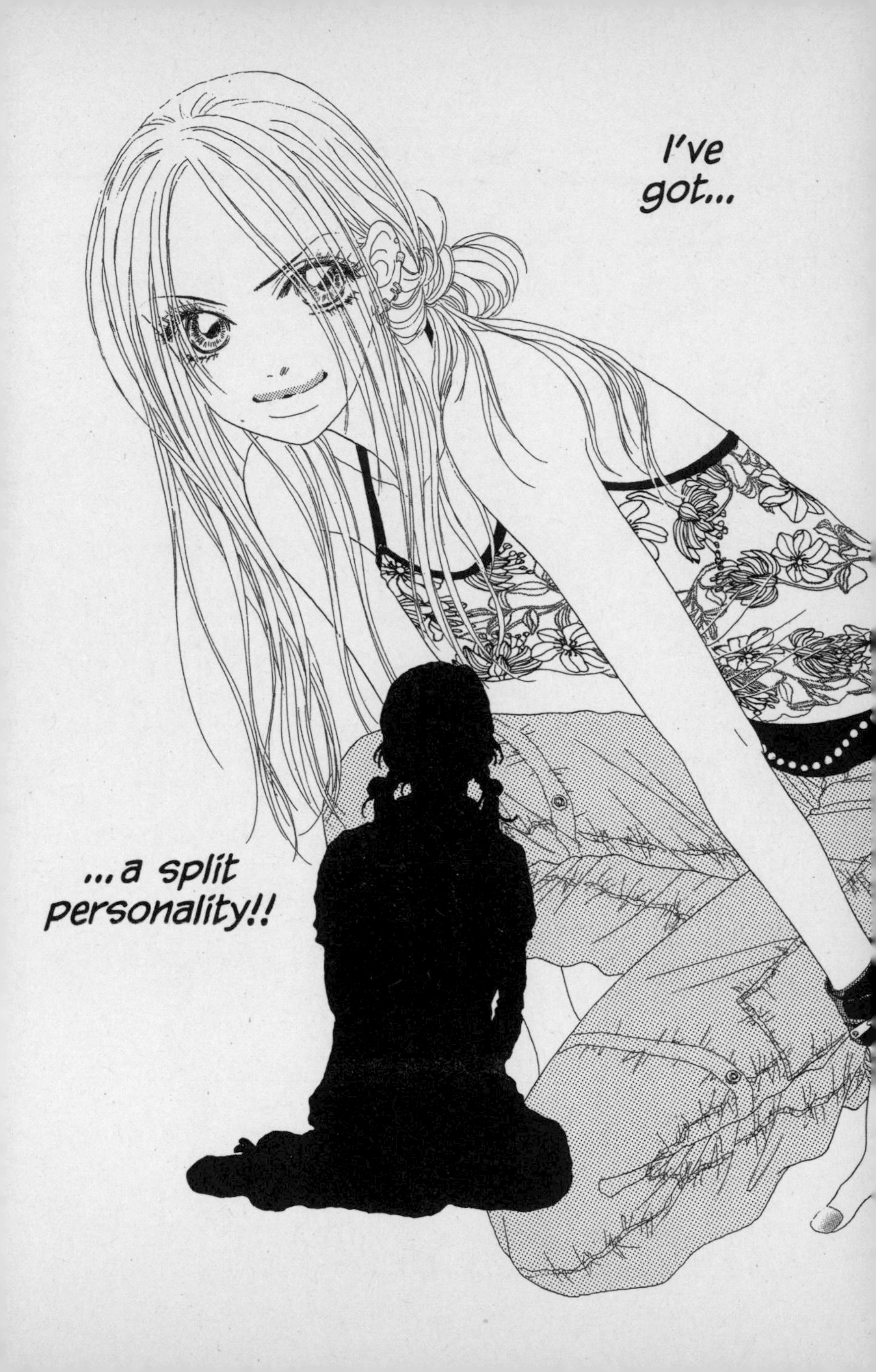
I've got...
...a split personality!!

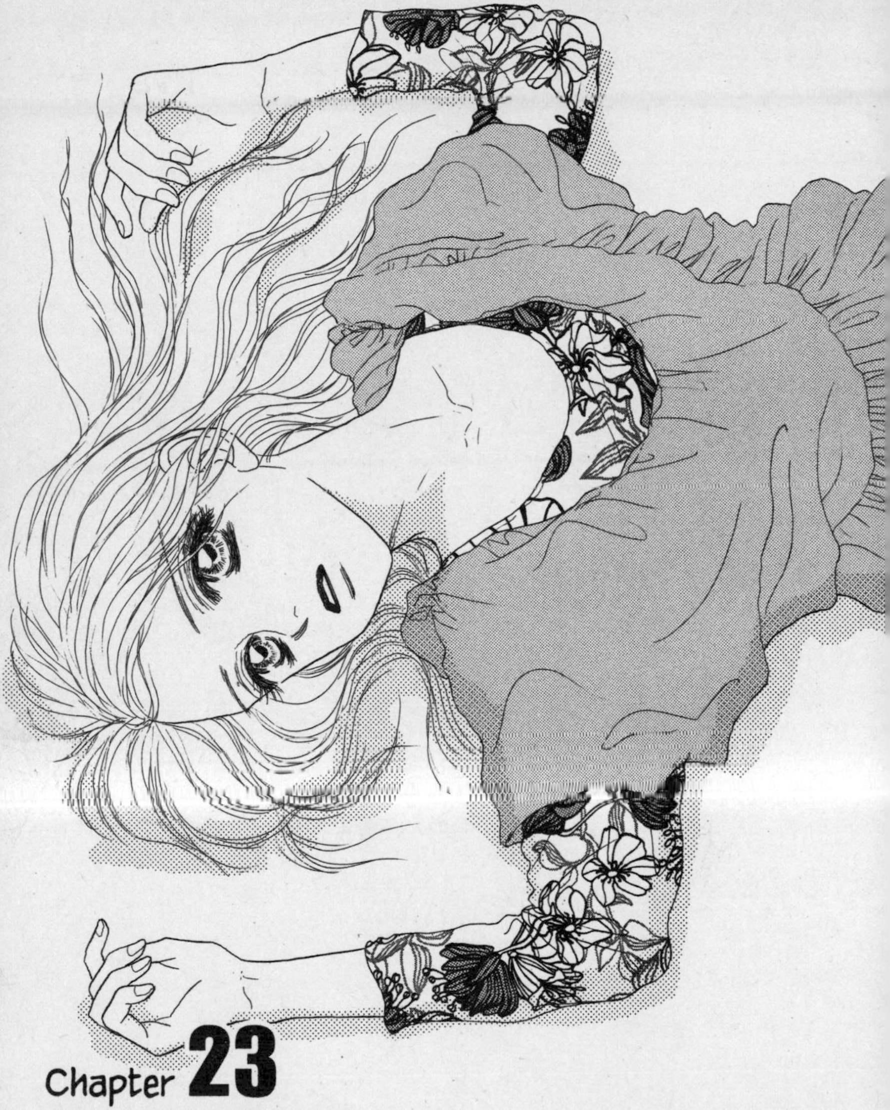

Chapter 23
Yaya's Breakdown?!

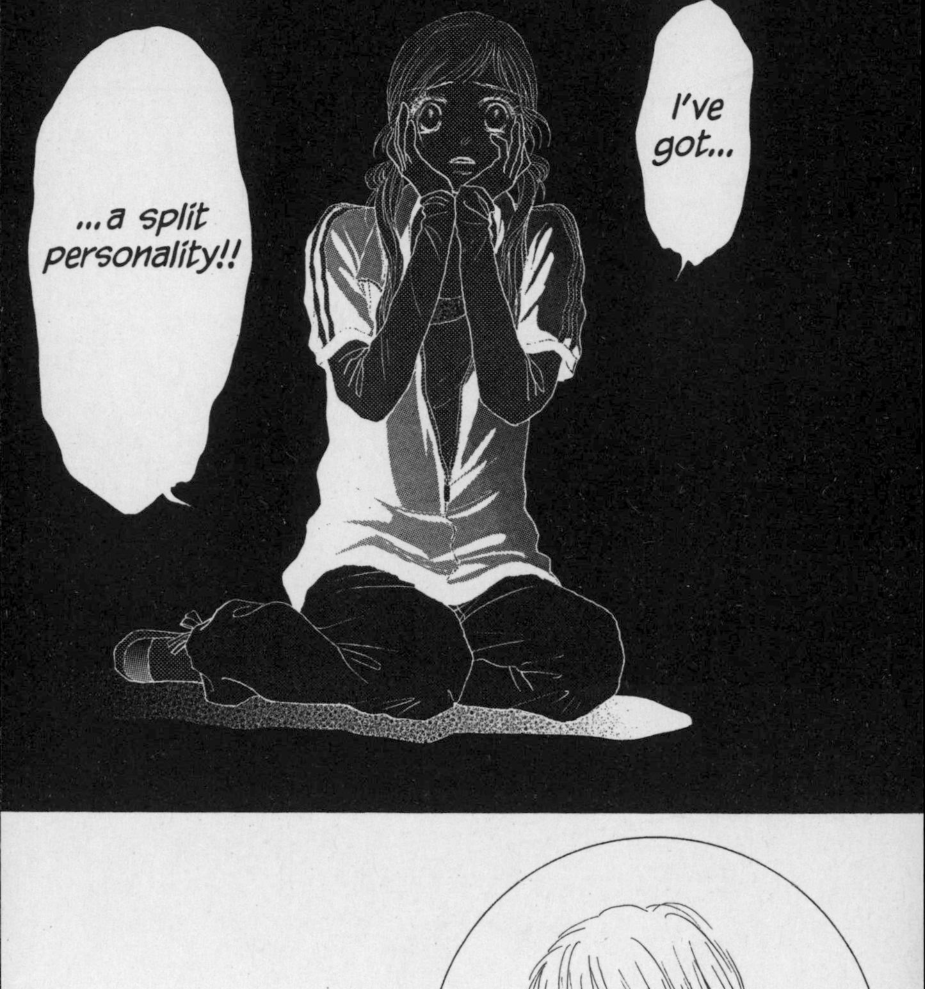
I've got...
...a split personality!!
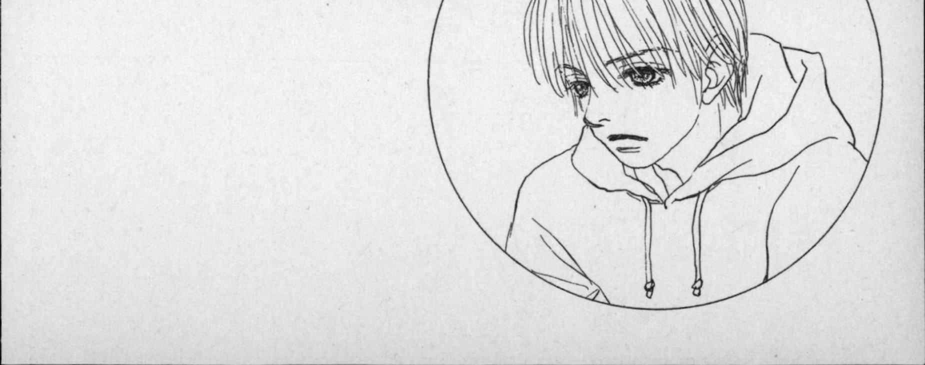

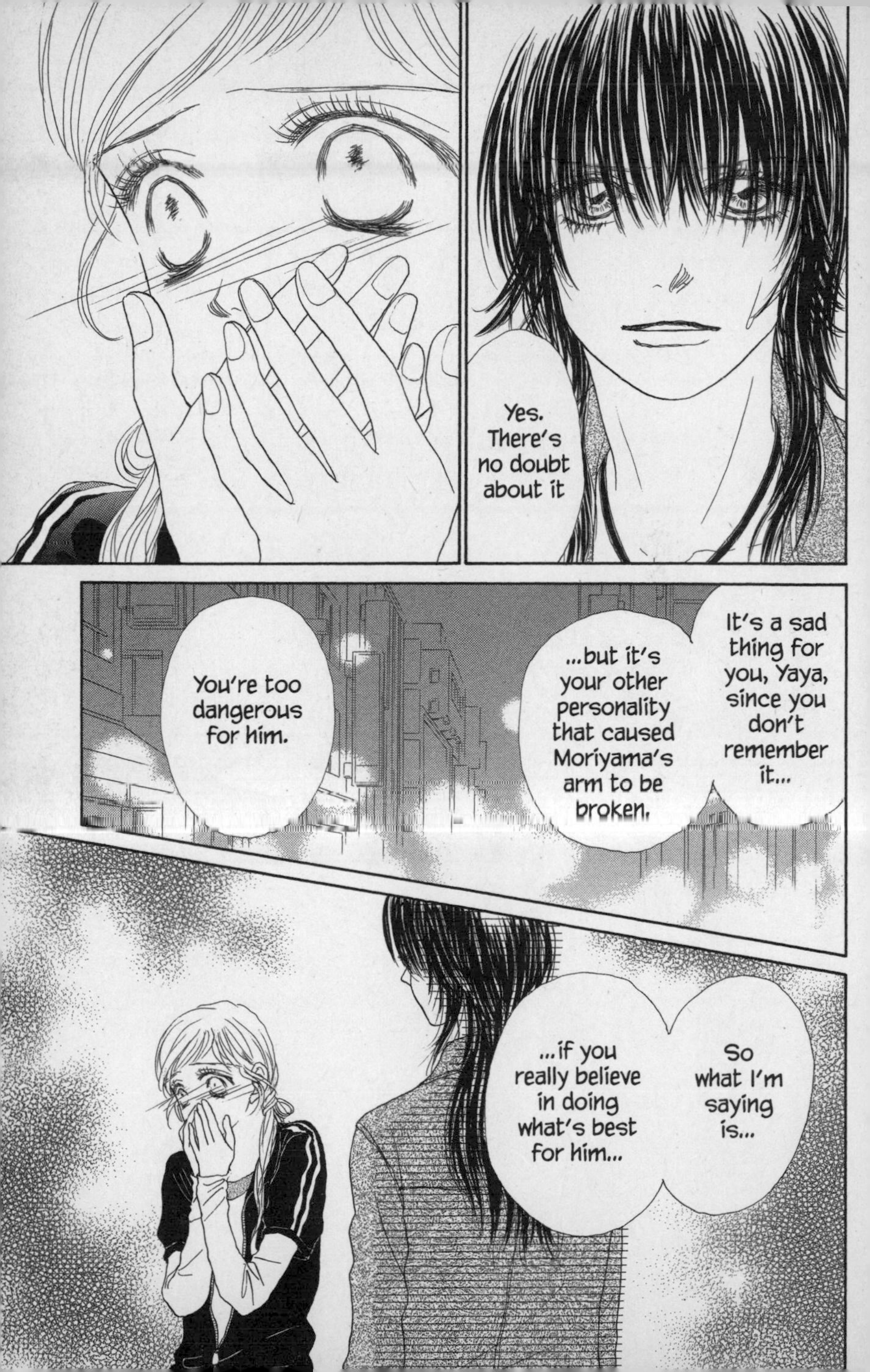
Yes. There's no doubt about it
It's a sad thing for you, Yaya, since you don't remember it...
...but it's your other personality that caused Moriyama's arm to be broken.
You're too dangerous for him.
So what I'm saying is...
...if you really believe in doing what's best for him...

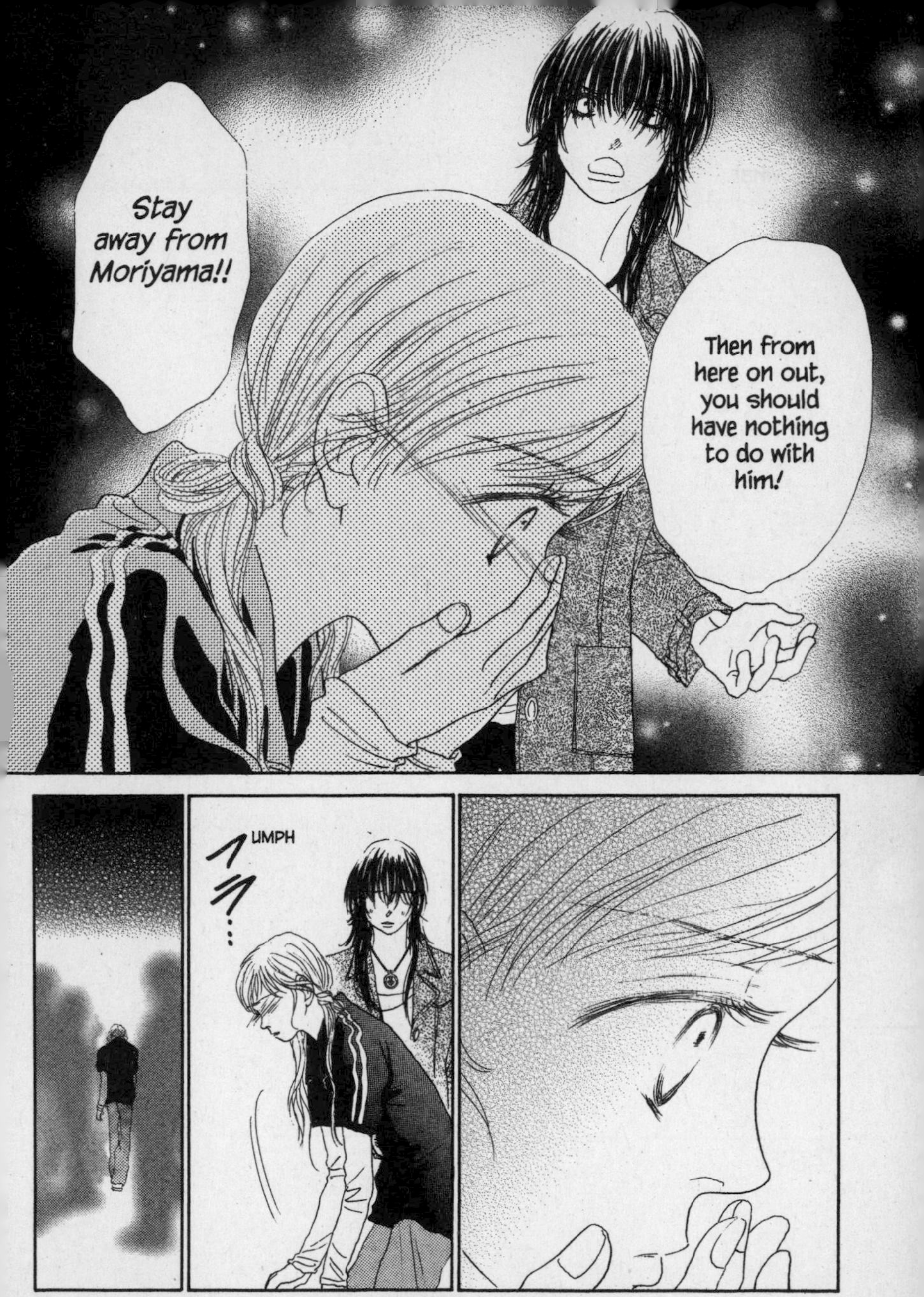
Stay away from Moriyama!!
Then from here on out, you should have nothing to do with him!
UMPH

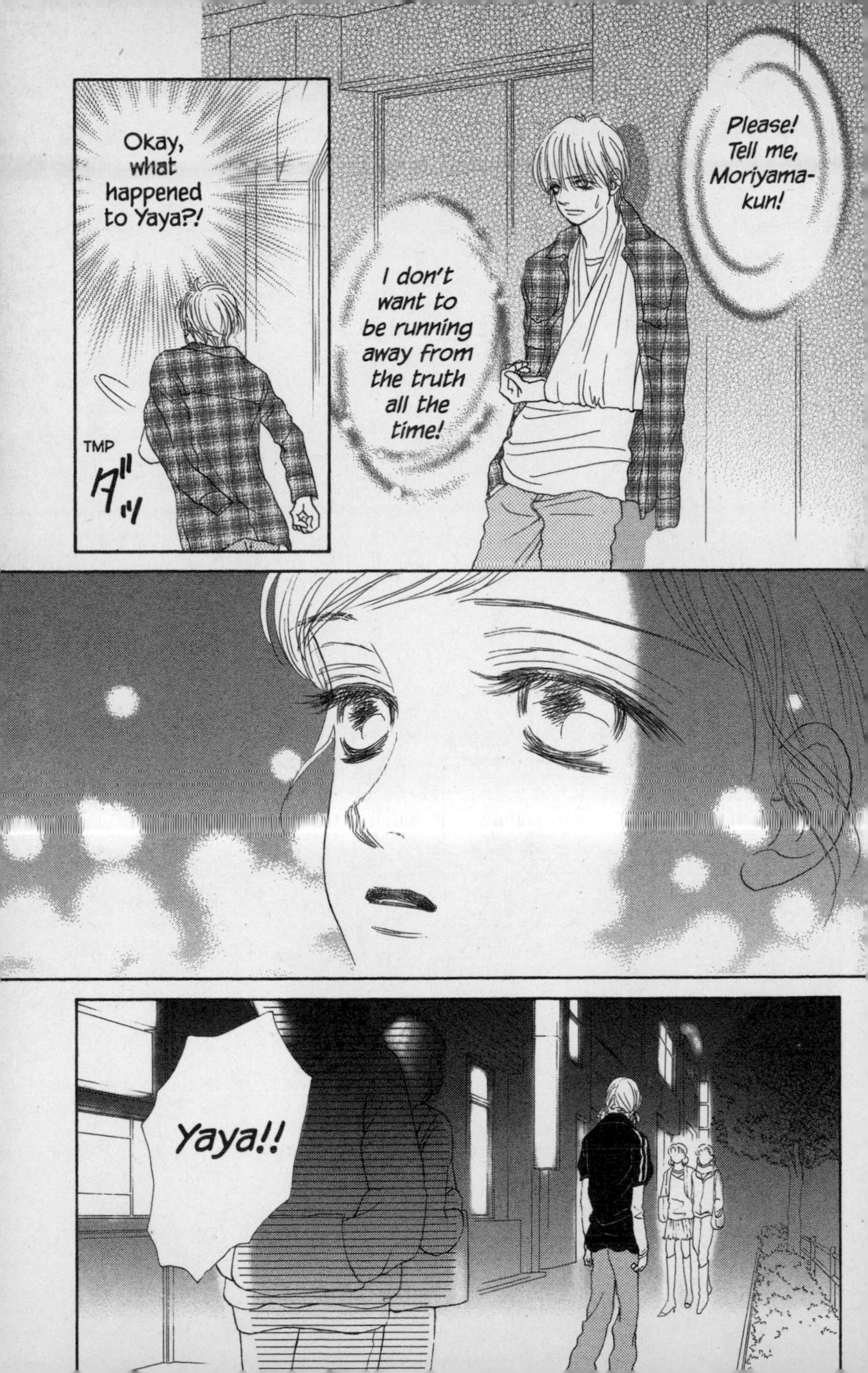
Please! Tell me, Moriyama-kun!
I don't want to be running away from the truth all the time!
Okay, what happened to Yaya?!
TMP
ダッ
Yaya!!

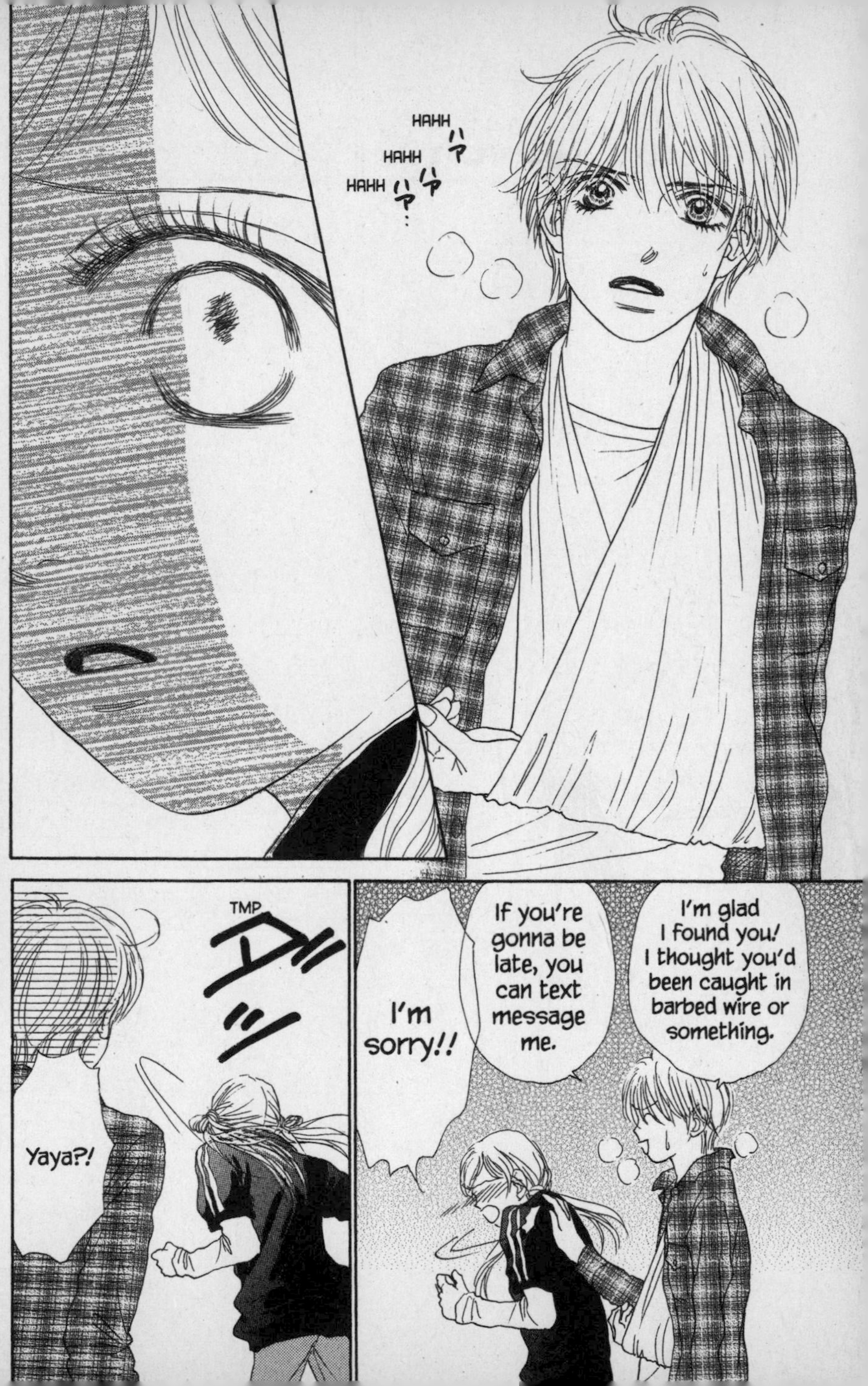
HAHH
HAHH
HAHH
I'm glad I found you! I thought you'd been caught in barbed wire or something.
If you're gonna be late, you can text message me.
I'm sorry!!
TMP
Yaya?!

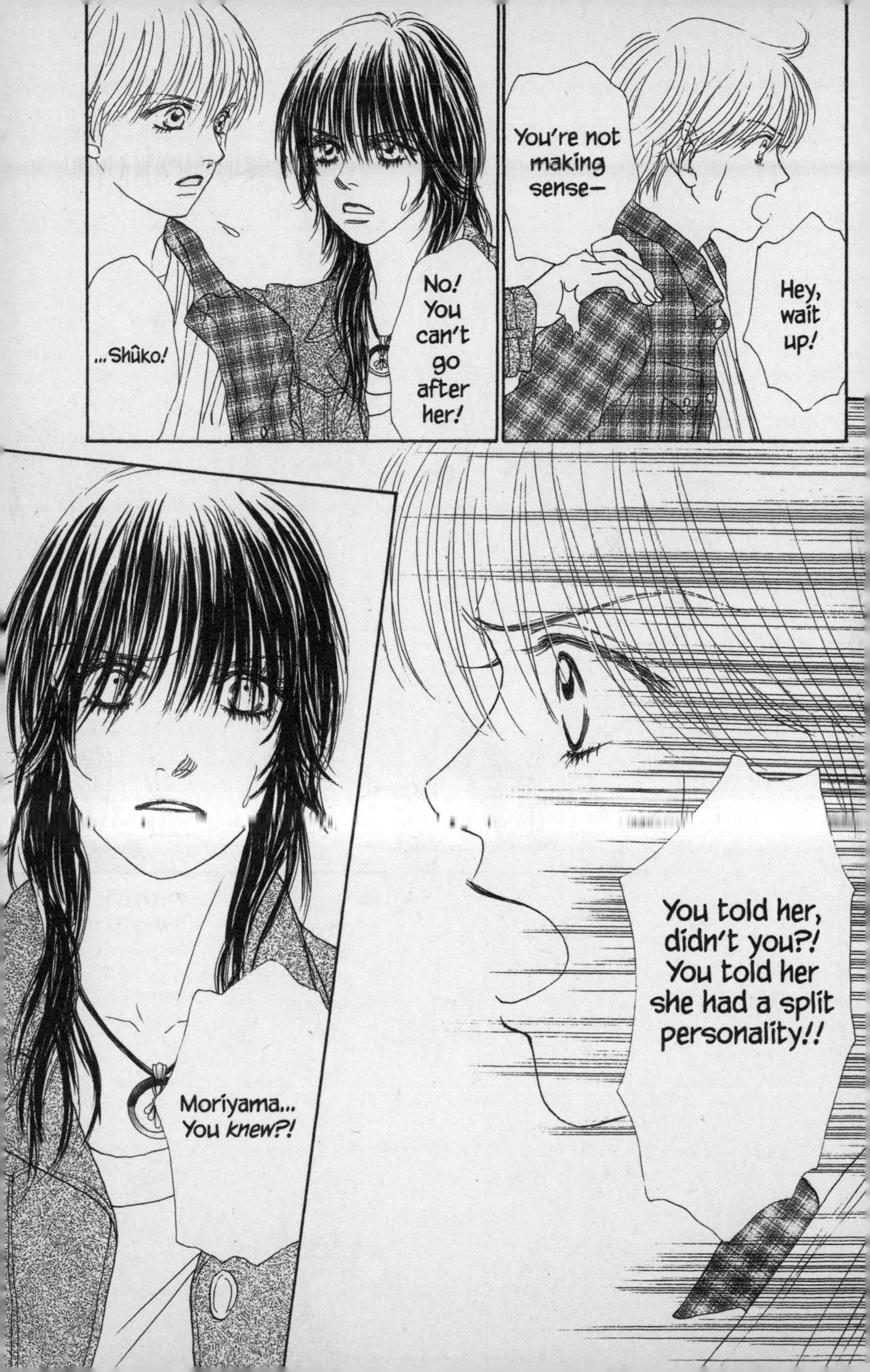
Hey, wait up!
You're not making sense—
No! You can't go after her!
...Shûko!
You told her, didn't you?! You told her she had a split personality!!
Moriyama... You knew?!

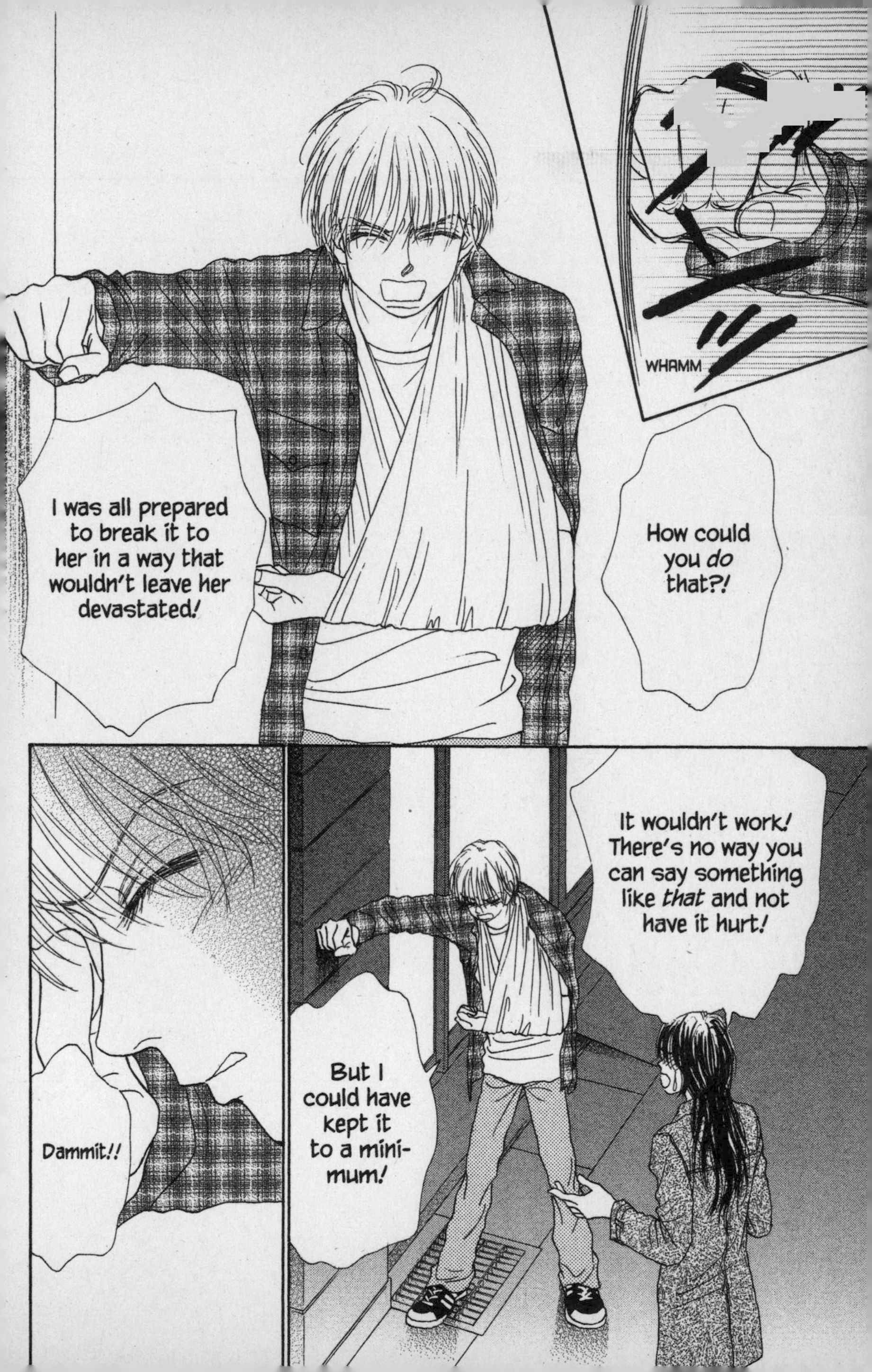
WHAMM
How could you *do* that?!
I was all prepared to break it to her in a way that wouldn't leave her devastated!
It wouldn't work! There's no way you can say something like *that* and not have it hurt!
But I could have kept it to a mini-mum!
Dammit!!

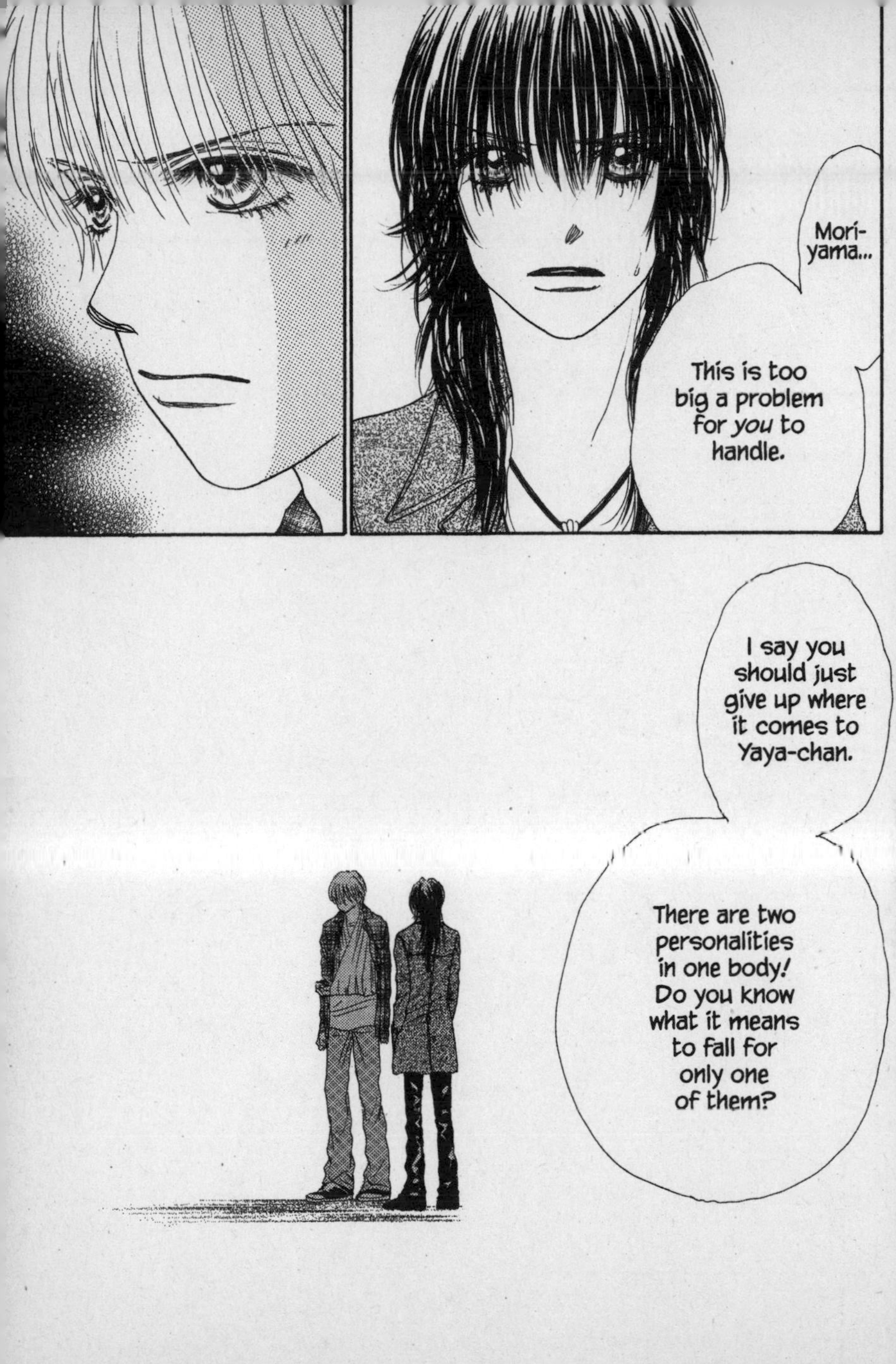
Mori-yama...
This is too big a problem for *you* to handle.
I say you should just give up where it comes to Yaya-chan.
There are two personalities in one body! Do you know what it means to fall for only one of them?

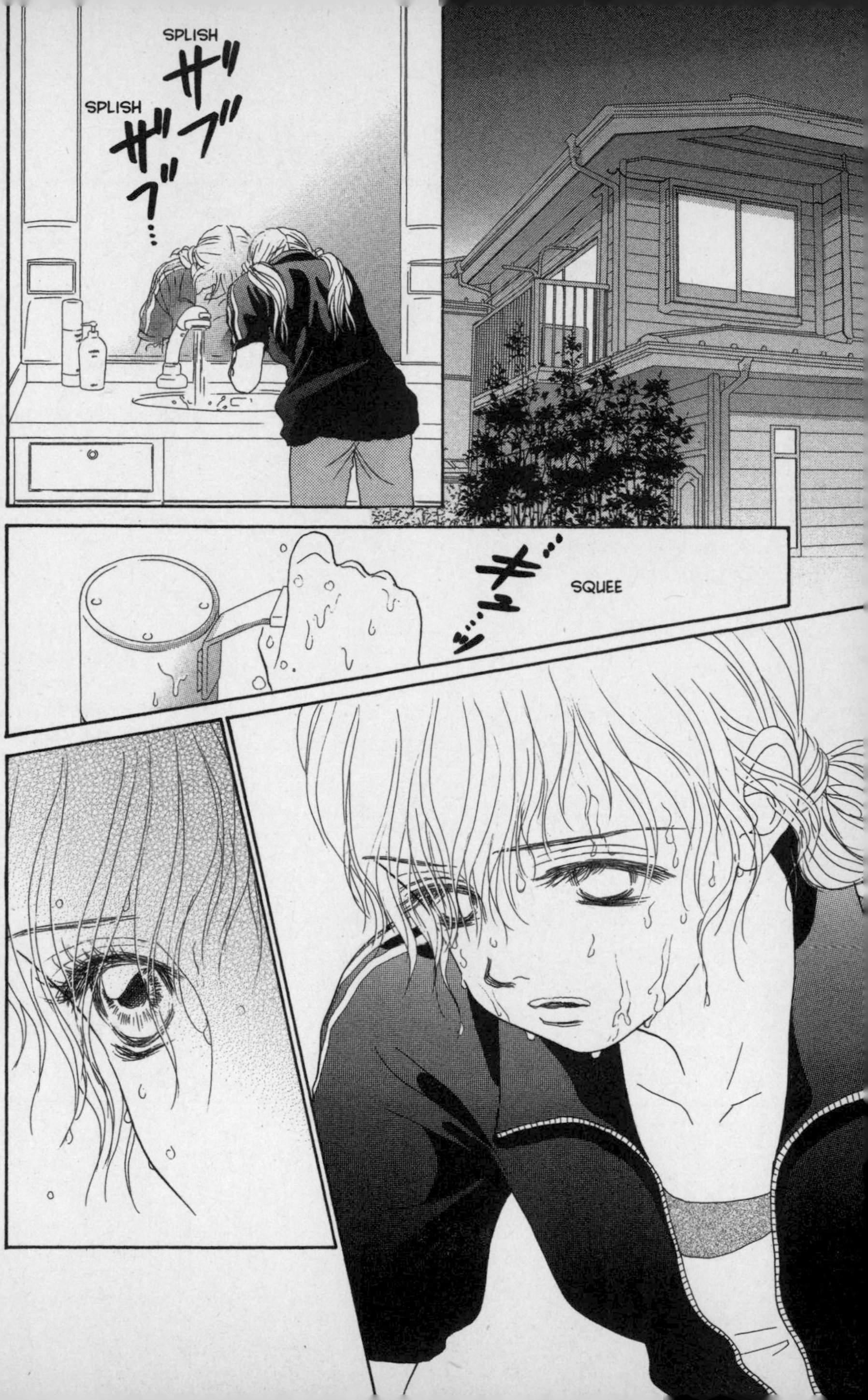
SPLISH
SPLISH
ザブザブ…
SQUEE
ギュッ

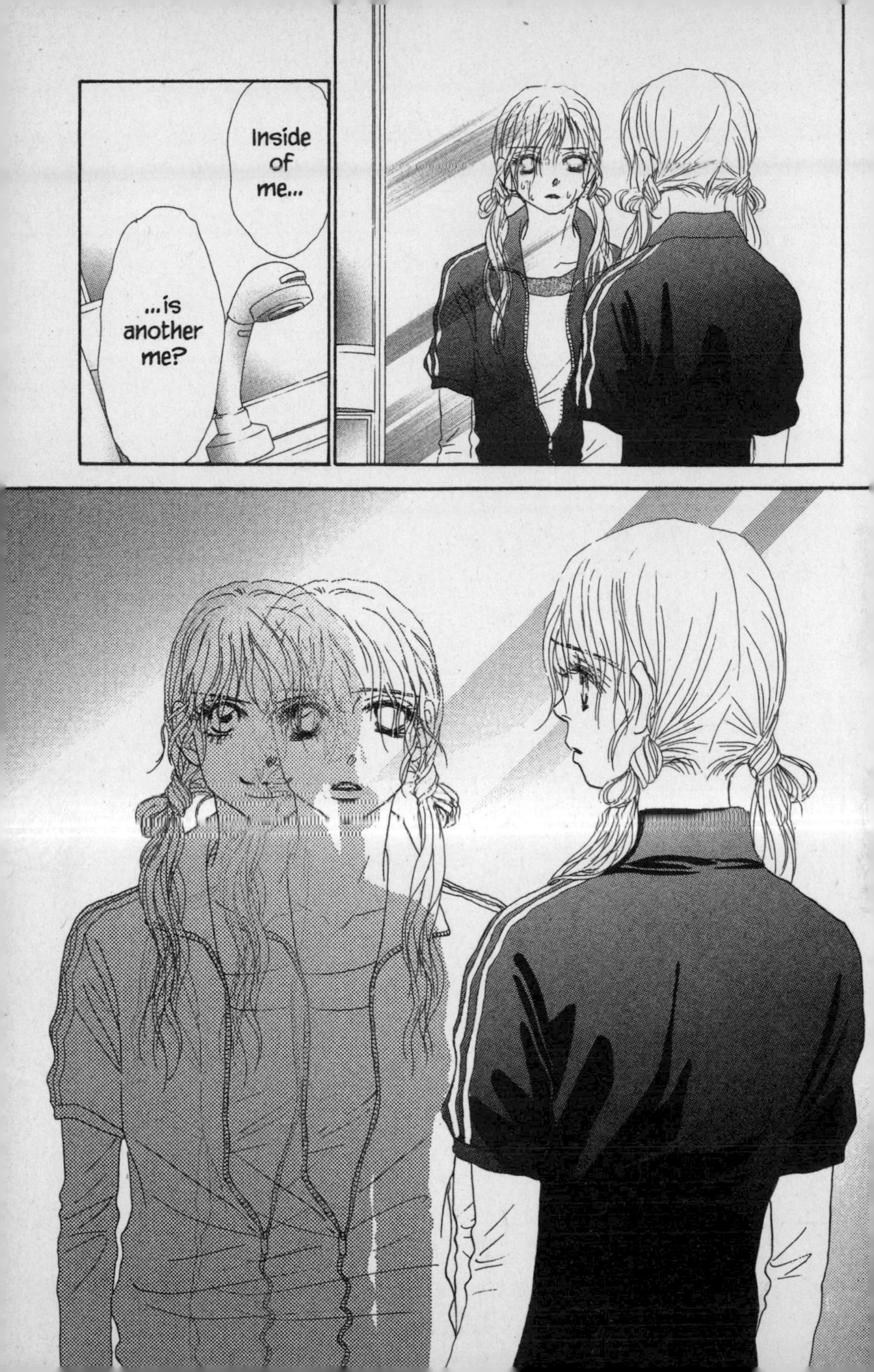
Inside of me...
...is another me?

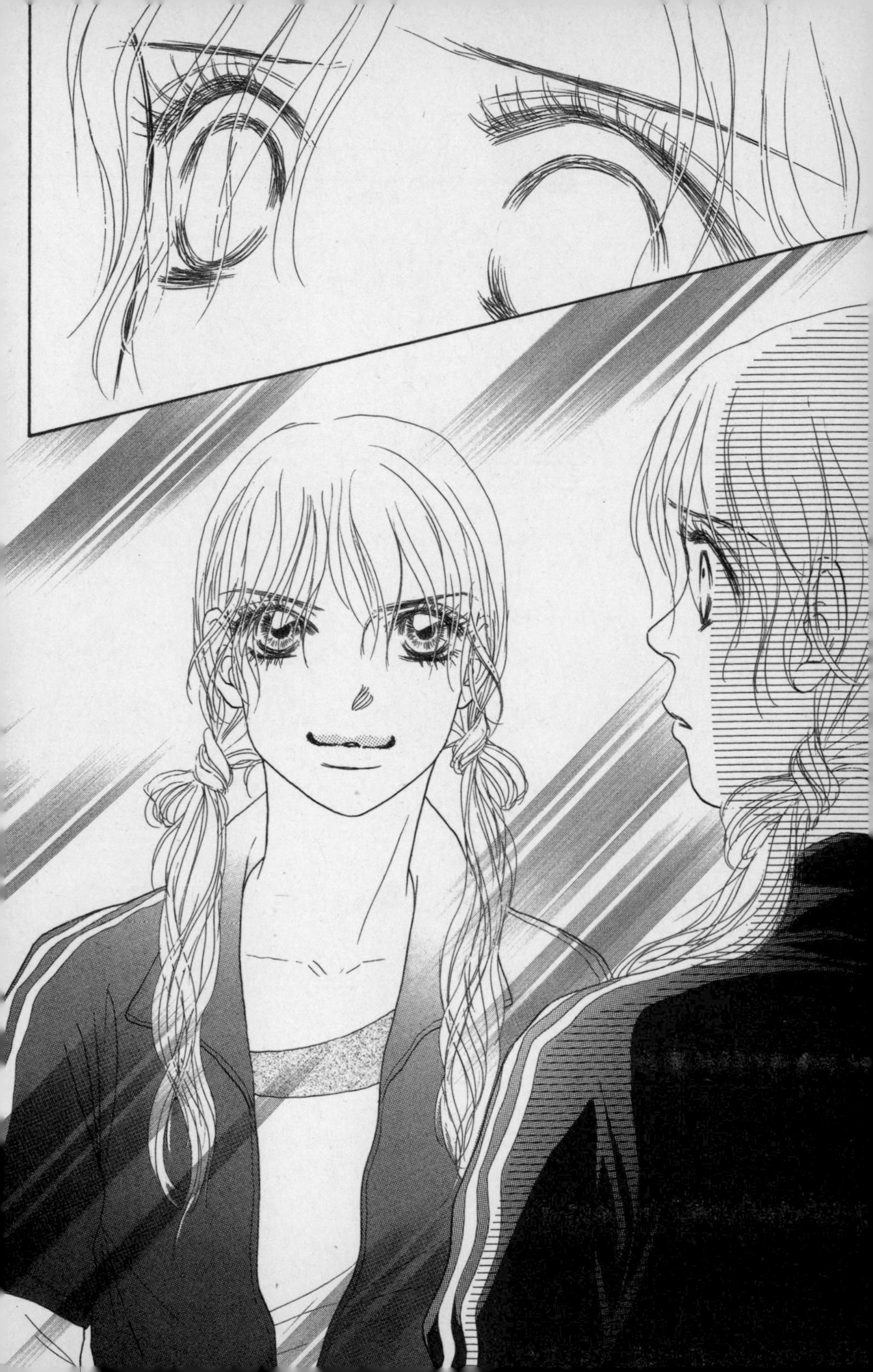

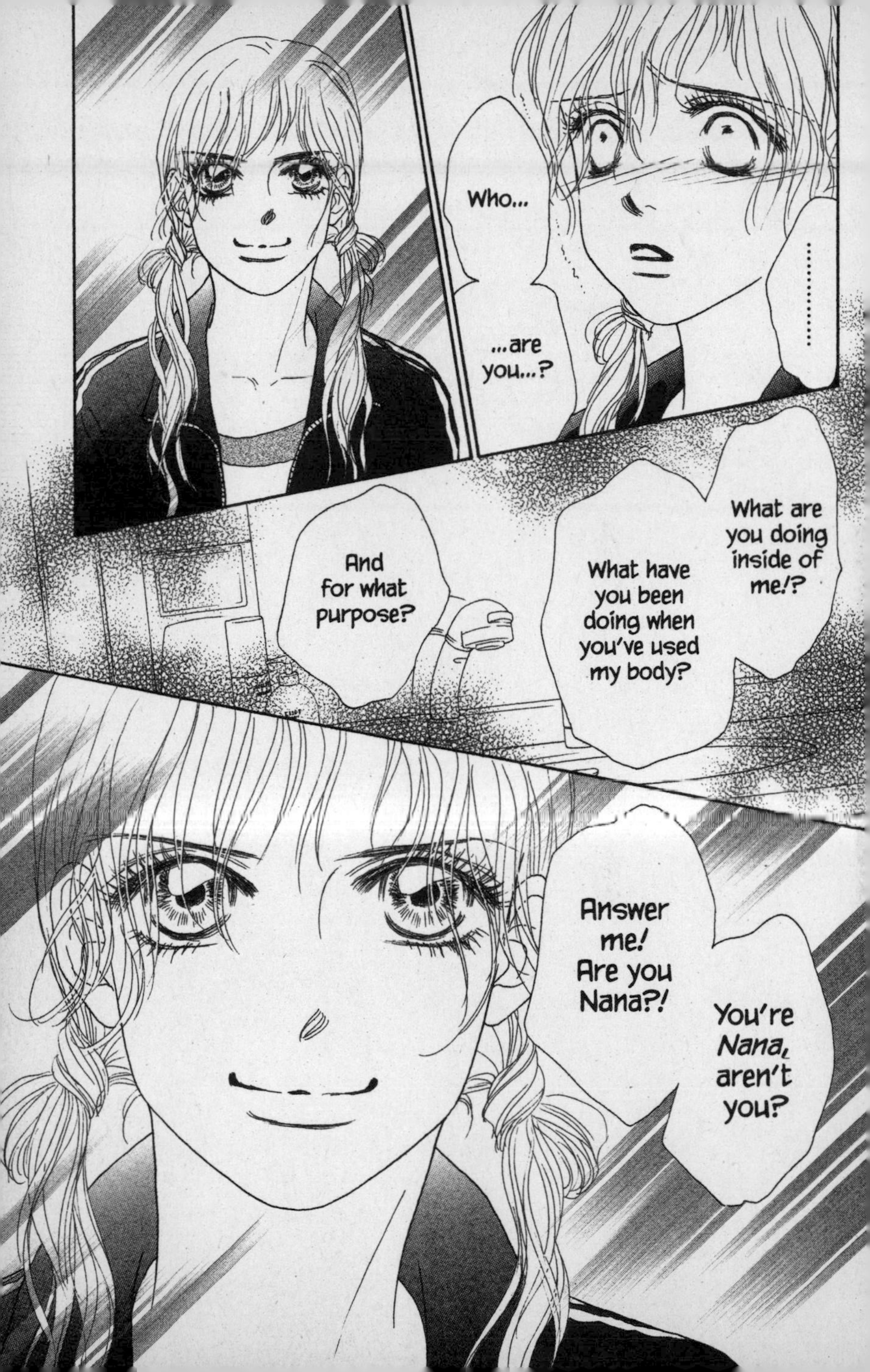
......
Who...
...are you...?
What are you doing inside of me!?
What have you been doing when you've used my body?
And for what purpose?
Answer me! Are you Nana?!
You're *Nana*, aren't you?

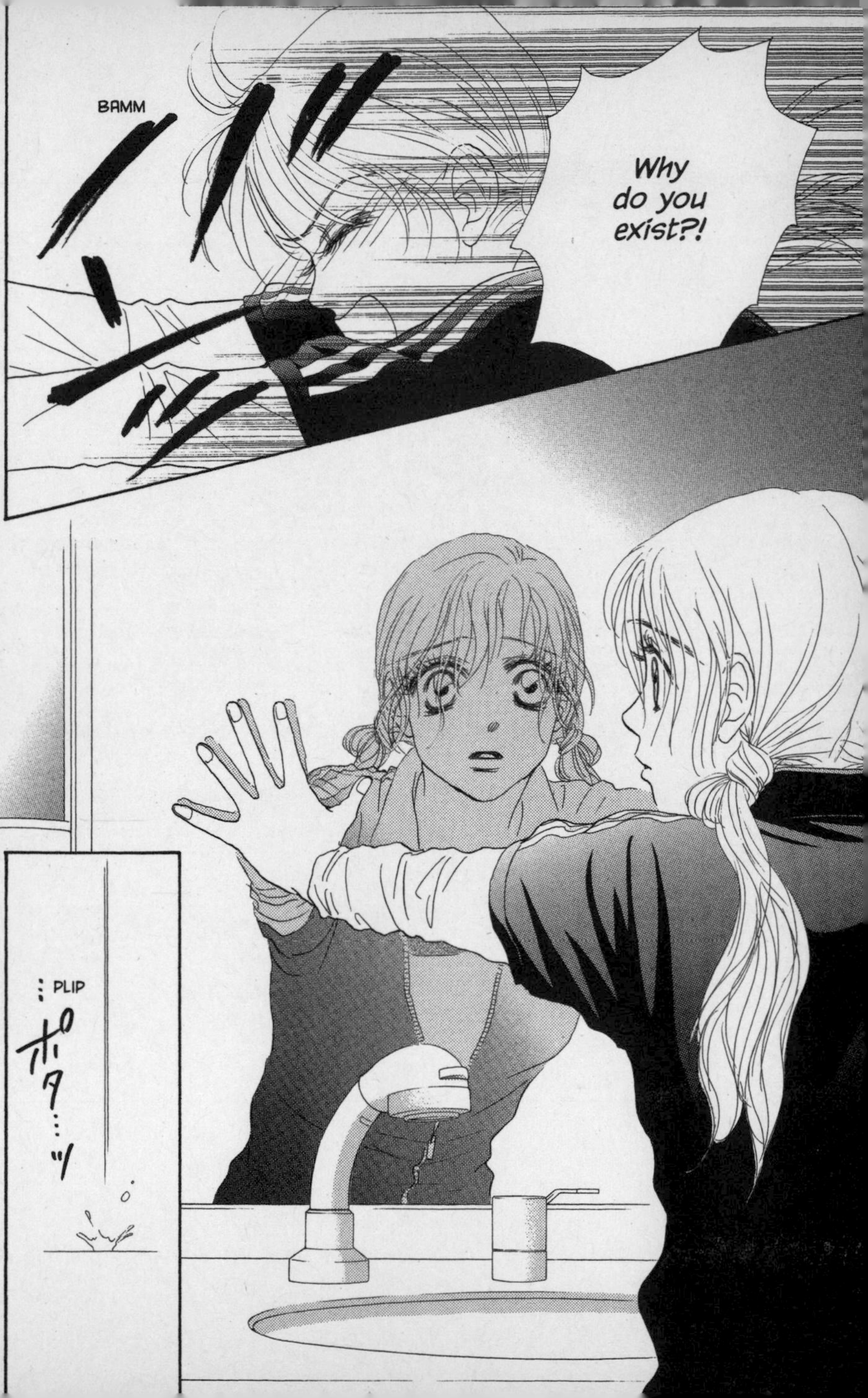
Why do you exist?!
BAMM
...PLIP
ポタ…ッ

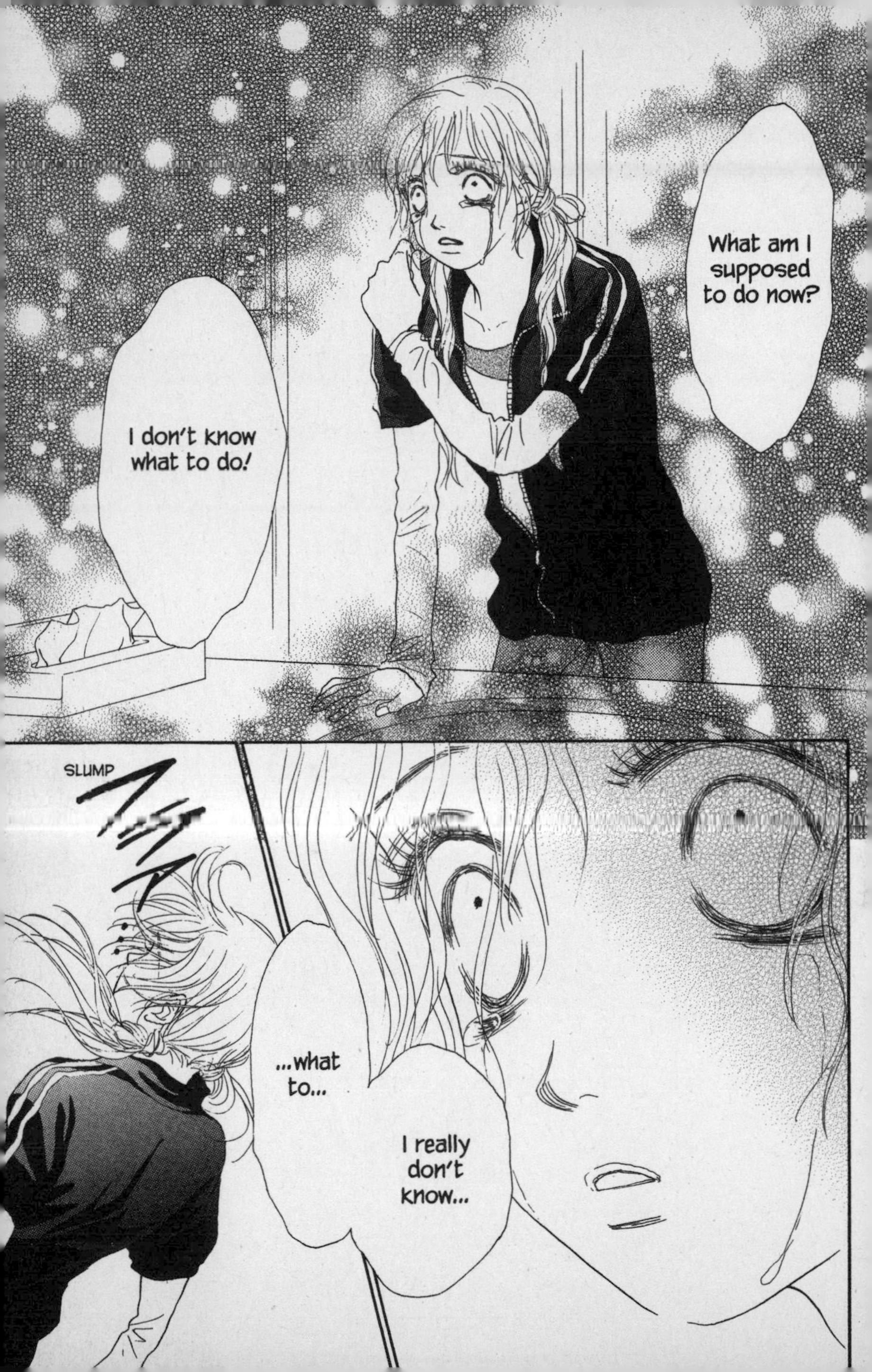
What am I supposed to do now?
I don't know what to do!
...what to...
I really don't know...
SLUMP

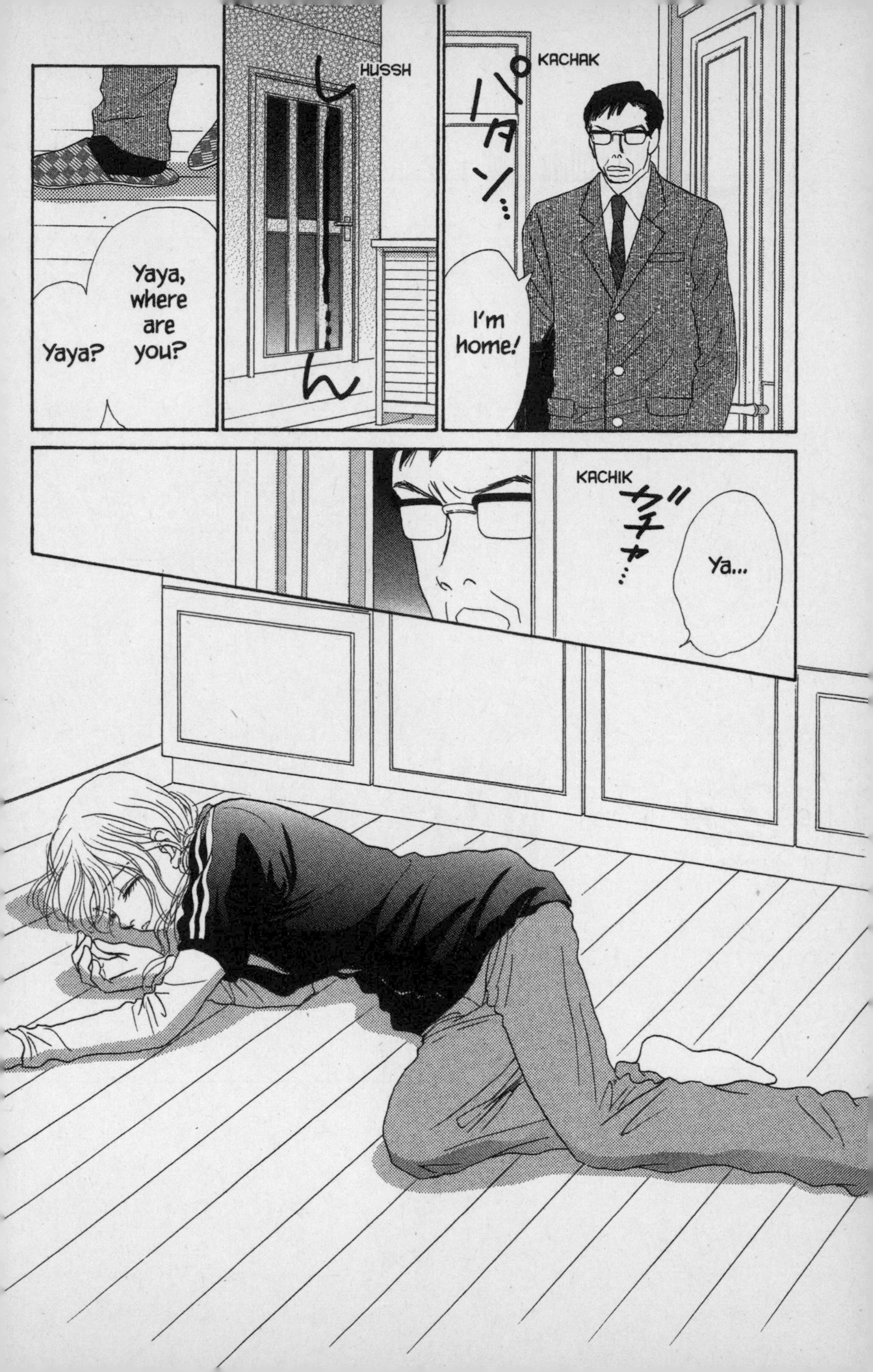
KACHAK
パタン…
I'm home!
HUSSH
しーん
Yaya, where are you?
Yaya?
KACHIK
ガチャ…
Ya...

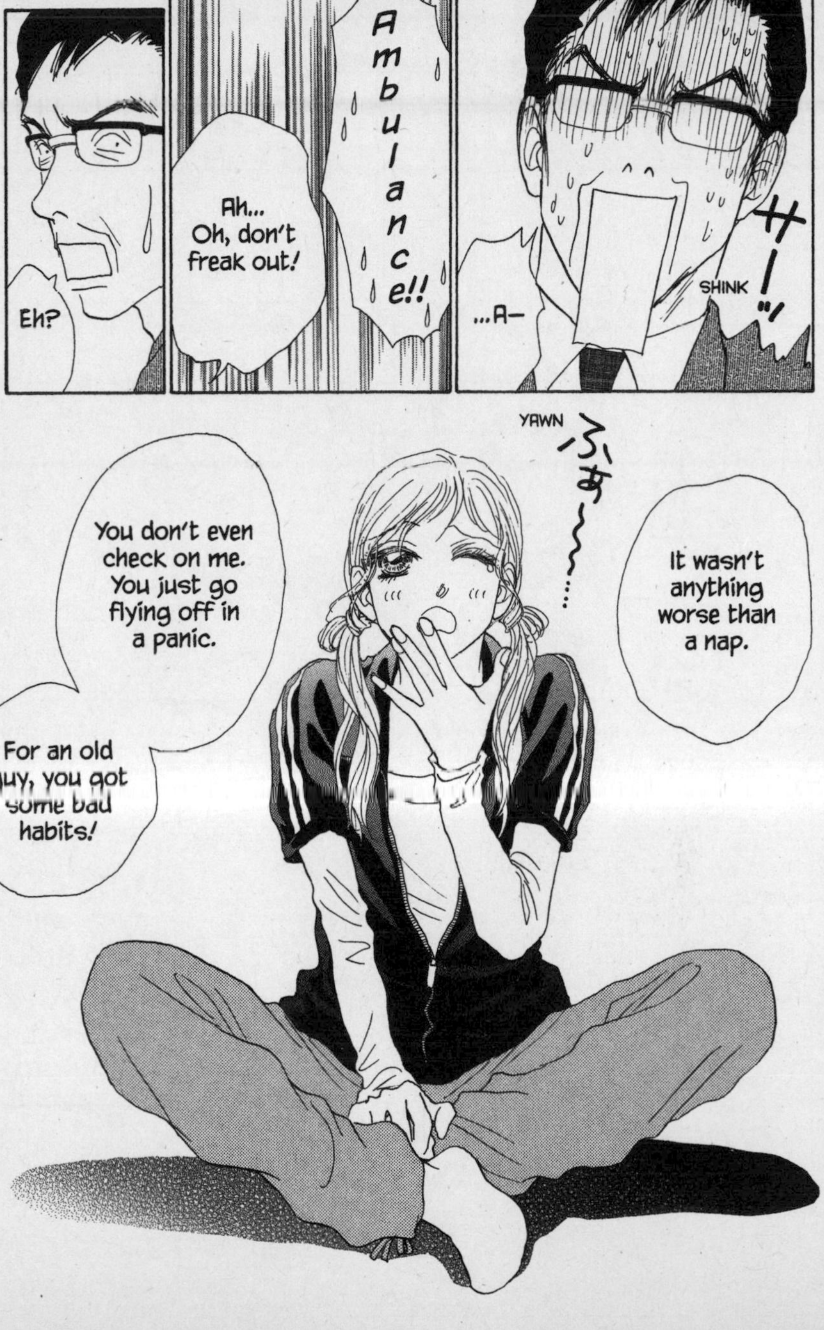
SHINK
サー
...A—
Ambulance!!
Ah... Oh, don't freak out!
Eh?
YAWN
ふぁ〜....
It wasn't anything worse than a nap.
You don't even check on me. You just go flying off in a panic.
For an old guy, you got some bad habits!

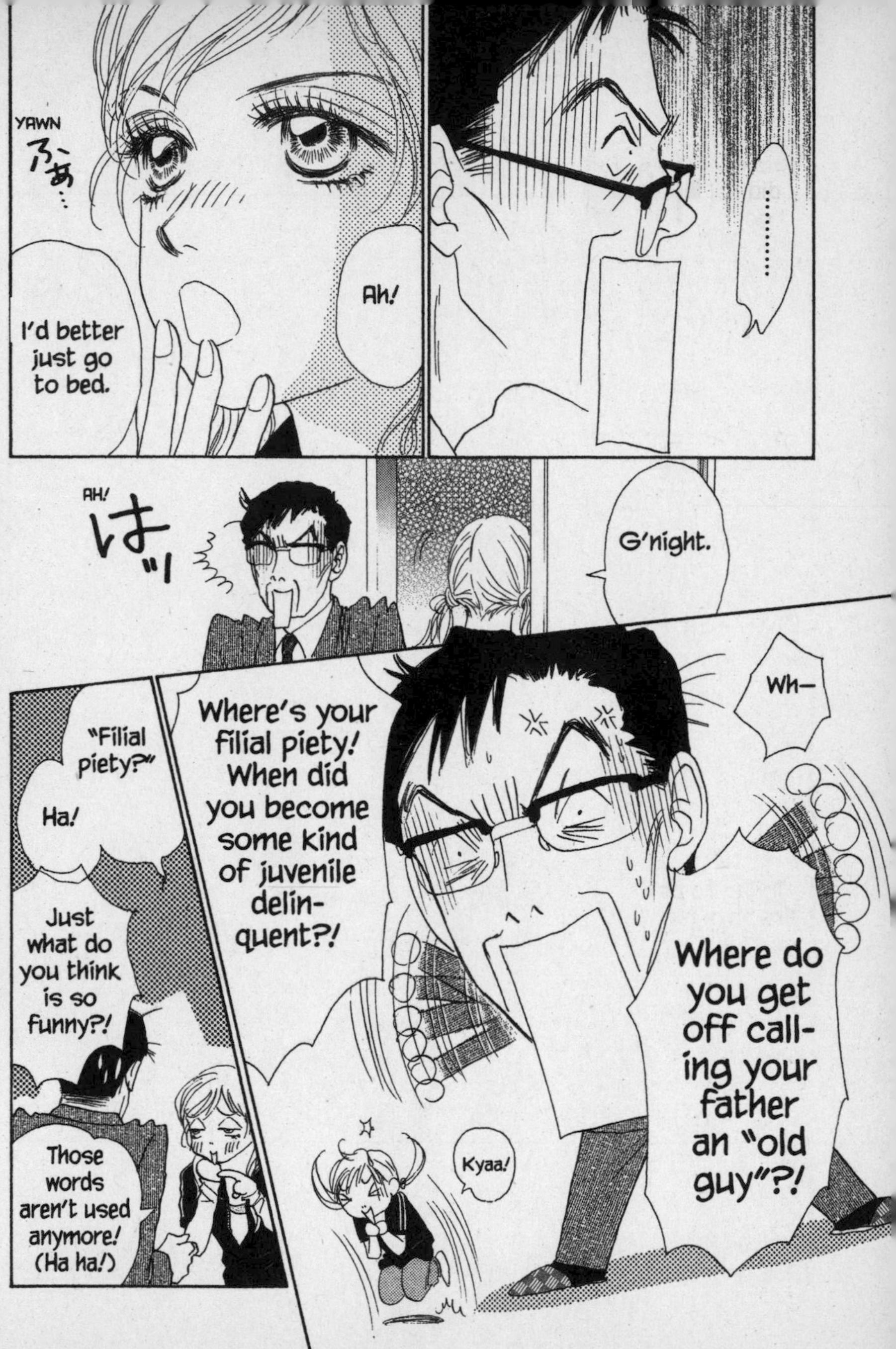
……
Ah!
YAWN
ふぁ…
I'd better just go to bed.
G'night.
AH!
はッ
Wh–
Where do you get off call-ing your father an "old guy"?!
Where's your filial piety! When did you become some kind of juvenile delin-quent?!
Kyaa!
"Filial piety?"
Ha!
Just what do you think is so funny?!
Those words aren't used anymore! (Ha ha!)

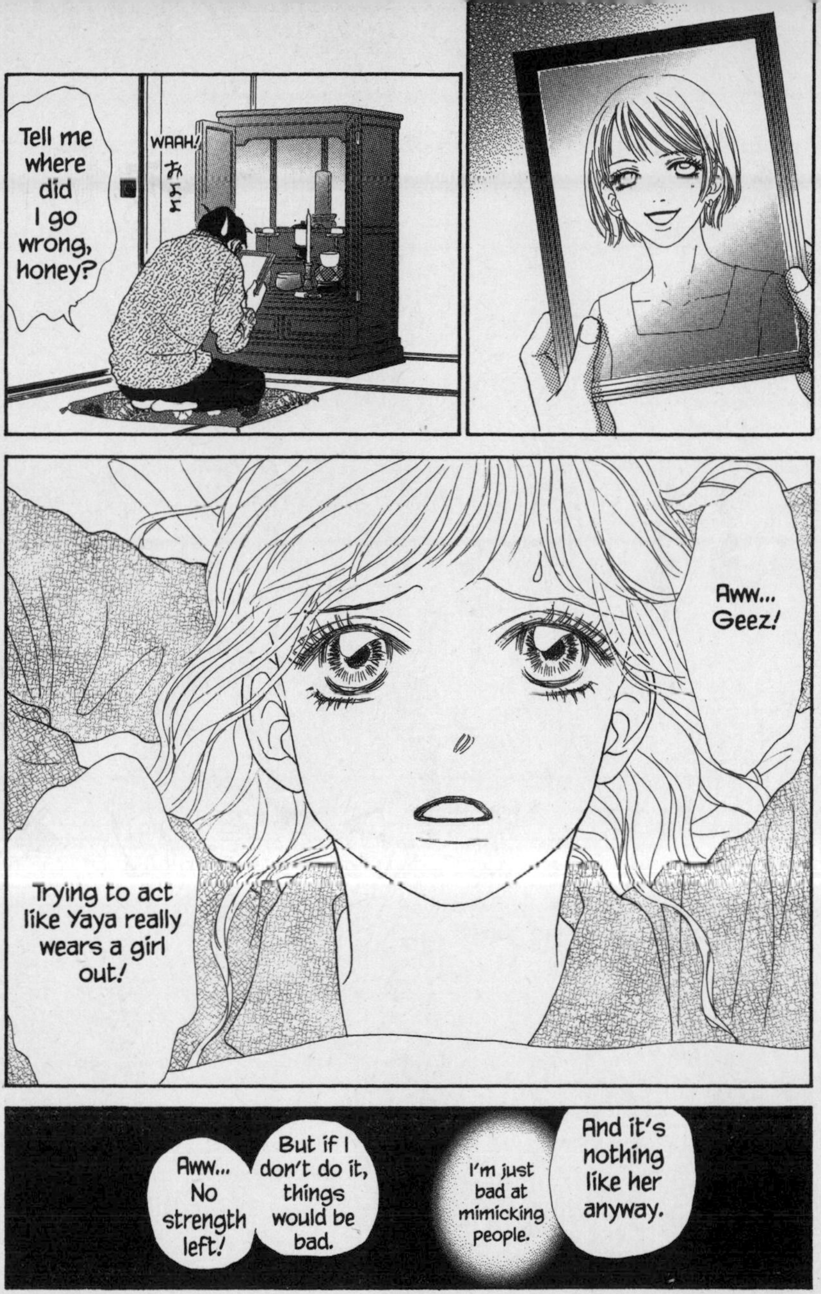
WAAH!
およよ
Tell me where did I go wrong, honey?
Aww... Geez!
Trying to act like Yaya really wears a girl out!
And it's nothing like her anyway.
I'm just bad at mimicking people.
But if I don't do it, things would be bad.
Aww... No strength left!

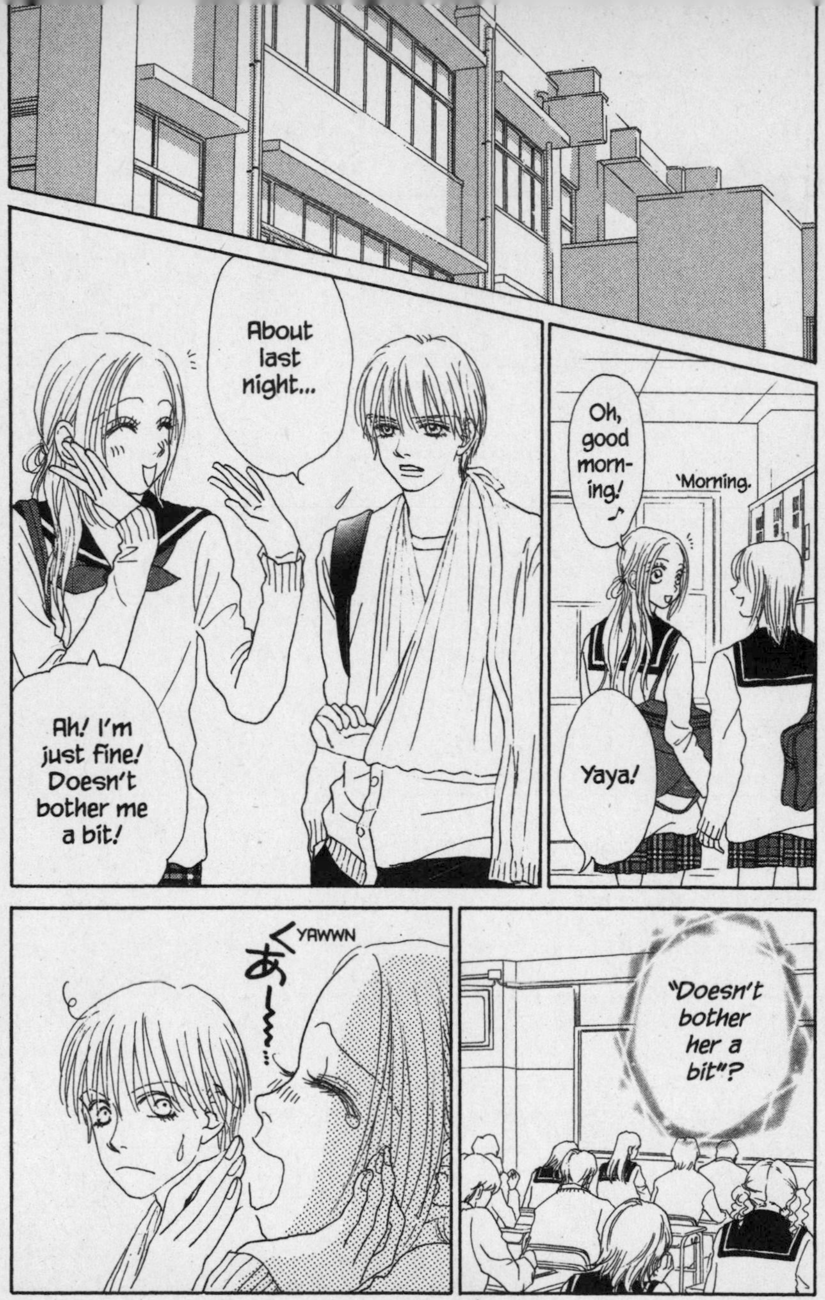
Oh, good morning! ♪
'Morning.
Yaya!
About last night...
Ah! I'm just fine! Doesn't bother me a bit!
"Doesn't bother her a bit"?
YAWWN
あ～～…

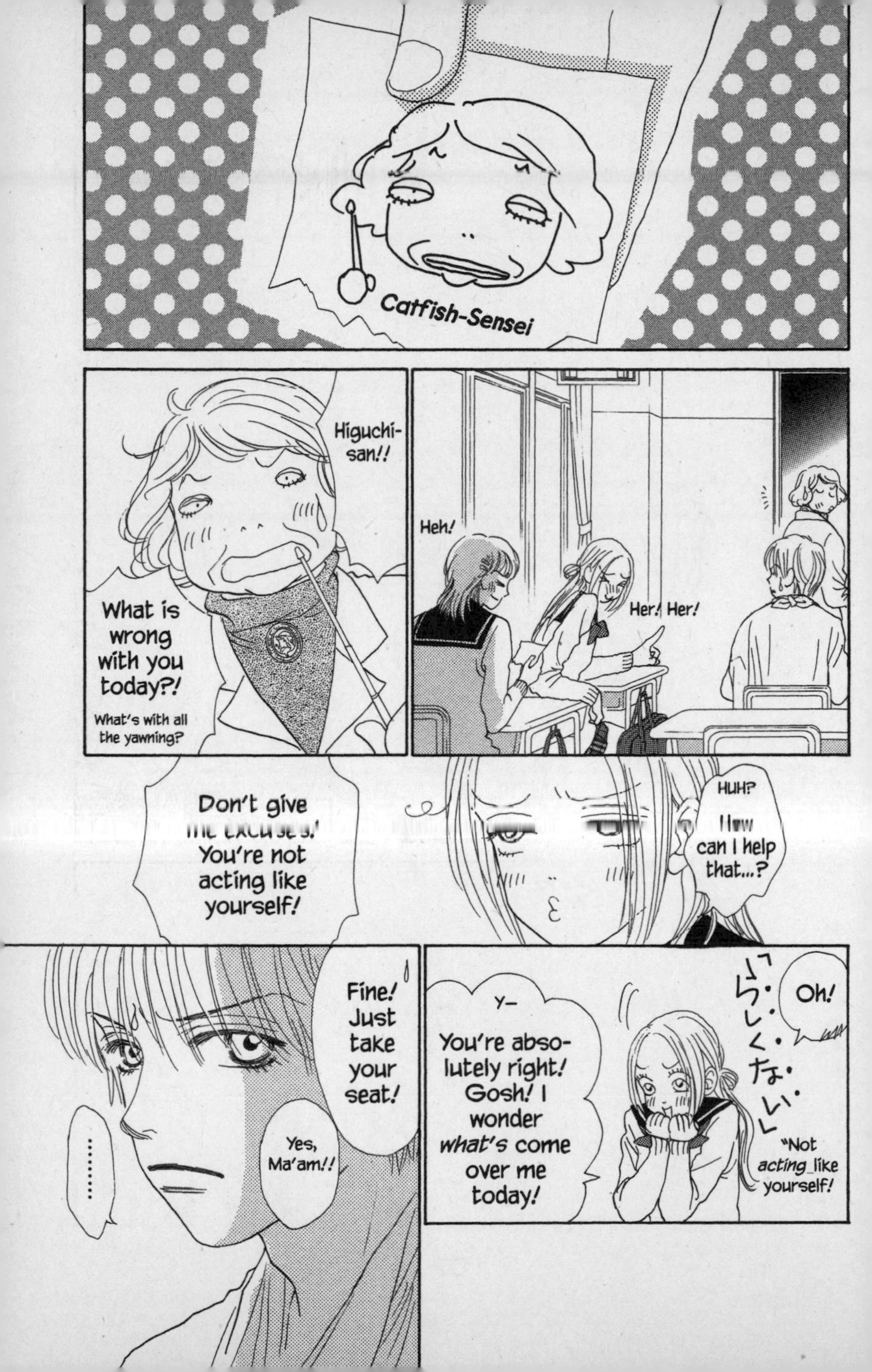
Catfish-Sensei
Heh!
Her! Her!
Higuchi-san!!
What is wrong with you today?!
What's with all the yawning?
HUH? How can I help that...?
Don't give me excuses! You're not acting like yourself!
Oh!
「ら・し・く・な・い」
"Not *acting* like yourself!
Y— You're absolutely right! Gosh! I wonder *what's* come over me today!
Fine! Just take your seat!
Yes, Ma'am!!
....

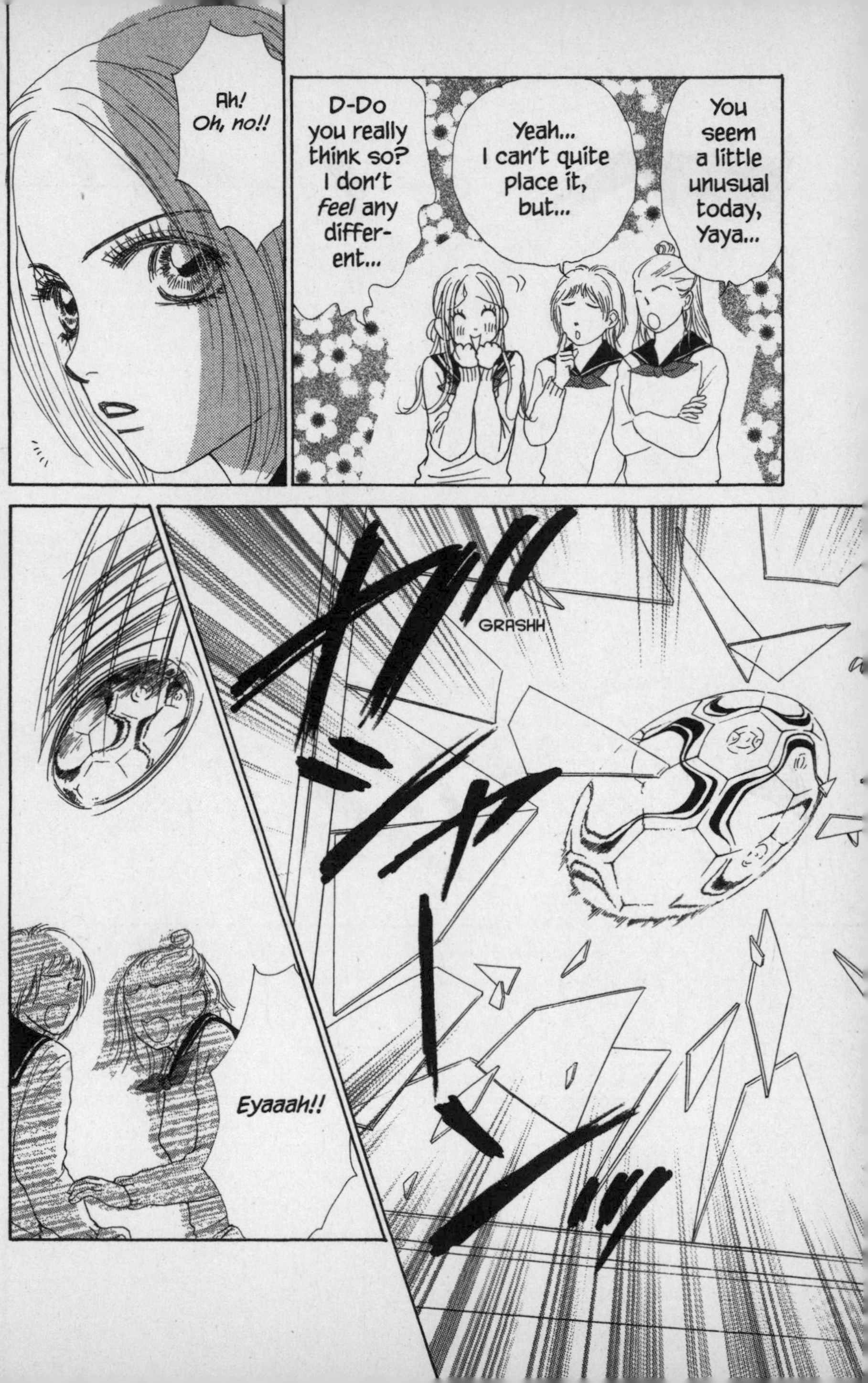
You seem a little unusual today, Yaya...
Yeah... I can't quite place it, but...
D-Do you really think so? I don't *feel* any differ-ent...
Ah! Oh, no!!
GRASHH
Eyaaah!!

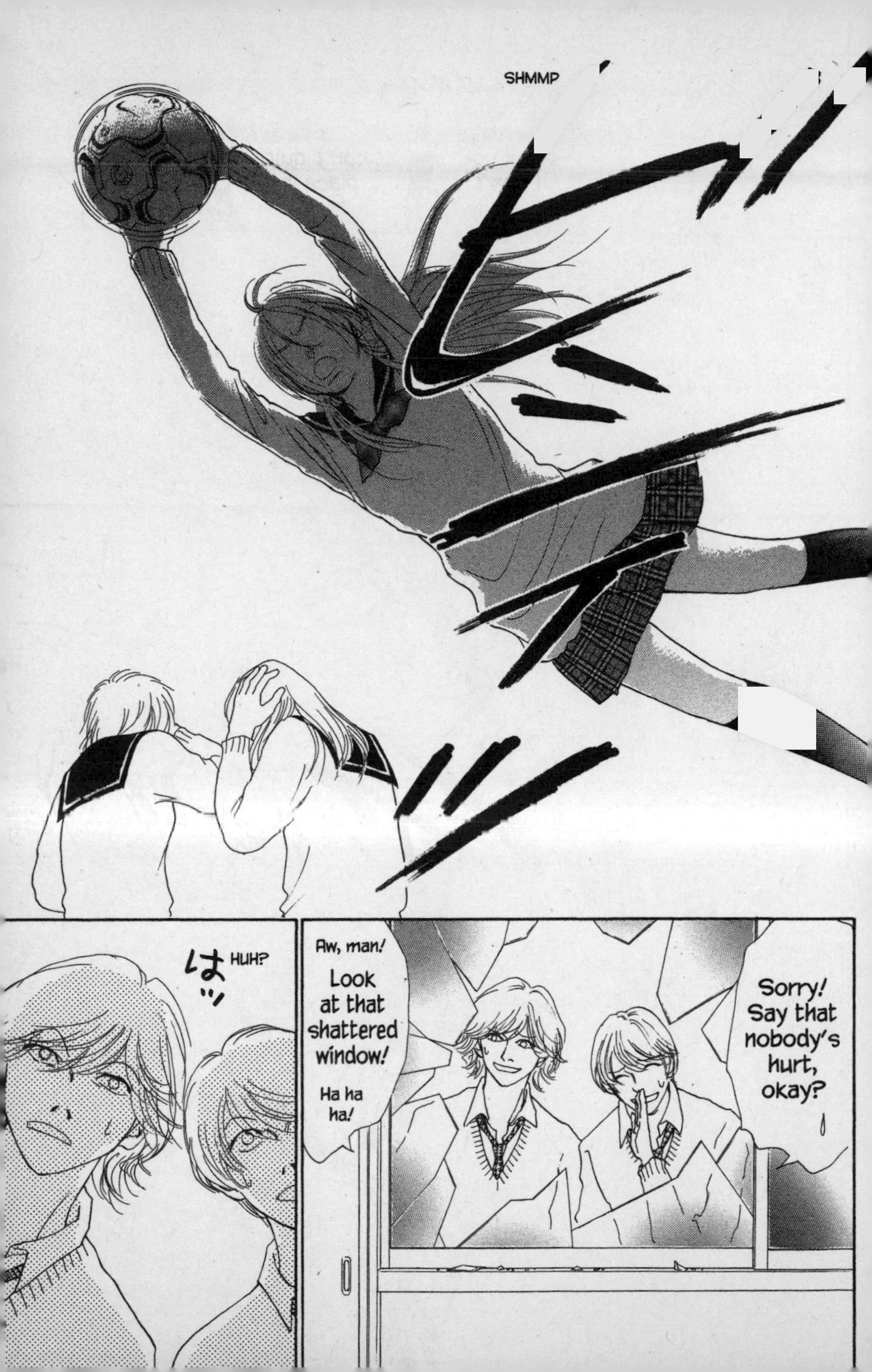
SHMMP
Sorry! Say that nobody's hurt, okay?
Aw, man! Look at that shattered window!
Ha ha ha!
はッ
HUH?

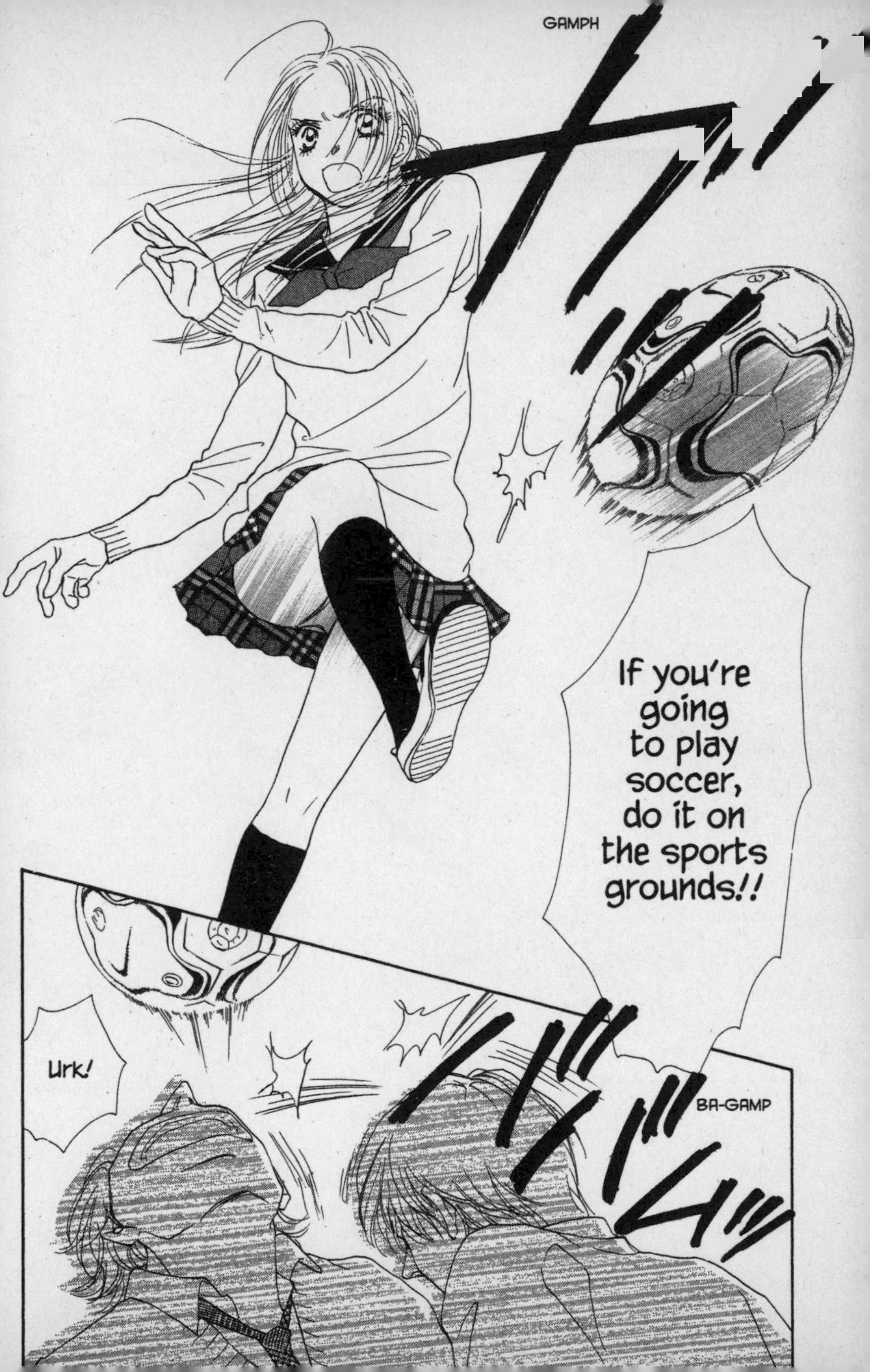
GAMPH
If you're going to play soccer, do it on the sports grounds!!
BA-GAMP
Urk!

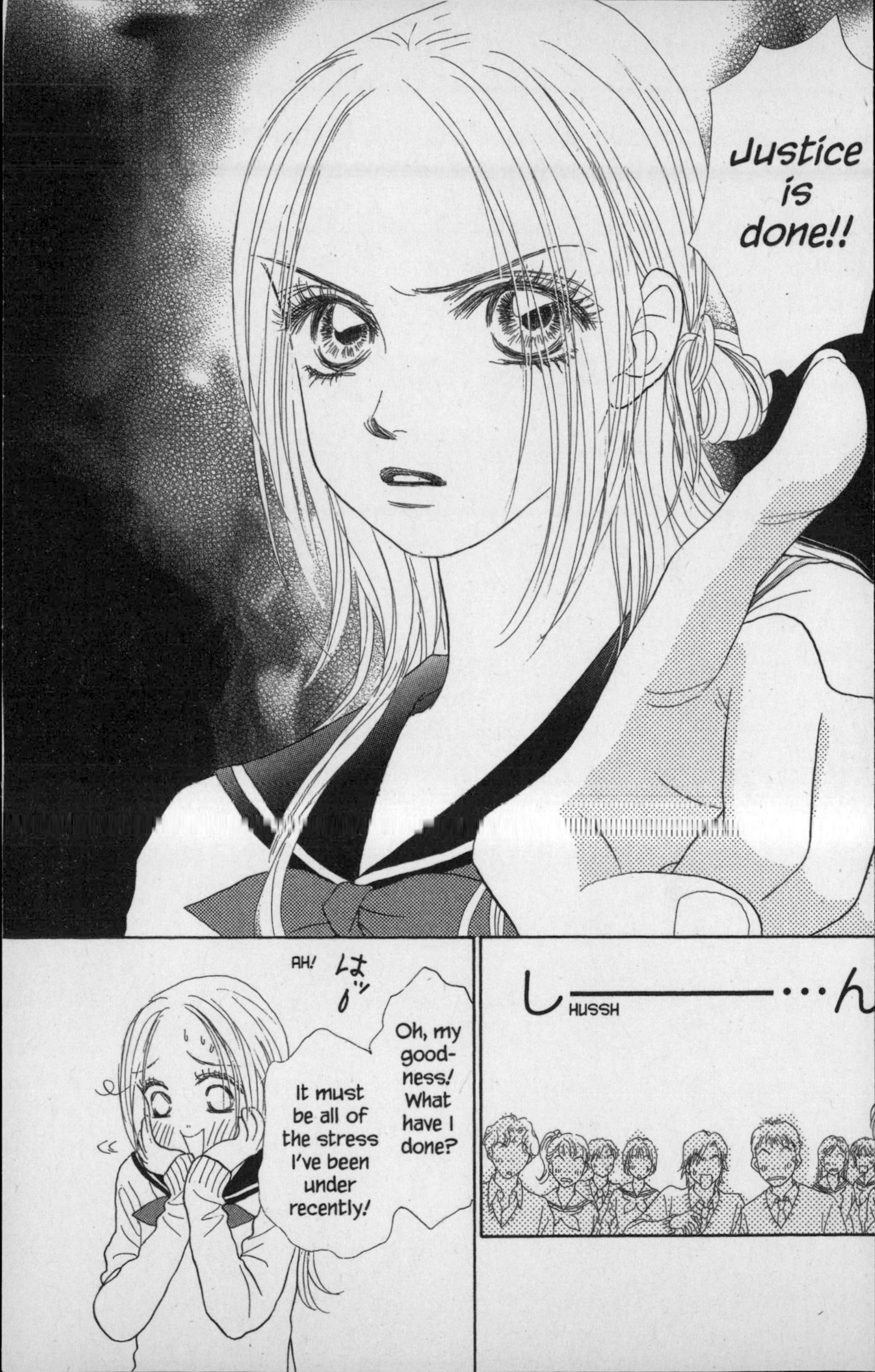
Justice is done!!
し————…ん
HUSSH
はッ
AH!
Oh, my goodness! What have I done?
It must be all of the stress I've been under recently!

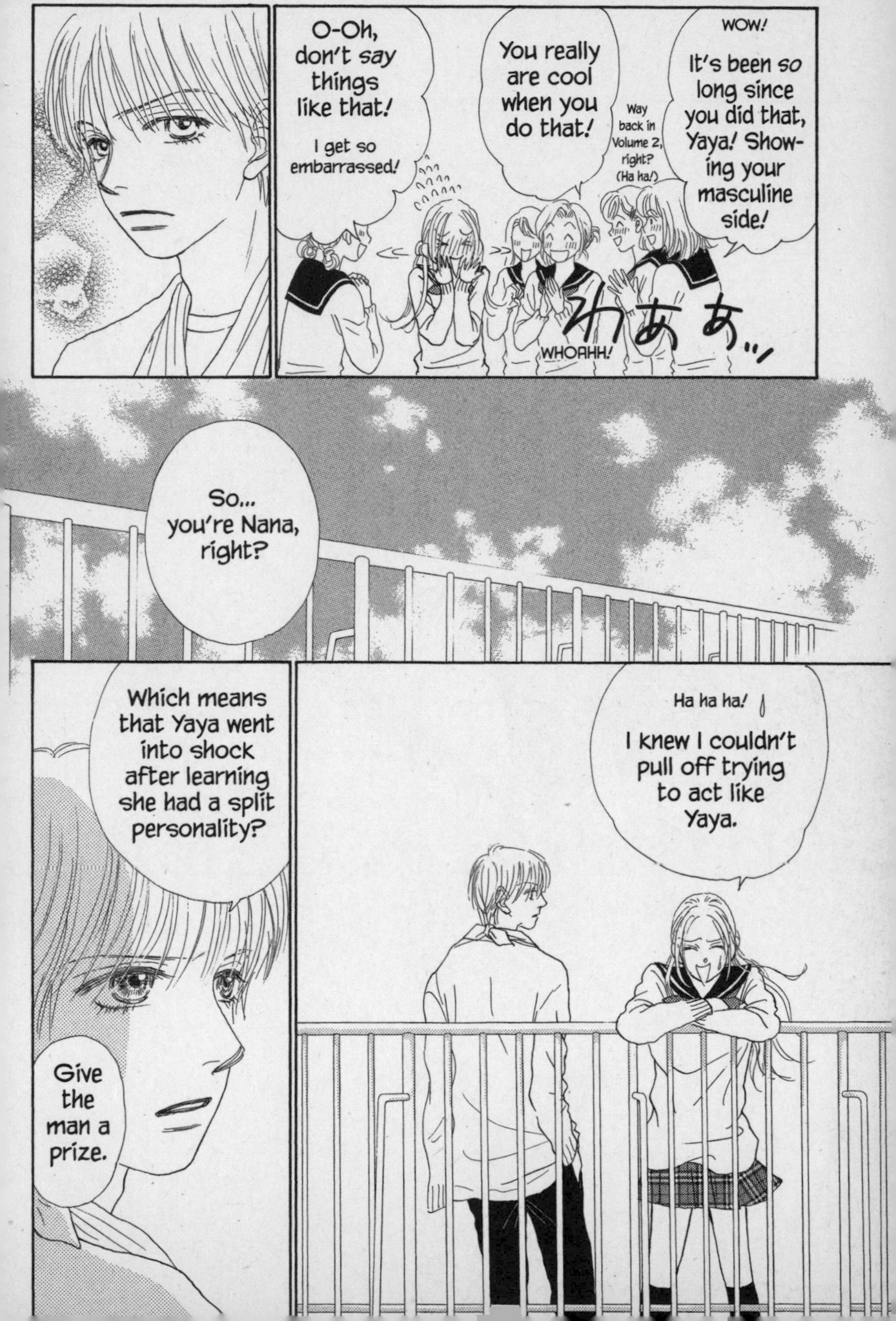
WOW!
It's been so long since you did that, Yaya! Showing your masculine side!
Way back in Volume 2, right? (Ha ha!)
You really are cool when you do that!
O-Oh, don't say things like that!
I get so embarrassed!
わあぁ
WHOAHH!
So... you're Nana, right?
Ha ha ha!
I knew I couldn't pull off trying to act like Yaya.
Which means that Yaya went into shock after learning she had a split personality?
Give the man a prize.

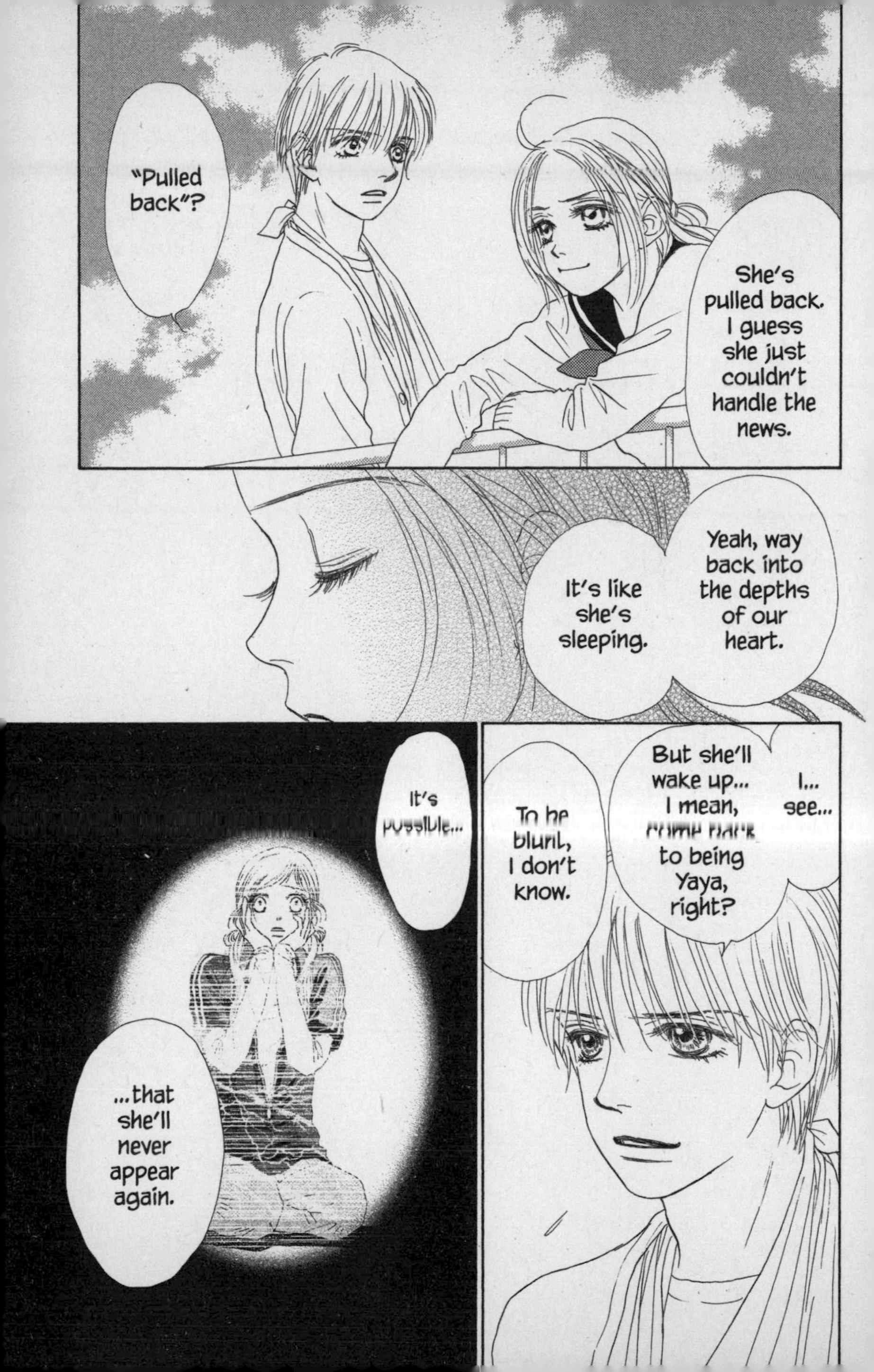
She's pulled back. I guess she just couldn't handle the news.
"Pulled back"?
Yeah, way back into the depths of our heart.
It's like she's sleeping.
I... see...
But she'll wake up... I mean, come back to being Yaya, right?
To be blunt, I don't know.
It's possible...
...that she'll never appear again.

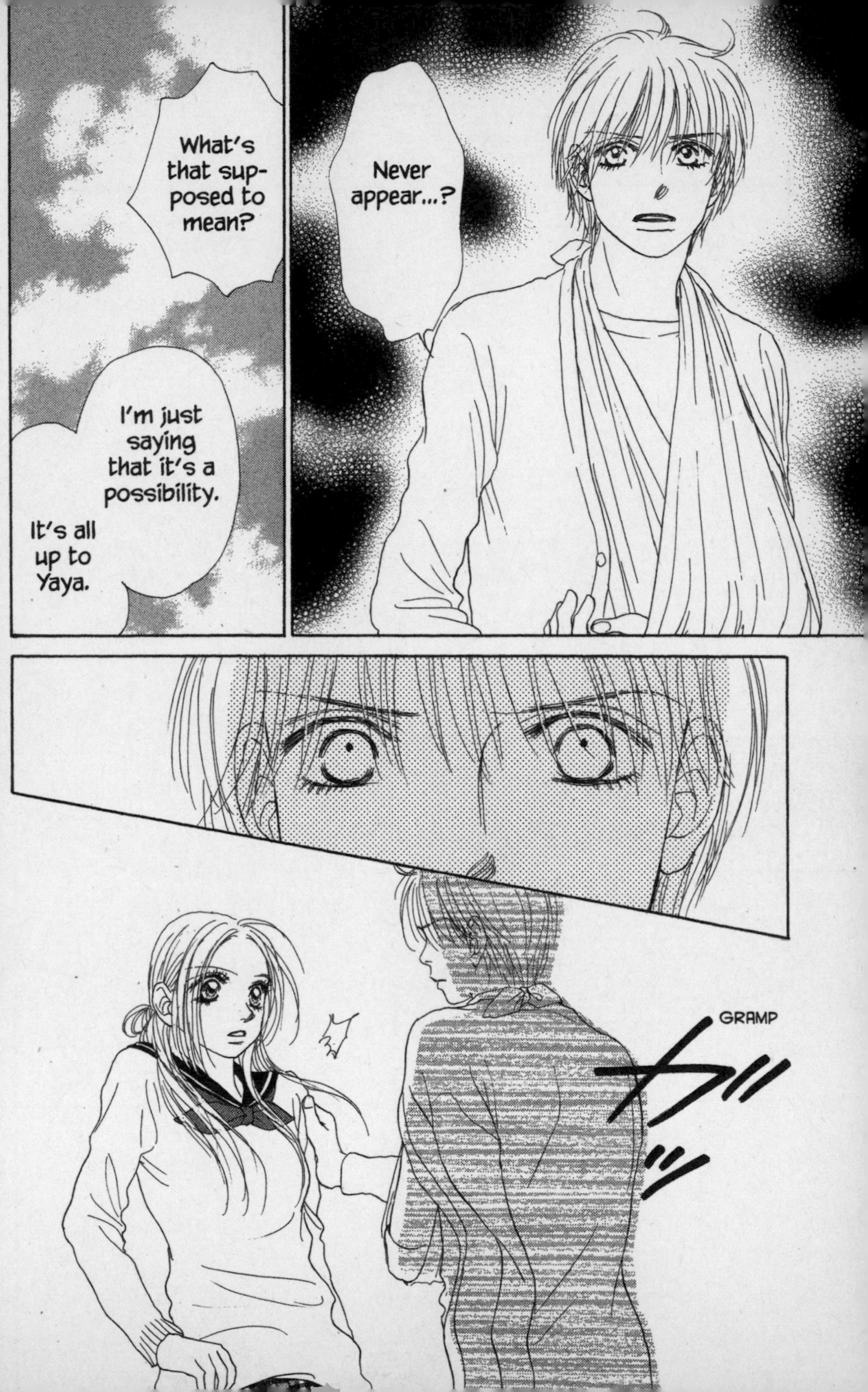
Never appear...?
What's that sup-posed to mean?
I'm just saying that it's a possibility.
It's all up to Yaya.
GRAMP

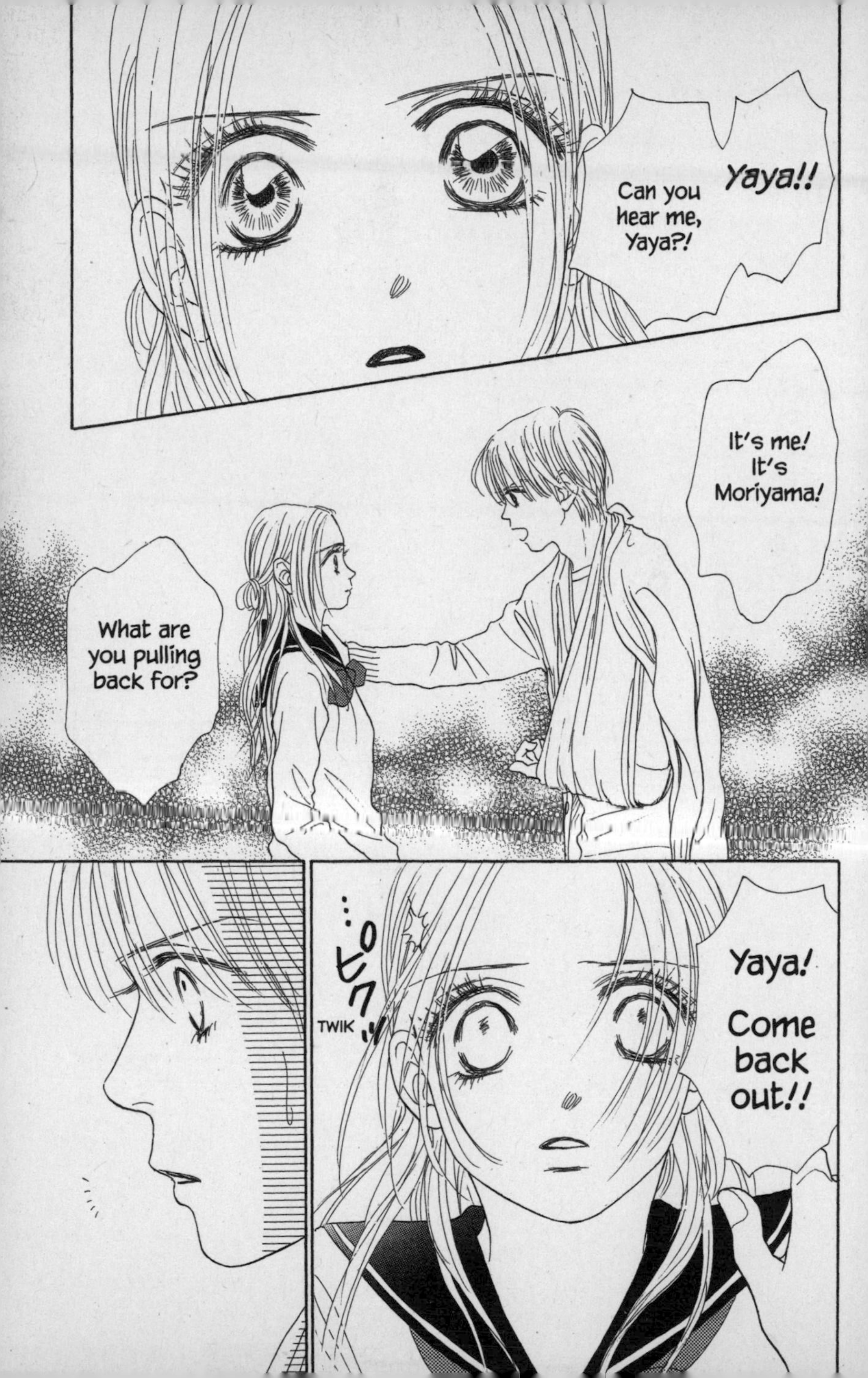
Yaya!!
Can you hear me, Yaya?!
It's me! It's Moriyama!
What are you pulling back for?
Yaya! Come back out!!
…ピクッ
TWIK

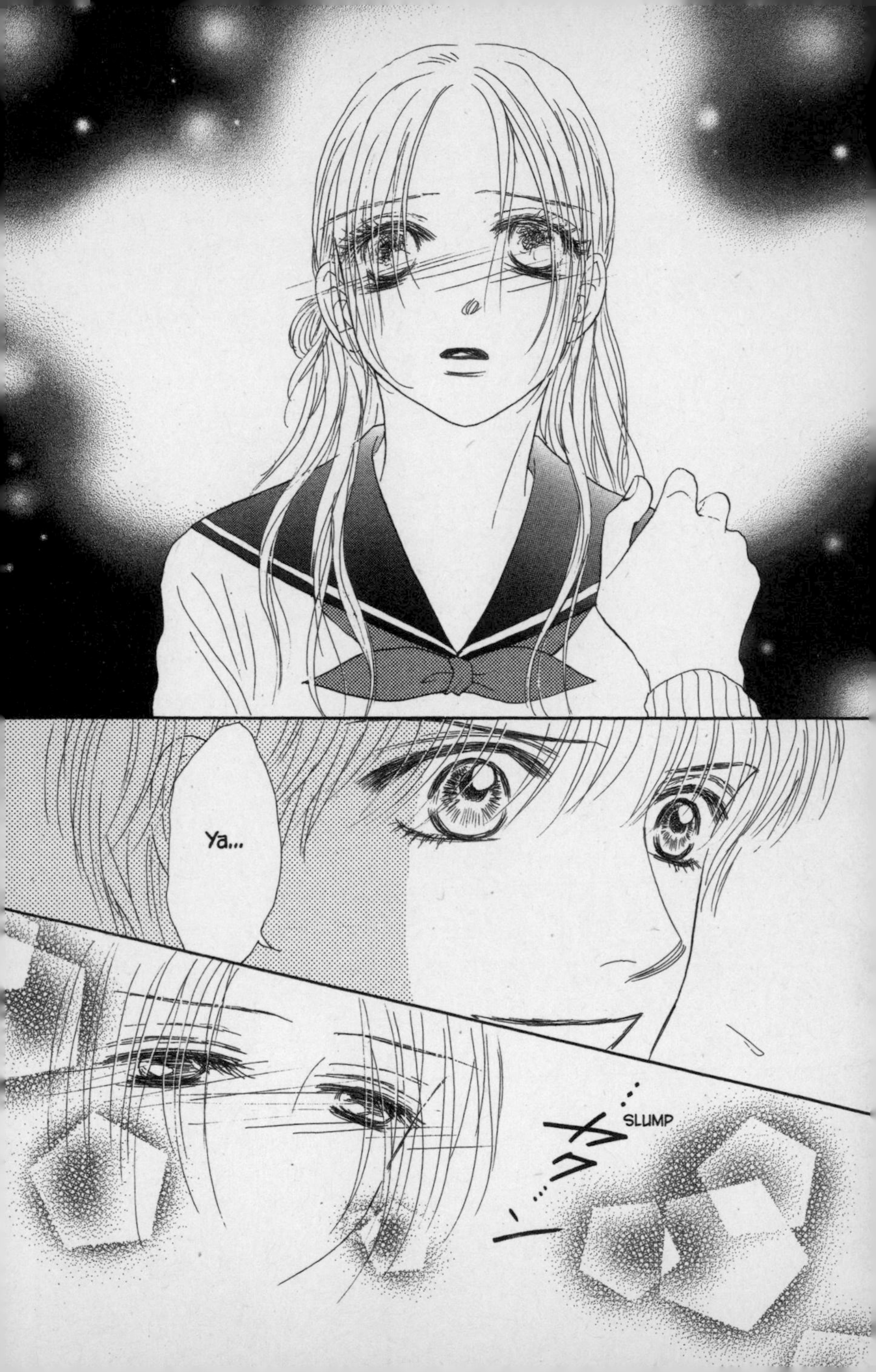
Ya...
SLUMP

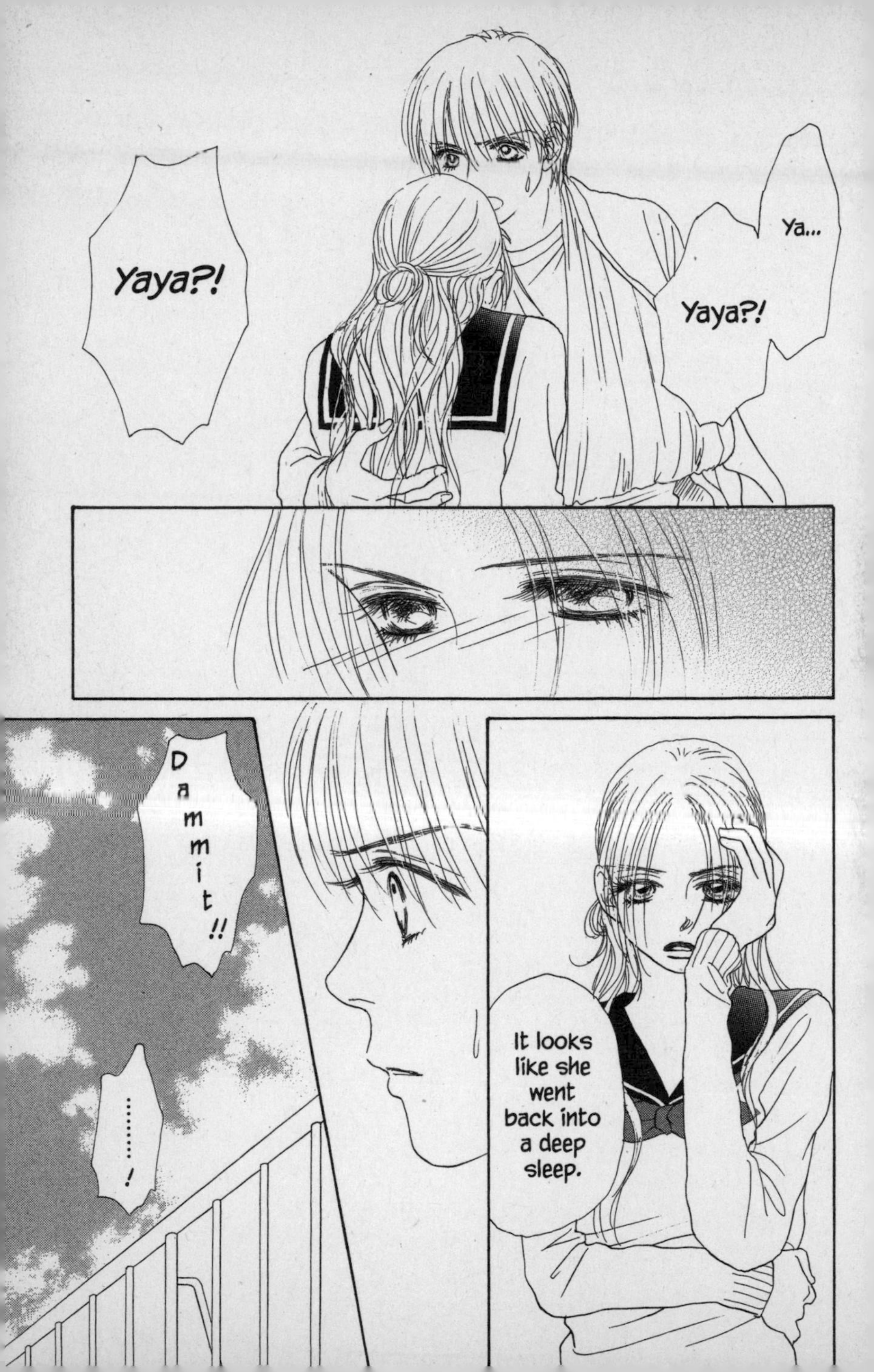
Ya... Yaya?!
Yaya?!
It looks like she went back into a deep sleep.
Dammit!!
......!

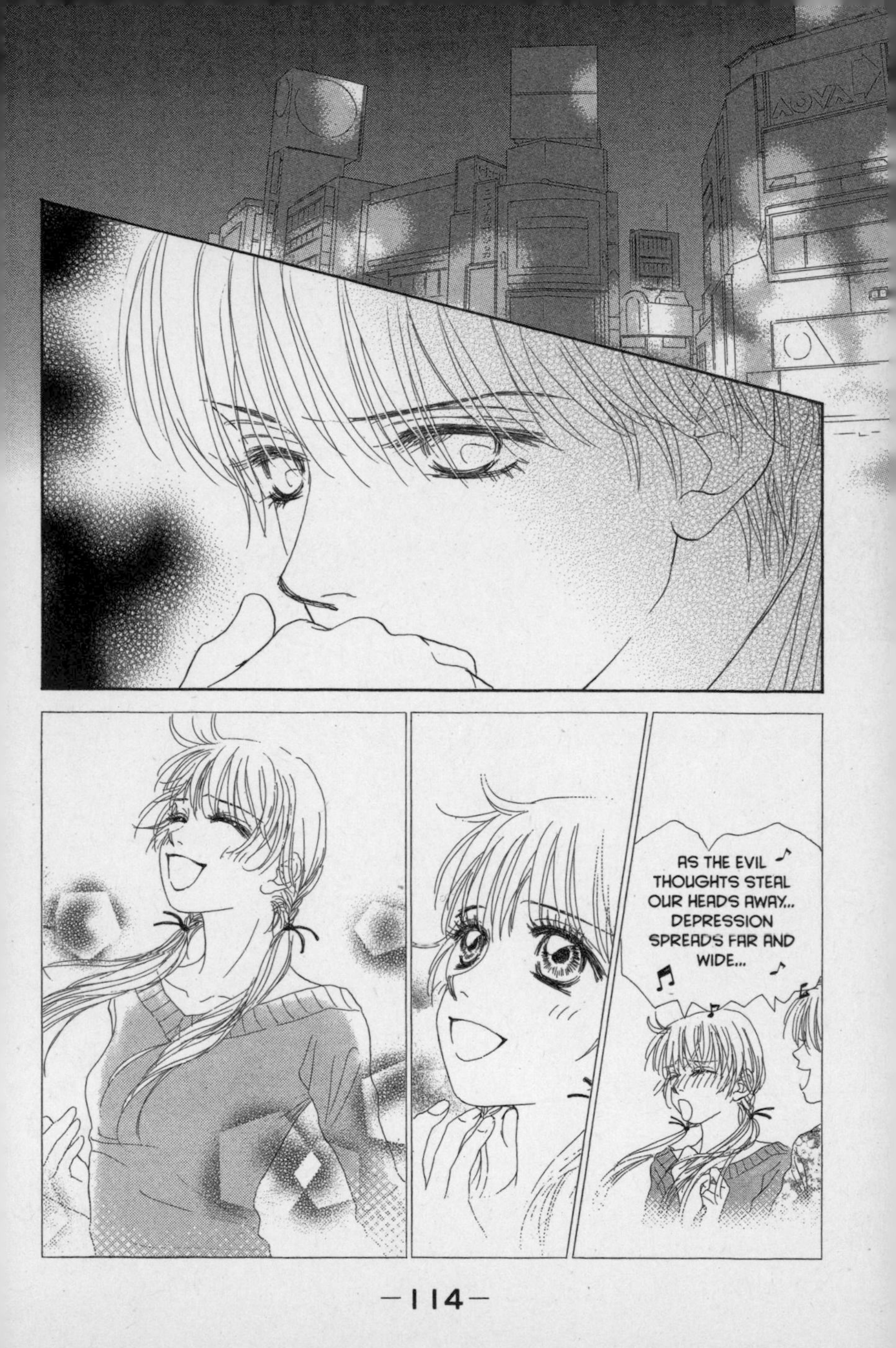
AS THE EVIL THOUGHTS STEAL OUR HEADS AWAY... DEPRESSION SPREADS FAR AND WIDE...

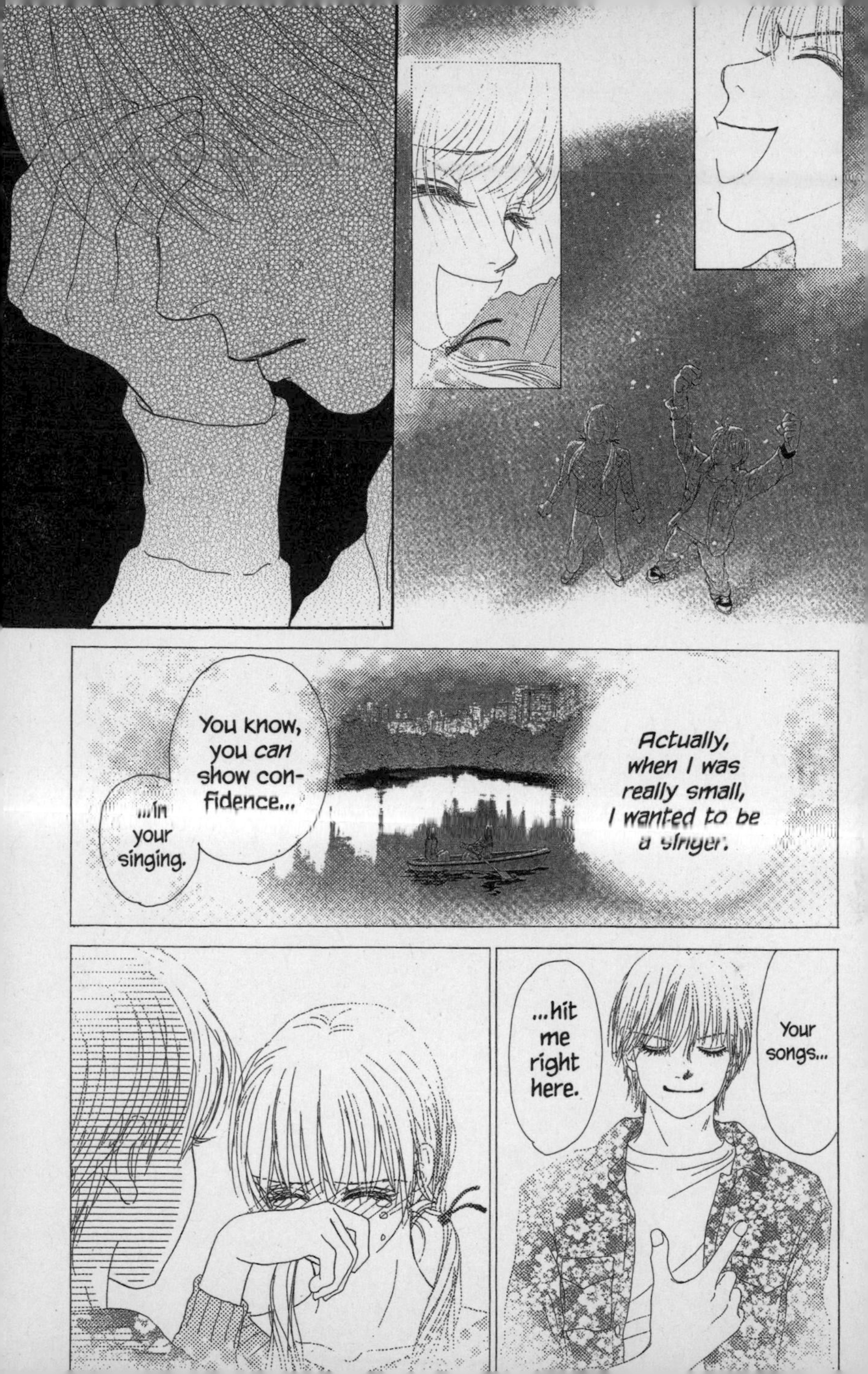
Actually, when I was really small, I wanted to be a singer.
You know, you can show confidence...
...in your singing.
Your songs...
...hit me right here.

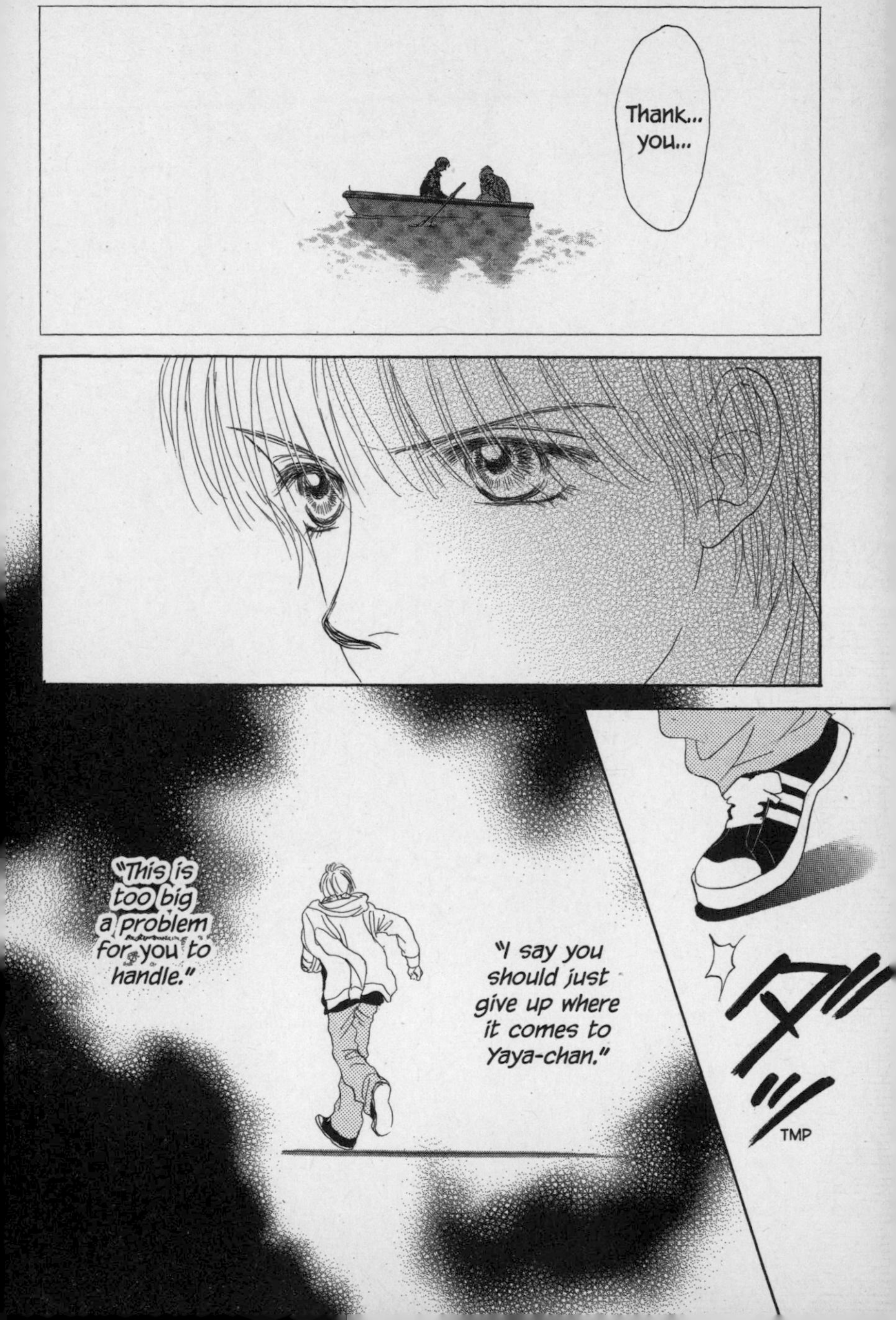
Thank... you...
TMP
"I say you should just give up where it comes to Yaya-chan."
"This is too big a problem for you to handle."

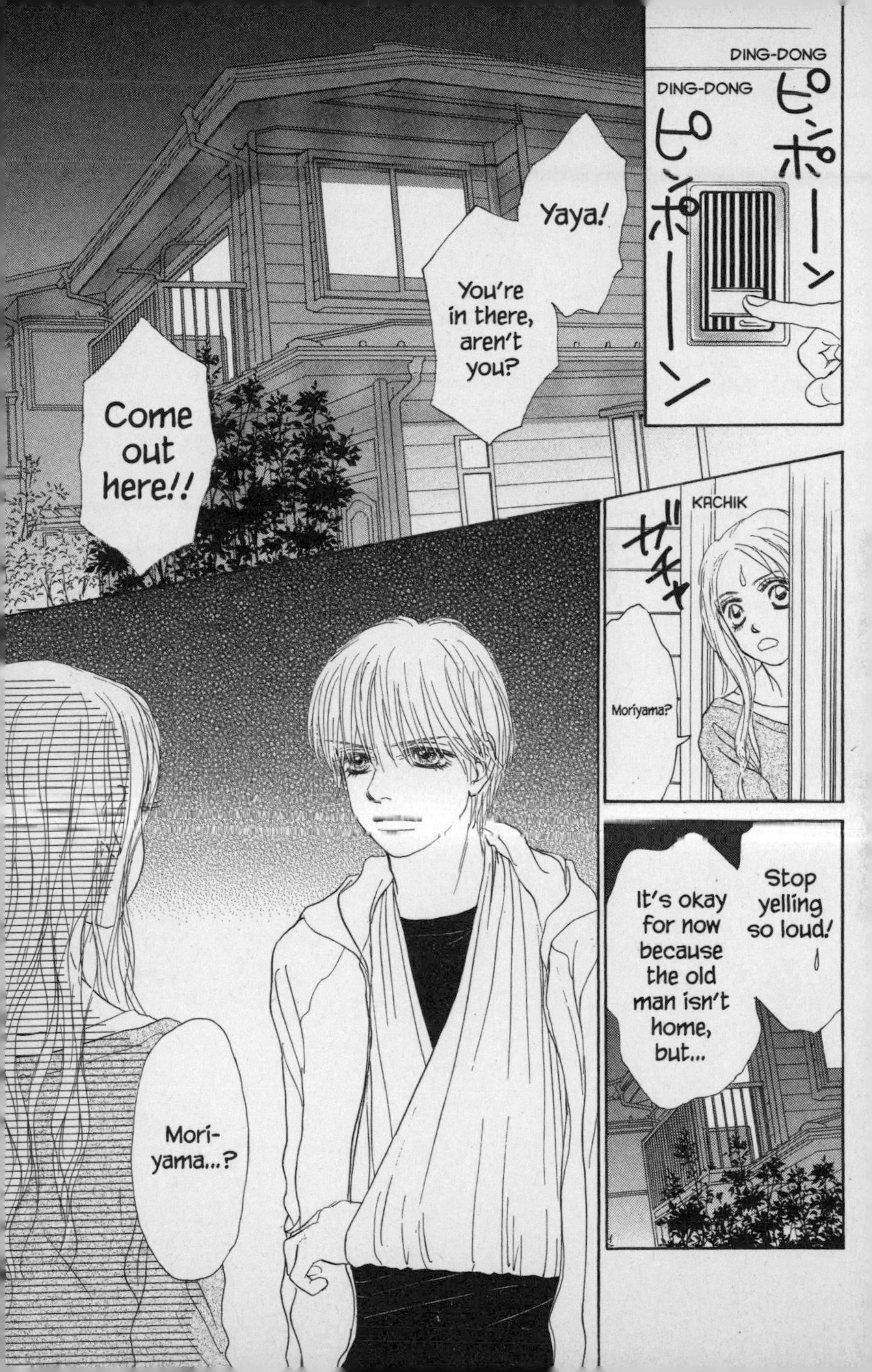
DING-DONG
ピンポーン
DING-DONG
ピンポーン
Yaya!
You're in there, aren't you?
Come out here!!
KACHIK
ガチャ
Moriyama?
Stop yelling so loud!
It's okay for now because the old man isn't home, but...
Mori-yama...?

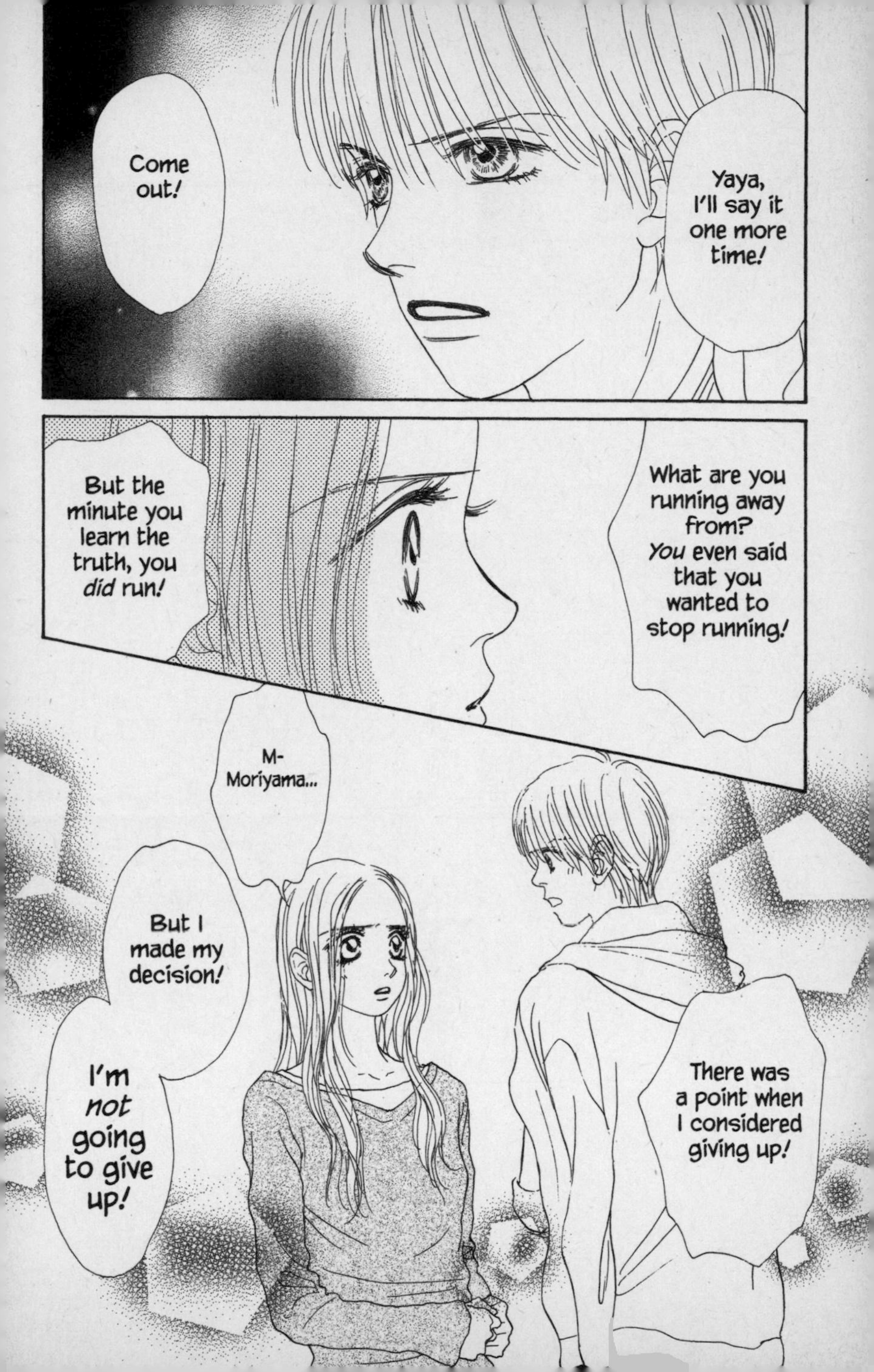
Yaya, I'll say it one more time!
Come out!
What are you running away from? *You* even said that you wanted to stop running!
But the minute you learn the truth, you *did* run!
M- Moriyama...
There was a point when I considered giving up!
But I made my decision!
I'm *not* going to give up!

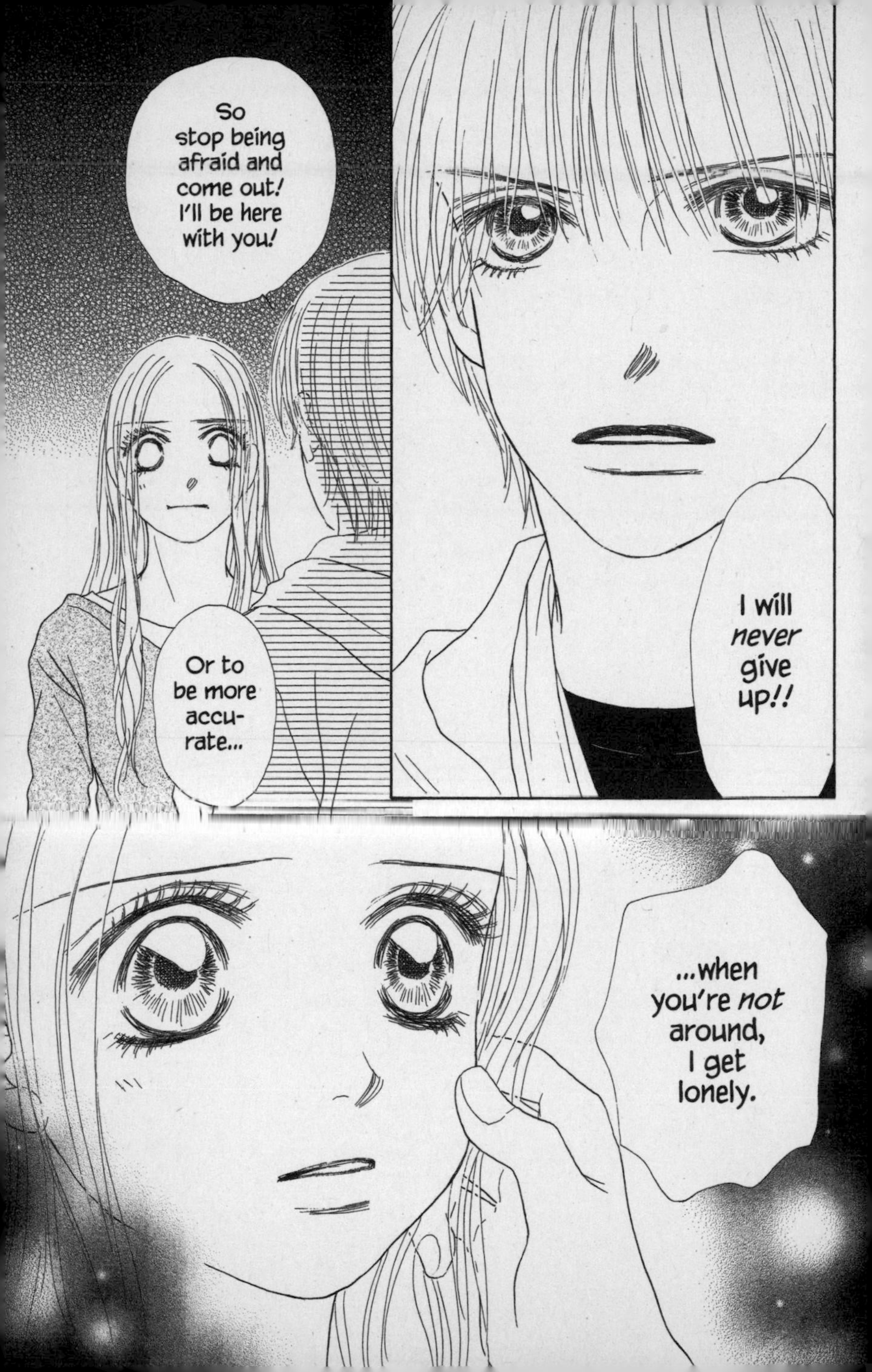
I will *never* give up!!
So stop being afraid and come out! I'll be here with you!
Or to be more accurate...
...when you're *not* around, I get lonely.

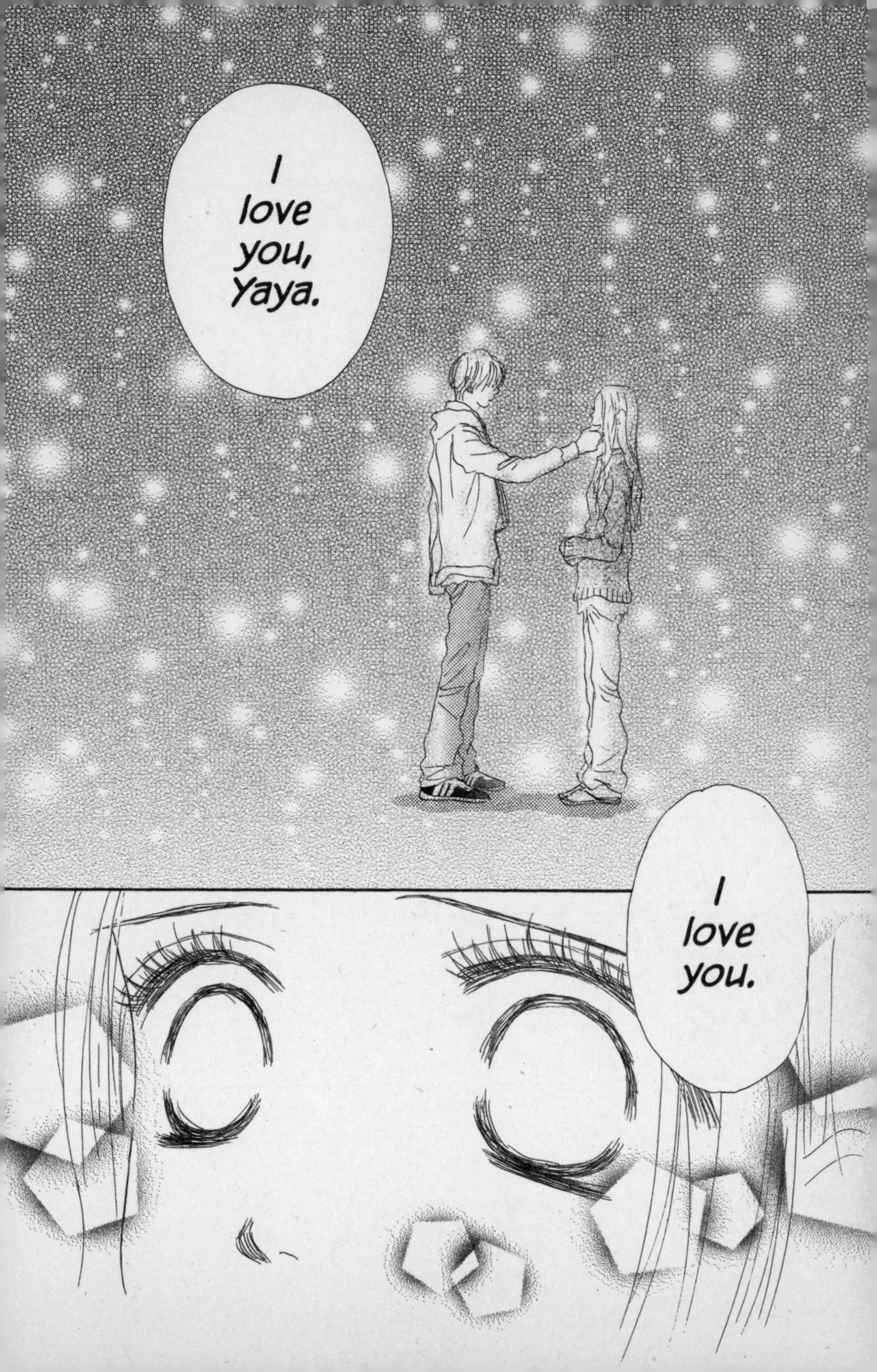
I love you, Yaya.
I love you.

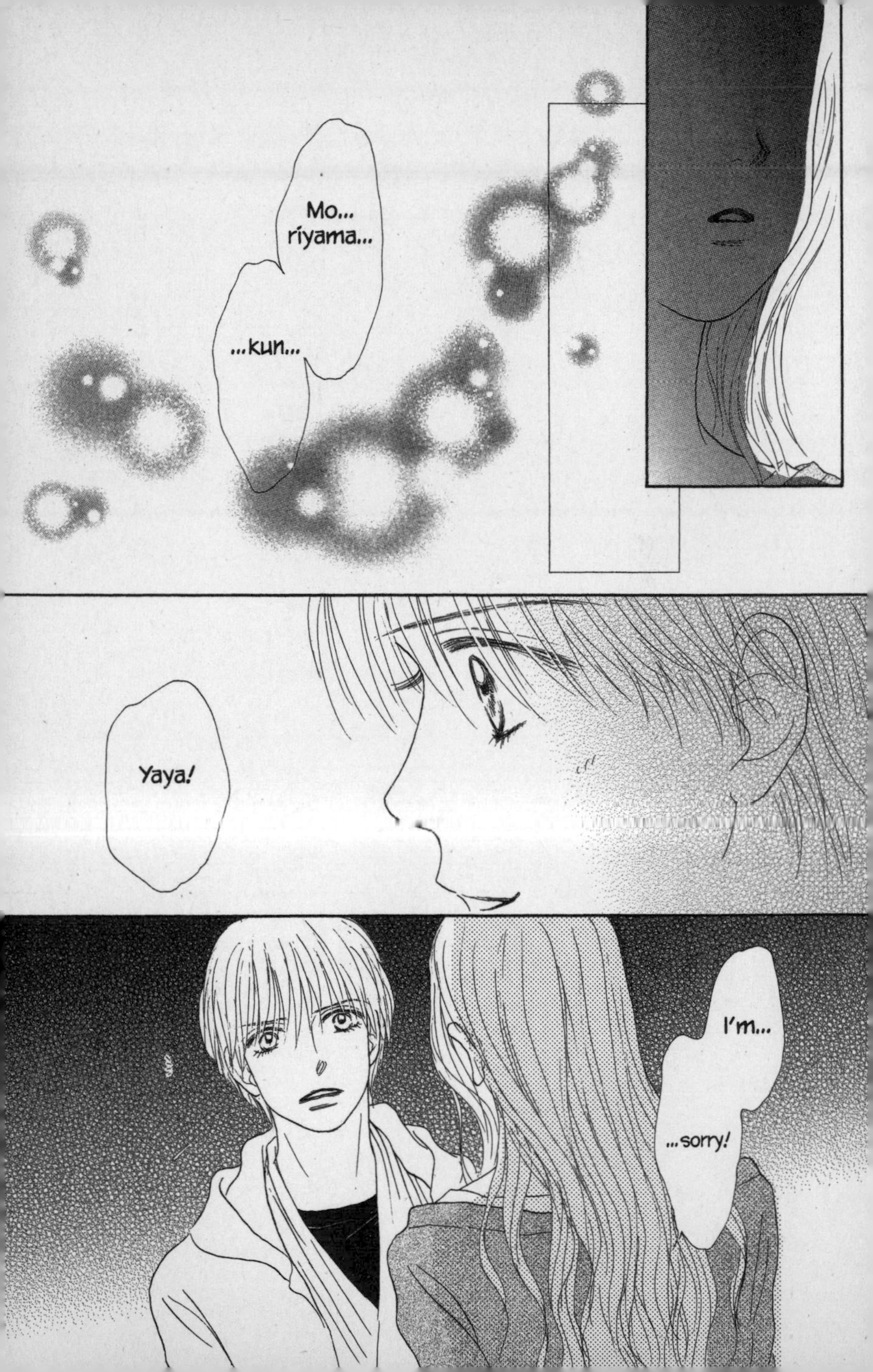
Mo... riyama...
...kun...
Yaya!
I'm...
...sorry!

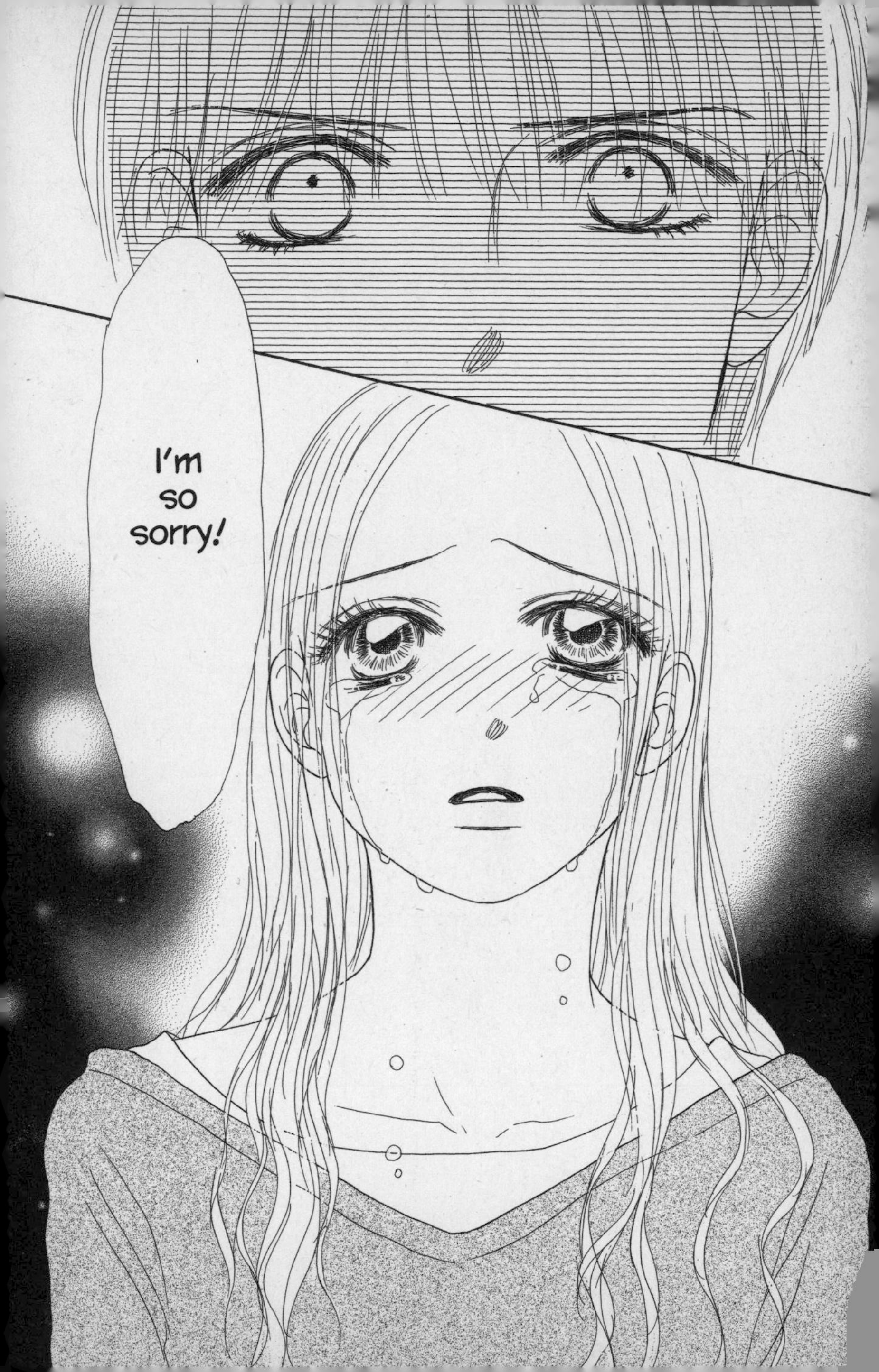
I'm so sorry!

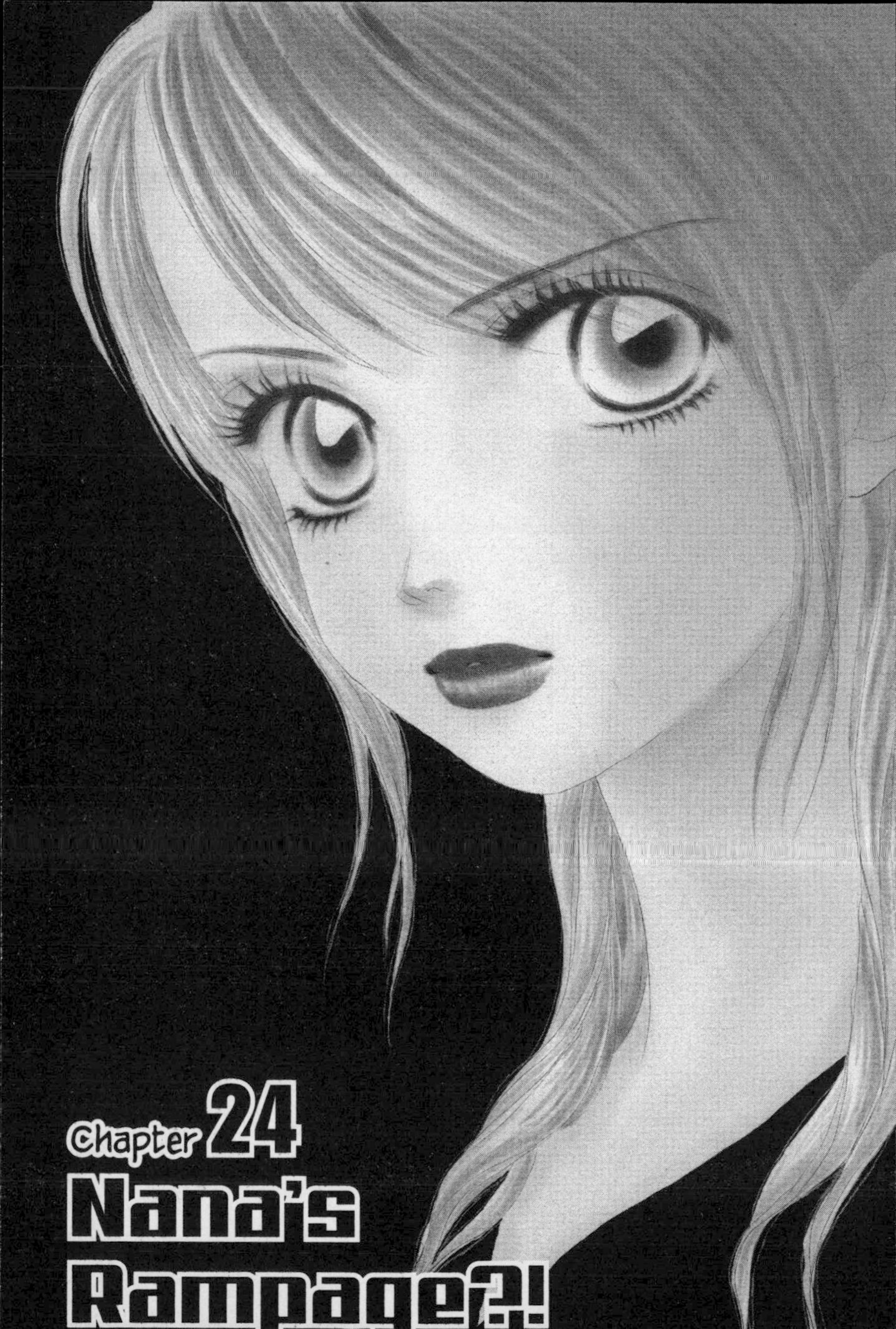
Chapter 24
Nana's Rampage?!

OTHELLO

オセロ。

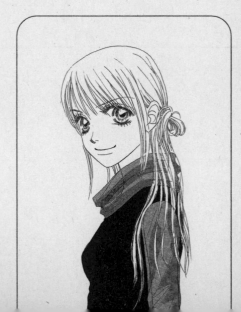

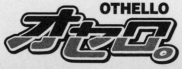

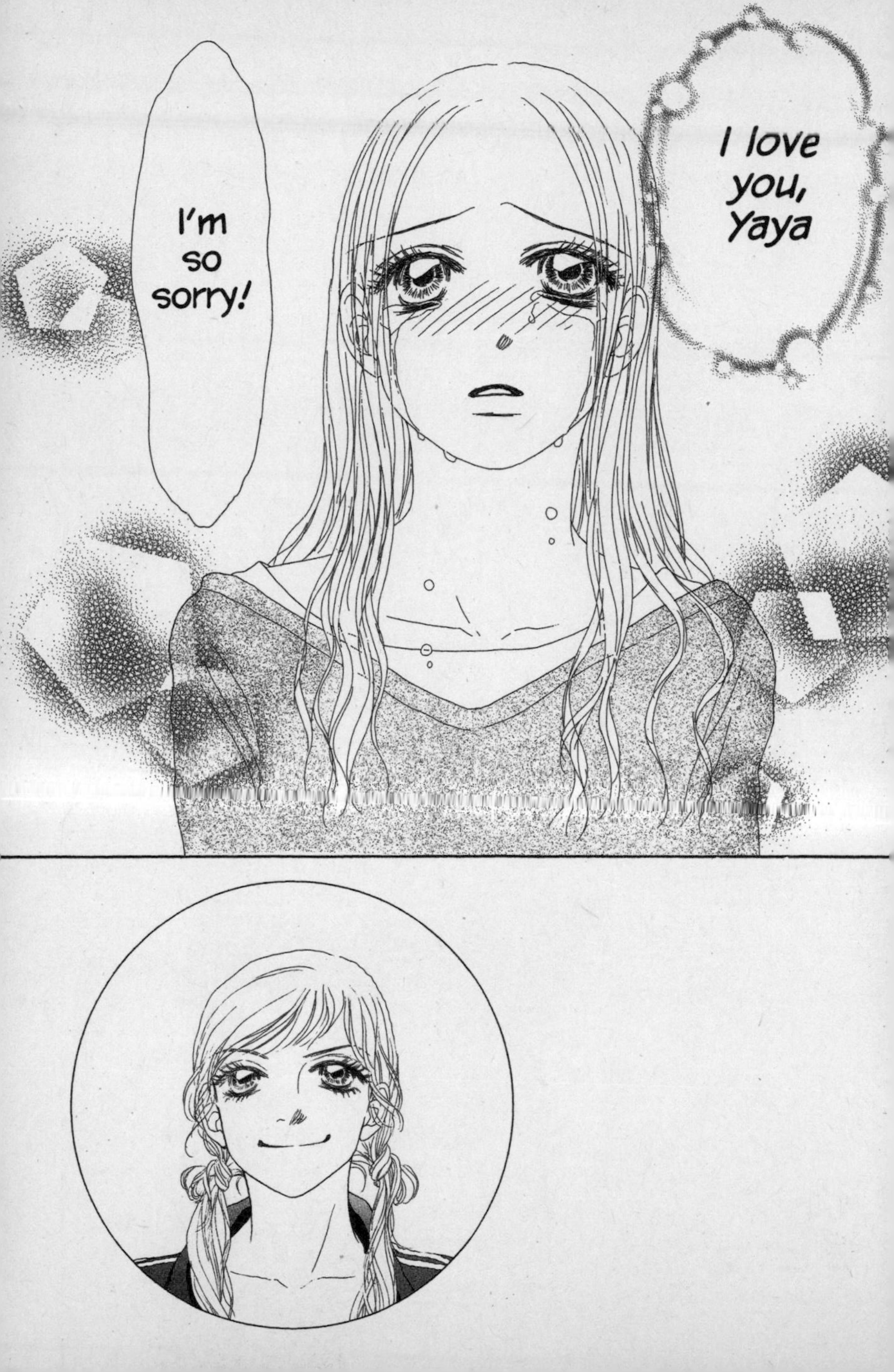
I love you, Yaya
I'm so sorry!

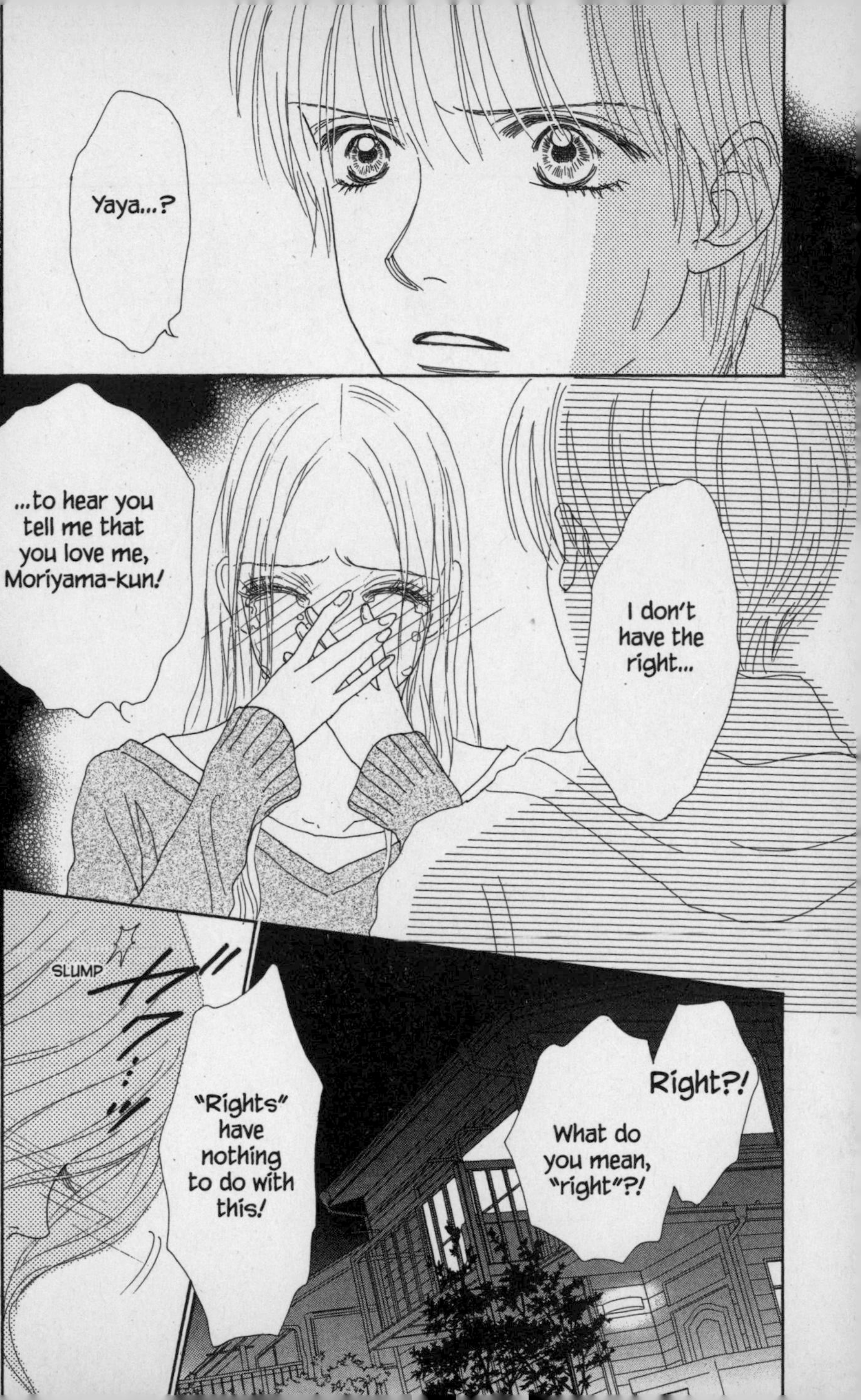
Yaya...?
I don't have the right...
...to hear you tell me that you love me, Moriyama-kun!
Right?! What do you mean, "right"?!
SLUMP
"Rights" have nothing to do with this!

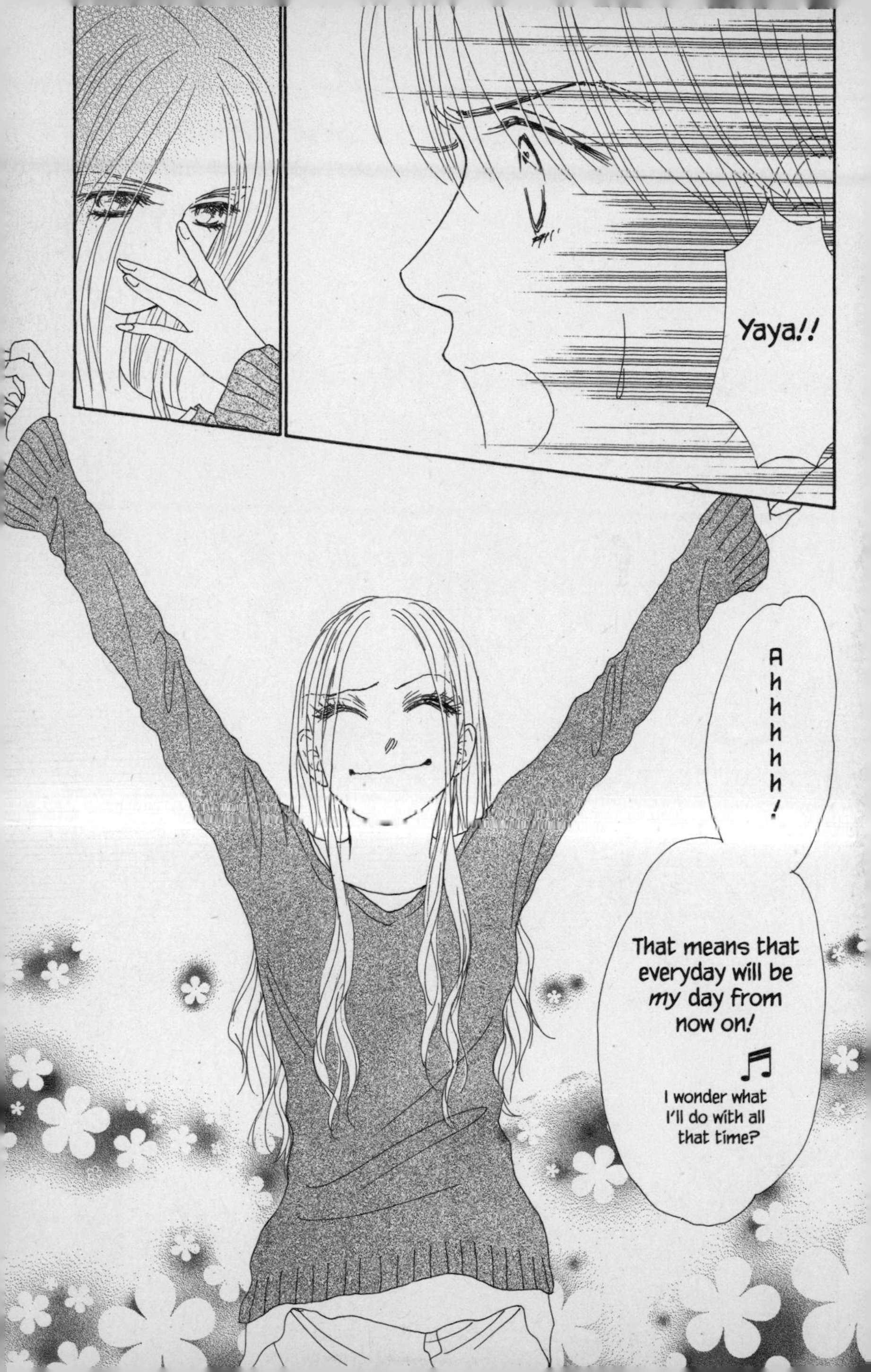
Yaya!!
Ahhhhh!
That means that everyday will be *my* day from now on! ♫
I wonder what I'll do with all that time?

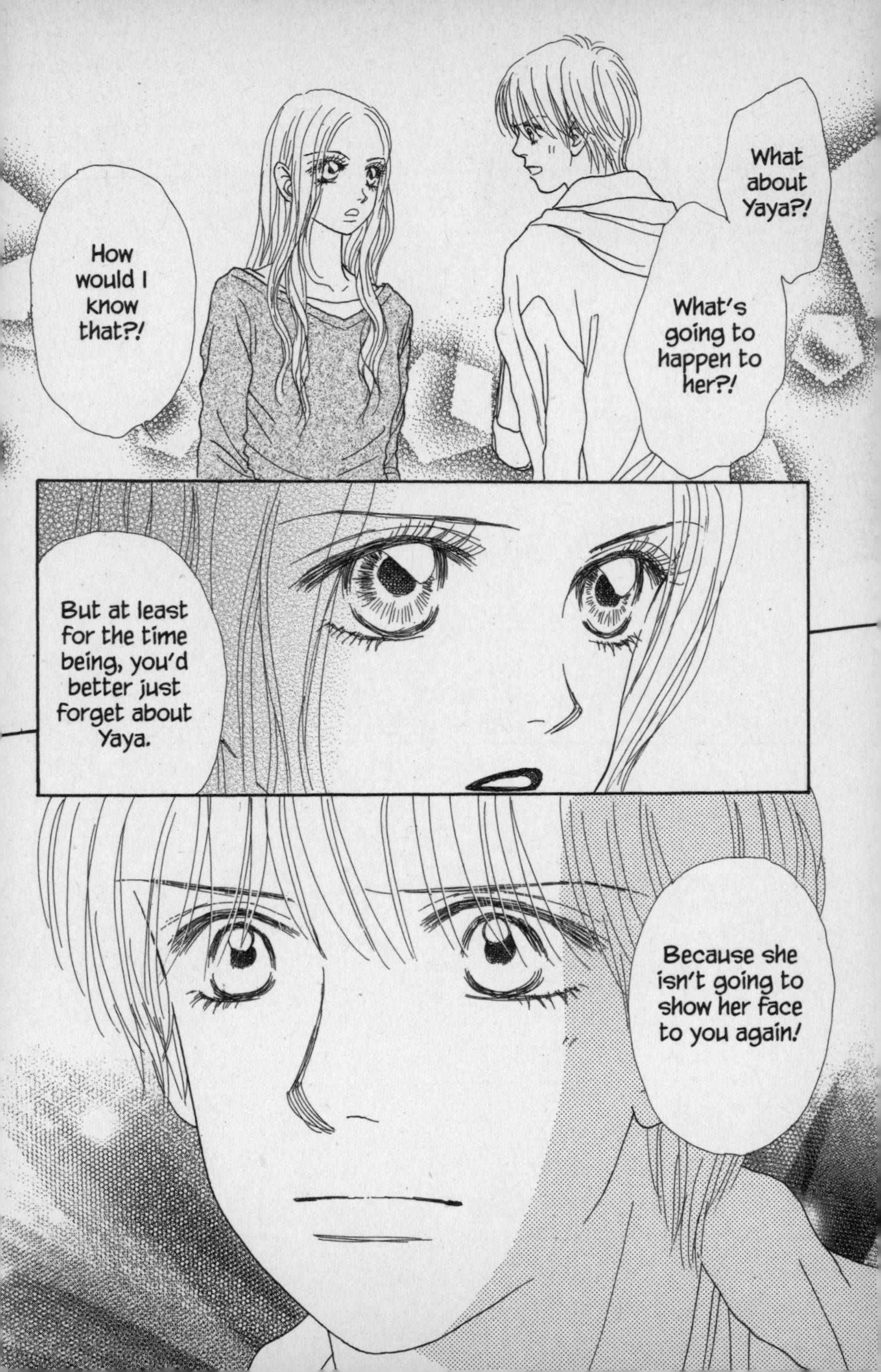
What about Yaya?!
What's going to happen to her?!
How would I know that?!
But at least for the time being, you'd better just forget about Yaya.
Because she isn't going to show her face to you again!

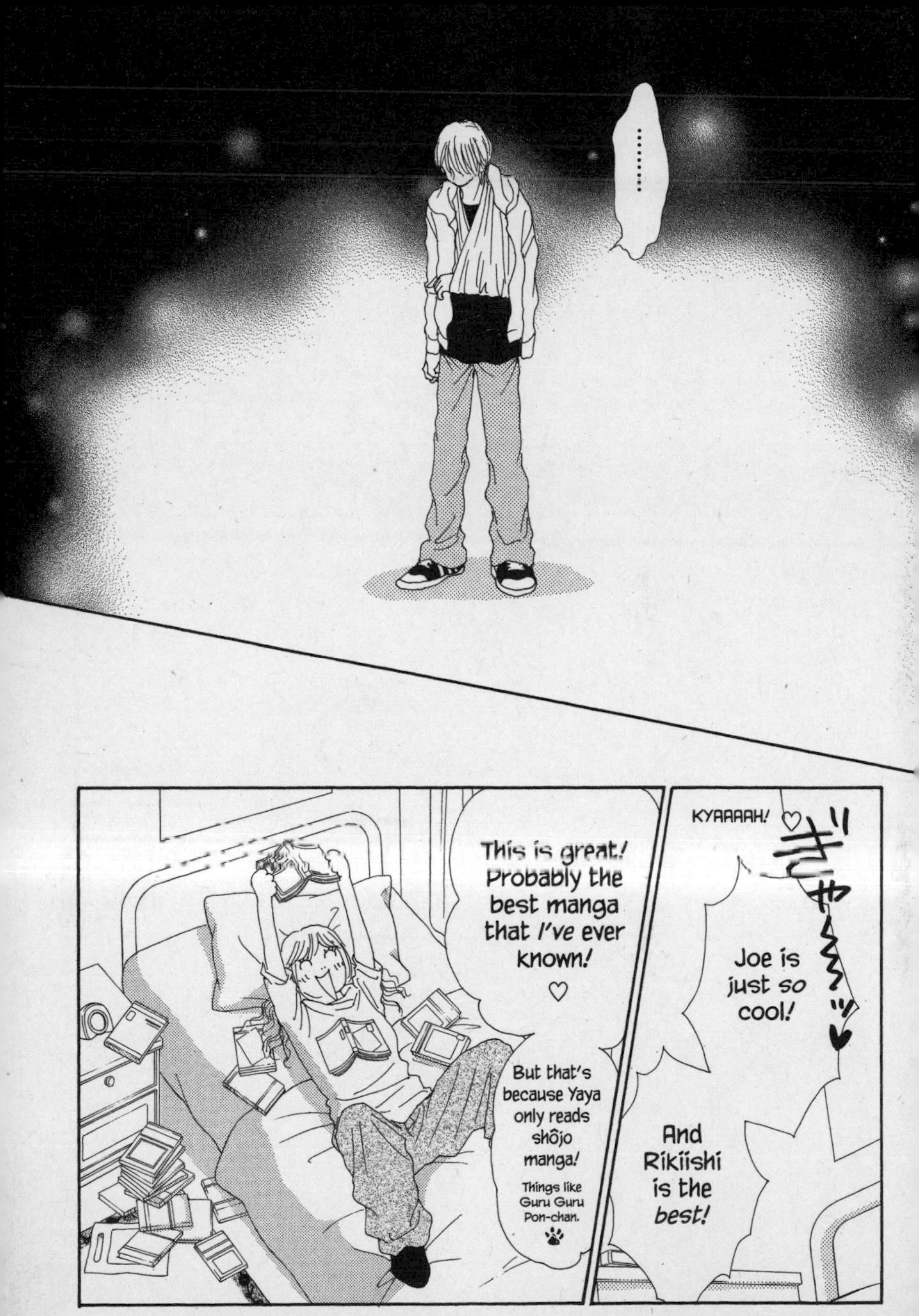
……
KYAAAAH! ♡
Joe is just so cool!
And Rikiishi is the best!
This is great! Probably the best manga that I've ever known! ♡
But that's because Yaya only reads shôjo manga!
Things like Guru Guru Pon-chan.

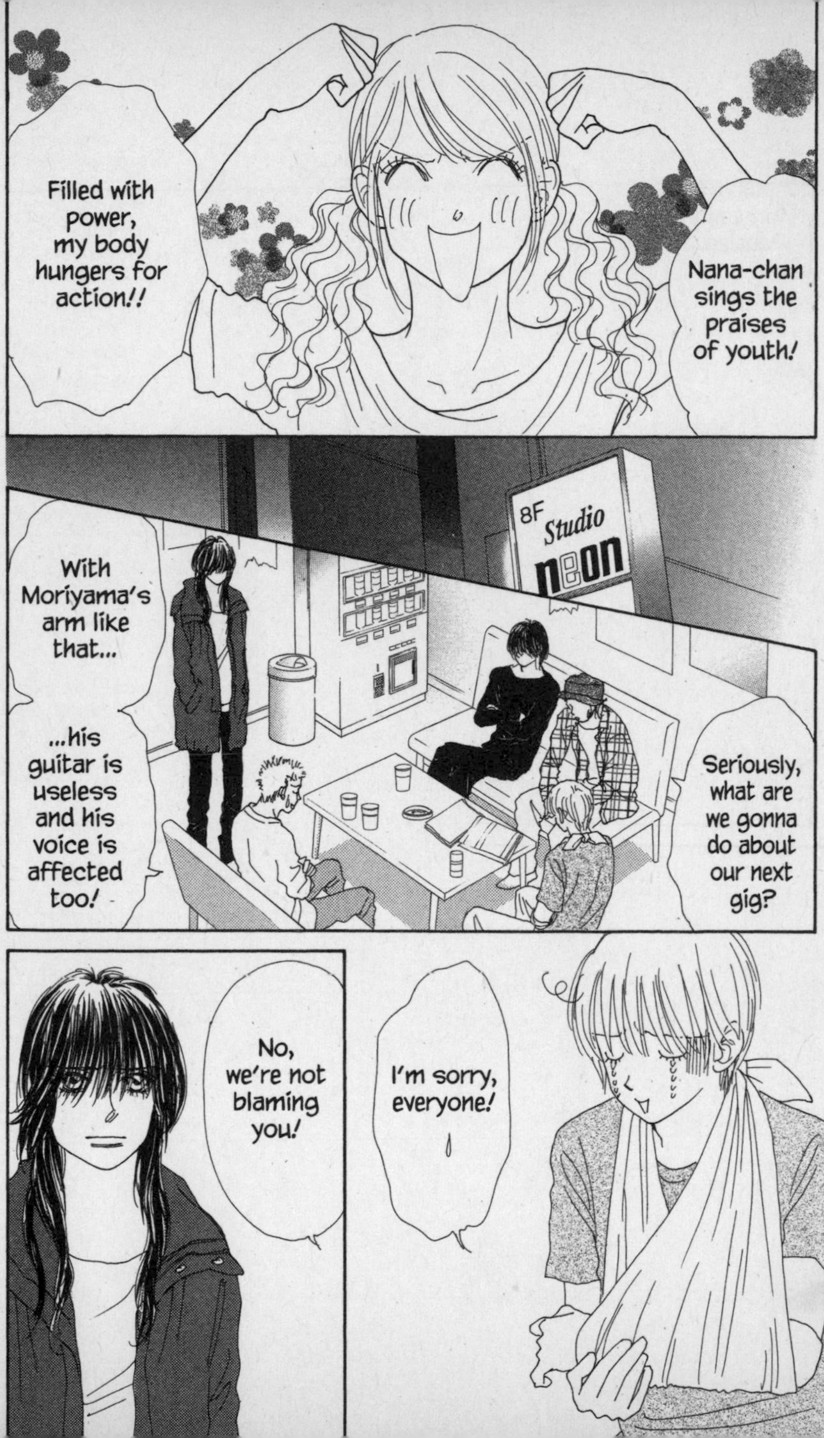
Nana-chan sings the praises of youth!
Filled with power, my body hungers for action!!
8F Studio neon
Seriously, what are we gonna do about our next gig?
With Moriyama's arm like that...
...his guitar is useless and his voice is affected too!
I'm sorry, everyone!
No, we're not blaming you!

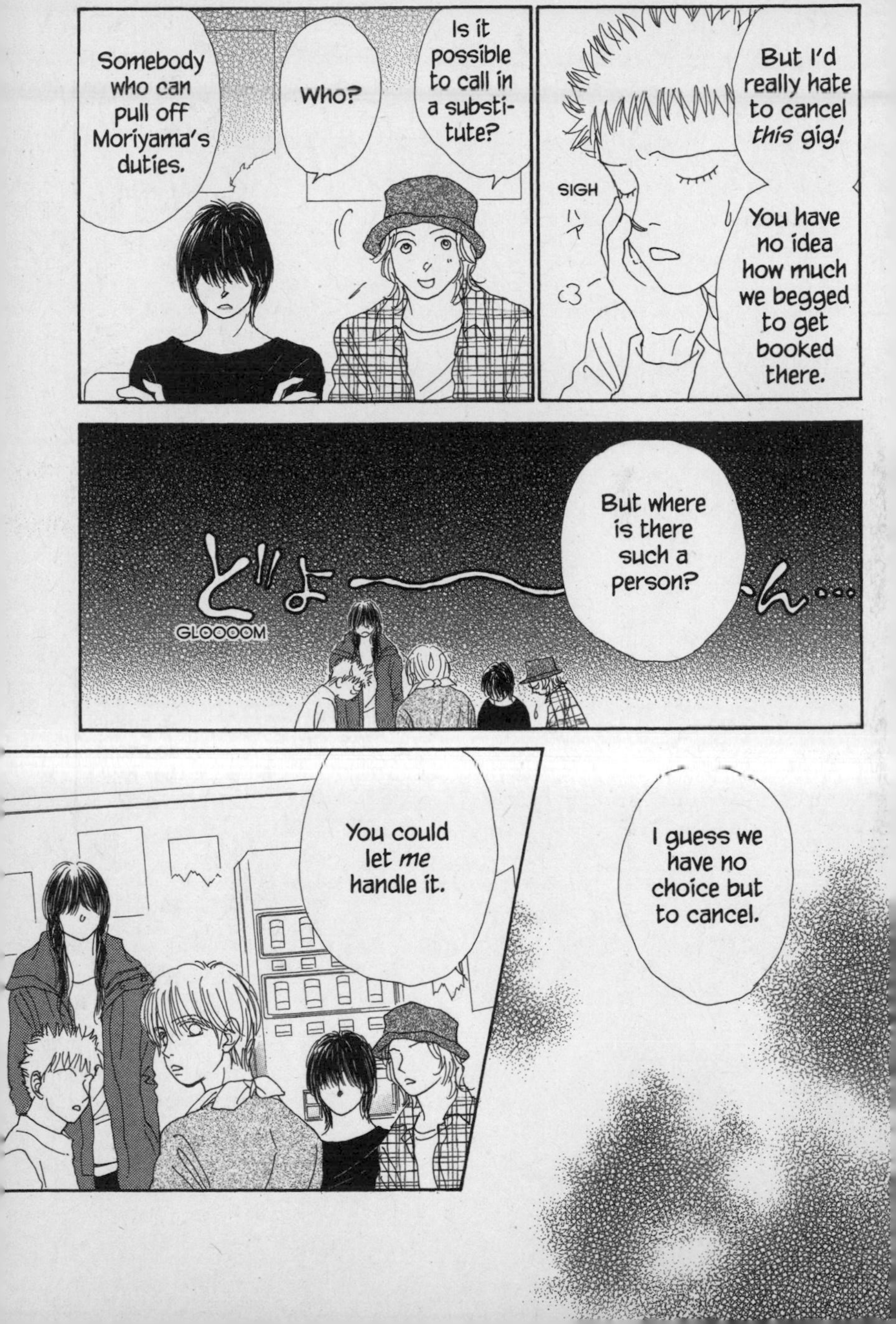

But I'd really hate to cancel *this* gig!
SIGH
You have no idea how much we begged to get booked there.
Is it possible to call in a substitute?
Who?
Somebody who can pull off Moriyama's duties.
But where is there such a person?
GLOOOOM
I guess we have no choice but to cancel.
You could let *me* handle it.

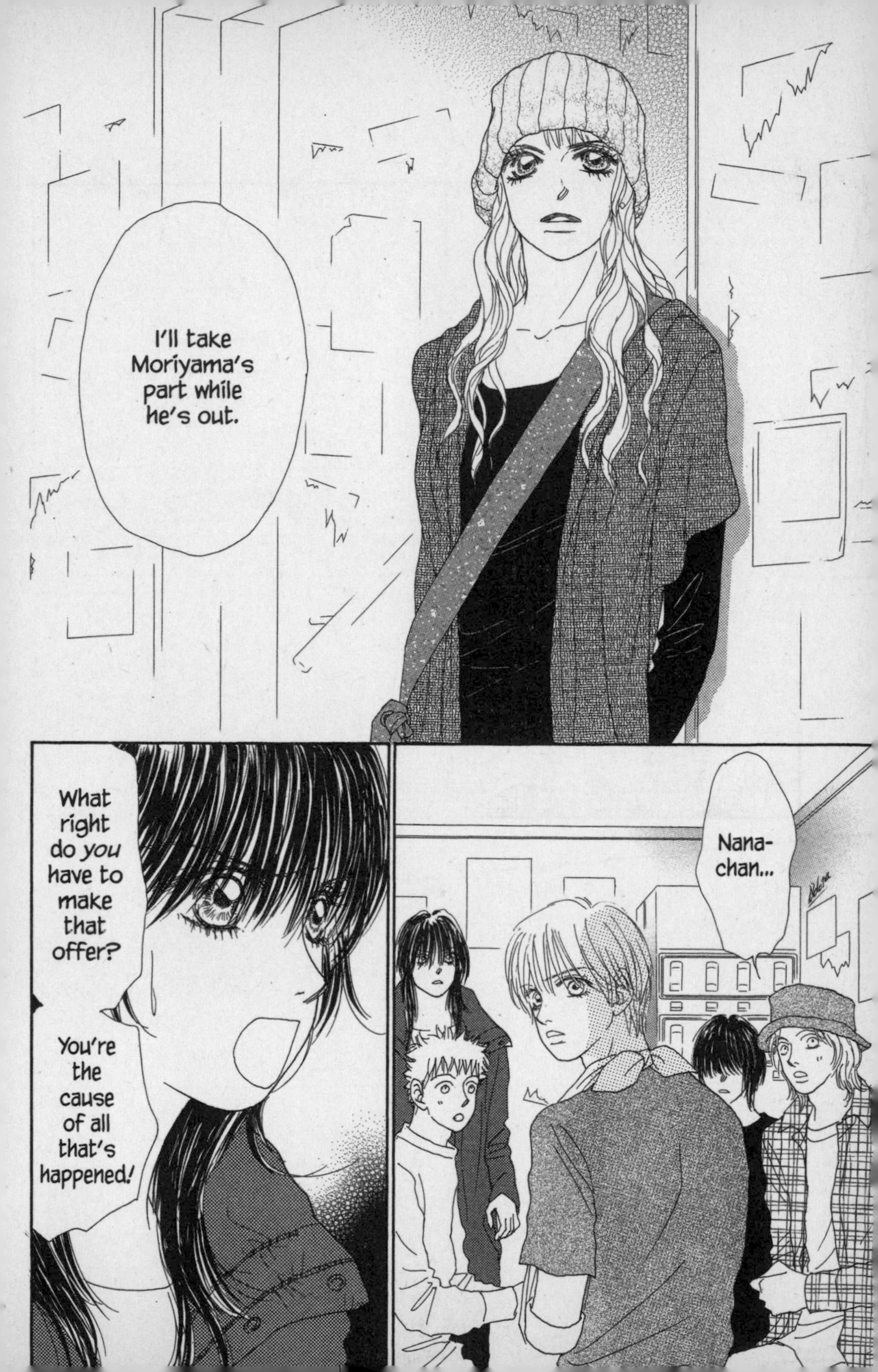

I'll take Moriyama's part while he's out.
Nana-chan...
What right do *you* have to make that offer?
You're the cause of all that's happened!

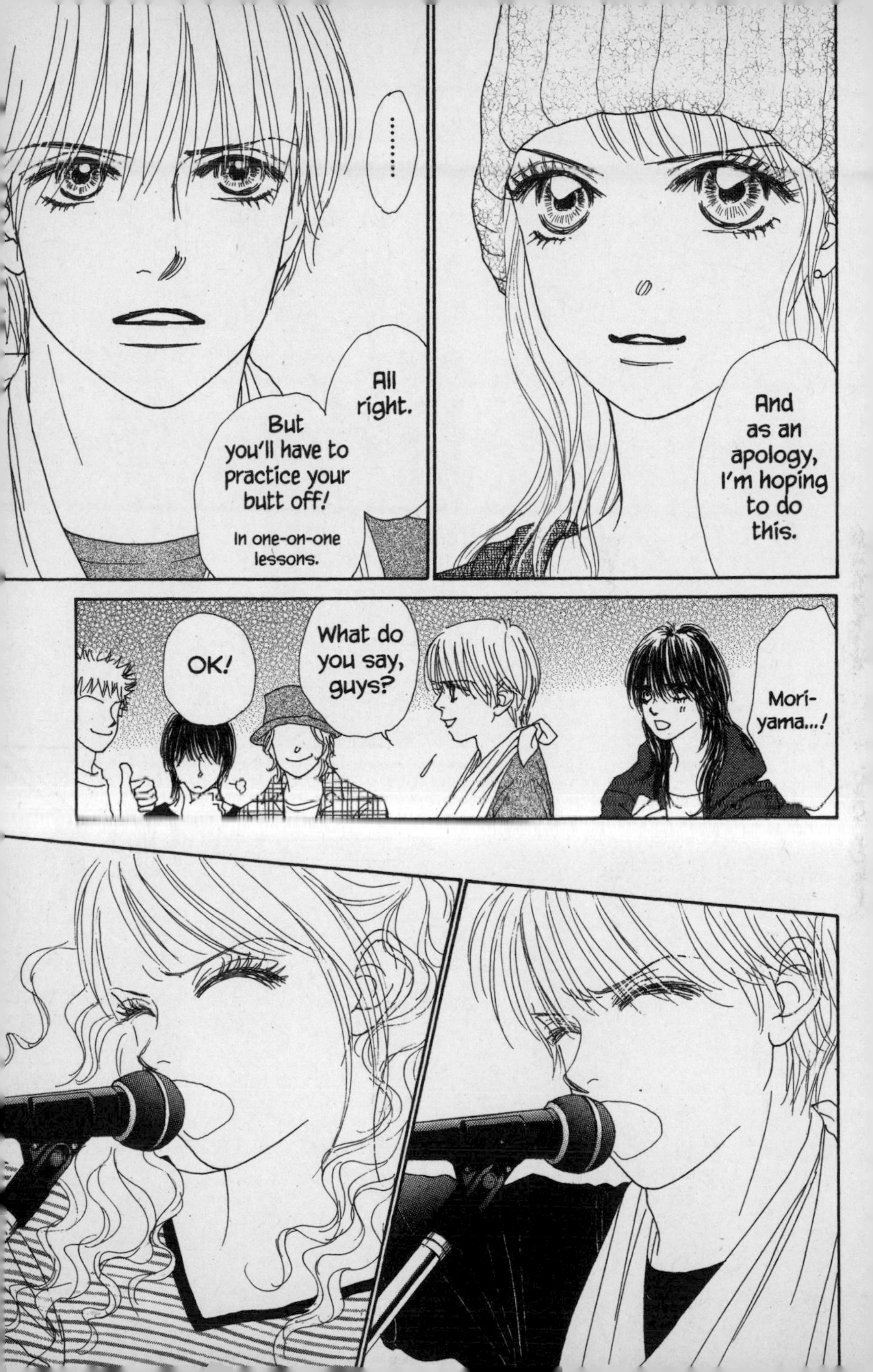
And as an apology, I'm hoping to do this.
......
All right.
But you'll have to practice your butt off!
In one-on-one lessons.
Mori-yama...!
What do you say, guys?
OK!

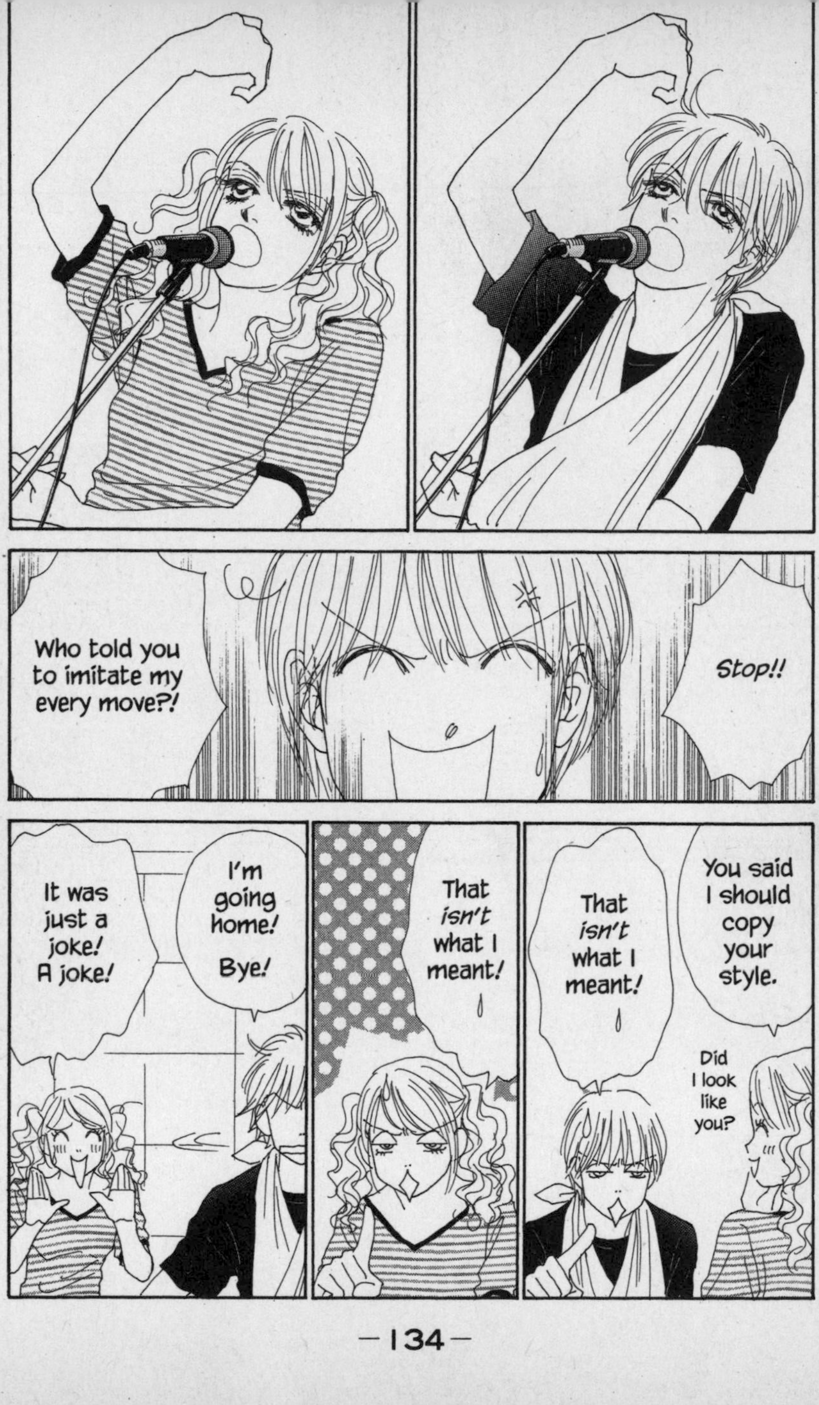

Stop!!
Who told you to imitate my every move?!
You said I should copy your style.
That *isn't* what I meant!
Did I look like you?
That *isn't* what I meant!
I'm going home! Bye!
It was just a joke! A joke!

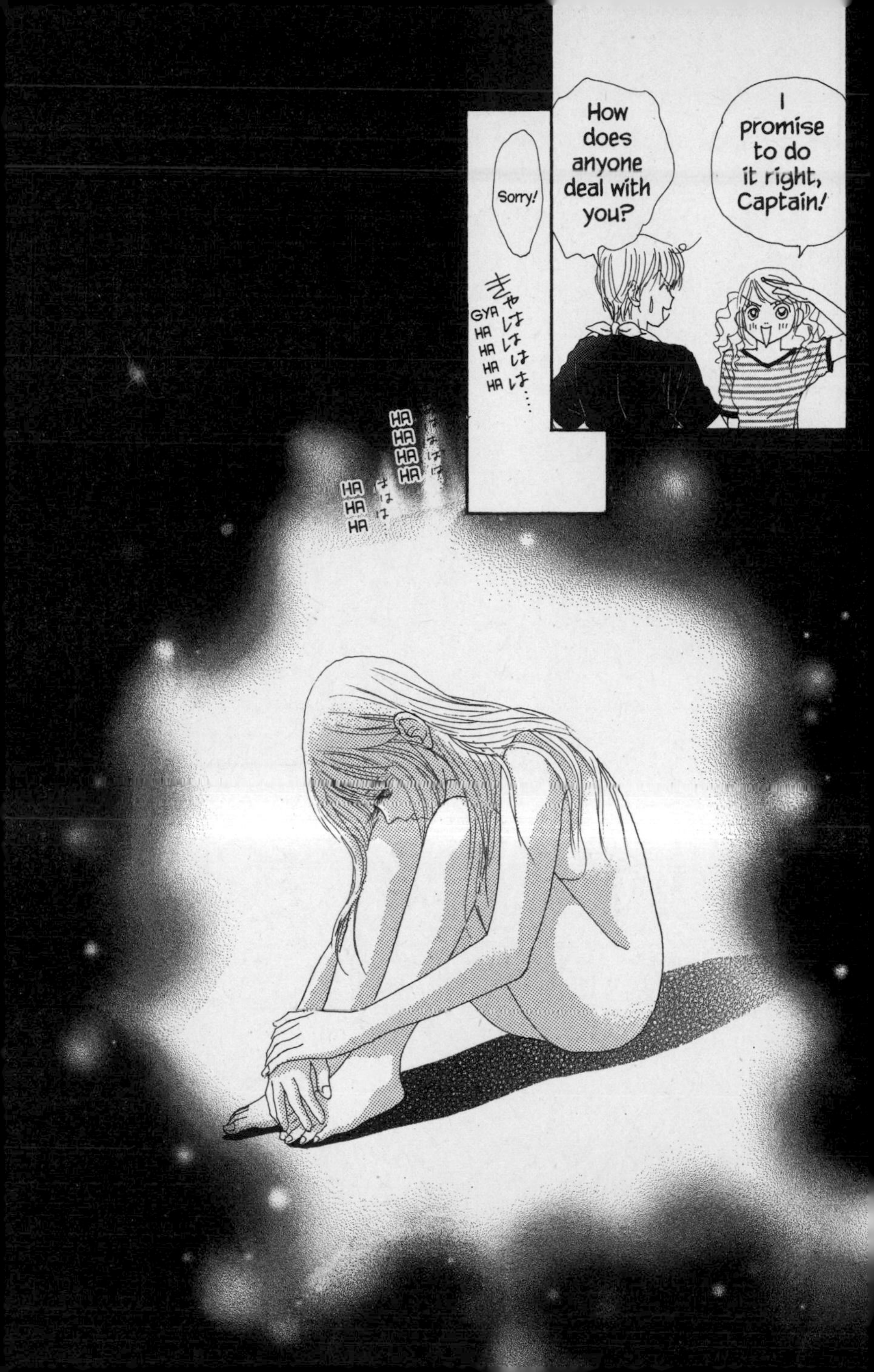

I promise to do it right, Captain!
How does anyone deal with you?
Sorry!
GYA HA HA HA HA
HA HA HA HA
HA HA HA

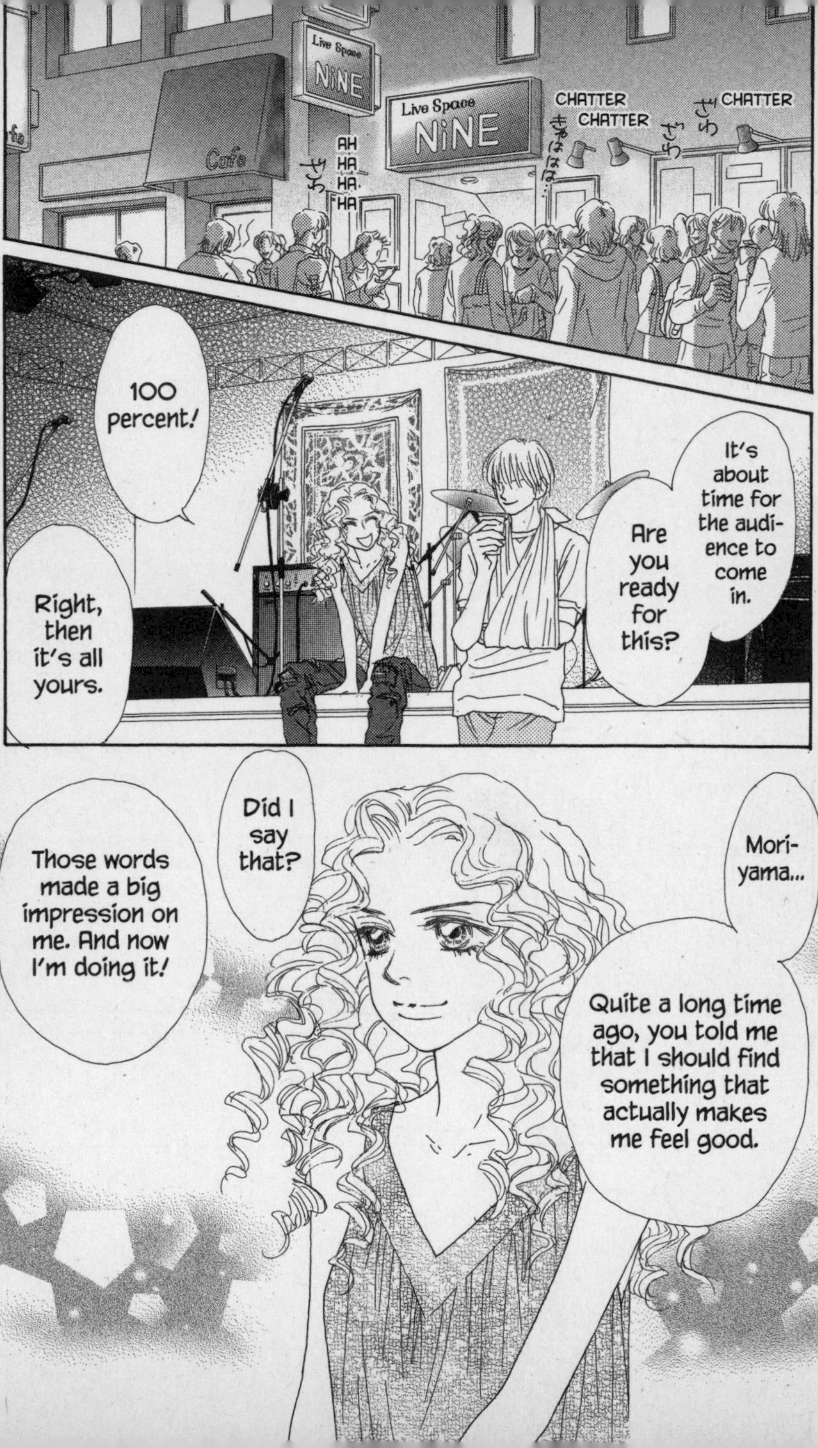
CHATTER
ざわ ざわ
CHATTER CHATTER
きゃははは…
Live Space NiNE
Live Space NiNE
AH HA HA HA
Cafe
It's about time for the audience to come in.
Are you ready for this?
100 percent!
Right, then it's all yours.
Mori-yama...
Quite a long time ago, you told me that I should find something that actually makes me feel good.
Did I say that?
Those words made a big impression on me. And now I'm doing it!

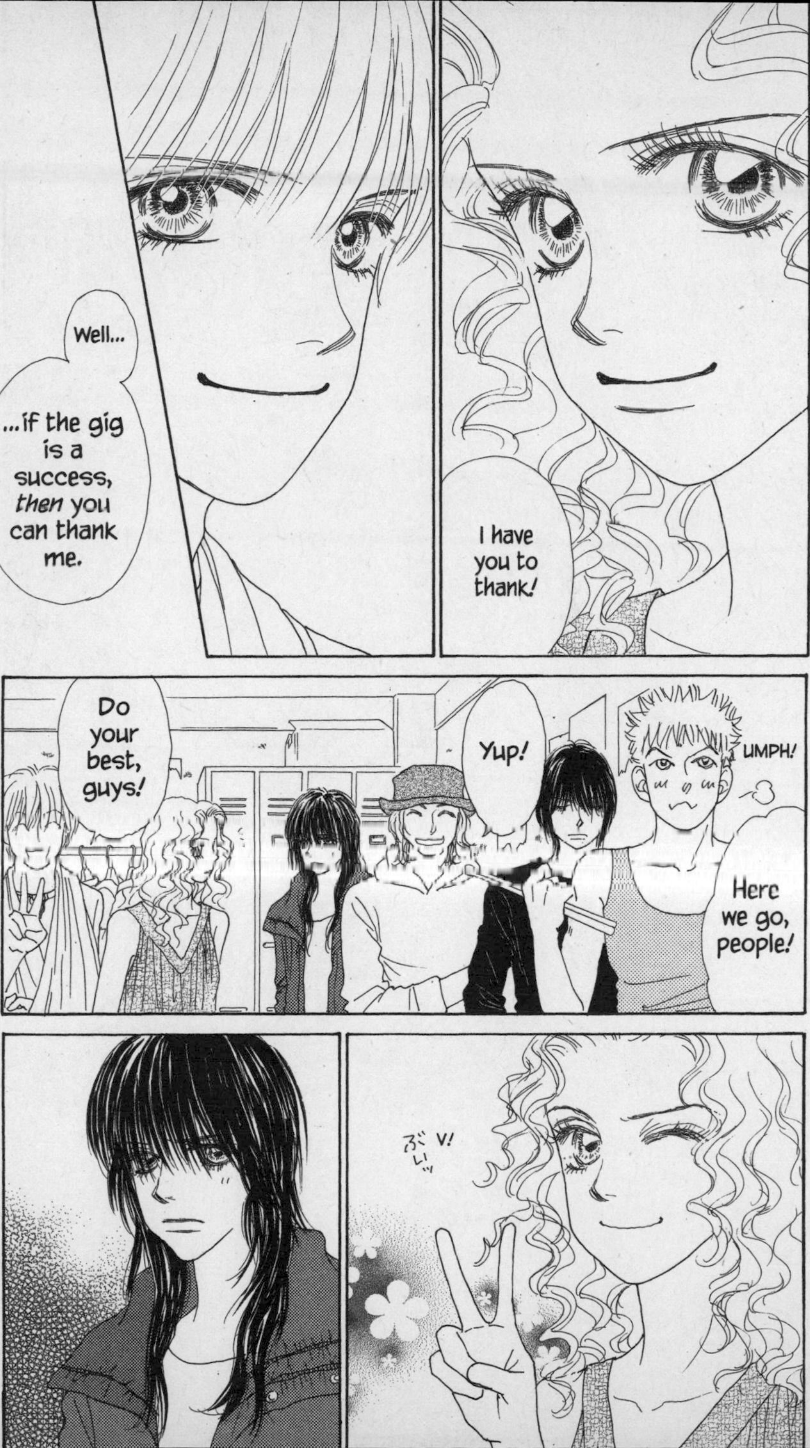
I have you to thank!
Well...
...if the gig is a success, *then* you can thank me.
Here we go, people!
UMPH!
Yup!
Do your best, guys!
ぶぃッ
V!

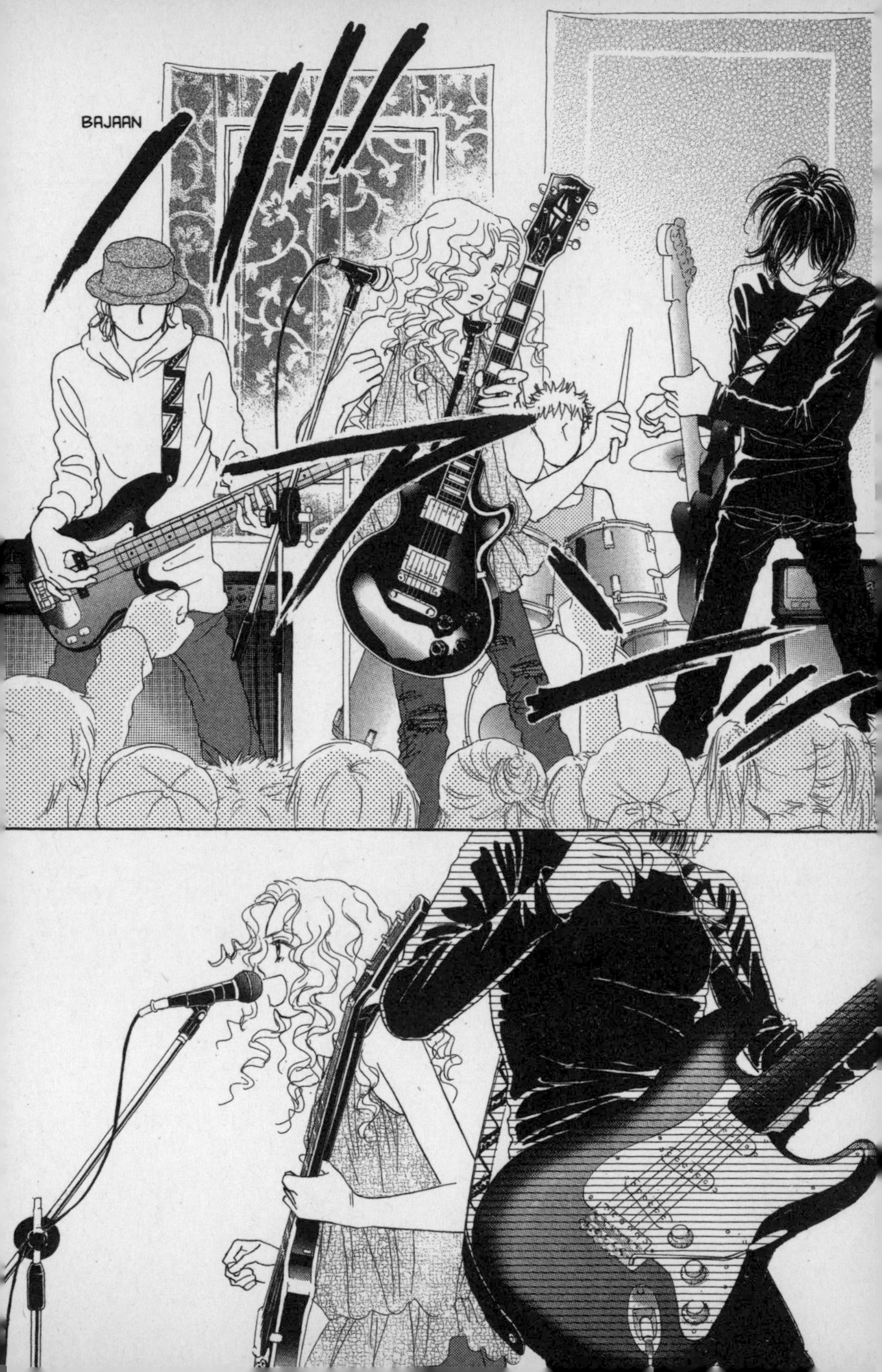
BAJAAN

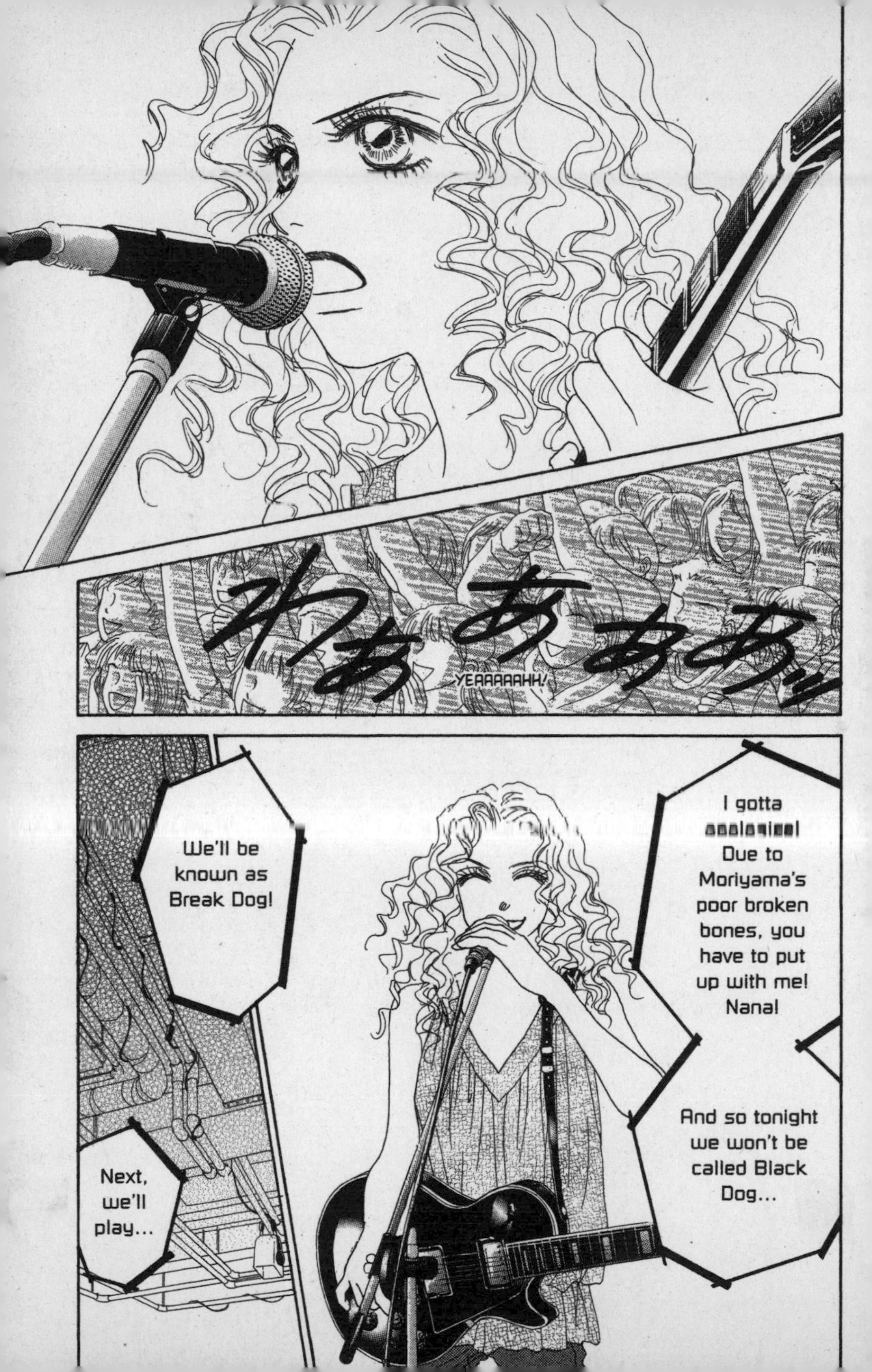
わあああッ
YEAAAAAH!
I gotta apologize! Due to Moriyama's poor broken bones, you have to put up with me! Nana!
And so tonight we won't be called Black Dog...
We'll be known as Break Dog!
Next, we'll play...

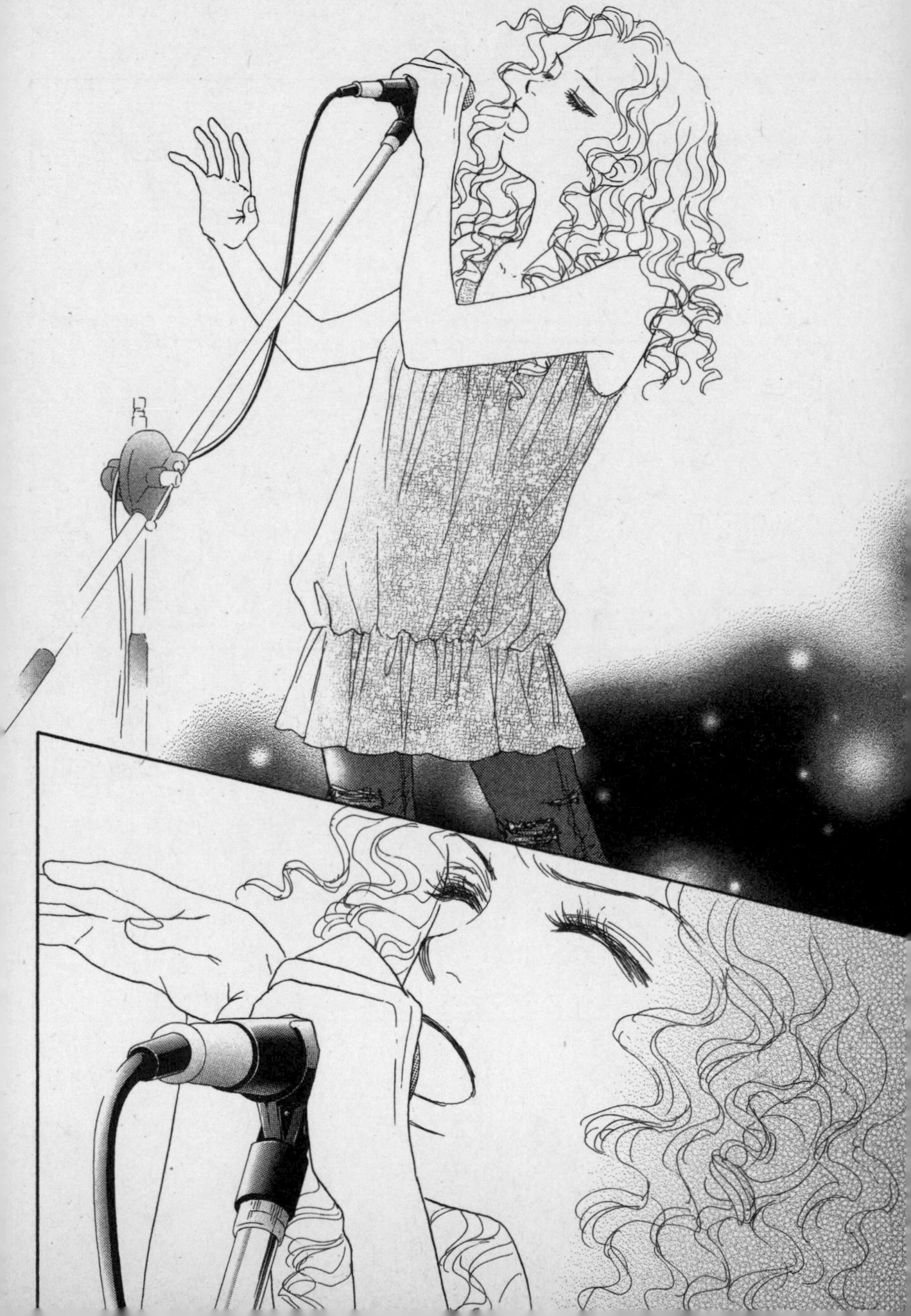

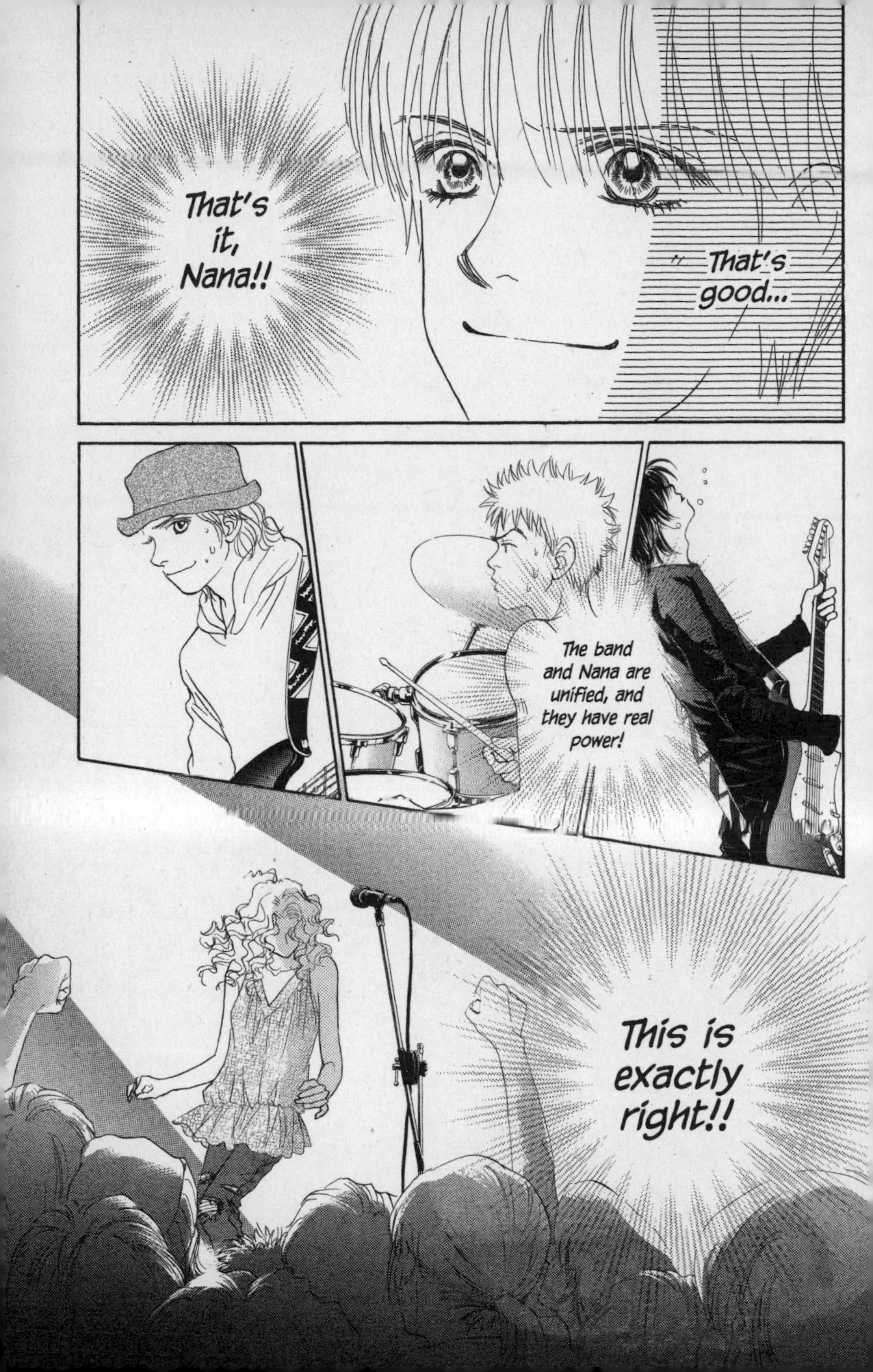

That's good...
That's it, Nana!!
The band and Nana are unified, and they have real power!
This is exactly right!!

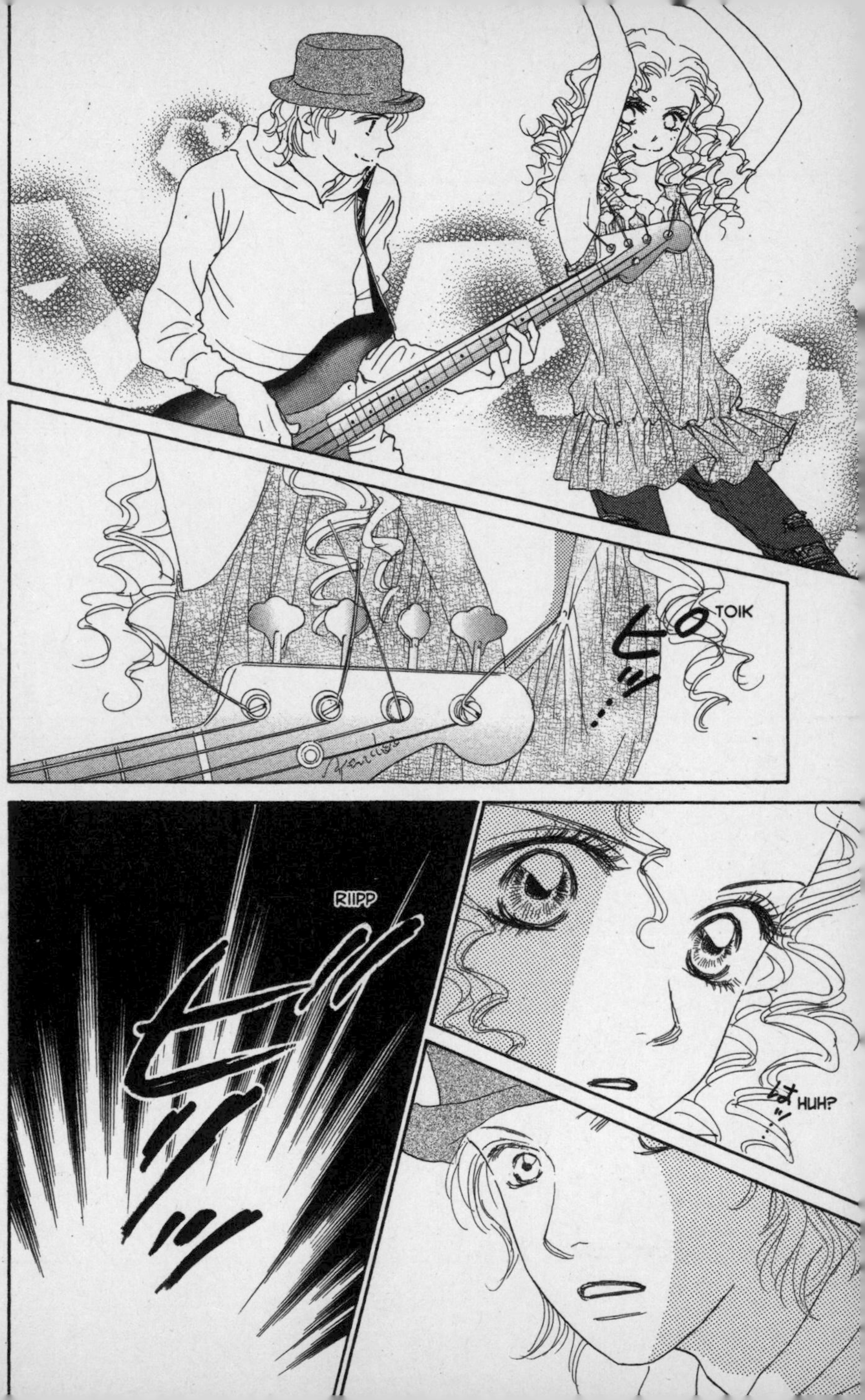
TOIK
HUH?
RIIPP

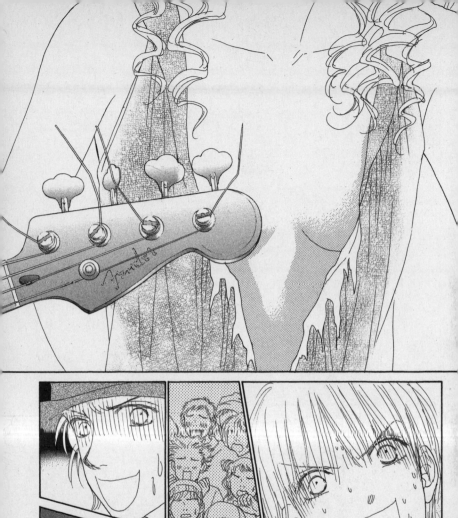

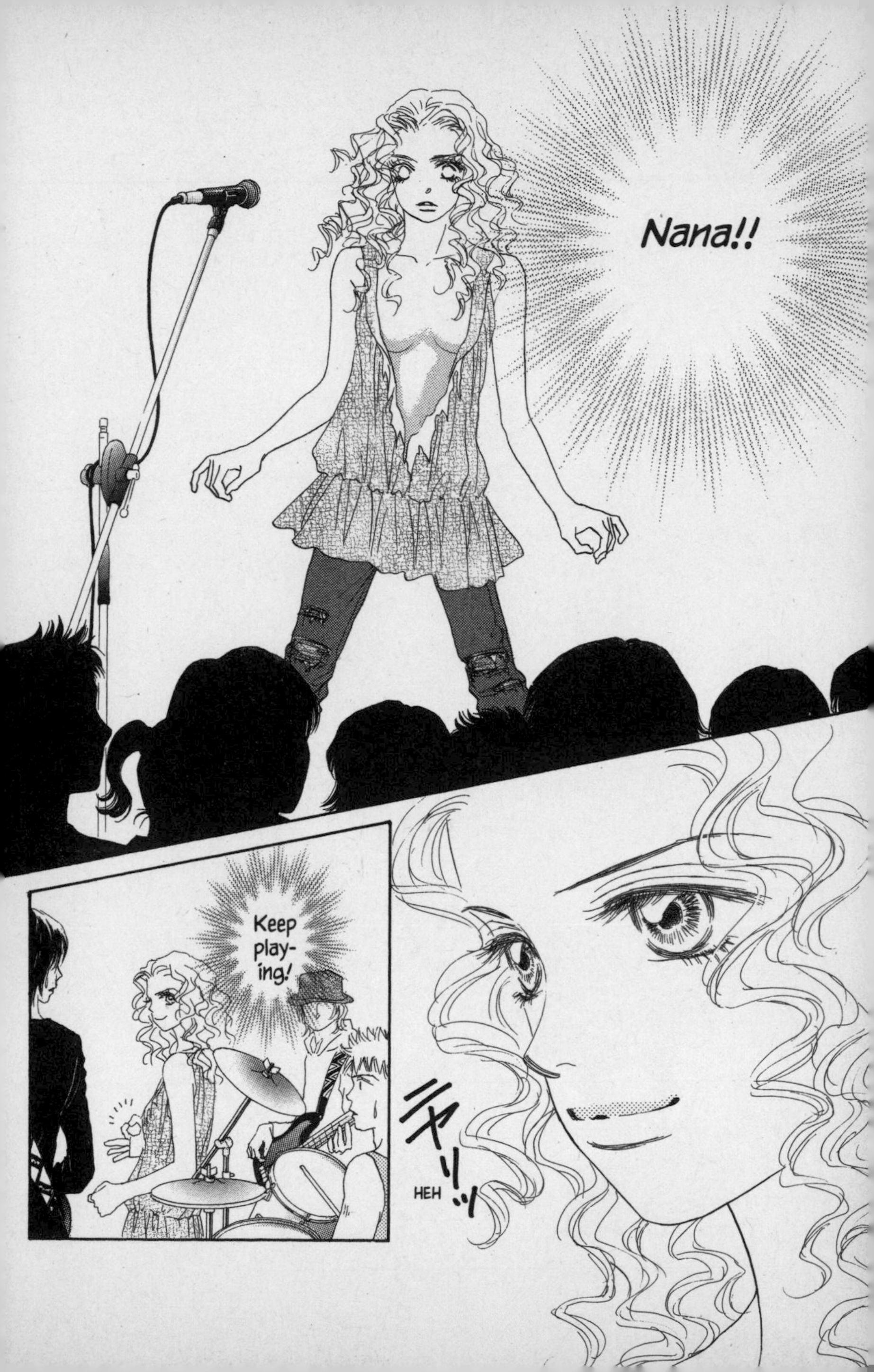
Nana!!
ニヤリッ
HEH
Keep playing!

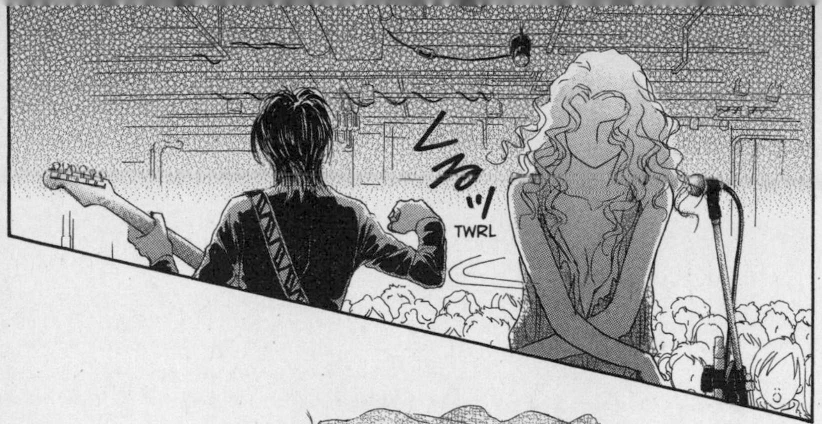
TWRL
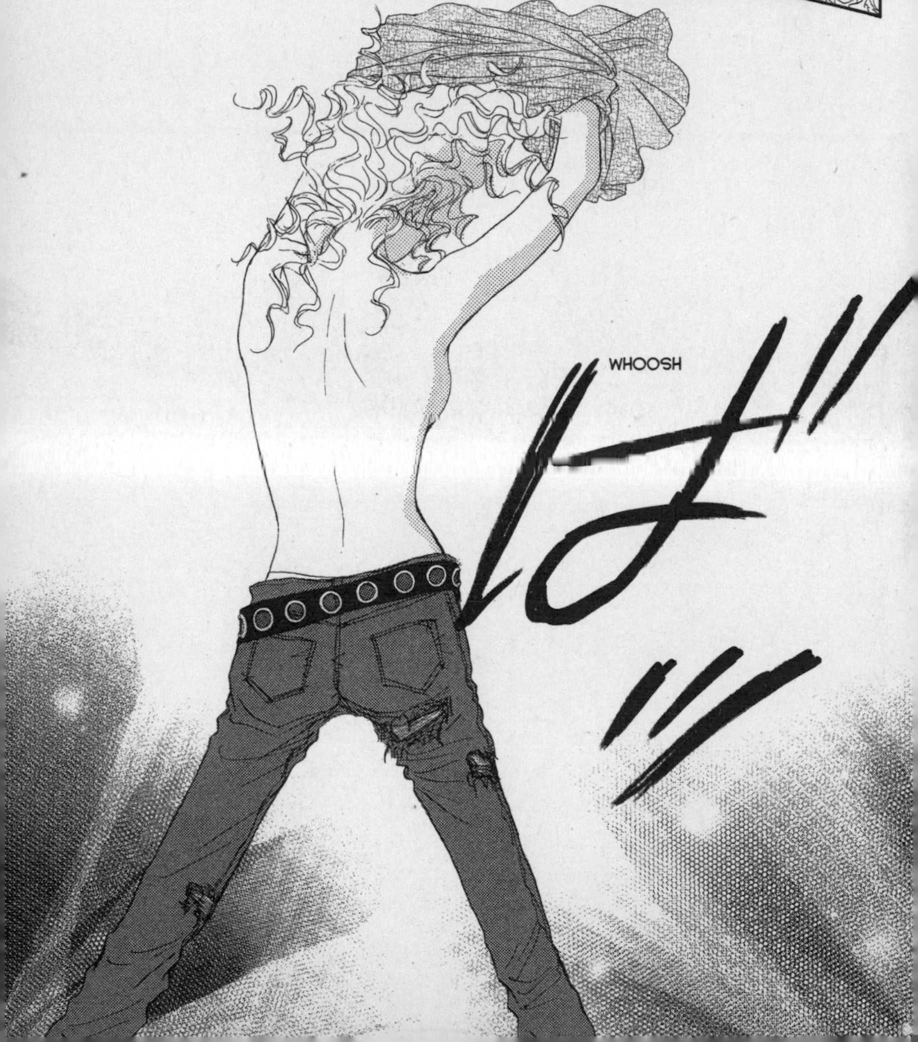
WHOOSH

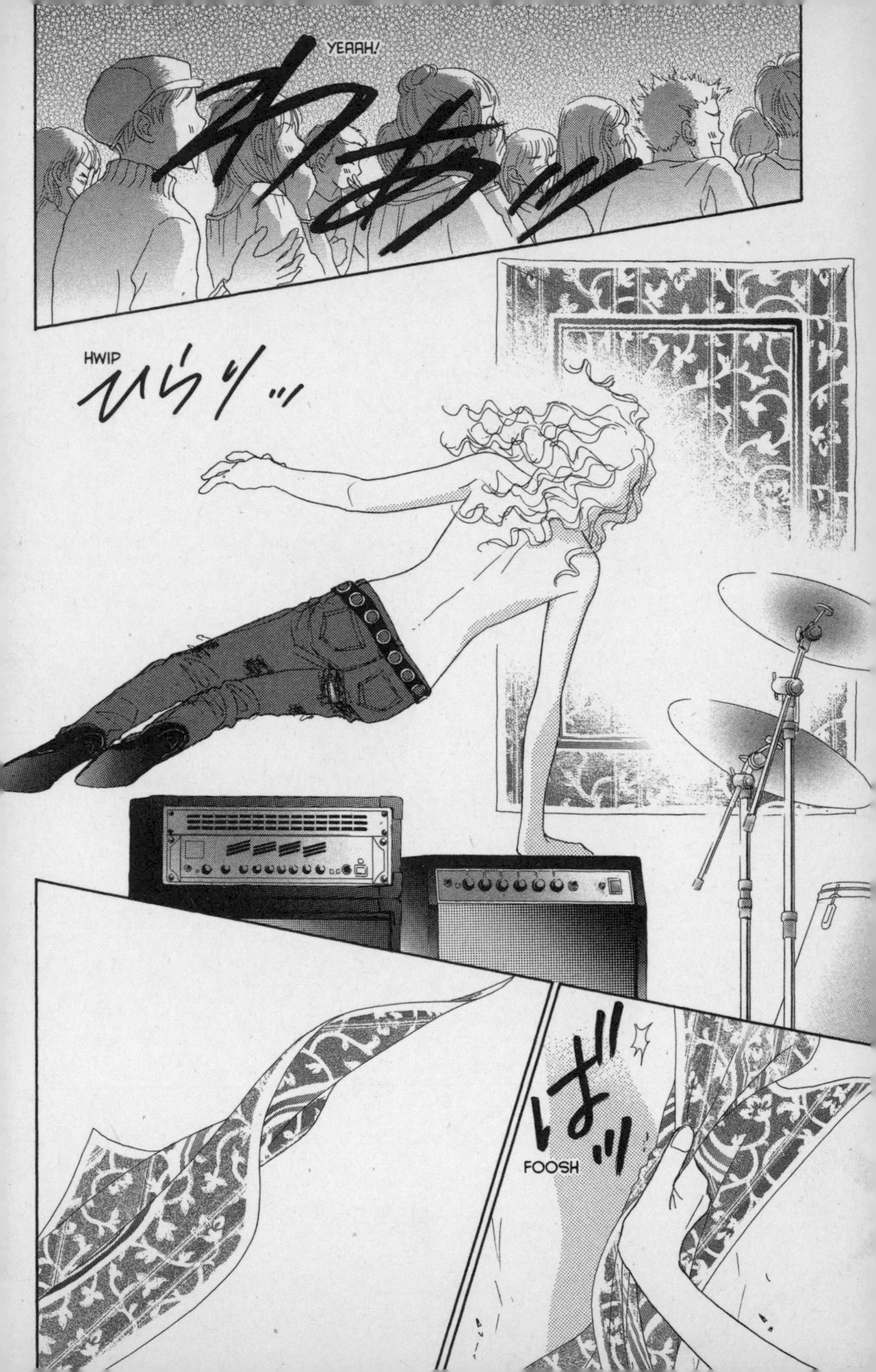
YEAAH!
HWIP
ひらりッ
ばッ
FOOSH

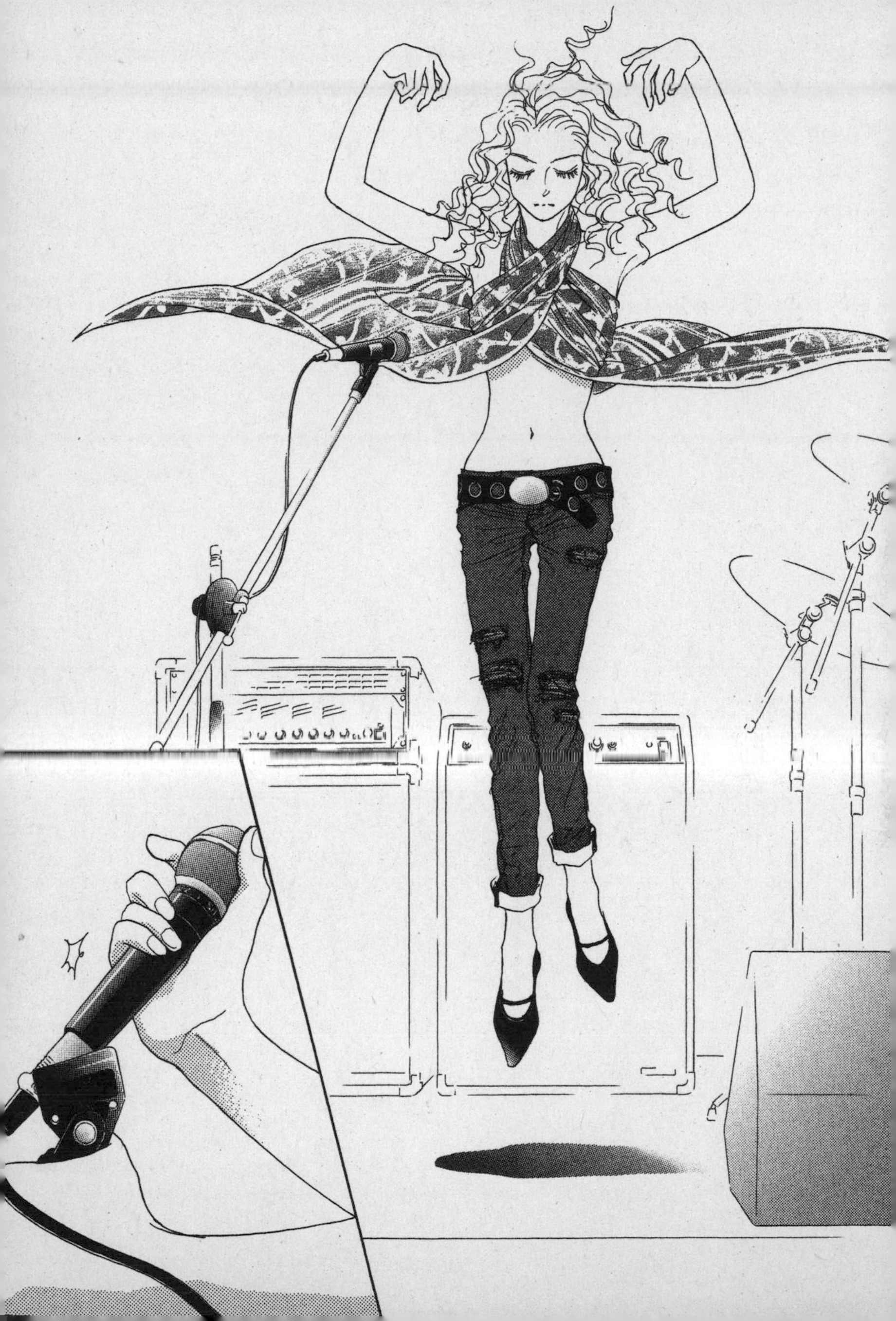

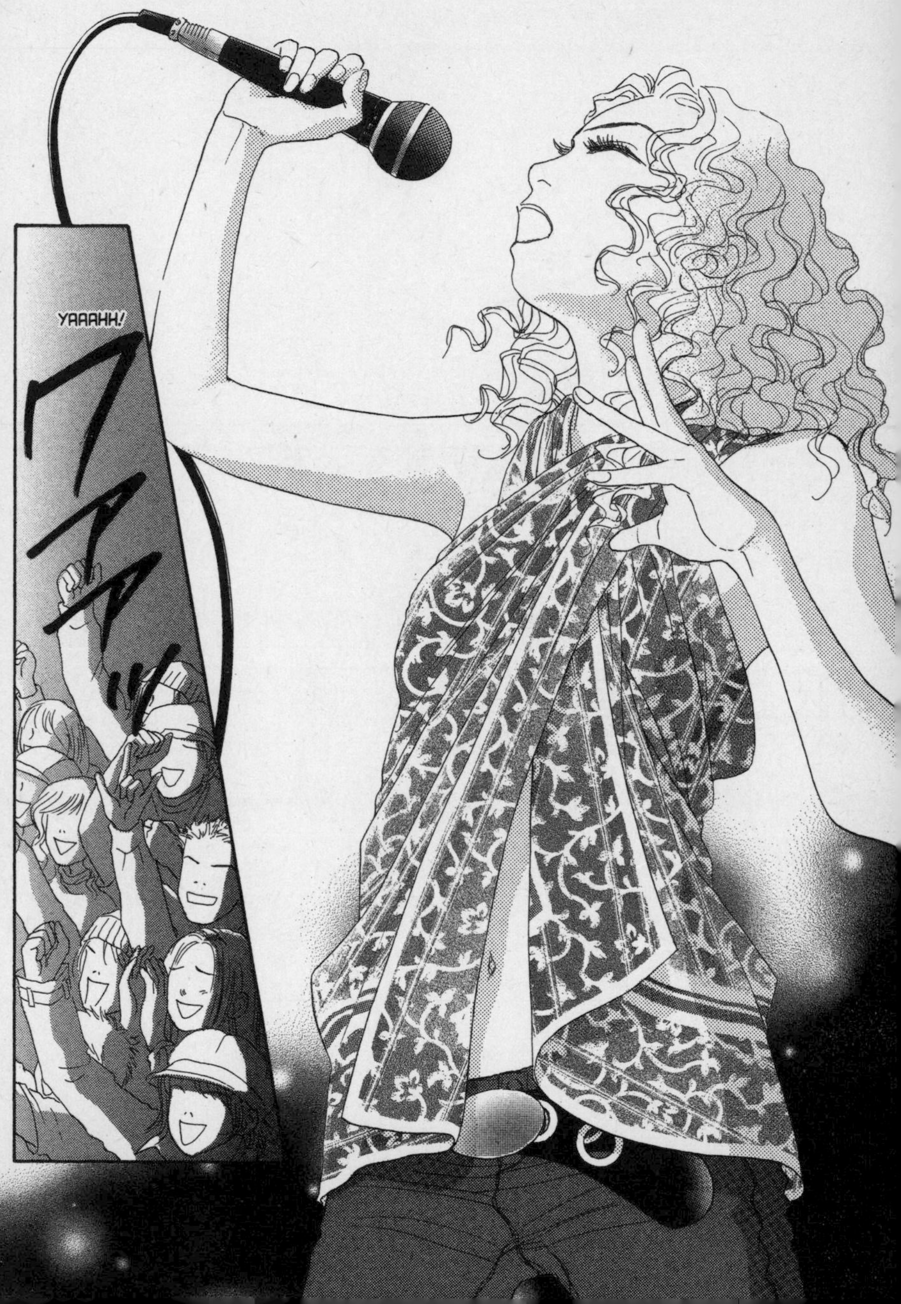
YAAAHH!

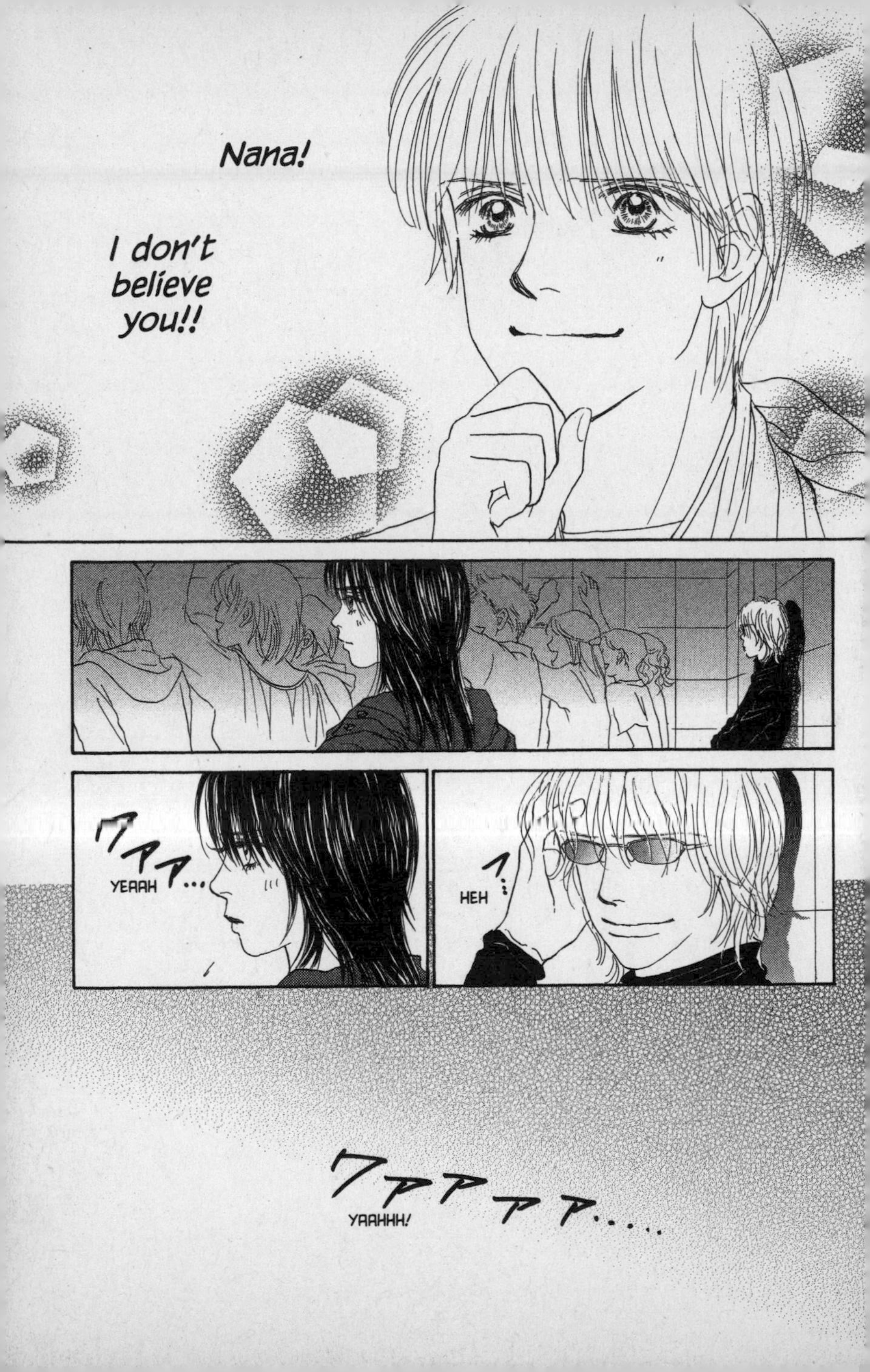
Nana!
I don't believe you!!
フ…
HEH
ワァァ…
YEAAH
ワァァァァァ….
YAAHHH!

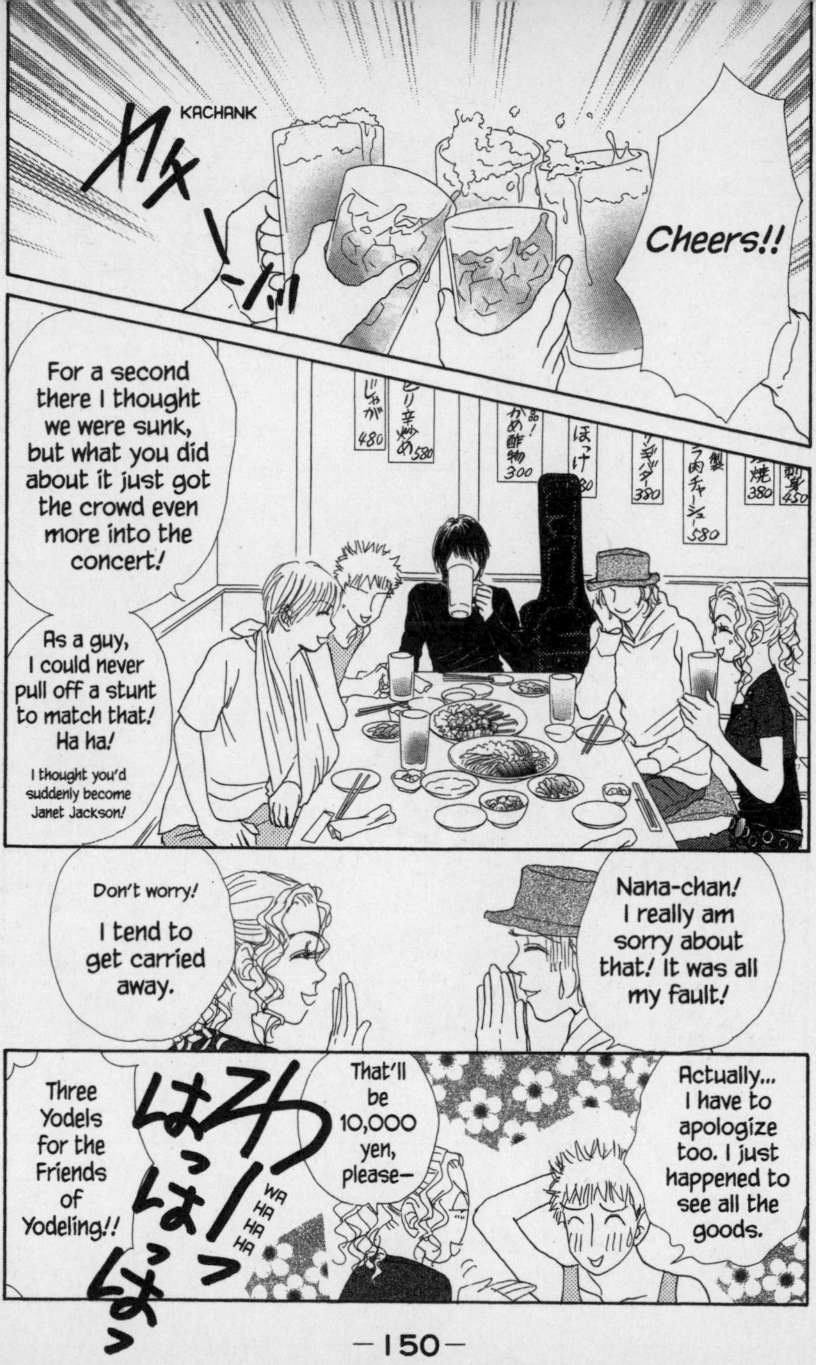
Cheers!!
KACHANK
For a second there I thought we were sunk, but what you did about it just got the crowd even more into the concert!
As a guy, I could never pull off a stunt to match that! Ha ha!
I thought you'd suddenly become Janet Jackson!
Nana-chan! I really am sorry about that! It was all my fault!
Don't worry!
I tend to get carried away.
Actually... I have to apologize too. I just happened to see all the goods.
That'll be 10,000 yen, please—
Three Yodels for the Friends of Yodeling!!
WA HA HA HA

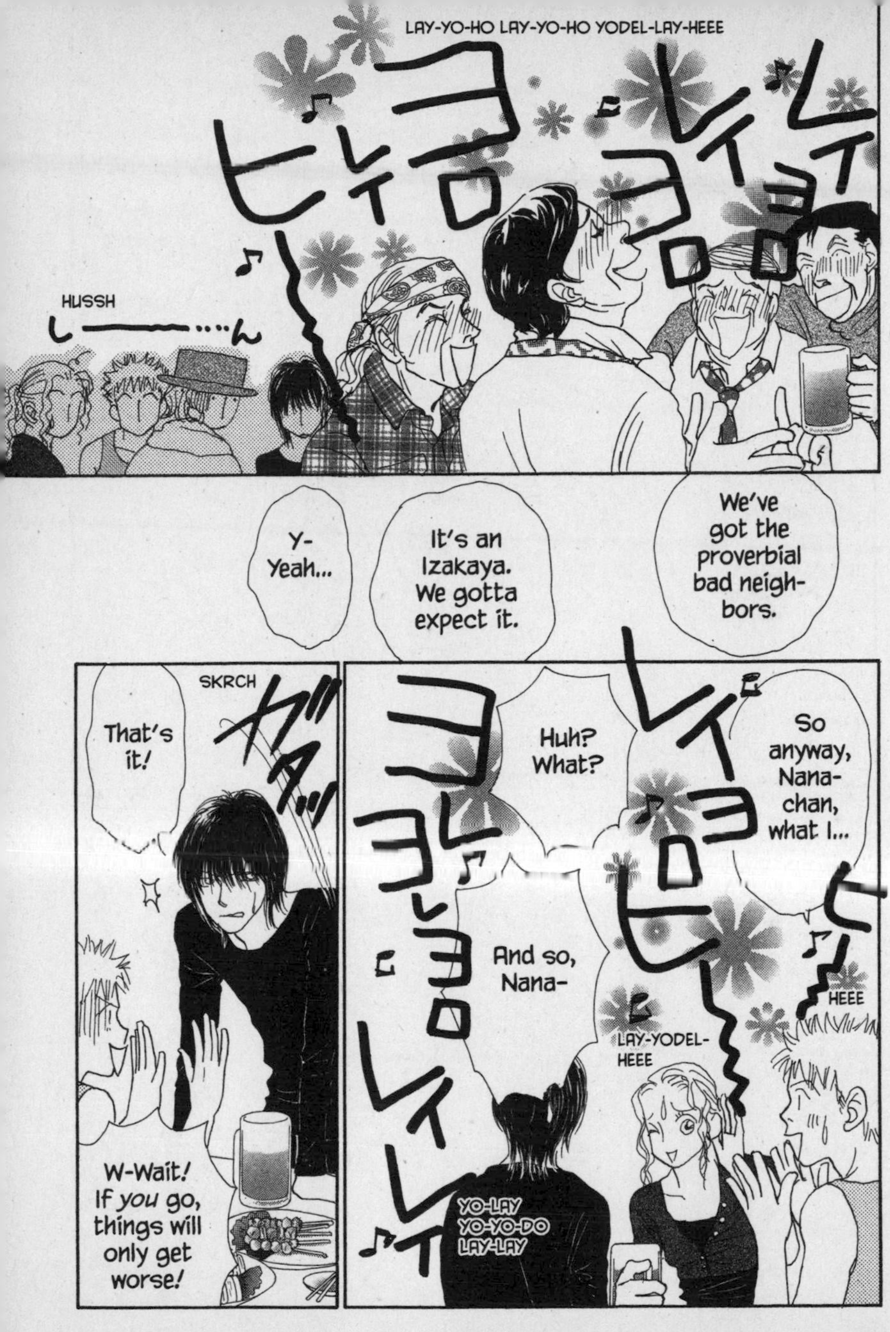
LAY-YO-HO LAY-YO-HO YODEL-LAY-HEEE
HUSSH
しーーー…ん
We've got the proverbial bad neighbors.
It's an Izakaya. We gotta expect it.
Y-Yeah...
So anyway, Nana-chan, what I...
Huh? What?
HEEE
LAY-YODEL-HEEE
And so, Nana-
YO-LAY YO-YO-DO LAY-LAY
SKRCH
That's it!
W-Wait! If *you* go, things will only get worse!

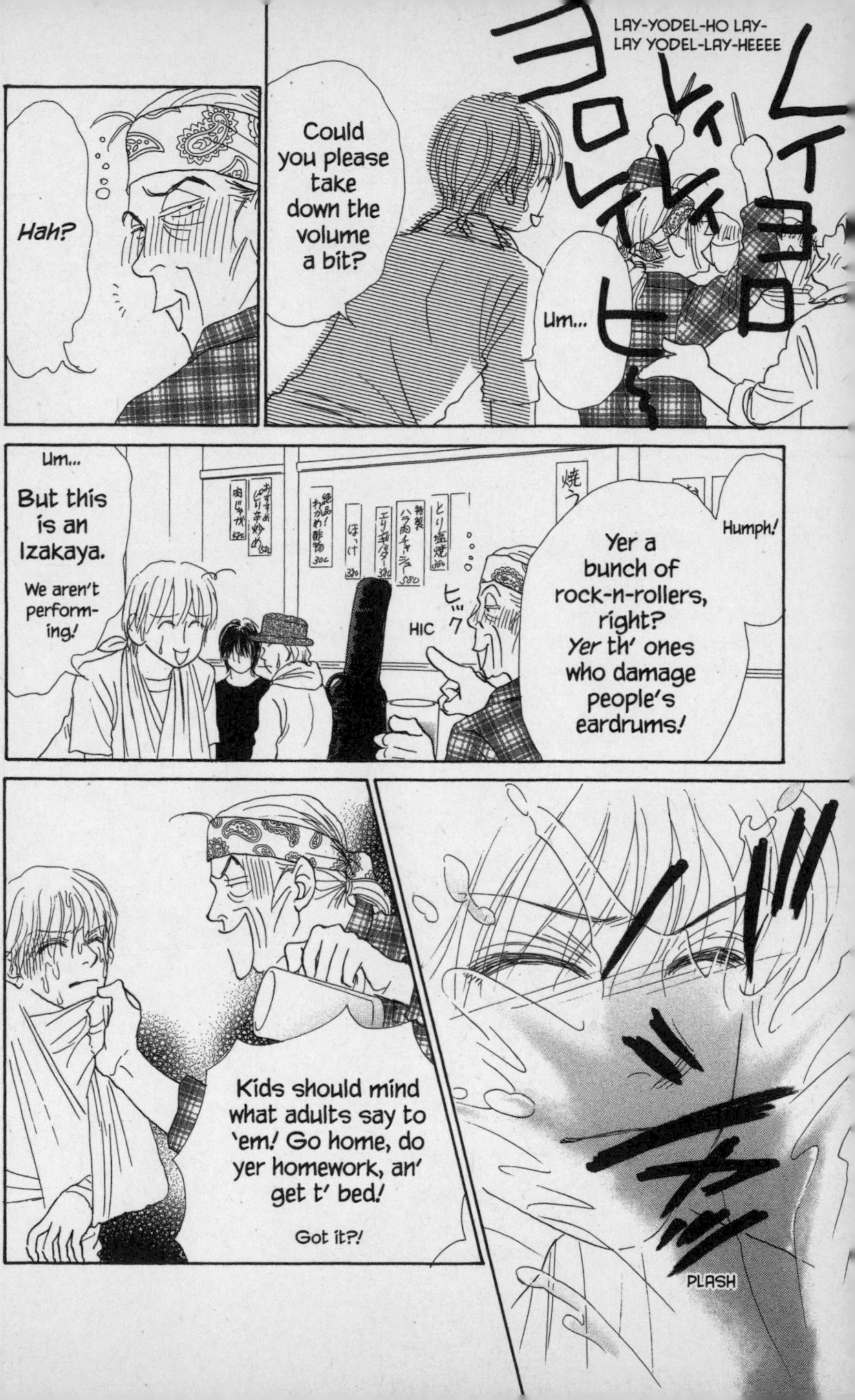
LAY-YODEL-HO LAY-LAY YODEL-LAY-HEEEE
Um...
Could you please take down the volume a bit?
Hah?
Humph!
Yer a bunch of rock-n-rollers, right? Yer th' ones who damage people's eardrums!
HIC
Um...
But this is an Izakaya.
We aren't performing!
PLASH
Kids should mind what adults say to 'em! Go home, do yer homework, an' get t' bed!
Got it?!

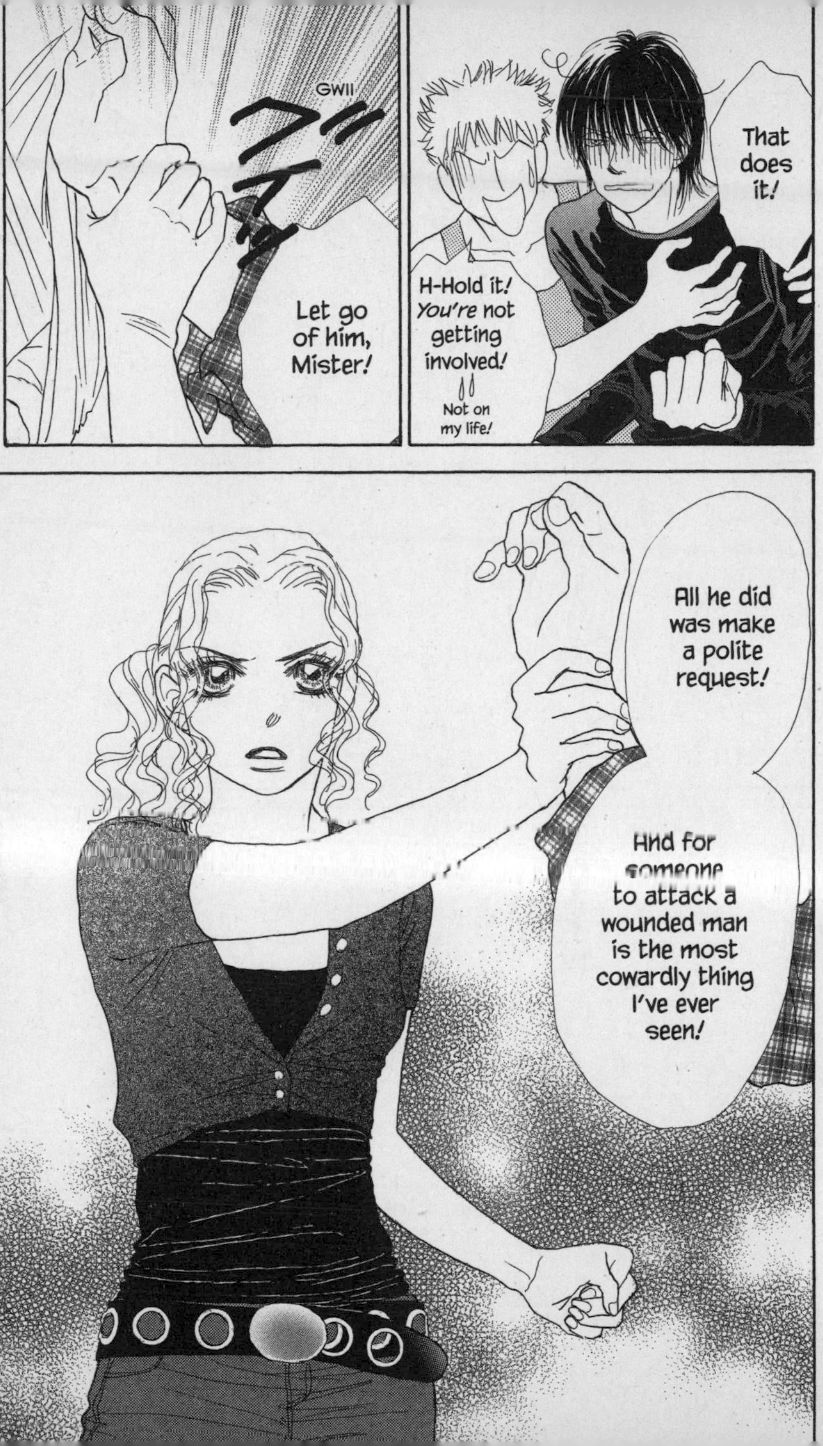
That does it!
H-Hold it! *You're* not getting involved!
Not on my life!
GWII
Let go of him, Mister!
All he did was make a polite request!
And for someone to attack a wounded man is the most cowardly thing I've ever seen!

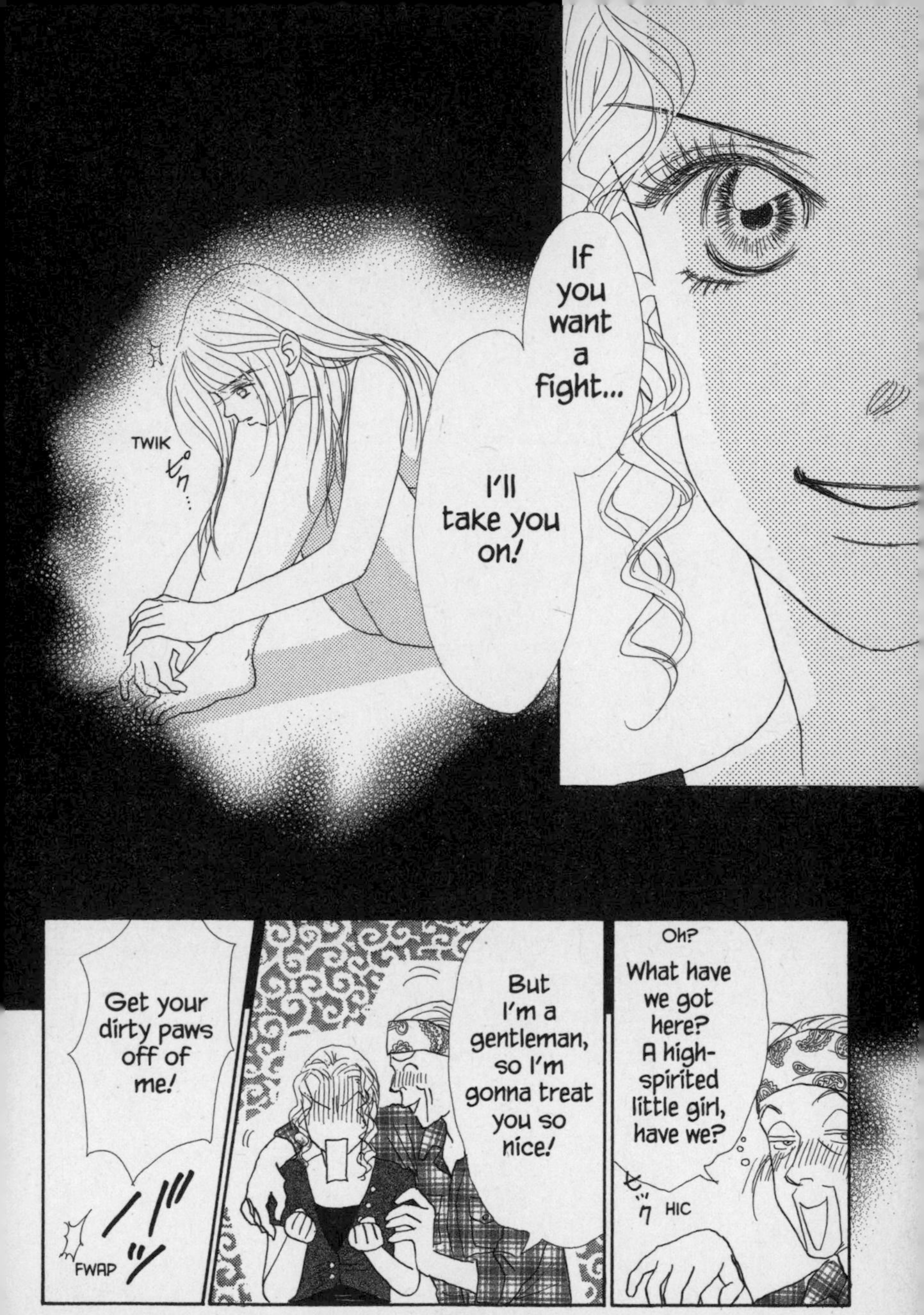

If you want a fight...
I'll take you on!
TWIK
Oh? What have we got here? A high-spirited little girl, have we?
HIC
But I'm a gentleman, so I'm gonna treat you so nice!
Get your dirty paws off of me!
FWAP

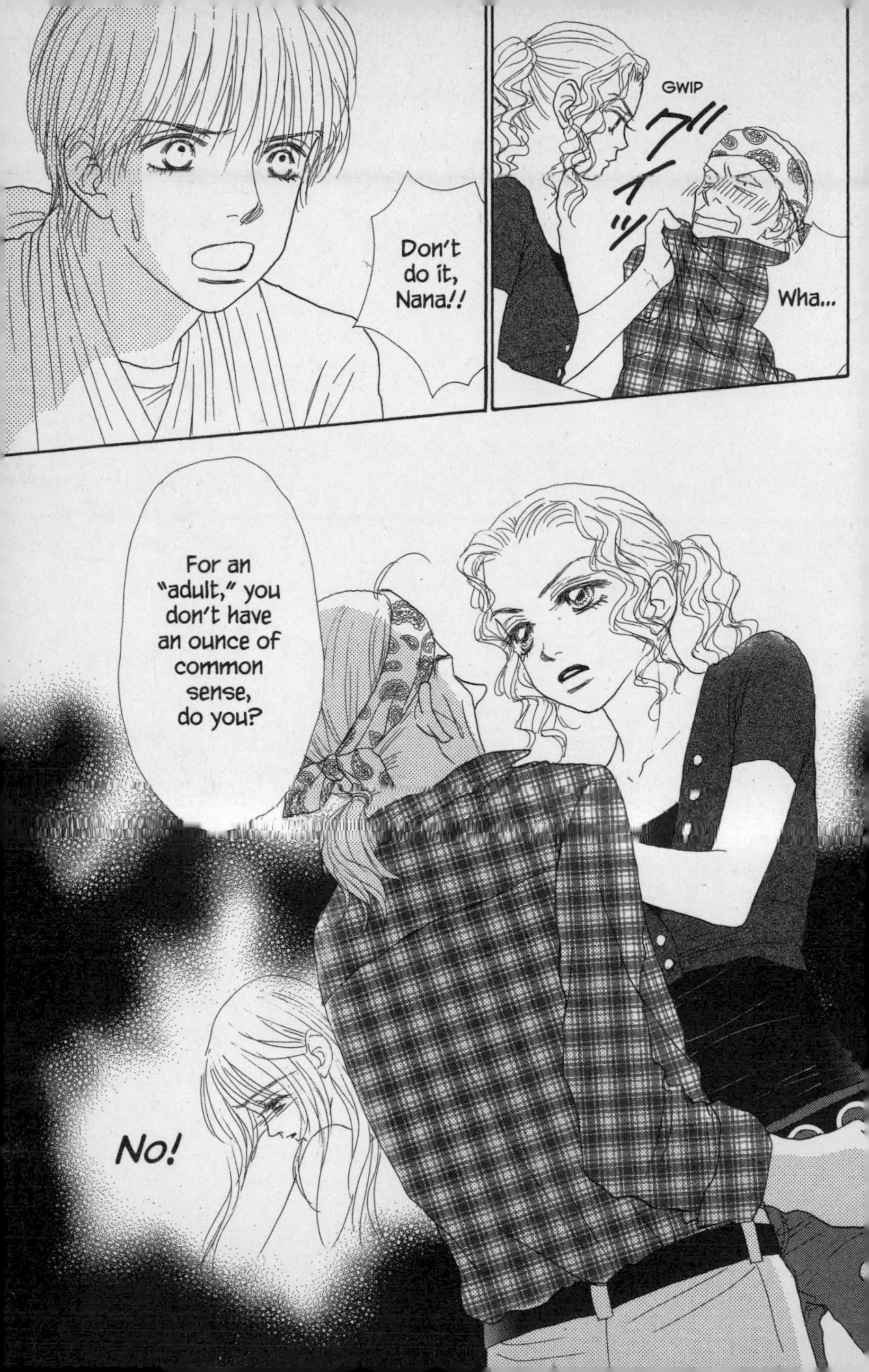
GWIP
グイッ
Wha...
Don't do it, Nana!!
For an "adult," you don't have an ounce of common sense, do you?
No!

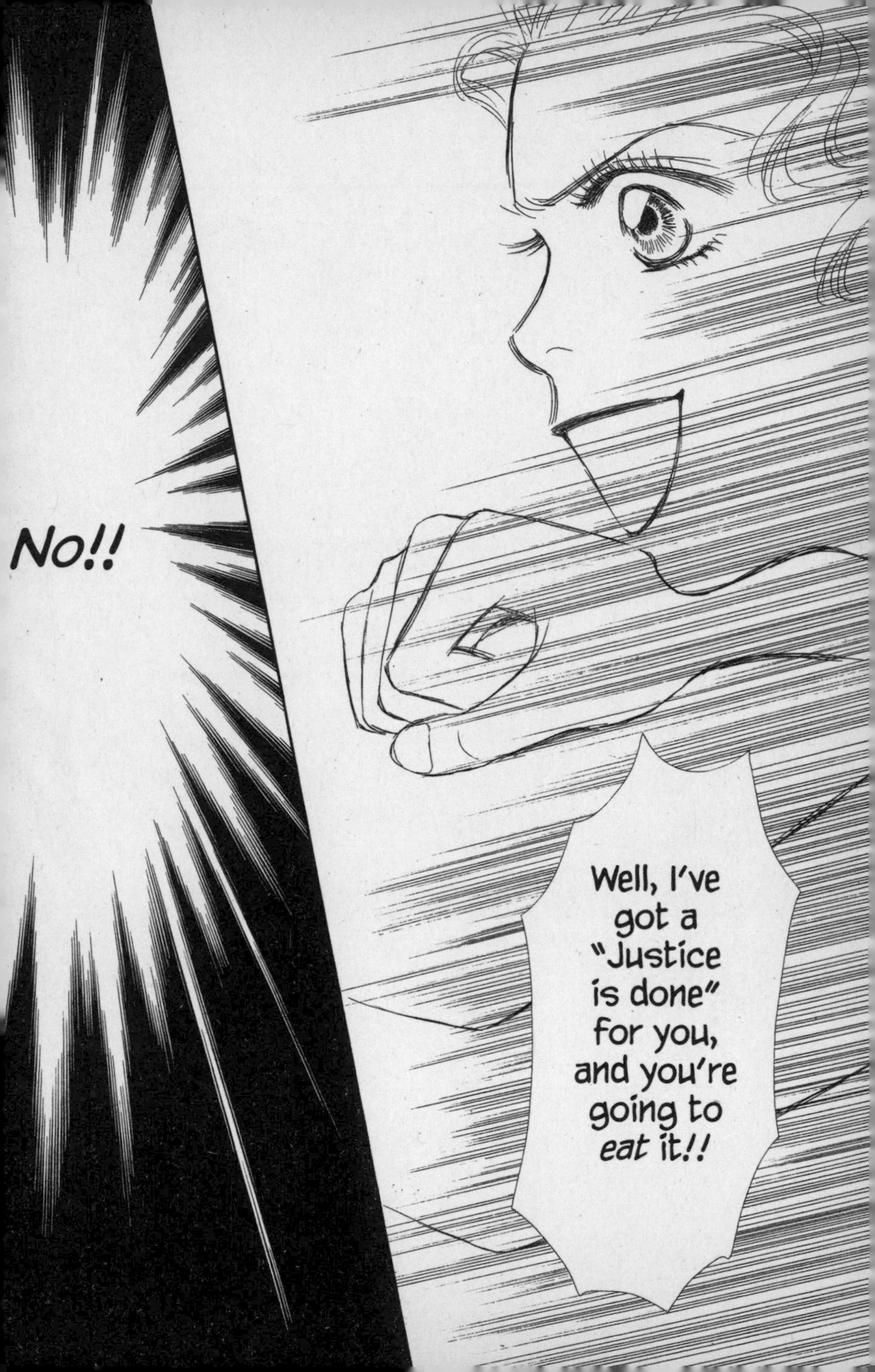
Well, I've got a "Justice is done" for you, and you're going to *eat* it!!
No!!

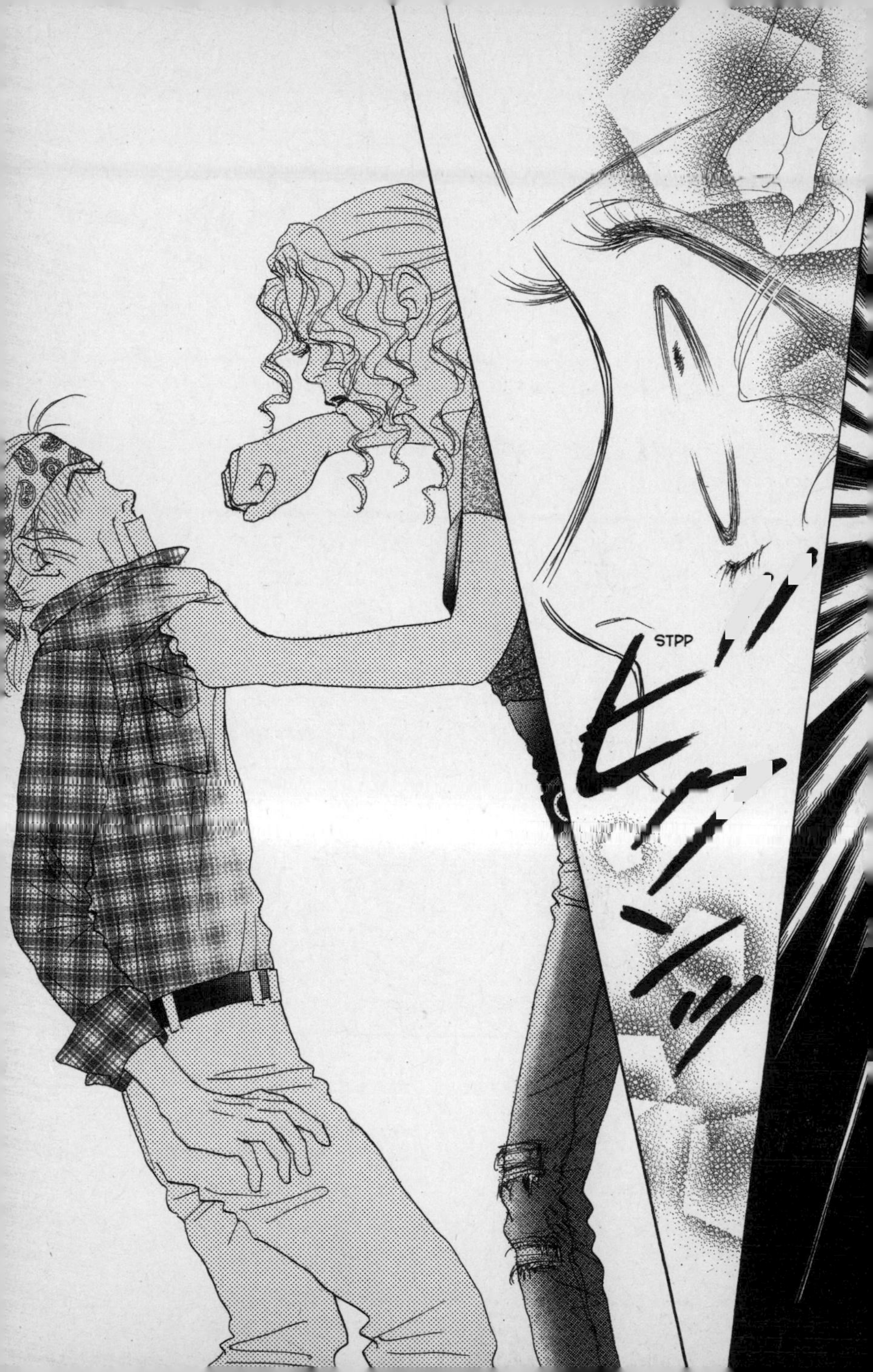
STPP

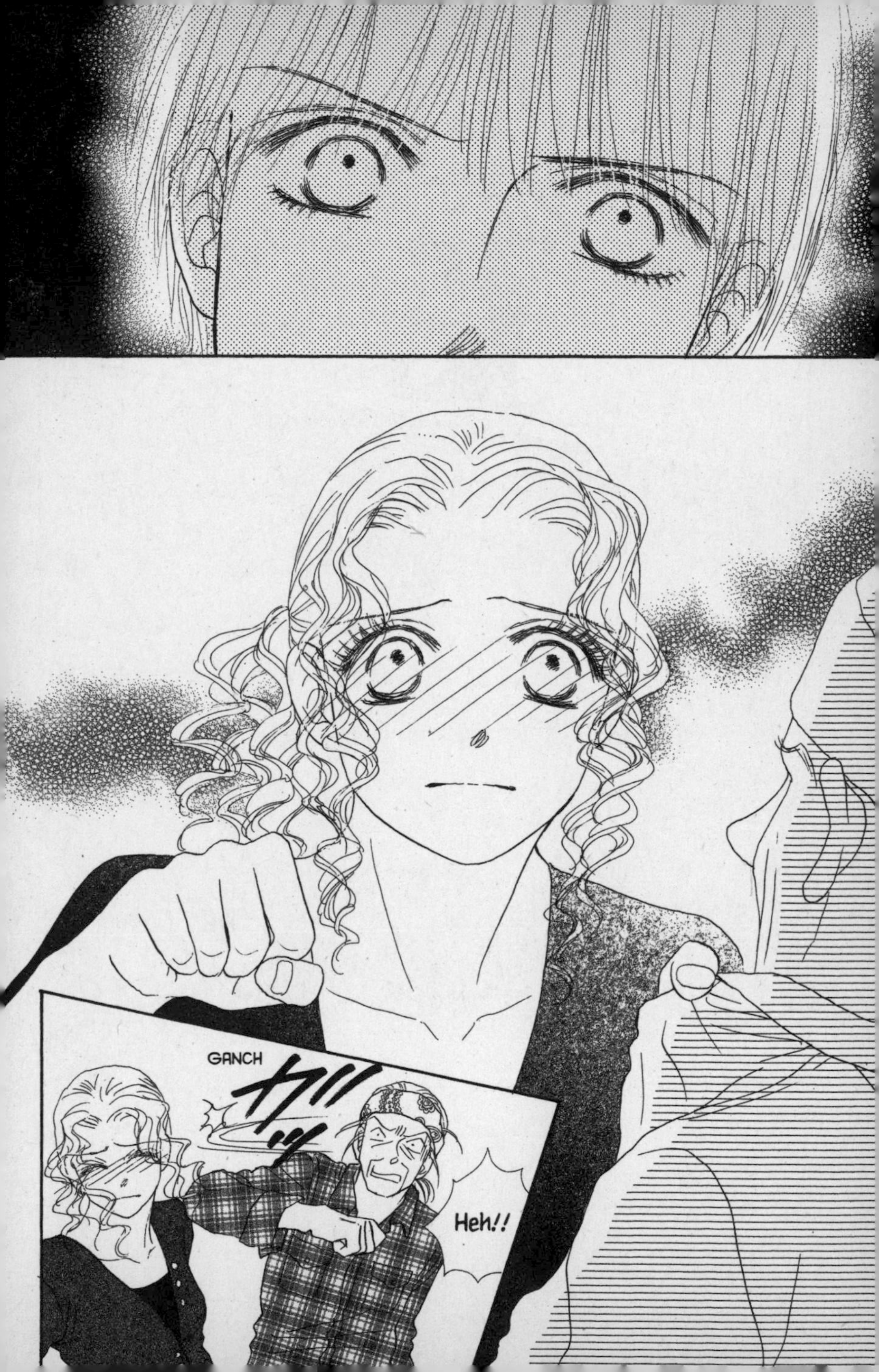
GANCH
Heh!!

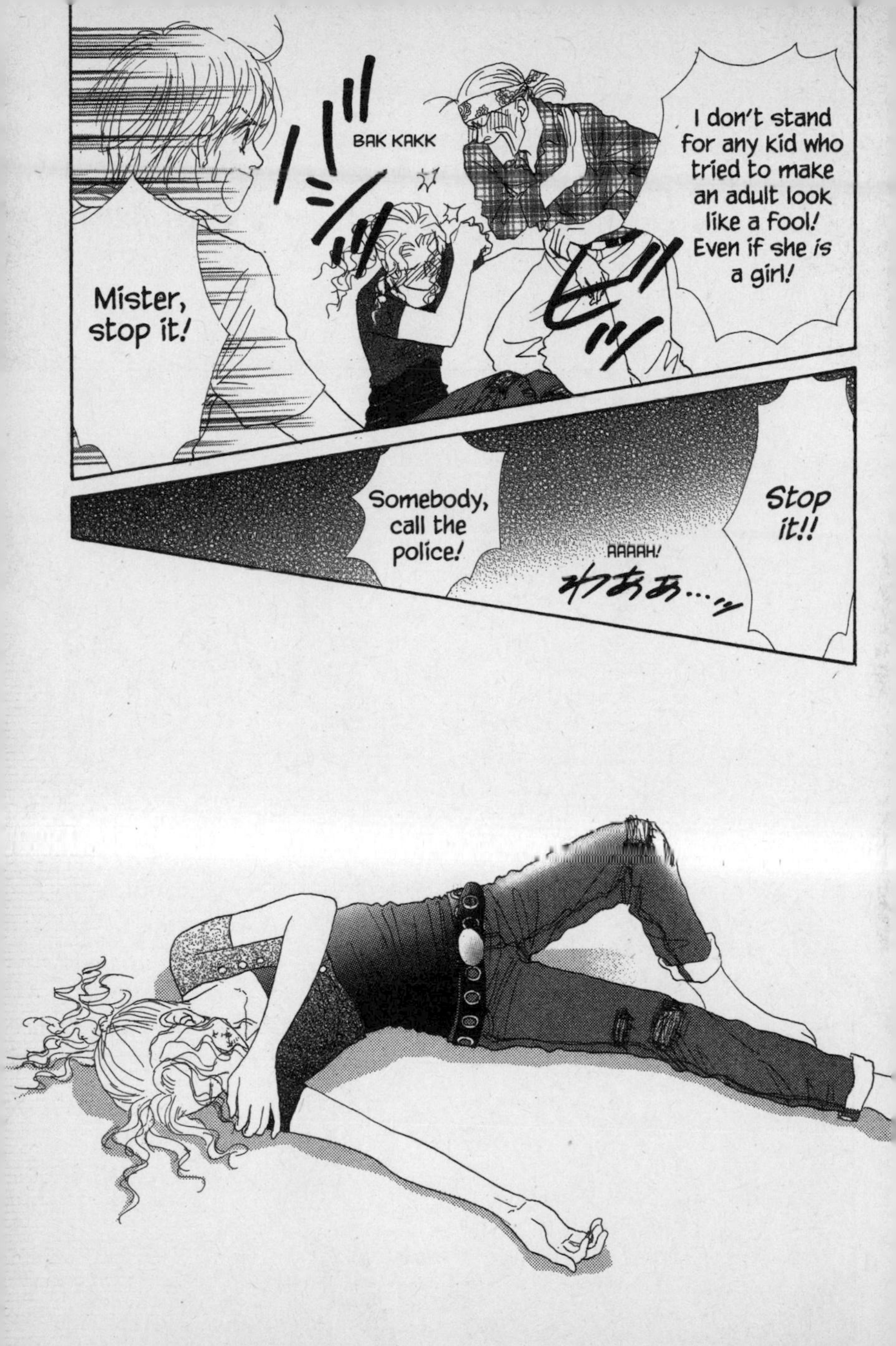
I don't stand for any kid who tried to make an adult look like a fool! Even if she *is* a girl!
BAK KAKK
Mister, stop it!
Stop it!!
AAAAH!
わあぁ…ッ
Somebody, call the police!

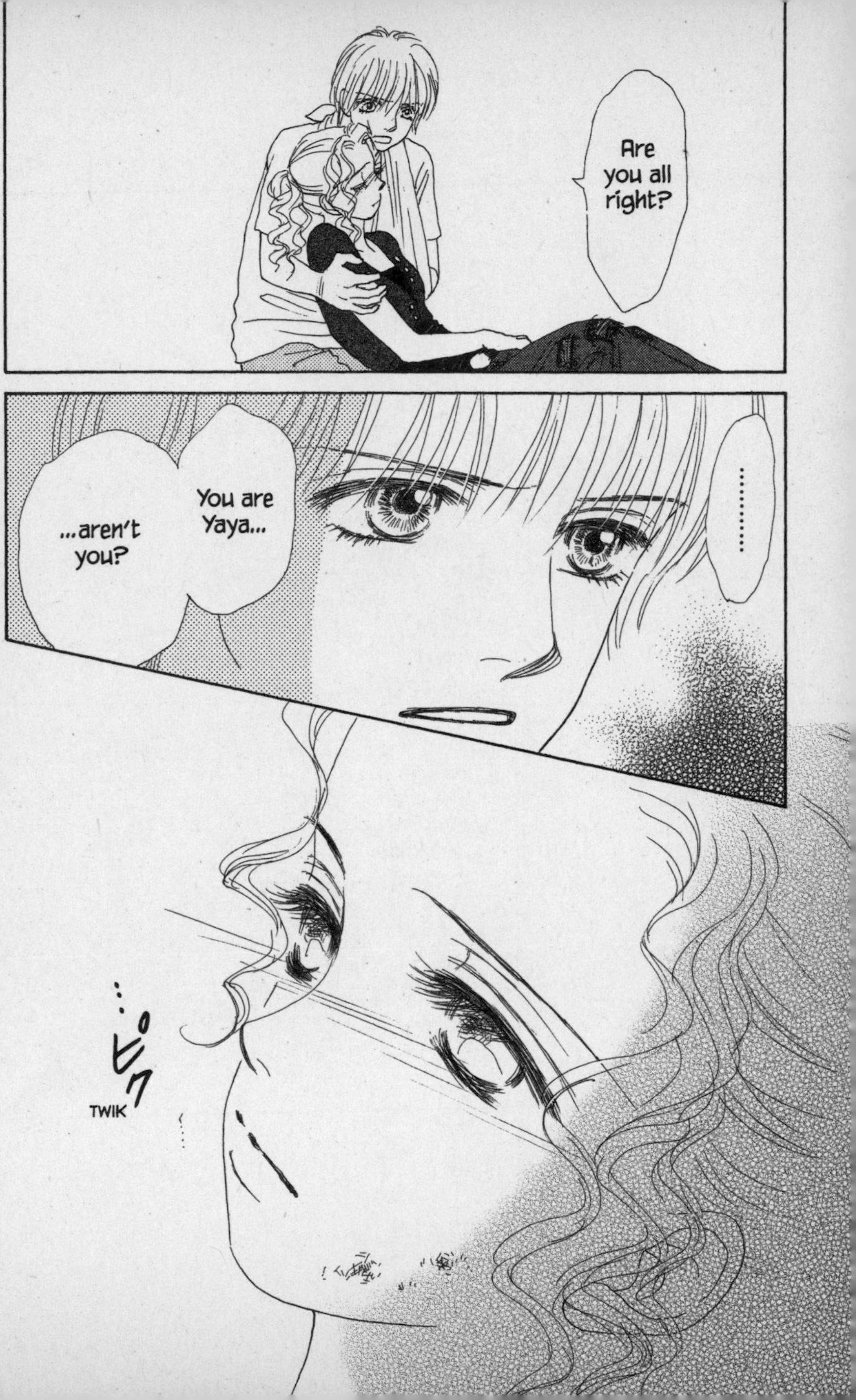
Are you all right?
......
You are Yaya...
...aren't you?
...ピク
TWIK
......

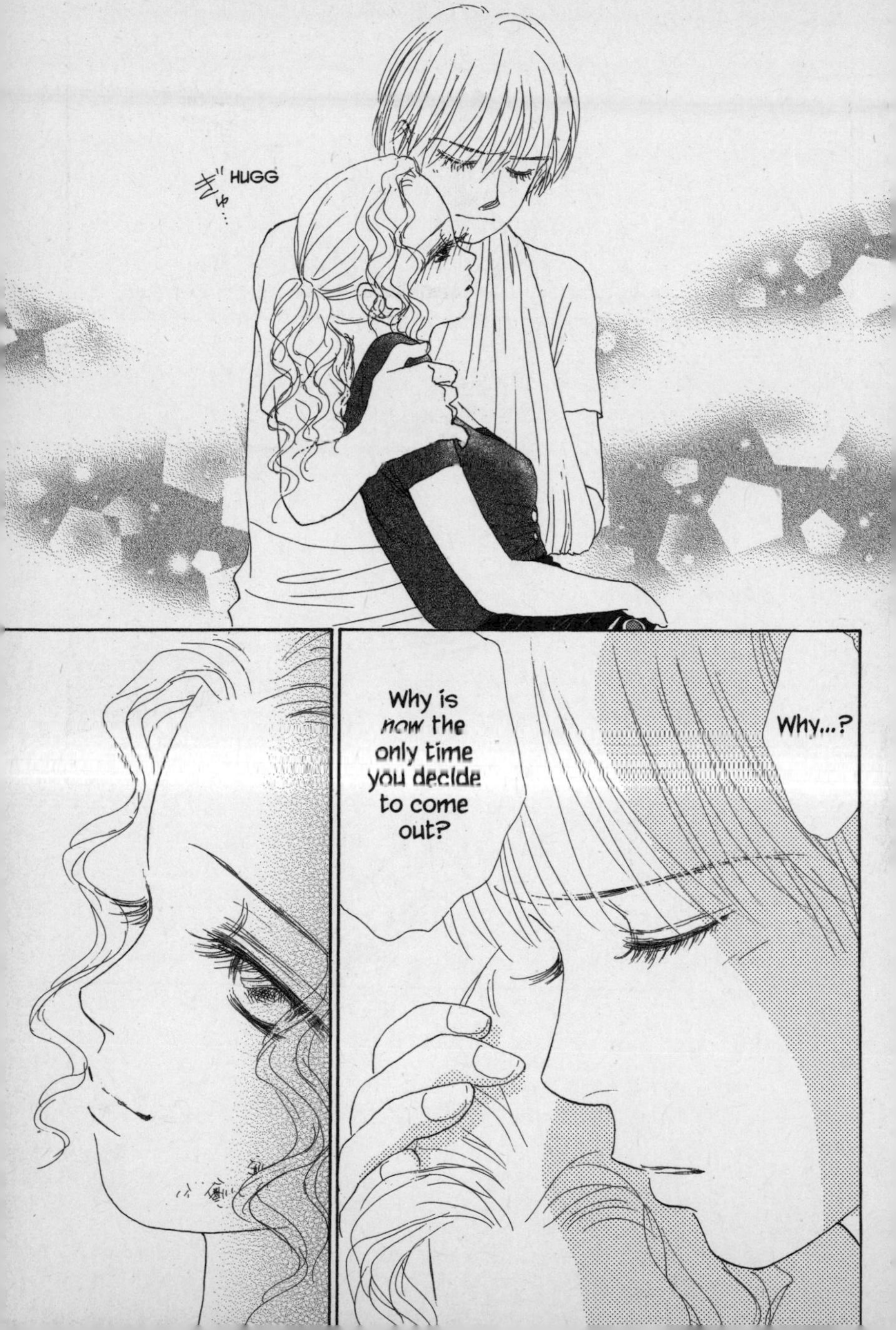
ぎゅ…
HUGG
Why...?
Why is *now* the only time you decide to come out?

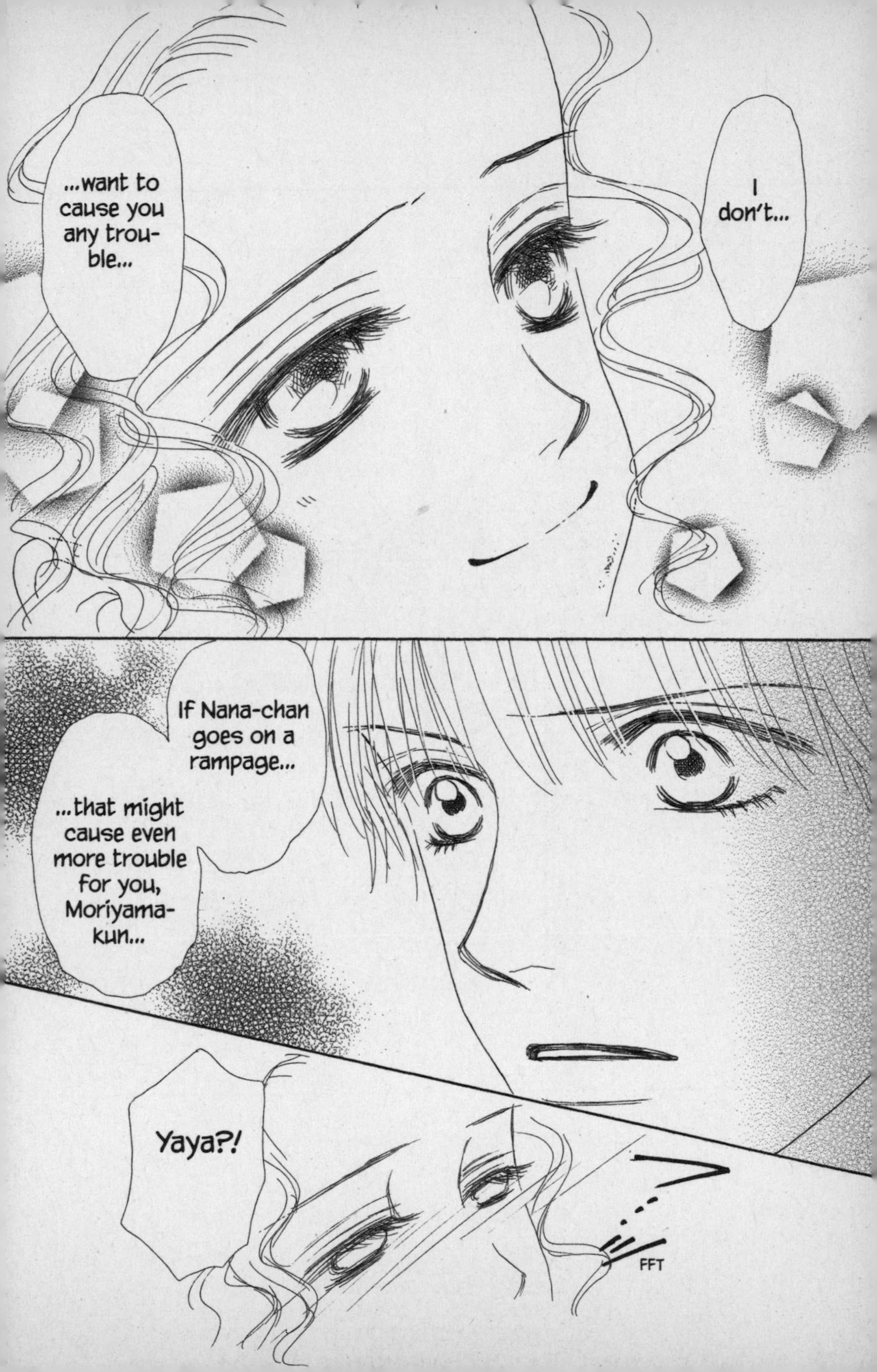
I don't...
...want to cause you any trouble...
If Nana-chan goes on a rampage...
...that might cause even more trouble for you, Moriyama-kun...
Yaya?!
FFT

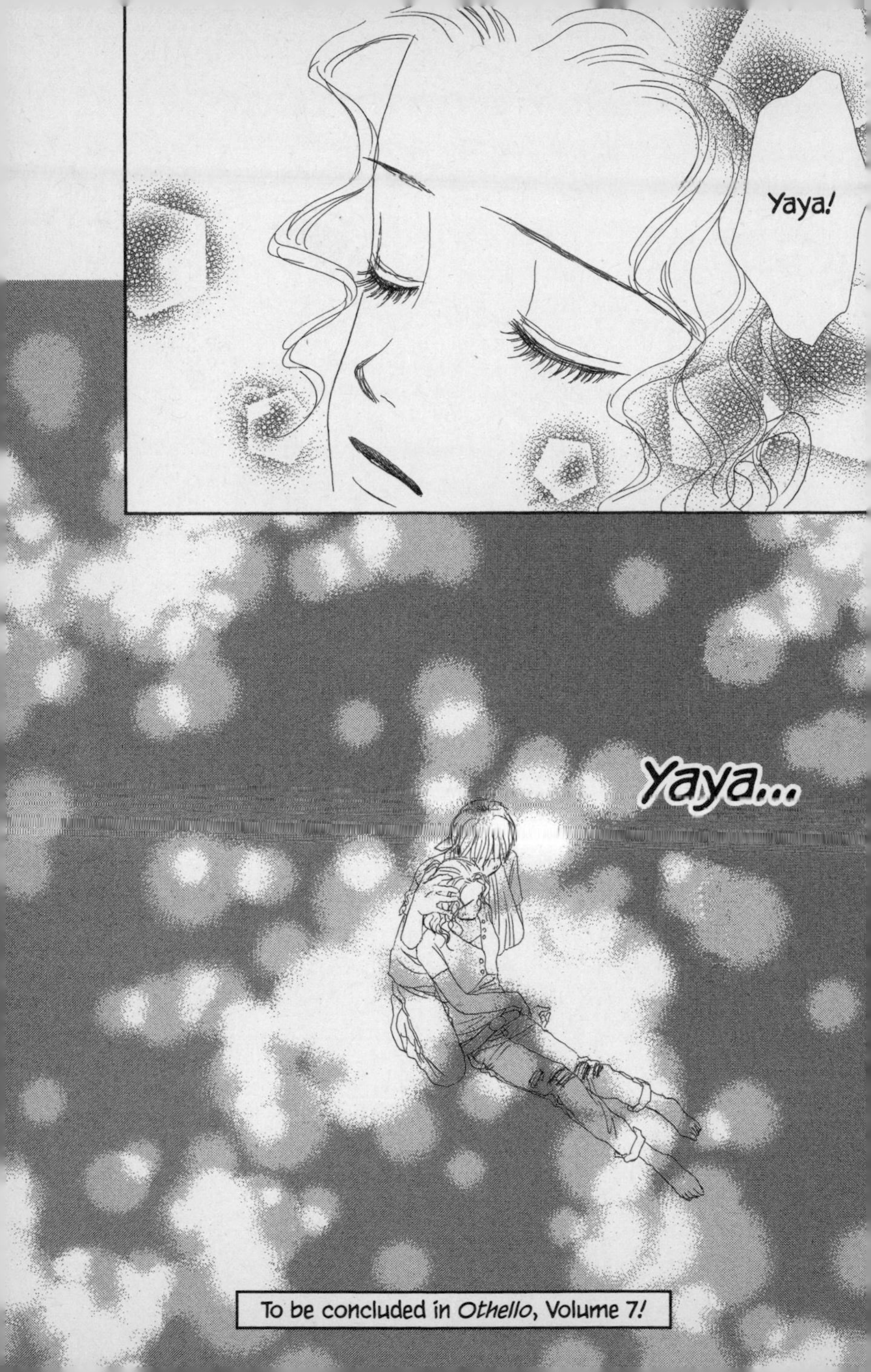
Yaya!
Yaya...
To be concluded in *Othello*, Volume 7!

About the Author

Satomi Ikezawa's previous work before *Othello* is *Guru Guru Pon-chan*. She currently continues to work on *Othello*, which is being serialized in the Kodansha weekly manga magazine, *Bessatsu Friend*.

Ikezawa won the 24th Kodansha Manga Prize in 2000 for *Guru Guru Pon-chan*.

She has two Labradors, named Guts and Ponta.

Translation Notes

Japanese is a tricky language for most Westerners, and translation is often more art than science. For your edification and reading pleasure, here are notes on some of the places where we could have gone in a different direction in our translation of the work, or where a Japanese cultural reference is used.

The meaning of the title Othello

We've had a bunch of questions come in asking how *Othello* relates to Shakespeare's play of the same name. Well, one could make a case for people who stab others in the back while claiming to be friends (Seri, Moe, and Hano-chan for the manga, Iago for Shakespeare), but it is more likely that the play wasn't the basis for the manga at all.

Rather, it's the game, Othello. Similar to the traditional Japanese board game of Go, and invented by a Japanese game designer, Othello is estimated to have 60 million players in Japan. And the constant switching between the white side and the black side of the Othello stones would correspond well to Yaya's sudden change into Nana and back again.

Hanging All Over a Guy (beta-beta suru), Page 23

Japan is generally pretty reserved when it comes to public displays of affection, so when a girl hangs on a guys arm in public, it's a very open statement that they're going out together. In this instance, since they haven't even gone on a date yet, Nana hanging on to Moriyama like that indicates a more intimate relationship than he is willing to acknowledge.

Stan Hansen, Page 36

With a wrestling history of 27 years and nearly 130 tours of Japan, Stan Hansen is one of Japan's greatest wrestling stars, most famous for playing the foreign "heel" in the ring. The ornery Texan reigned three times as the Triple Crown Heavyweight champion, twice won the Carnival Championships, and once the AWA world title.

"Hair on edge," Page 58

Her insults have really set our hair on edge!
We've been taking a lot of crap from that staff member girl of yours!

Finally! A Japanese pun that works in English!! As many people know, since English is a combination of Germanic and Latin-based languages, a translator can sometimes find a pun that works both in the original and in the translation from many western languages. But since the Japanese and English languages have had little influence on each other before the American occupation of Japan a half a century ago, there are few words or phrases in Japanese that would have the same two meanings as the English word or phrase that would be required for a direct translation of a pun. Here, we have one unusual example. In Japanese, the word *tosaka* means "to be offended at," but it can also mean a "head crest" (like the guy's mohawk). And to "set one's hair on edge" in English can mean "to be annoyed," but also refer to the guy's spiky mohawk. We never said it was a *good* pun—but these things are very exciting to a translator!

Home Shrine, Page 101

Because the majority of Japanese citizens practice rights for both the Shinto religion and Buddhism, most Japanese families have a small Buddhist shrine in their homes venerating departed family members and their ancestors.

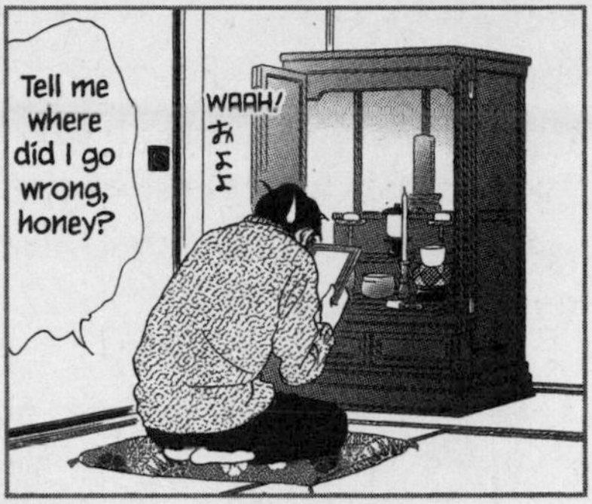
Tell me where did I go wrong, honey?
WAAH!
およよ

Ashita no Joe, Page 129

Perhaps the most popular manga of the '70s, Ashita no Joe ("Tomorrow's Joe") is a boxing manga that took Japan by storm. Joe is a struggling boxer out of the slums of Tokyo who gets himself mixed up with criminals and sent to jail. There he meets another convict, Toru Rikiishi, and the two train to become rivals for the title of Japan's greatest boxer.

Break Dog, Page 139

This is probably a comment on Moriyama's broken arm, but since "L" and "R" sound the same to Japanese ears, the Japanese spelling for "Black" and "Break" are very similar.

Signs on the wall, Page 150

Instead of menus, the more traditional Japanese bars and restaurants hang signs for their menu items on the wall on wooden plaques with the item and the price.

Janet Jackson, Page 150

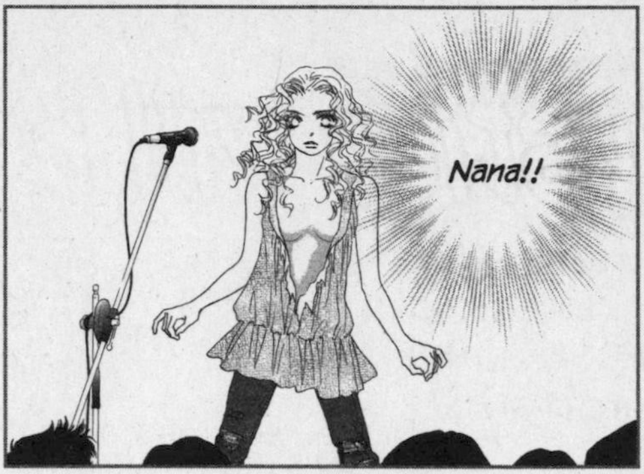
Nana!!

No, there was no substitution of American pop-culture references in this phrase. Moriyama does say "Janet Jackson" there. Since the book was first published in Japan in April of 2004, there was plenty of time for America's obsession with Janet Jackson's controversial "wardrobe malfunction" to reach Japanese shores.

Izakaya, Page 151

Izakaya are halfway between American bars and Chinese Dim-Sum restaurants. In America one thinks of a bar as a place for drinks, and if there is any food, it is simple snacks like peanuts or pretzels. But in Japan, the Izakaya serve a wide variety of cooked and prepared foods with their drinks. The foods are made to order, and usually around 300-500 yen per dish and are made to be shared among all the drinkers in the party. When one thinks of Japanese businessmen going for drinks after work, Izakaya are the places they usually go.

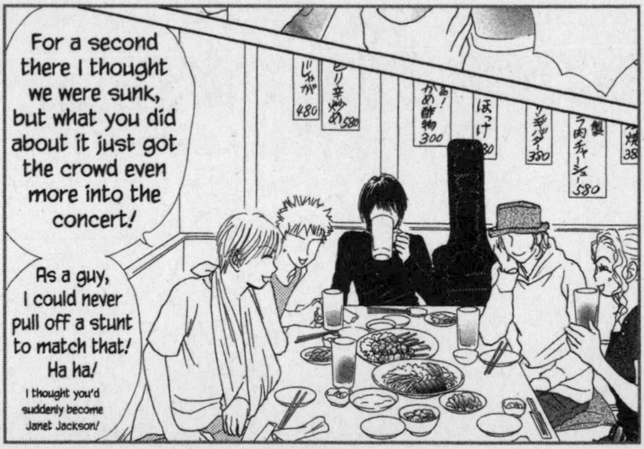
For a second there I thought we were sunk, but what you did about it just got the crowd even more into the concert!
As a guy, I could never pull off a stunt to match that! Ha ha!
I thought you'd suddenly become Janet Jackson!

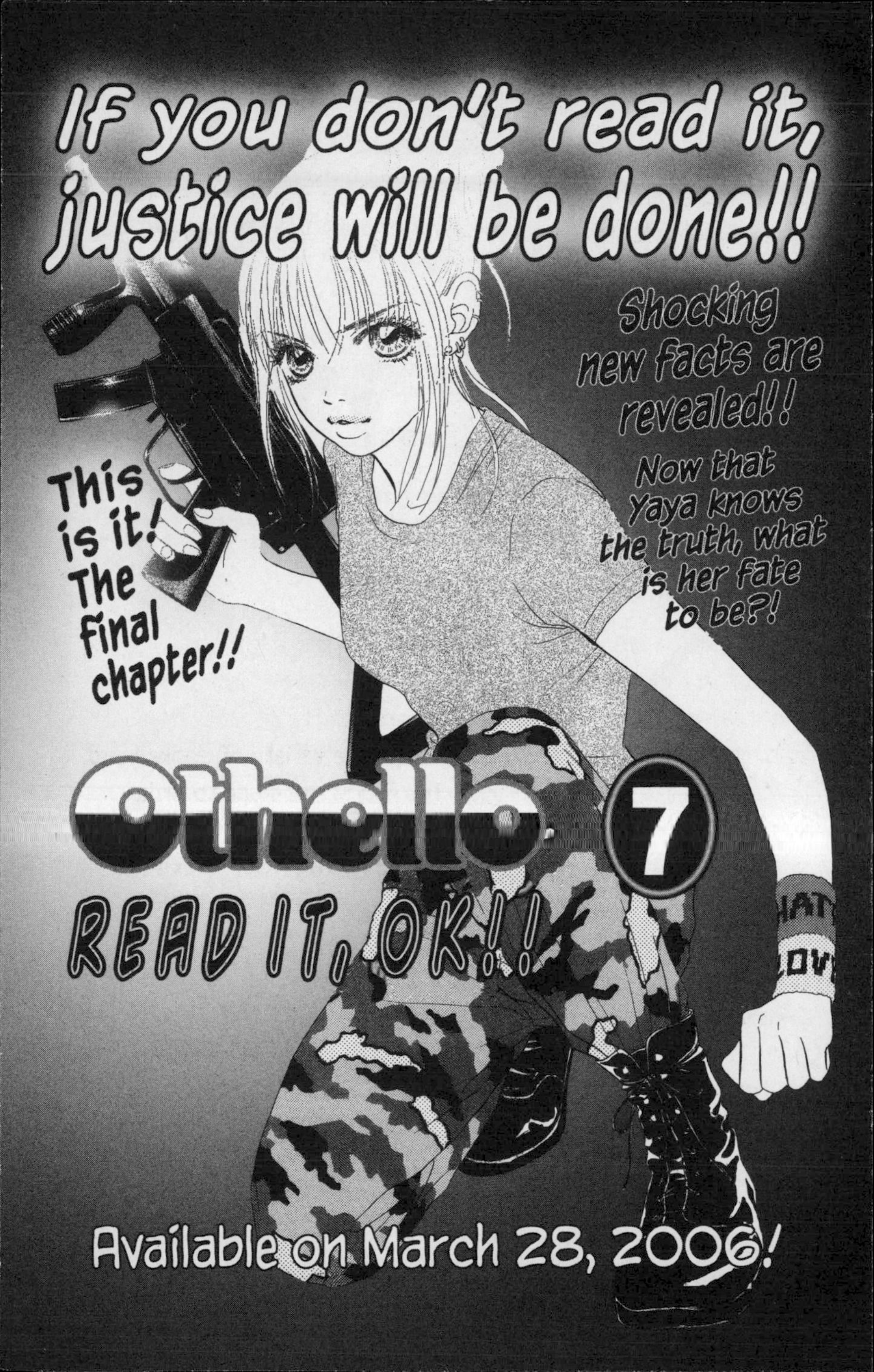
If you don't read it, justice will be done!!
Shocking new facts are revealed!!
Now that Yaya knows the truth, what is her fate to be?!
This is it! The final chapter!!
Othello 7
READ IT, OK!!
Available on March 28, 2006!

TOMARE!

[STOP!]

You are going the wrong way!

Manga is a completely different
type of reading experience.

To start at the *beginning,* go to the *end!*

That's right! Authentic manga is read the traditional Japanese
way—from right to left. Exactly the *opposite* of how American
books are read. It's easy to follow: Just go to the other end of
the book, and read each page—and each panel—from right side
to left side, starting at the top right. Now you're experiencing
manga as it was meant to be.